I was invited as a guest to the Leipzig book fair in Germany. It was amazing! The German fans were both super polite and passionate. Also, I had heard over and over about how German food is bad, but it was great!

—Tite Kubo

BLEACH is author Tite Kubo's second title. Kubo made his debut with *ZOMBIEPOWDER.*, a four-volume series for *WEEKLY SHONEN JUMP*. To date, *BLEACH* has been translated into numerous languages and has also inspired an animated TV series that began airing in the U.S. in 2006. Beginning its serialization in 2001, *BLEACH* is still a mainstay in the pages of *WEEKLY SHONEN JUMP*. In 2005, *BLEACH* was awarded the prestigious Shogakukan Manga Award in the *shonen* (boys) category.

BLEACH
VOL. 59: THE BATTLE
SHONEN JUMP Manga Edition

STORY AND ART BY
TITE KUBO

Translation/Joe Yamazaki
Touch-up Art & Lettering/Mark McMurray
Design/Kam Li
Editor/Alexis Kirsch

Printed in the U.S.A.

Published by VIZ Media, LLC
P.O. Box 77010
San Francisco, CA 94107

10 9 8 7 6 5 4 3 2 1
First printing, February 2014

www.viz.com

THE WORLD'S
MOST POPULAR MANGA
www.shonenjump.com

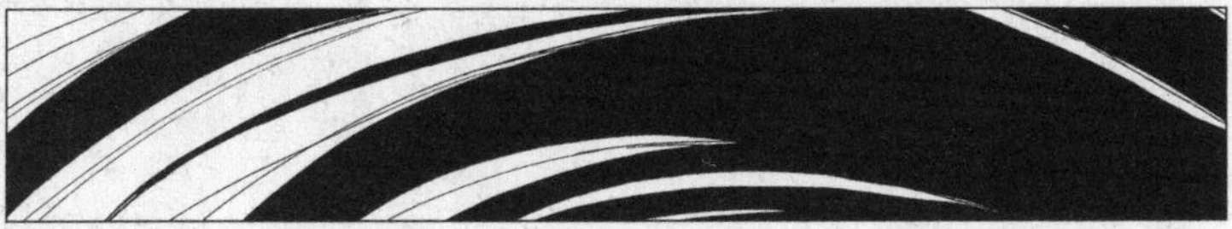

Battle is everything

BLEACH 59 THE BATTLE

Shonen Jump Manga

ALL STARS ★ AND

曳舟桐生
ヒキフネキリオ

KIRIO HIKIFUNE

RENJI ABARAI

阿散井恋次
アバライレンジ

黒崎一護
クロサキイチゴ

ICHIGO KUROSAKI

plot

Ichigo Kurosaki meets Soul Reaper Rukia Kuchiki and ends up helping her eradicate Hollows. After developing his powers as a Soul Reaper, Ichigo enters battle against Aizen and his dark ambitions! Ichigo finally defeats Aizen in exchange for his powers as a Soul Reaper.

With the battle over, Ichigo regains his normal life. But his tranquil days end when he meets Ginjo, who offers to help Ichigo get his powers back. But it's all a plot by Ginjo to steal Ichigo's new powers! Ginjo, who was the first ever Deputy Soul Reaper, then reveals to Ichigo the truth behind the deputy badge. However, even after learning the Soul Society's plans for him, Ichigo chooses to continue protecting his friends and defeats Ginjo.

The Vandenreich suddenly launches a full-on invasion of the Soul Society. The Vandenreich's king, Yhwach, then kills Captain General Yamamoto. With the enemy gone, the Soul Reapers assess the damage as Squad Zero makes their appearance. Their mission is to rebuild the Soul Society and take Ichigo back to the royal palace!

BLEACH

KENPACHI ZARAKI

更木剣八
ザラキケンパチ

京楽春水
キョウラクシュンスイ

SHUNSUI KYORAKU

OH-ETSU NIMAIYA

二枚屋王悦
ニマイヤオウエツ

STORIES

BLEACH 59

THE BATTLE

CONTENTS

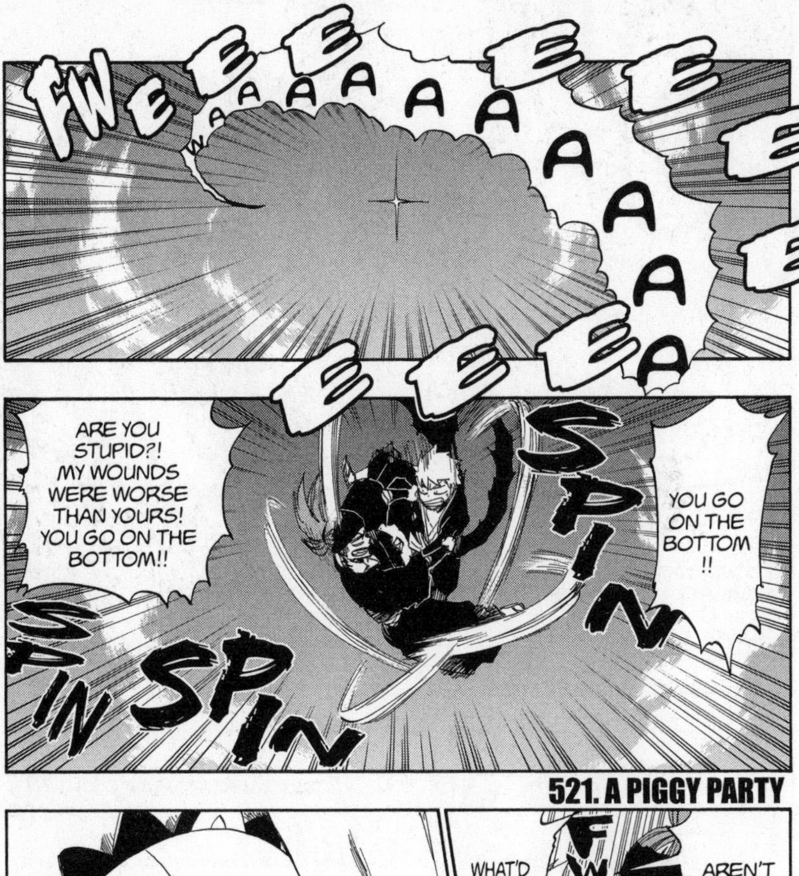
FWEEEEEEEEEEEEEE
WAAAAAAAAAAA
YOU GO ON THE BOTTOM !!
ARE YOU STUPID?! MY WOUNDS WERE WORSE THAN YOURS! YOU GO ON THE BOTTOM!!
SPIN
SPIN
SPIN

521. A PIGGY PARTY

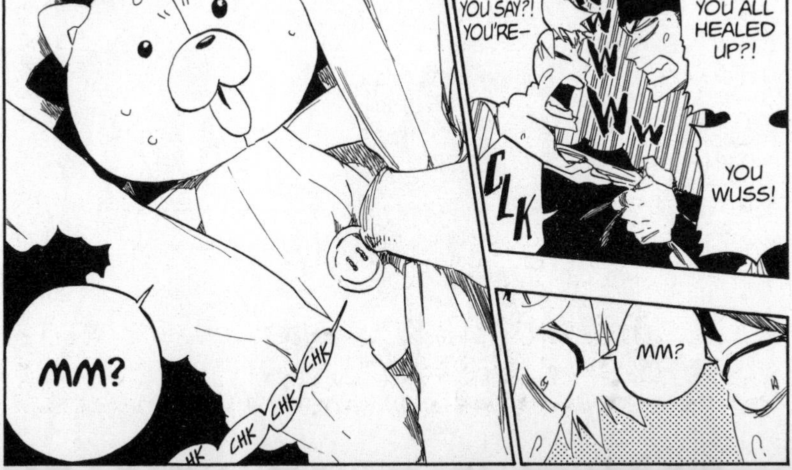
AREN'T YOU ALL HEALED UP?!
WHAT'D YOU SAY?! YOU'RE-
FWWWWWW
YOU WUSS!
CLK
MM?
MM?
CHK CHK CHK CHK HK

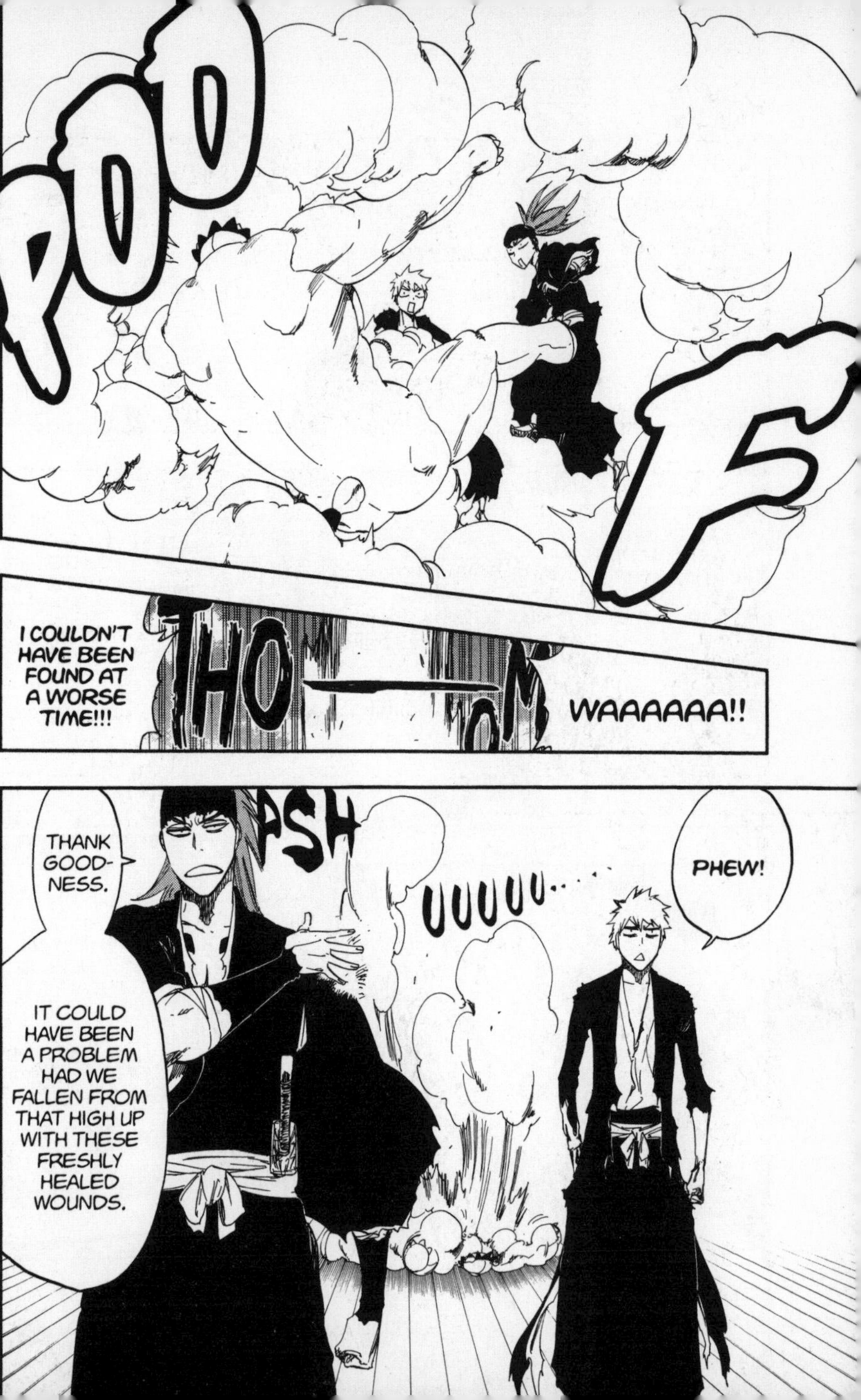
POOF
WAAAAAA!!
THO—OM
I COULDN'T HAVE BEEN FOUND AT A WORSE TIME!!!
PHEW!
UUUUU...
PSH
THANK GOODNESS.
IT COULD HAVE BEEN A PROBLEM HAD WE FALLEN FROM THAT HIGH UP WITH THESE FRESHLY HEALED WOUNDS.

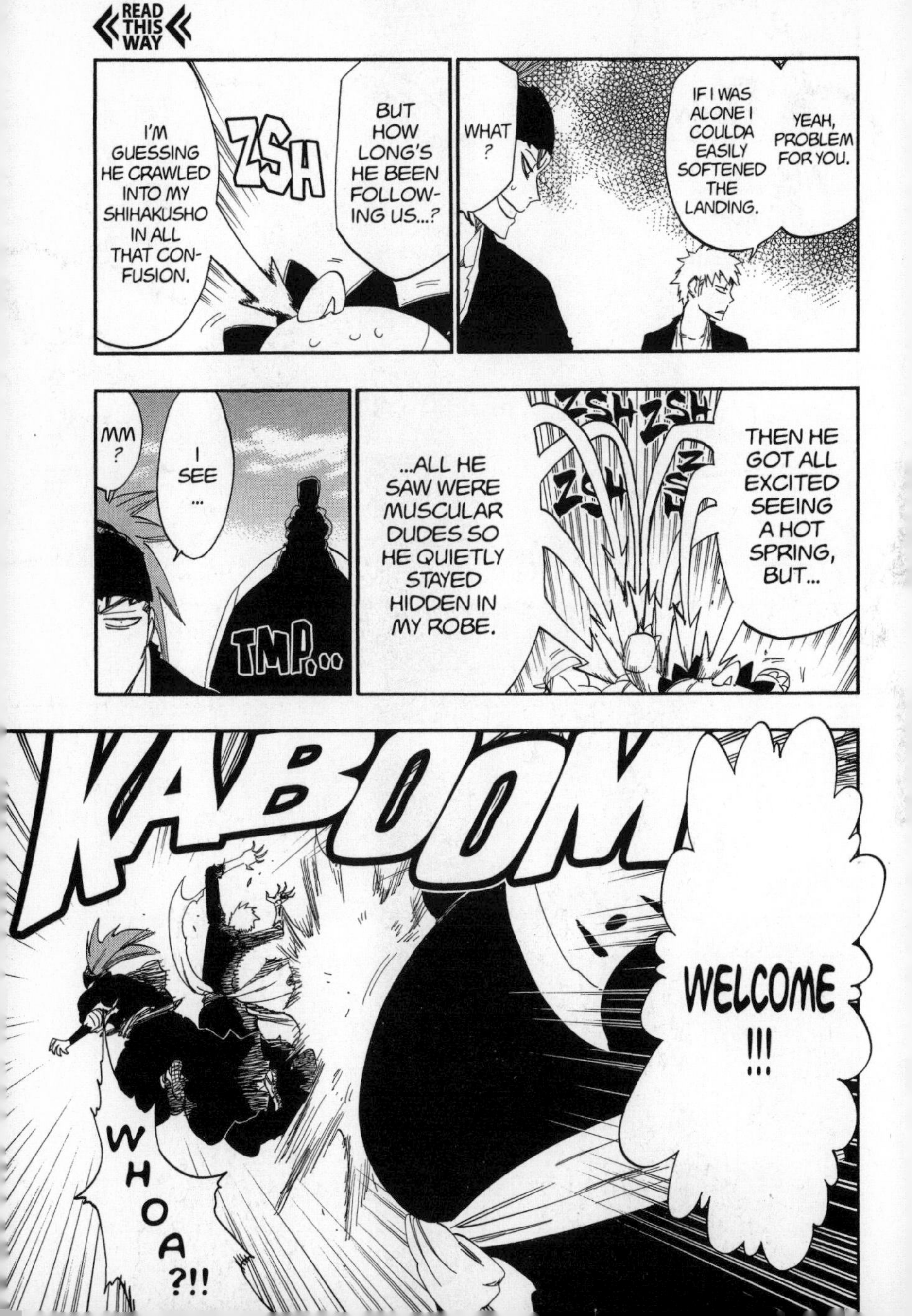
READ THIS WAY
YEAH, PROBLEM FOR YOU.
IF I WAS ALONE I COULDA EASILY SOFTENED THE LANDING.
WHAT?
BUT HOW LONG'S HE BEEN FOLLOWING US...?
ZSH
I'M GUESSING HE CRAWLED INTO MY SHIHAKUSHO IN ALL THAT CONFUSION.
ZSH ZSH
ZSH
ZSH
THEN HE GOT ALL EXCITED SEEING A HOT SPRING, BUT...
...ALL HE SAW WERE MUSCULAR DUDES SO HE QUIETLY STAYED HIDDEN IN MY ROBE.
I SEE...
MM?
TMP..
KABOOM
WELCOME!!!
WHOA?!!

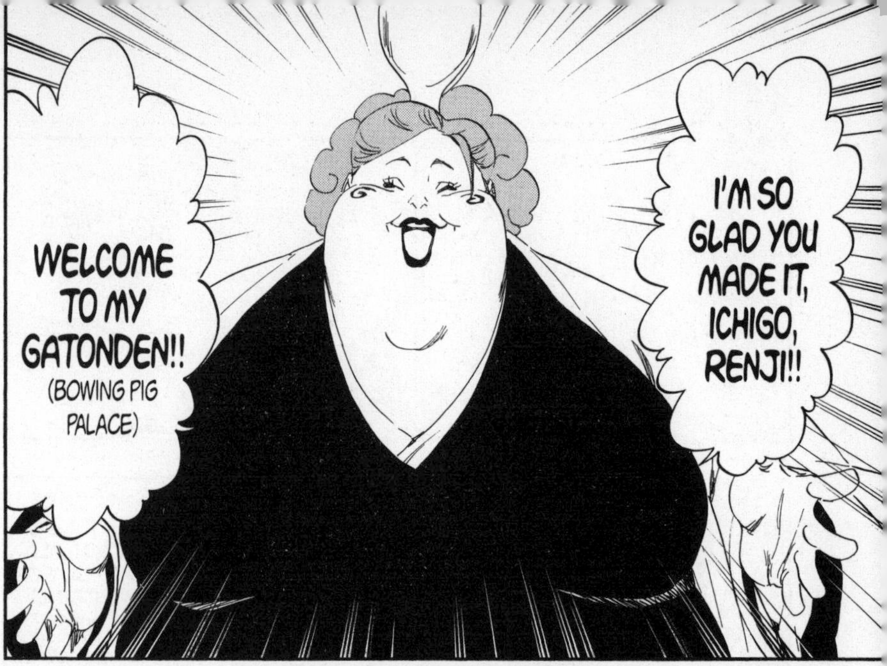
I'M SO GLAD YOU MADE IT, ICHIGO, RENJI!!
WELCOME TO MY GATONDEN!! (BOWING PIG PALACE)

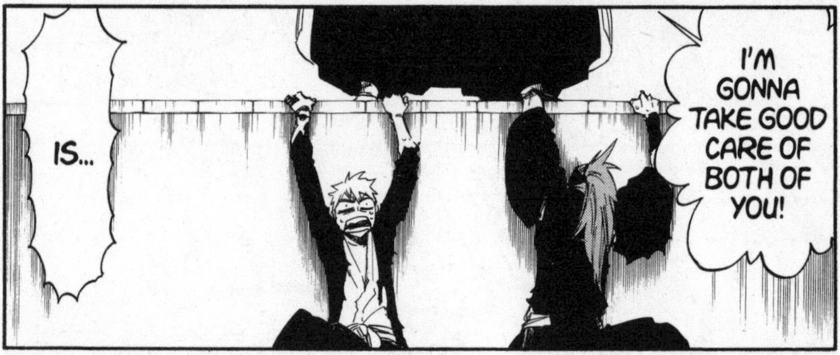
I'M GONNA TAKE GOOD CARE OF BOTH OF YOU!
IS...

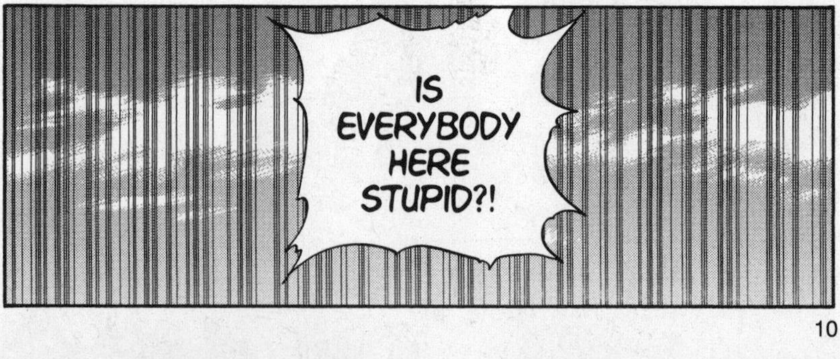
IS EVERYBODY HERE STUPID?!

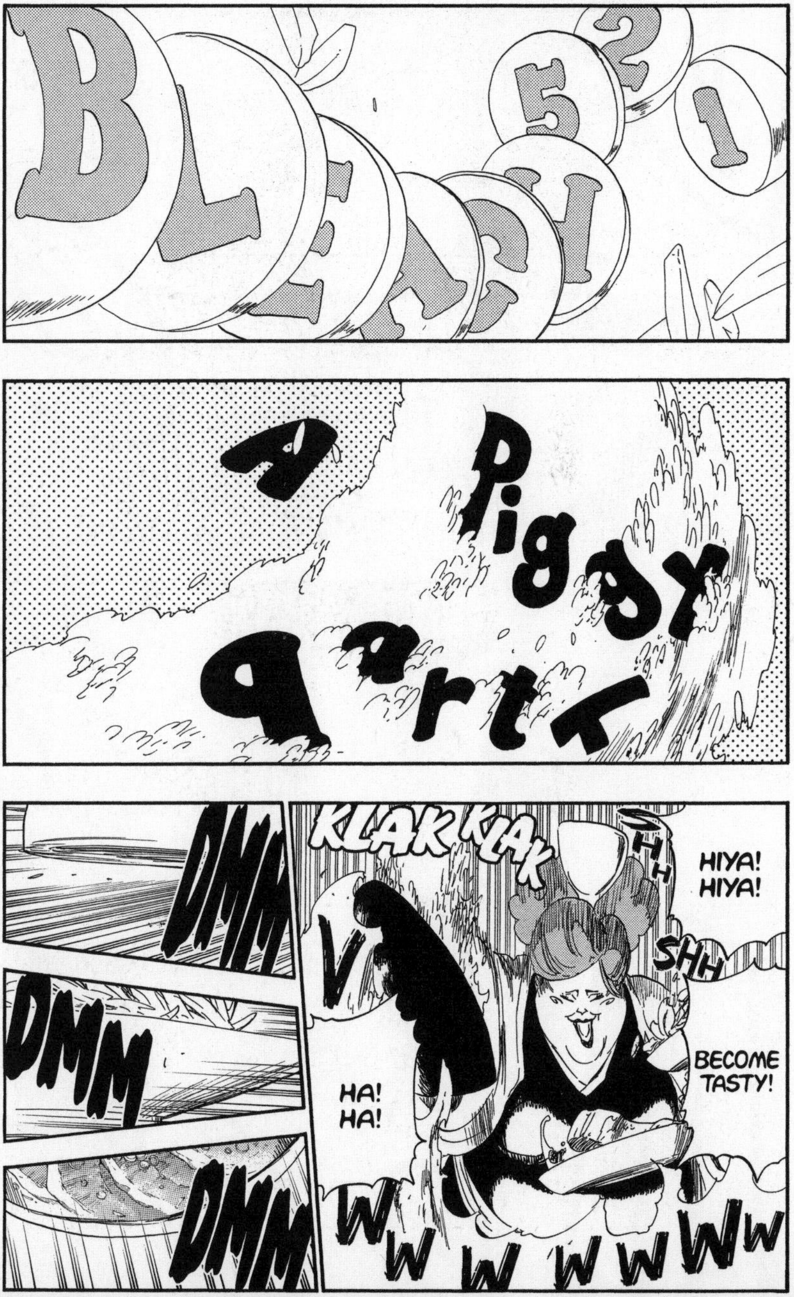
BLEACH 521
A Piggy Party
KLAK KLAK
SHH
HIYA! HIYA!
SHH
BECOME TASTY!
HA! HA!
VWWWWWWW
DMM
DMM
DMM

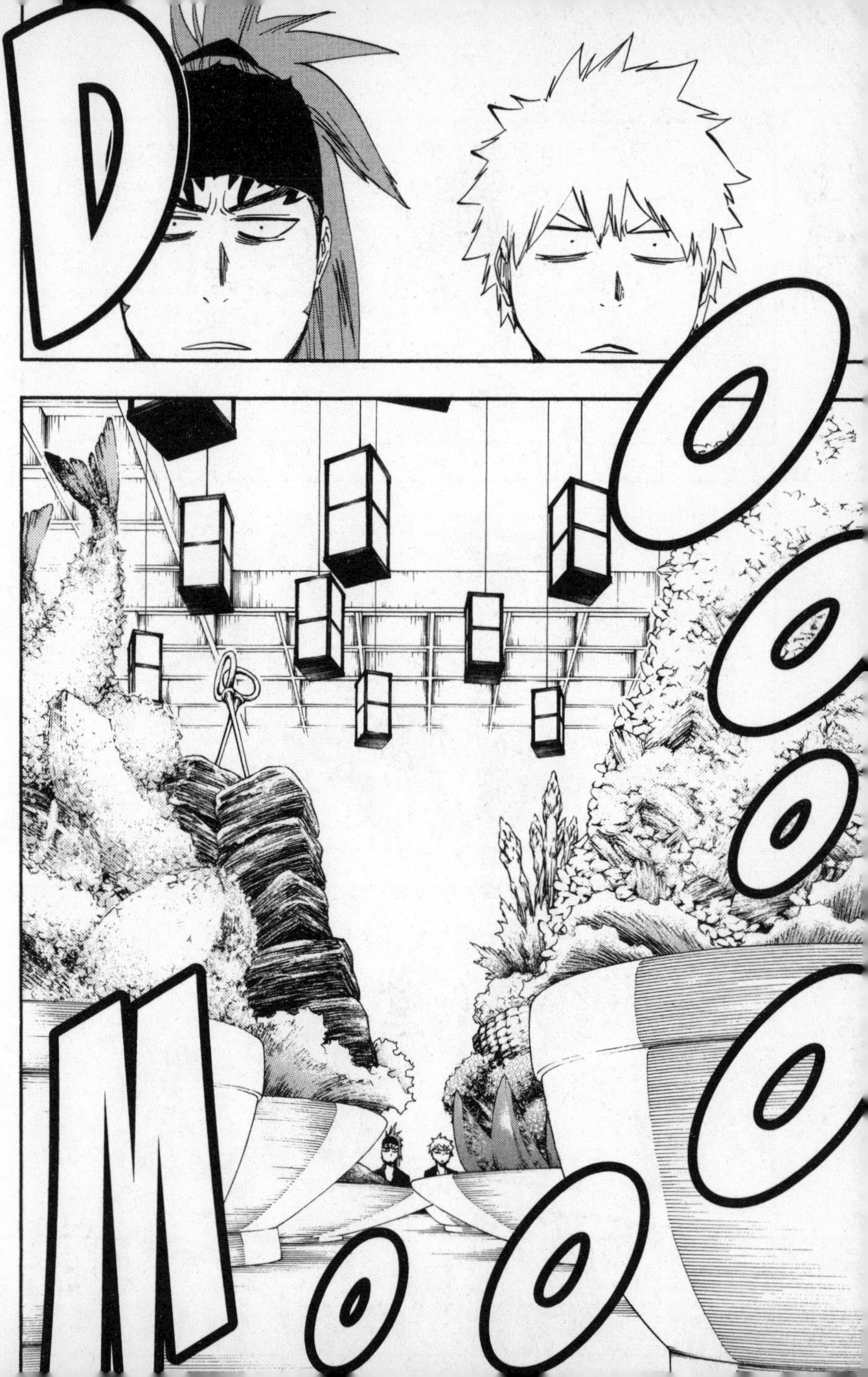
DOOOOO
MOOO

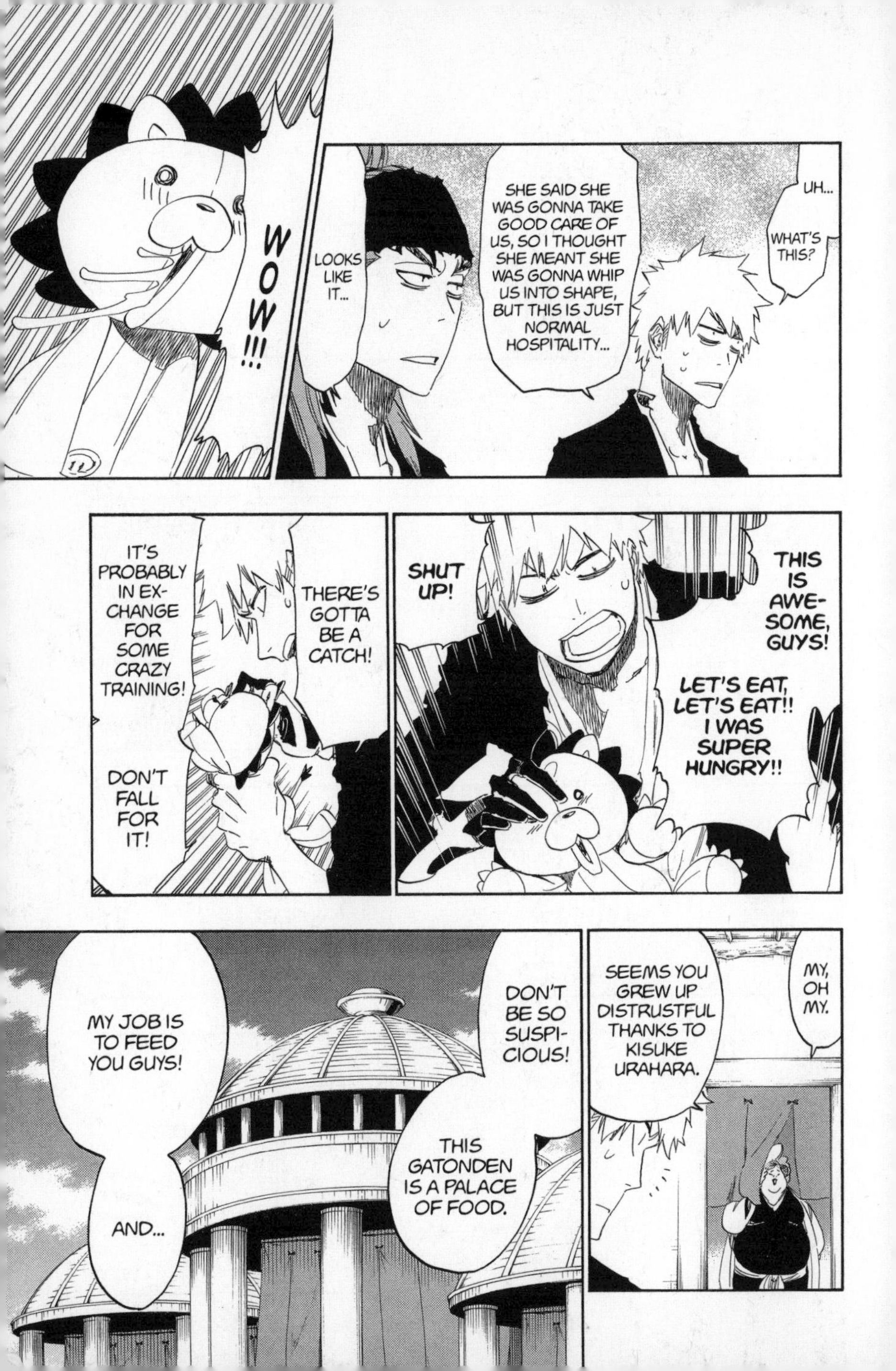

UH...
WHAT'S THIS?
SHE SAID SHE WAS GONNA TAKE GOOD CARE OF US, SO I THOUGHT SHE MEANT SHE WAS GONNA WHIP US INTO SHAPE, BUT THIS IS JUST NORMAL HOSPITALITY...
LOOKS LIKE IT...
WOW!!!
THIS IS AWE-SOME, GUYS!
LET'S EAT, LET'S EAT!! I WAS SUPER HUNGRY!!
SHUT UP!
THERE'S GOTTA BE A CATCH!
IT'S PROBABLY IN EX-CHANGE FOR SOME CRAZY TRAINING!
DON'T FALL FOR IT!
MY, OH MY.
SEEMS YOU GREW UP DISTRUSTFUL THANKS TO KISUKE URAHARA.
DON'T BE SO SUSPI-CIOUS!
MY JOB IS TO FEED YOU GUYS!
AND...
THIS GATONDEN IS A PALACE OF FOOD.

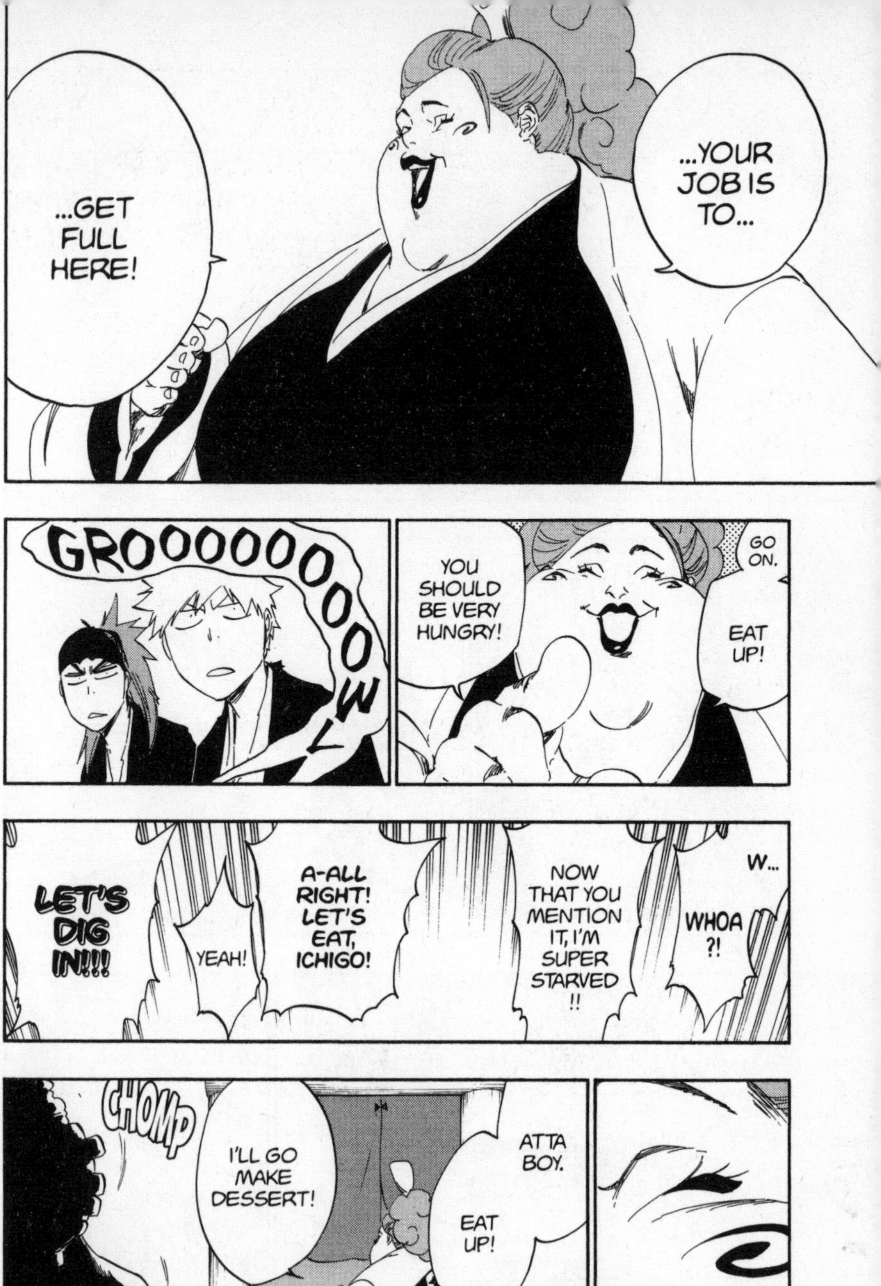
...YOUR JOB IS TO...
...GET FULL HERE!
GO ON.
YOU SHOULD BE VERY HUNGRY!
EAT UP!
GROOOOOOOOOWL
W...
WHOA?!
NOW THAT YOU MENTION IT, I'M SUPER STARVED!!
A-ALL RIGHT! LET'S EAT, ICHIGO!
YEAH!
LET'S DIG IN!!!
ATTA BOY.
EAT UP!
I'LL GO MAKE DESSERT!
CHOMP
CHOMP

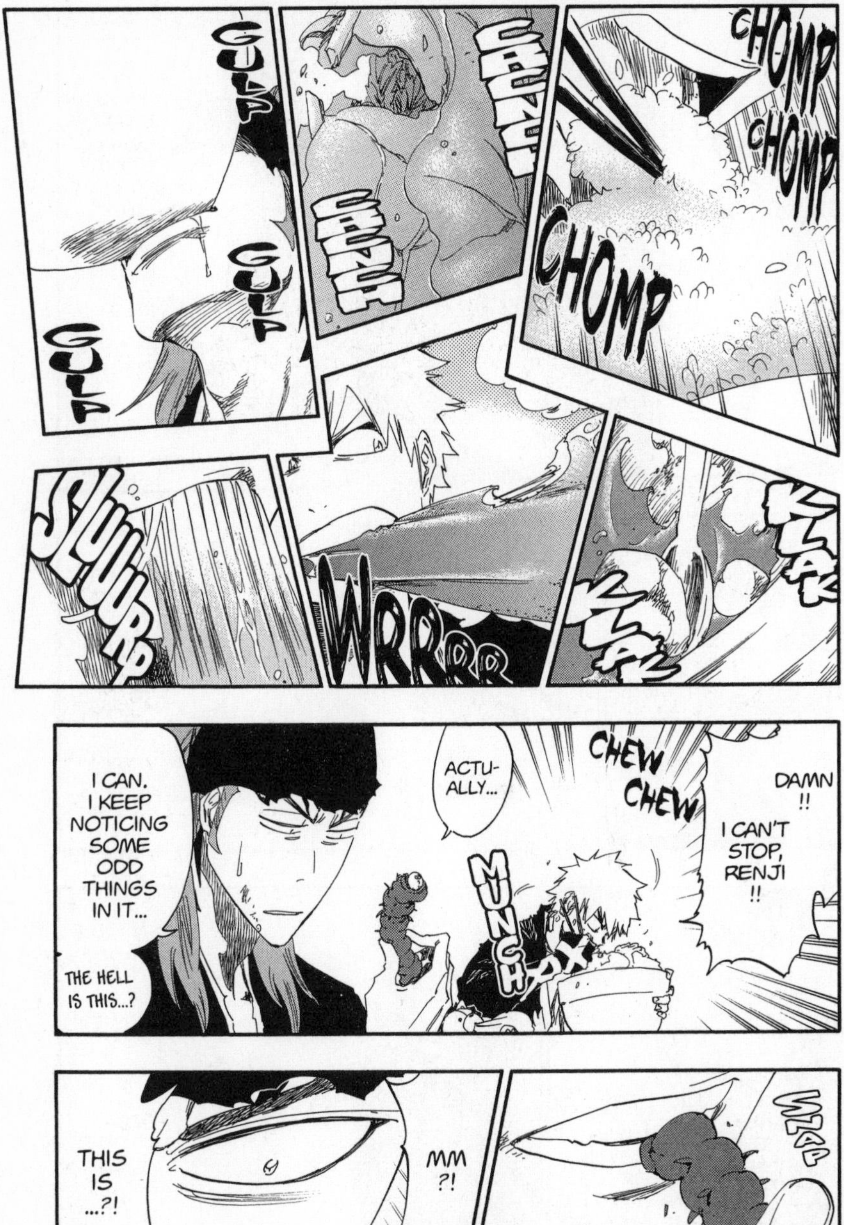
CHOMP
CHOMP
CHOMP
CHOMP
CRUNCH
CRUNCH
GULP
GULP
GULP
KLAK
KLAK
WRRRRR
SLUUURP
DAMN!!
I CAN'T STOP, RENJI!!
CHEW CHEW
MUNCH
ACTUALLY...
I CAN. I KEEP NOTICING SOME ODD THINGS IN IT...
THE HELL IS THIS...?
SZAP
MM?!
THIS IS ...?!

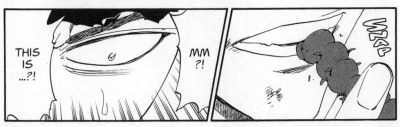

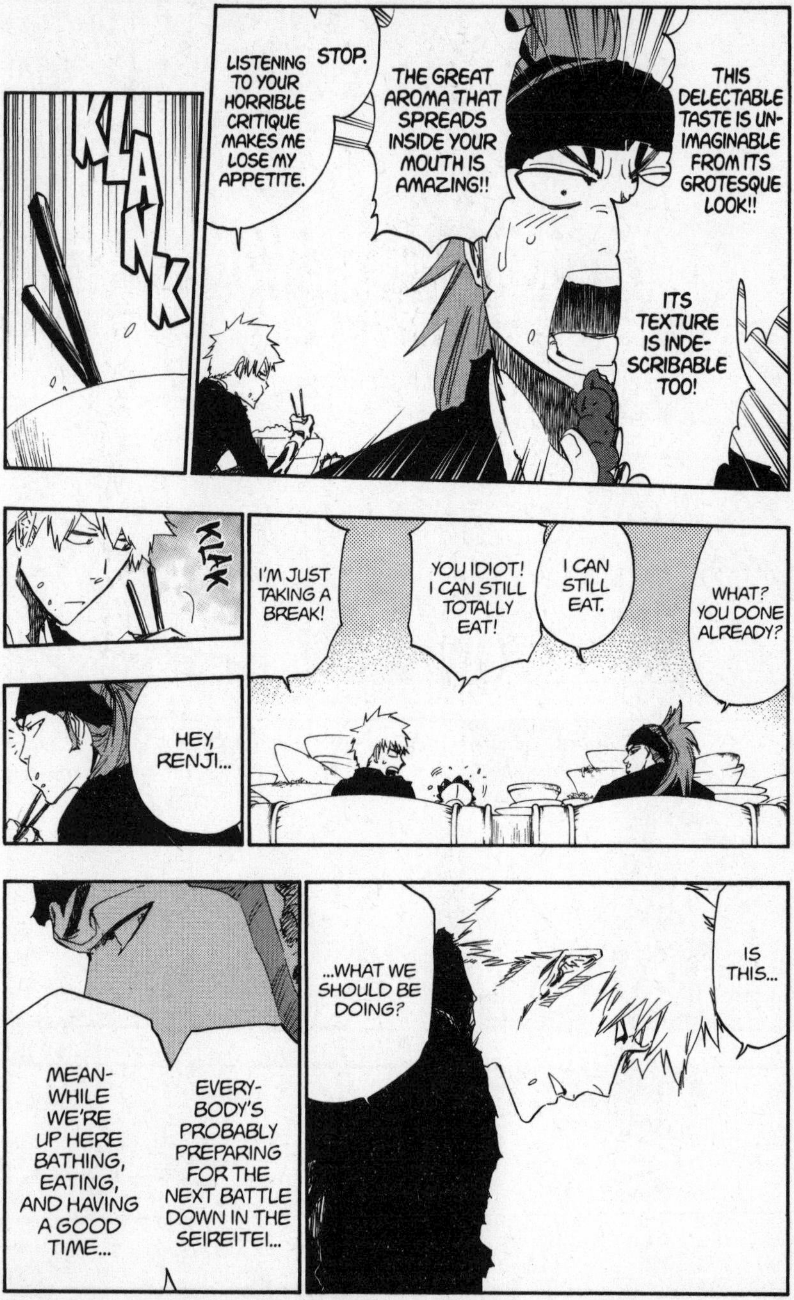
THIS DELECTABLE TASTE IS UNIMAGINABLE FROM ITS GROTESQUE LOOK!!
THE GREAT AROMA THAT SPREADS INSIDE YOUR MOUTH IS AMAZING!!
ITS TEXTURE IS INDESCRIBABLE TOO!
STOP.
LISTENING TO YOUR HORRIBLE CRITIQUE MAKES ME LOSE MY APPETITE.
KLANK
WHAT? YOU DONE ALREADY?
I CAN STILL EAT.
YOU IDIOT! I CAN STILL TOTALLY EAT!
I'M JUST TAKING A BREAK!
KLAK
HEY, RENJI...
IS THIS...
...WHAT WE SHOULD BE DOING?
EVERYBODY'S PROBABLY PREPARING FOR THE NEXT BATTLE DOWN IN THE SEIREITEI...
MEANWHILE WE'RE UP HERE BATHING, EATING, AND HAVING A GOOD TIME...

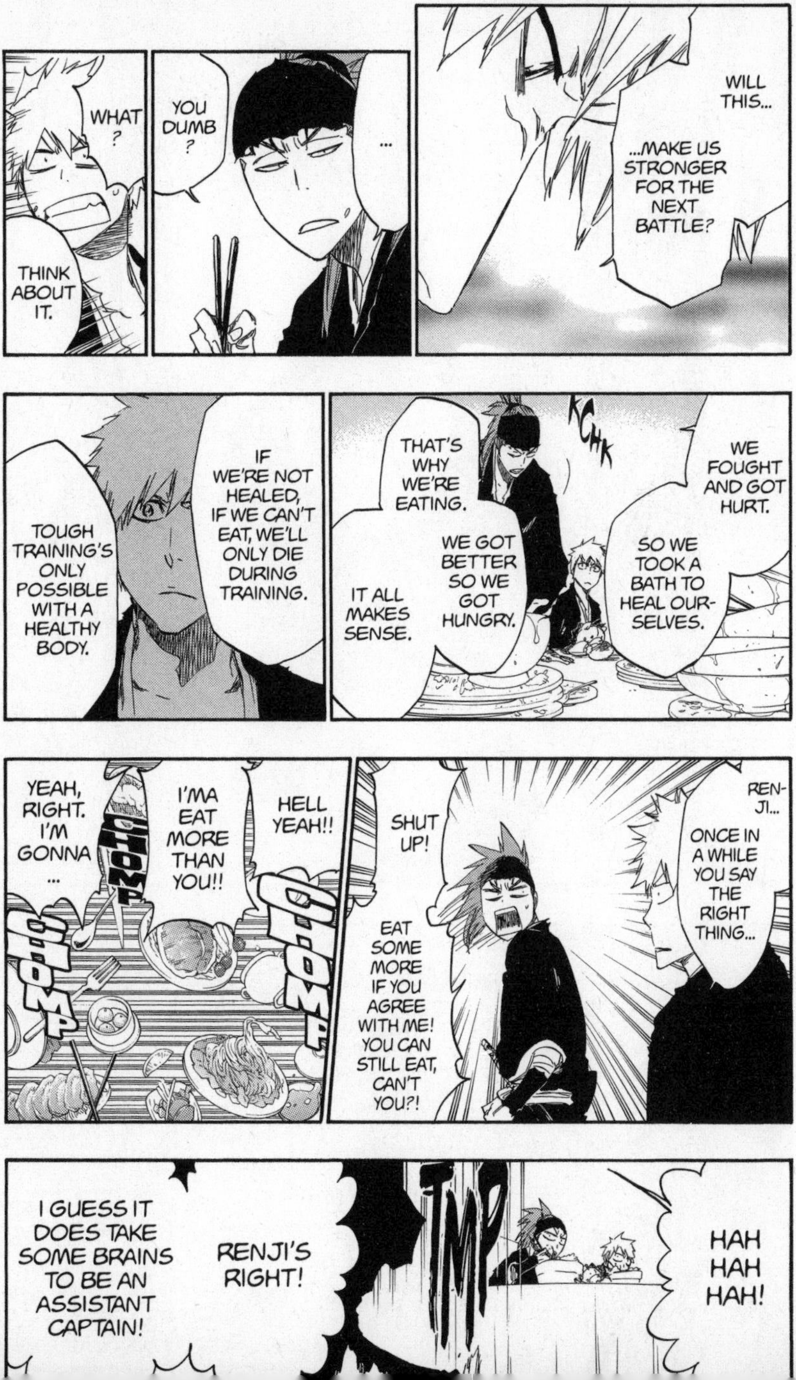
WILL THIS...
...MAKE US STRONGER FOR THE NEXT BATTLE?
...
YOU DUMB?
WHAT?
THINK ABOUT IT.
WE FOUGHT AND GOT HURT.
SO WE TOOK A BATH TO HEAL OUR-SELVES.
KCHK
THAT'S WHY WE'RE EATING.
WE GOT BETTER SO WE GOT HUNGRY.
IT ALL MAKES SENSE.
IF WE'RE NOT HEALED, IF WE CAN'T EAT, WE'LL ONLY DIE DURING TRAINING.
TOUGH TRAINING'S ONLY POSSIBLE WITH A HEALTHY BODY.
RENJI...
ONCE IN A WHILE YOU SAY THE RIGHT THING...
SHUT UP!
EAT SOME MORE IF YOU AGREE WITH ME! YOU CAN STILL EAT, CAN'T YOU?!
HELL YEAH!!
CHOMP
I'MA EAT MORE THAN YOU!!
CHOMP
YEAH, RIGHT. I'M GONNA...
CHOMP
HAH HAH HAH!
RENJI'S RIGHT!
I GUESS IT DOES TAKE SOME BRAINS TO BE AN ASSISTANT CAPTAIN!

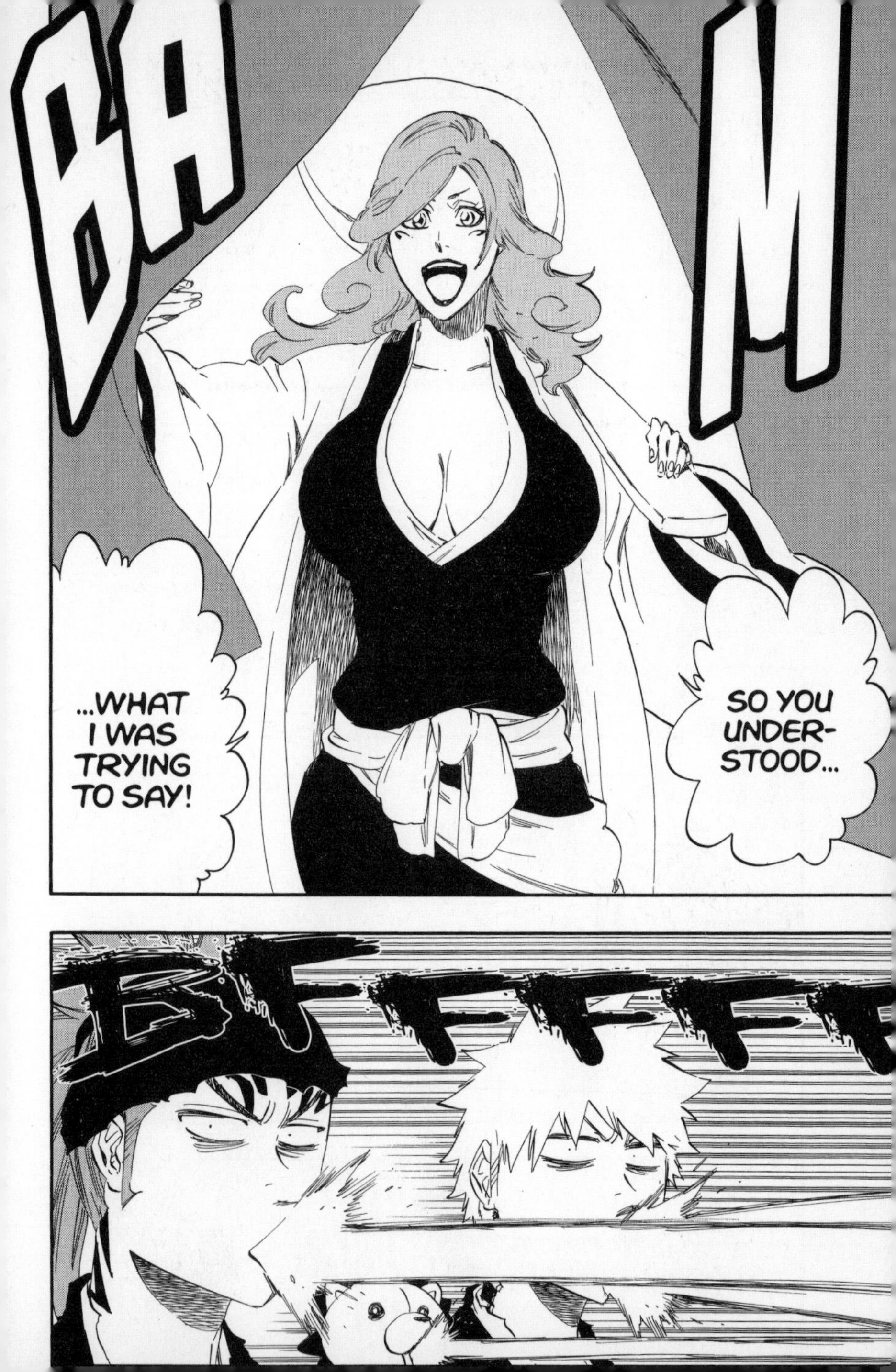
BAM
SO YOU UNDER-STOOD...
...WHAT I WAS TRYING TO SAY!
BFFFF

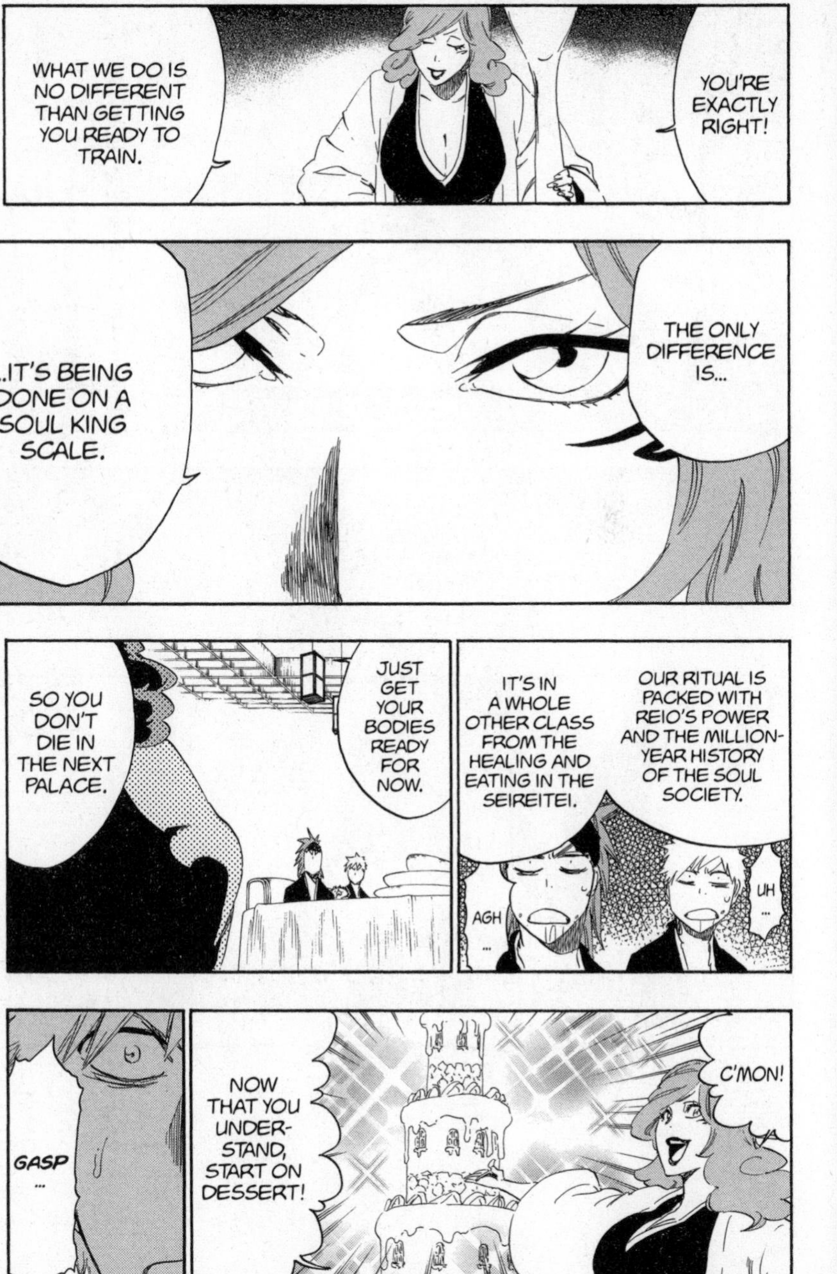
YOU'RE EXACTLY RIGHT!
WHAT WE DO IS NO DIFFERENT THAN GETTING YOU READY TO TRAIN.
THE ONLY DIFFERENCE IS...
...IT'S BEING DONE ON A SOUL KING SCALE.
OUR RITUAL IS PACKED WITH REIO'S POWER AND THE MILLION-YEAR HISTORY OF THE SOUL SOCIETY.
IT'S IN A WHOLE OTHER CLASS FROM THE HEALING AND EATING IN THE SEIREITEI.
UH...
AGH...
JUST GET YOUR BODIES READY FOR NOW.
SO YOU DON'T DIE IN THE NEXT PALACE.
C'MON!
NOW THAT YOU UNDER-STAND, START ON DESSERT!
GASP...

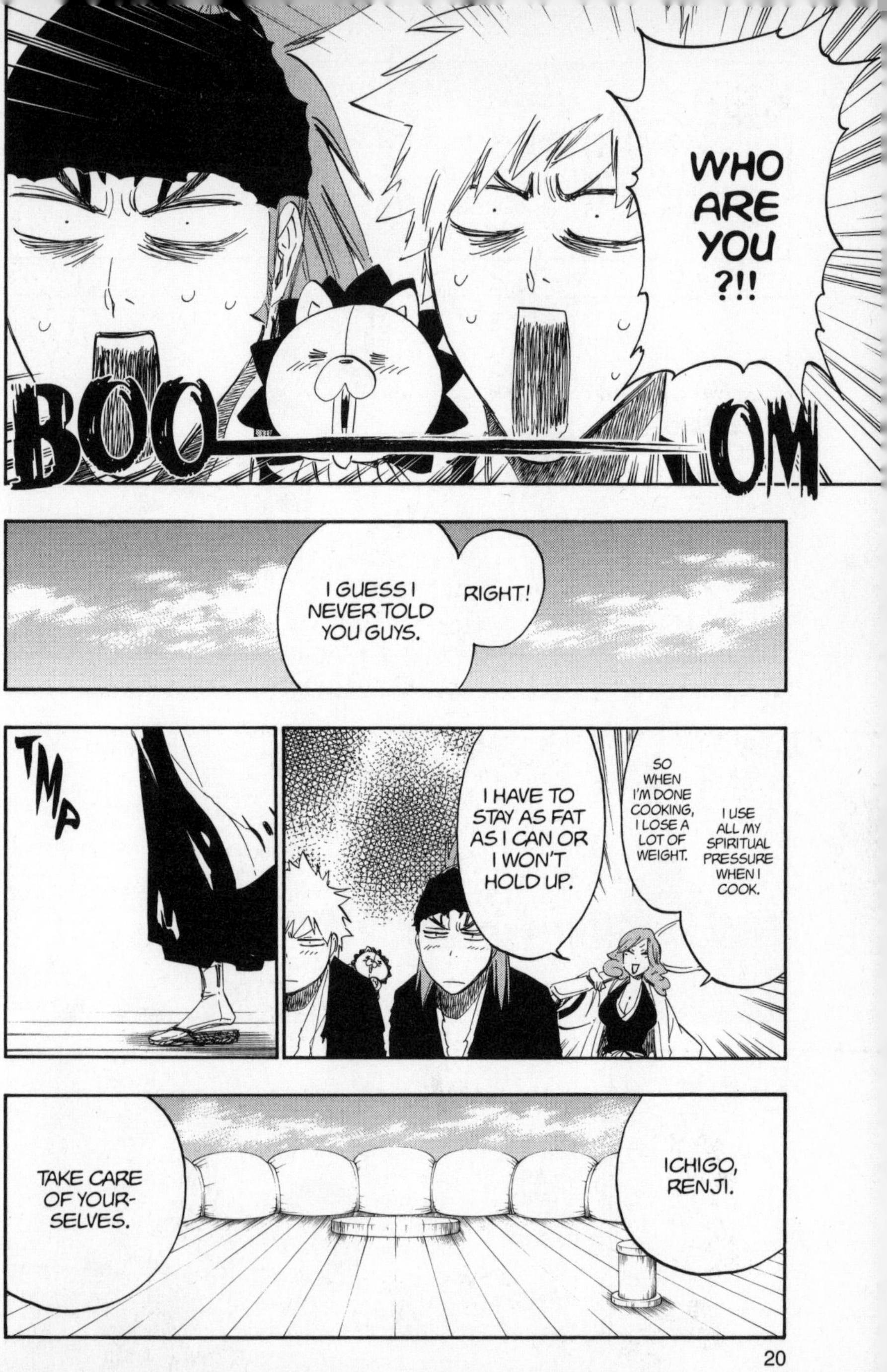
WHO ARE YOU ?!!
BOOOM
RIGHT!
I GUESS I NEVER TOLD YOU GUYS.
I USE ALL MY SPIRITUAL PRESSURE WHEN I COOK.
SO WHEN I'M DONE COOKING, I LOSE A LOT OF WEIGHT.
I HAVE TO STAY AS FAT AS I CAN OR I WON'T HOLD UP.
TMP
ICHIGO, RENJI.
TAKE CARE OF YOURSELVES.

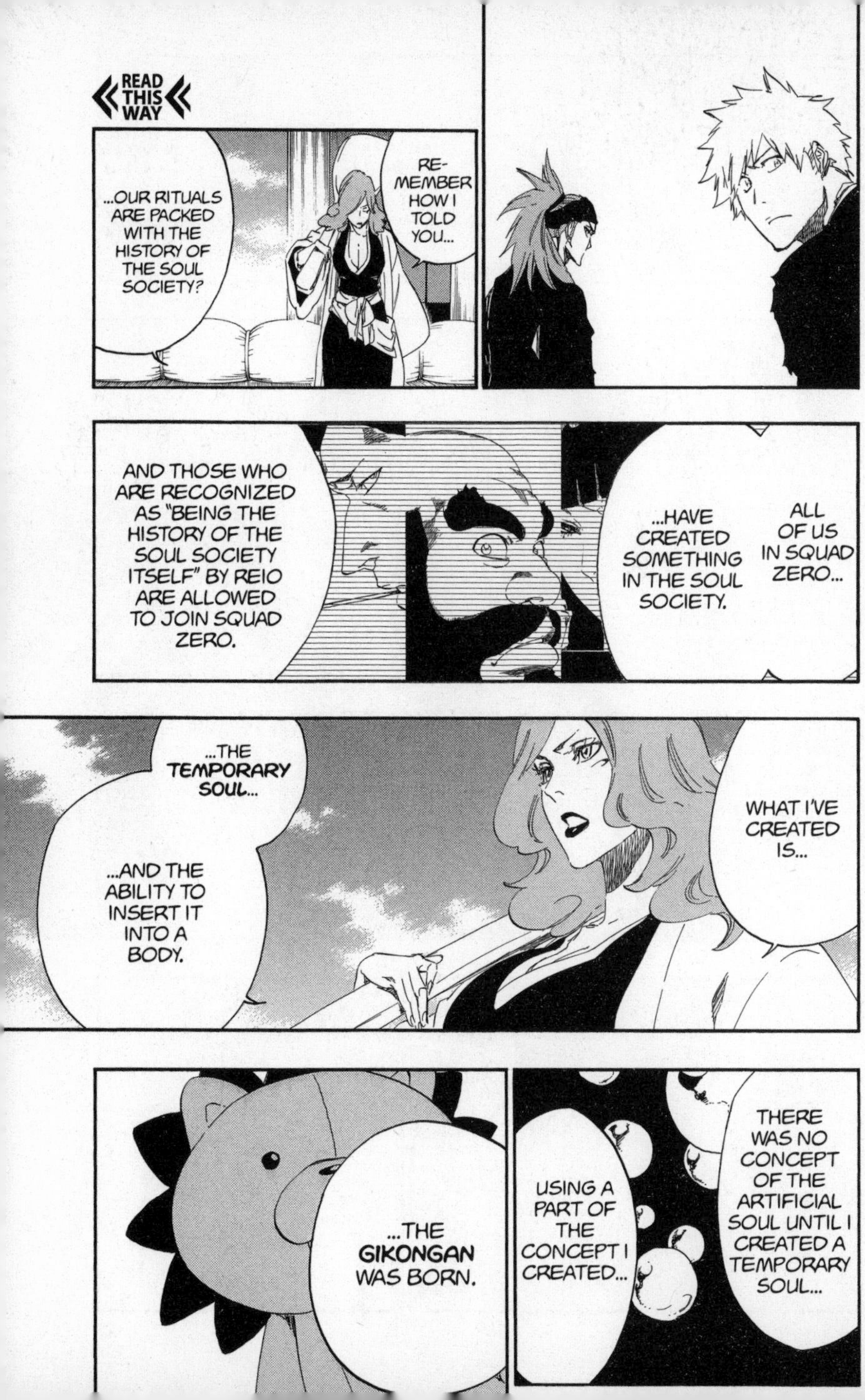
READ THIS WAY
RE-MEMBER HOW I TOLD YOU...
...OUR RITUALS ARE PACKED WITH THE HISTORY OF THE SOUL SOCIETY?
ALL OF US IN SQUAD ZERO...
...HAVE CREATED SOMETHING IN THE SOUL SOCIETY.
AND THOSE WHO ARE RECOGNIZED AS "BEING THE HISTORY OF THE SOUL SOCIETY ITSELF" BY REIO ARE ALLOWED TO JOIN SQUAD ZERO.
WHAT I'VE CREATED IS...
...THE TEMPORARY SOUL...
...AND THE ABILITY TO INSERT IT INTO A BODY.
THERE WAS NO CONCEPT OF THE ARTIFICIAL SOUL UNTIL I CREATED A TEMPORARY SOUL...
USING A PART OF THE CONCEPT I CREATED...
...THE GIKONGAN WAS BORN.

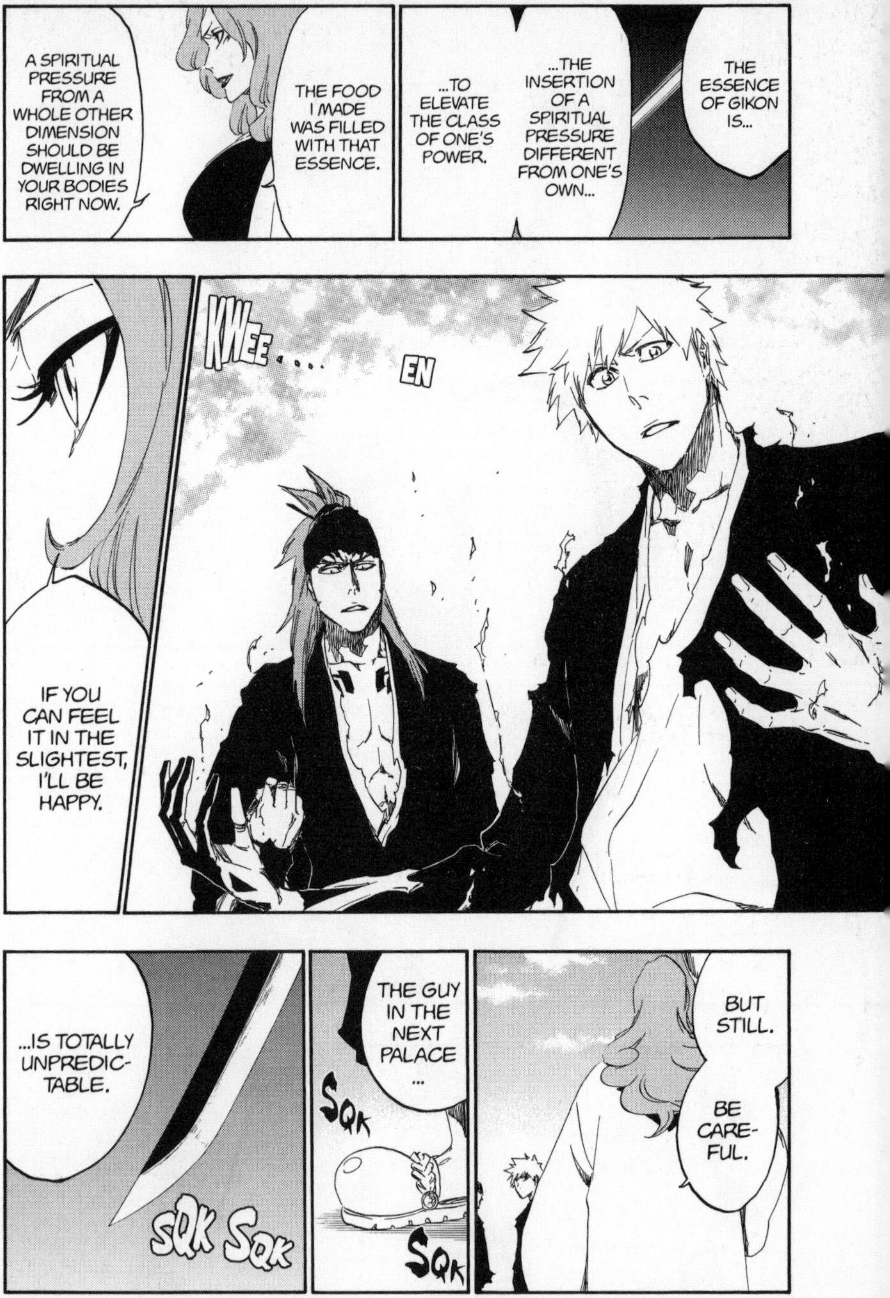
THE ESSENCE OF GIKON IS...
...THE INSERTION OF A SPIRITUAL PRESSURE DIFFERENT FROM ONE'S OWN...
...TO ELEVATE THE CLASS OF ONE'S POWER.
THE FOOD I MADE WAS FILLED WITH THAT ESSENCE.
A SPIRITUAL PRESSURE FROM A WHOLE OTHER DIMENSION SHOULD BE DWELLING IN YOUR BODIES RIGHT NOW.
KWEE.... EN
IF YOU CAN FEEL IT IN THE SLIGHTEST, I'LL BE HAPPY.
BUT STILL.
BE CARE-FUL.
THE GUY IN THE NEXT PALACE ...
SQK
SQK
...IS TOTALLY UNPREDIC-TABLE.
SQK SQK

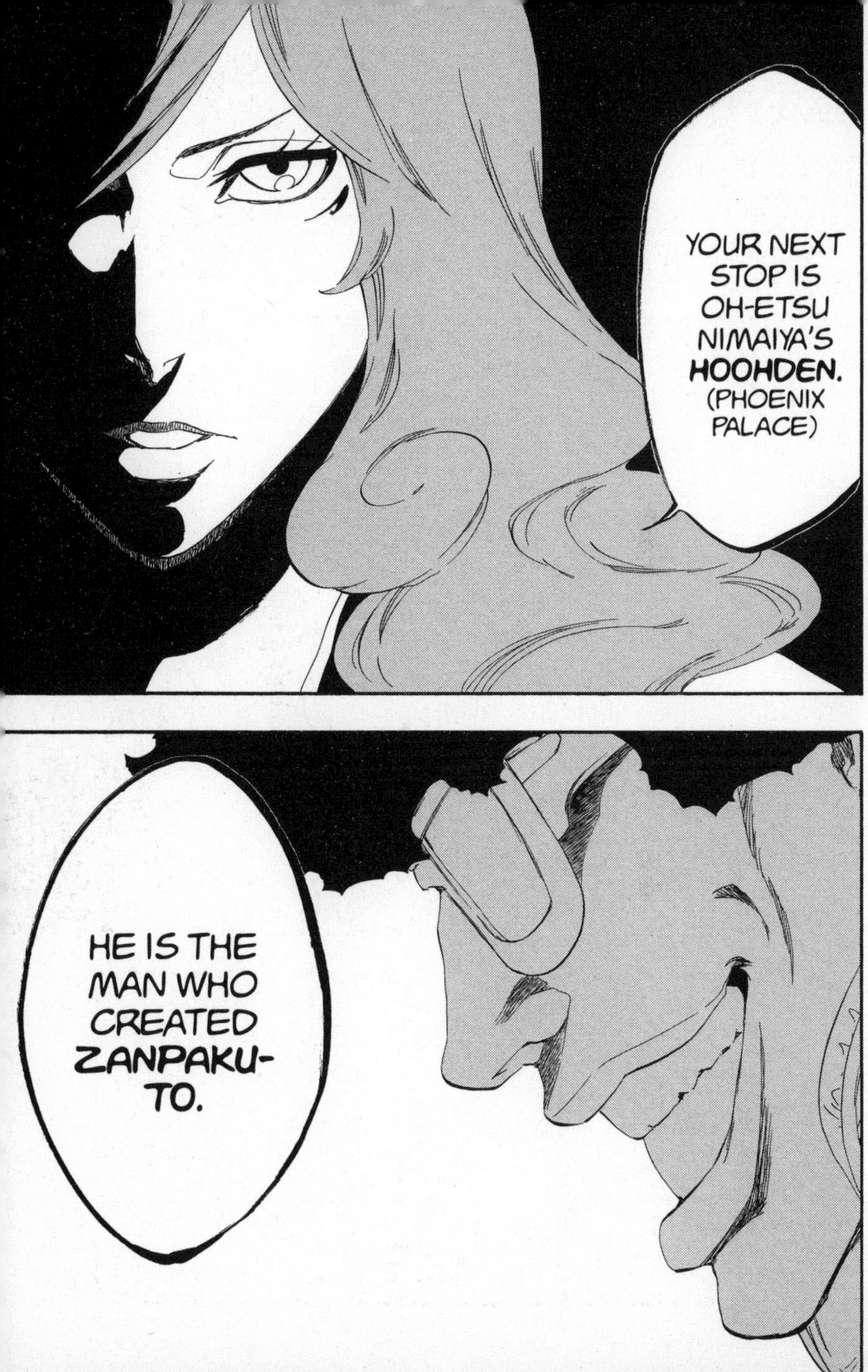
YOUR NEXT STOP IS OH-ETSU NIMAIYA'S **HOOHDEN.** (PHOENIX PALACE)
HE IS THE MAN WHO CREATED **ZANPAKU-TO.**

I BETTER GAIN
SOME MORE
WEIGHT.

522. LOVE IT

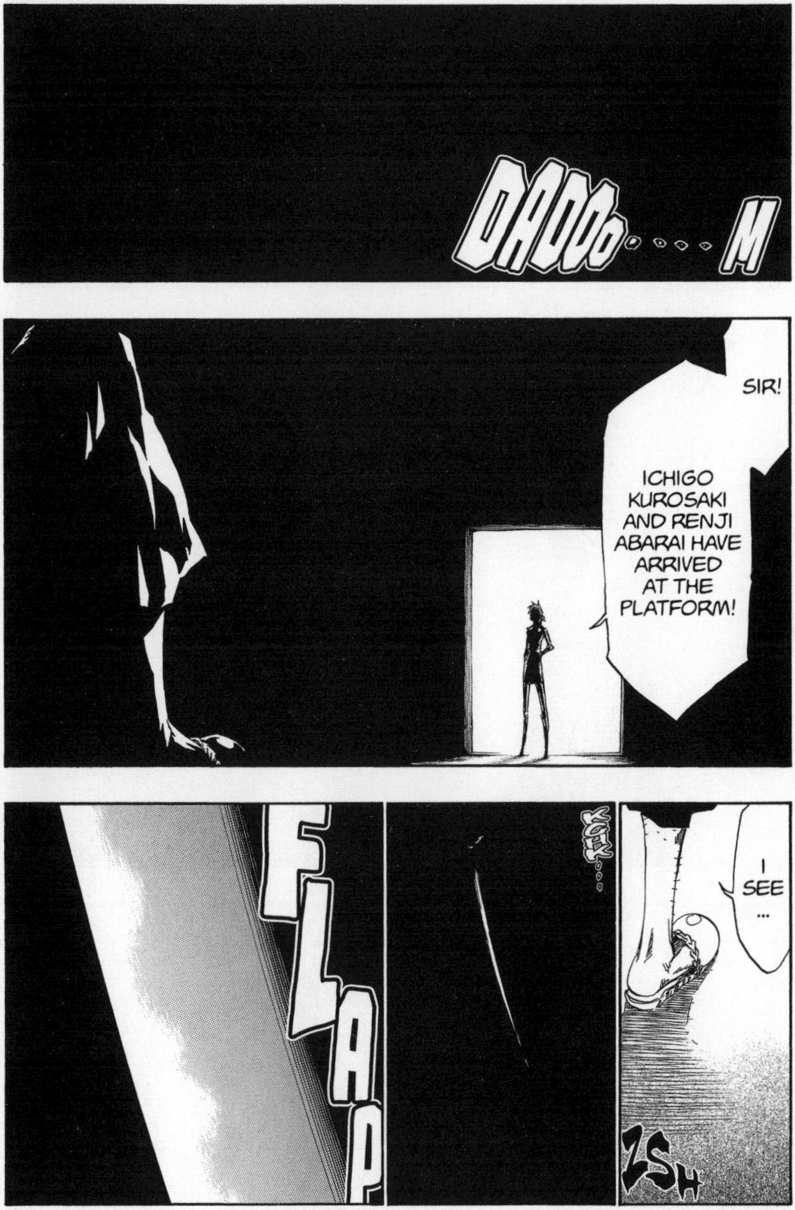
DADOO...M
SIR!
ICHIGO KUROSAKI AND RENJI ABARAI HAVE ARRIVED AT THE PLATFORM!
I SEE ...
ZSH
KCHK...
FLAP

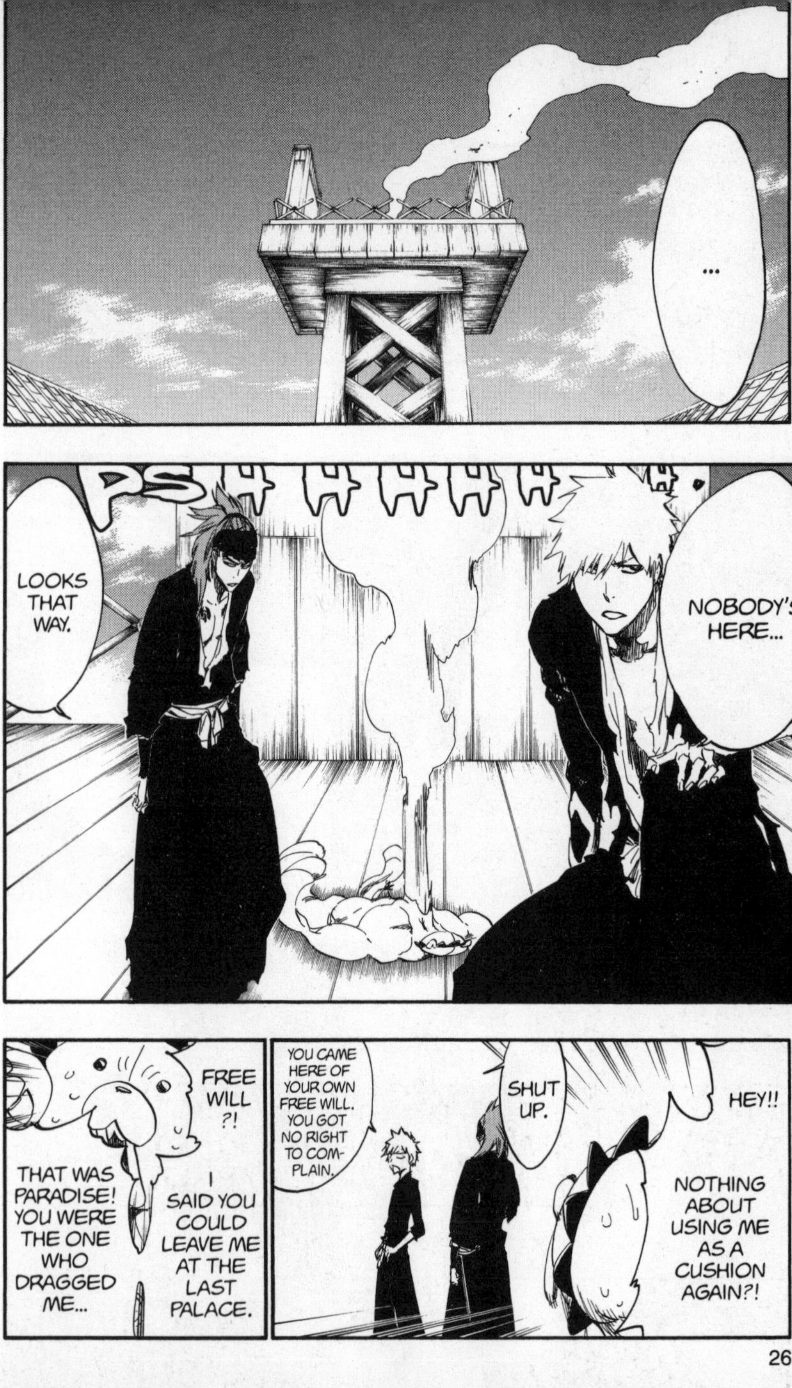
...
NOBODY'S HERE...
LOOKS THAT WAY.
HEY!!
NOTHING ABOUT USING ME AS A CUSHION AGAIN?!
SHUT UP.
YOU CAME HERE OF YOUR OWN FREE WILL. YOU GOT NO RIGHT TO COMPLAIN.
FREE WILL ?!
I SAID YOU COULD LEAVE ME AT THE LAST PALACE.
THAT WAS PARADISE! YOU WERE THE ONE WHO DRAGGED ME...

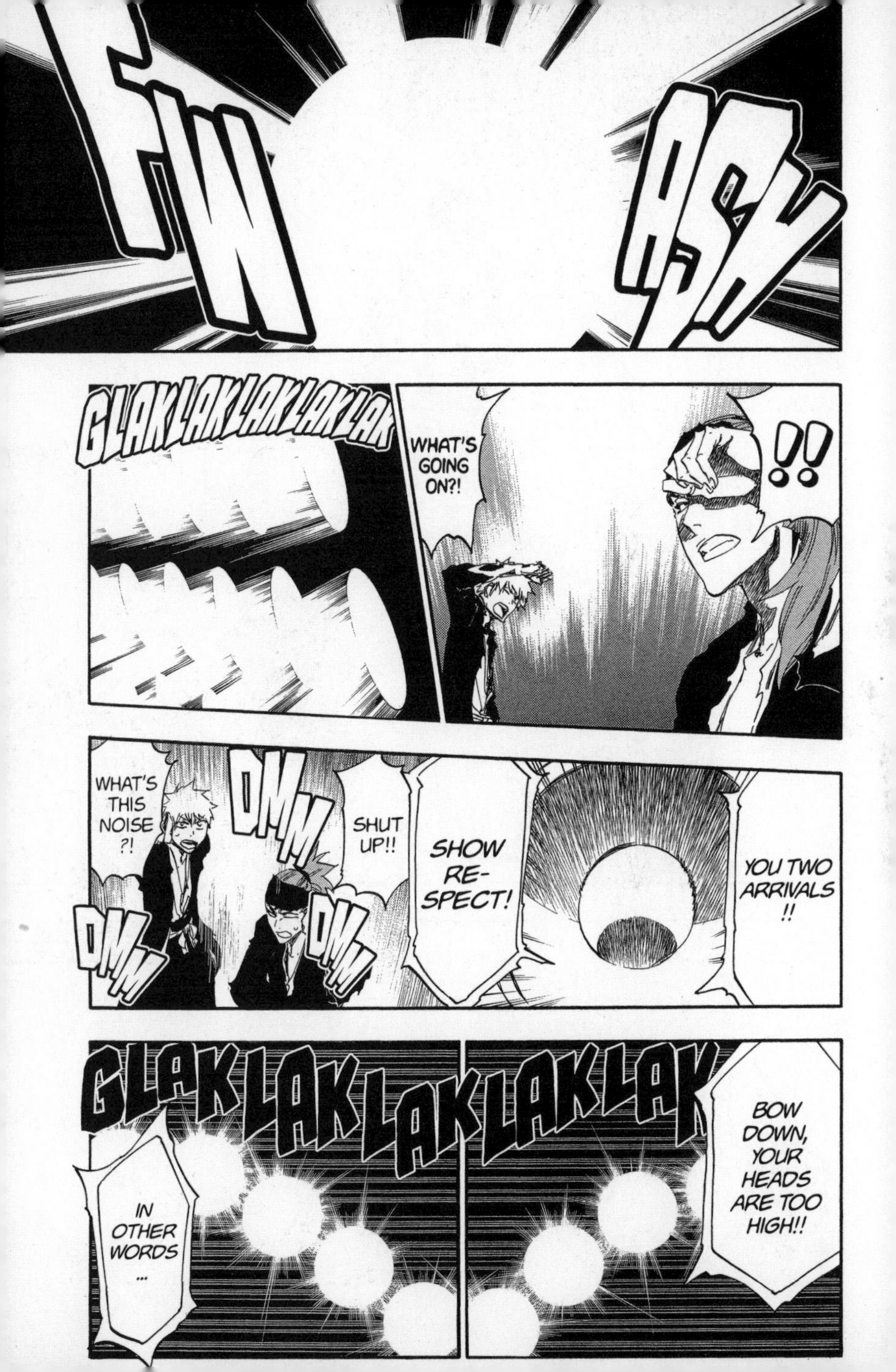
FLASH
!!
WHAT'S GOING ON?!
GLAKLAKLAKLAKLAK
YOU TWO ARRIVALS!!
SHOW RE-SPECT!
SHUT UP!!
DMM
WHAT'S THIS NOISE?!
DMM
DMM
BOW DOWN, YOUR HEADS ARE TOO HIGH!!
GLAKLAKLAKLAKLAK
IN OTHER WORDS...

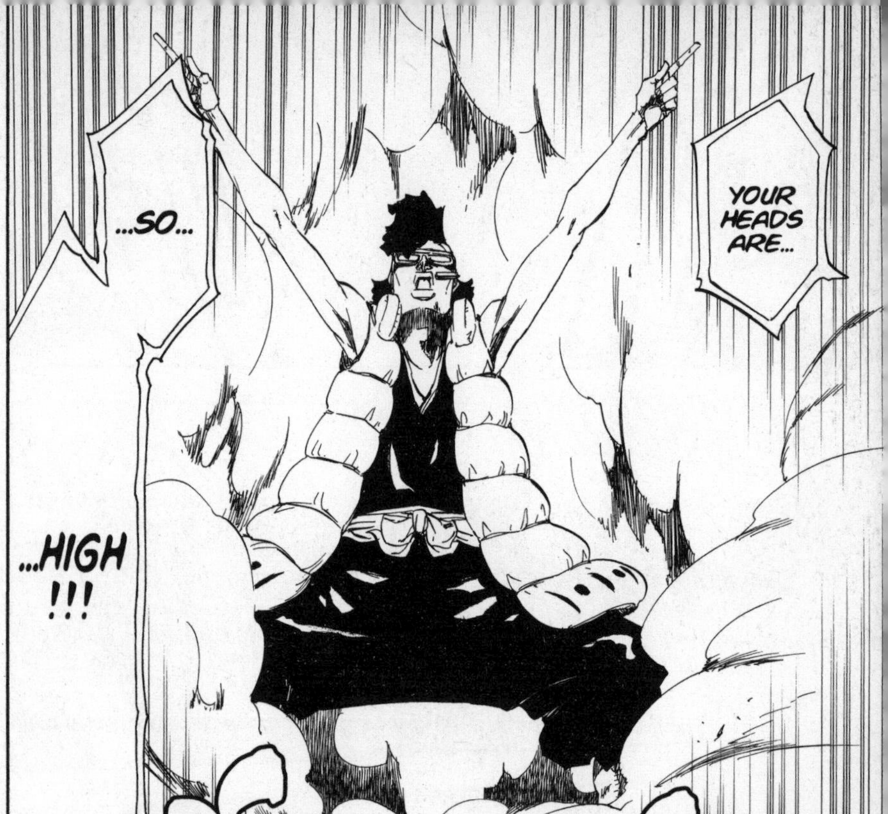
YOUR HEADS ARE...
...SO...
...HIGH !!!
PSS
SHHH
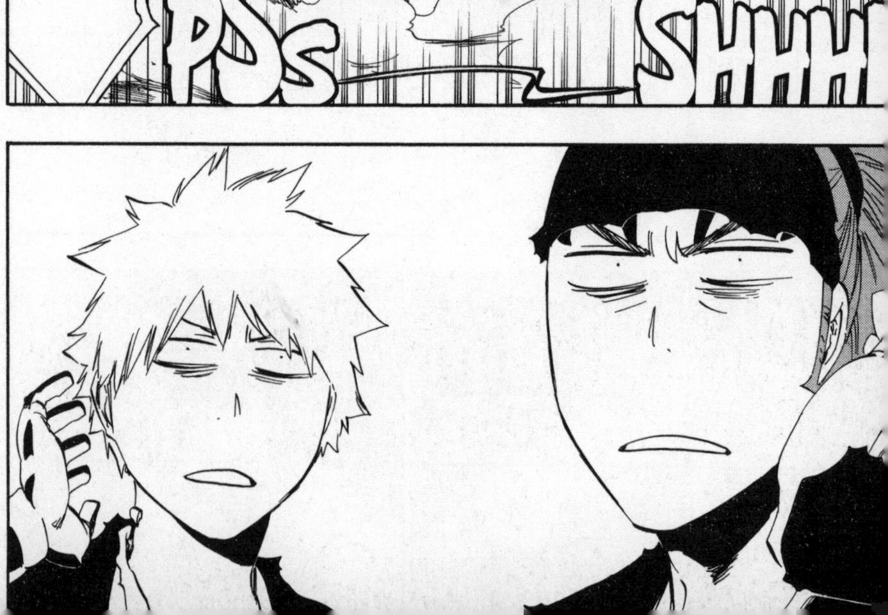

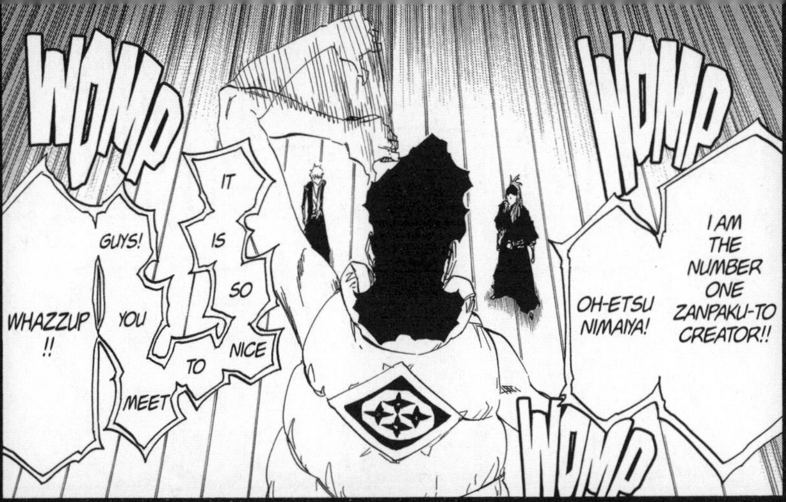
WOMP
WOMP
I AM THE NUMBER ONE ZANPAKU-TO CREATOR!!
OH-ETSU NIMAIYA!
IT IS SO NICE TO MEET YOU
GUYS!
WHAZZUP !!
WOMP

BLEACH 522.

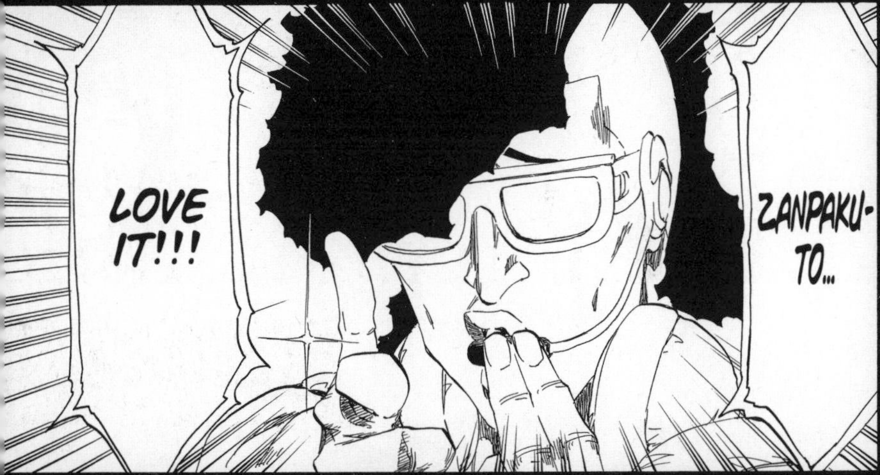
ZANPAKU-TO...
LOVE IT!!!

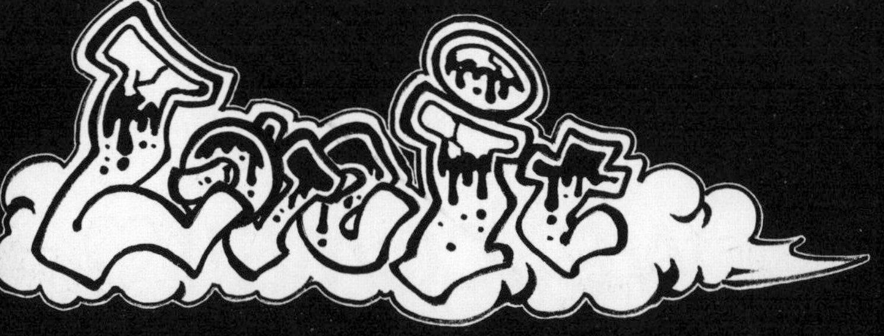

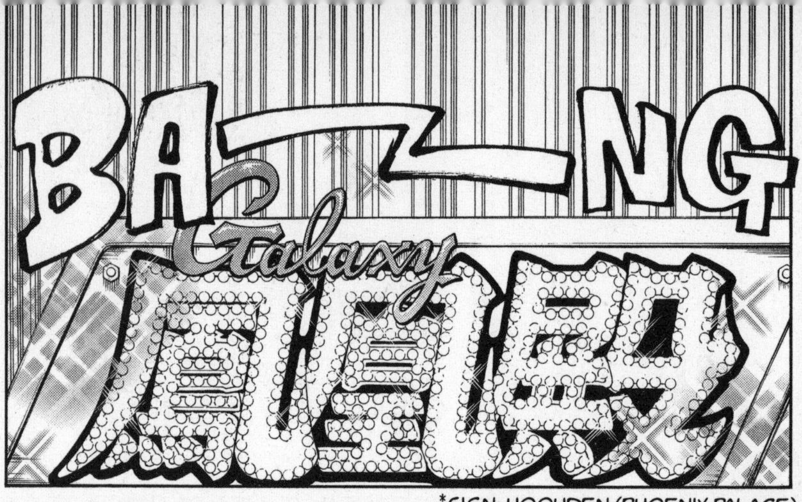
BA—NG
Galaxy
鳳凰殿
*SIGN: HOOHDEN (PHOENIX PALACE)

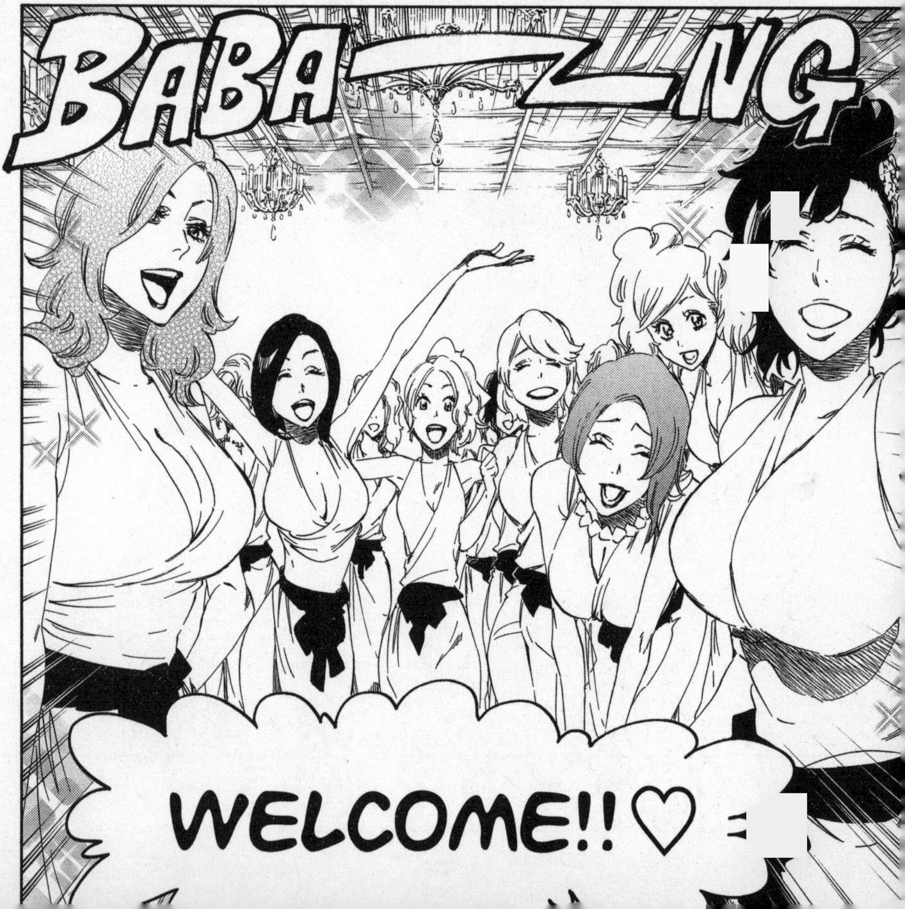
BABA—NG
WELCOME!! ♡

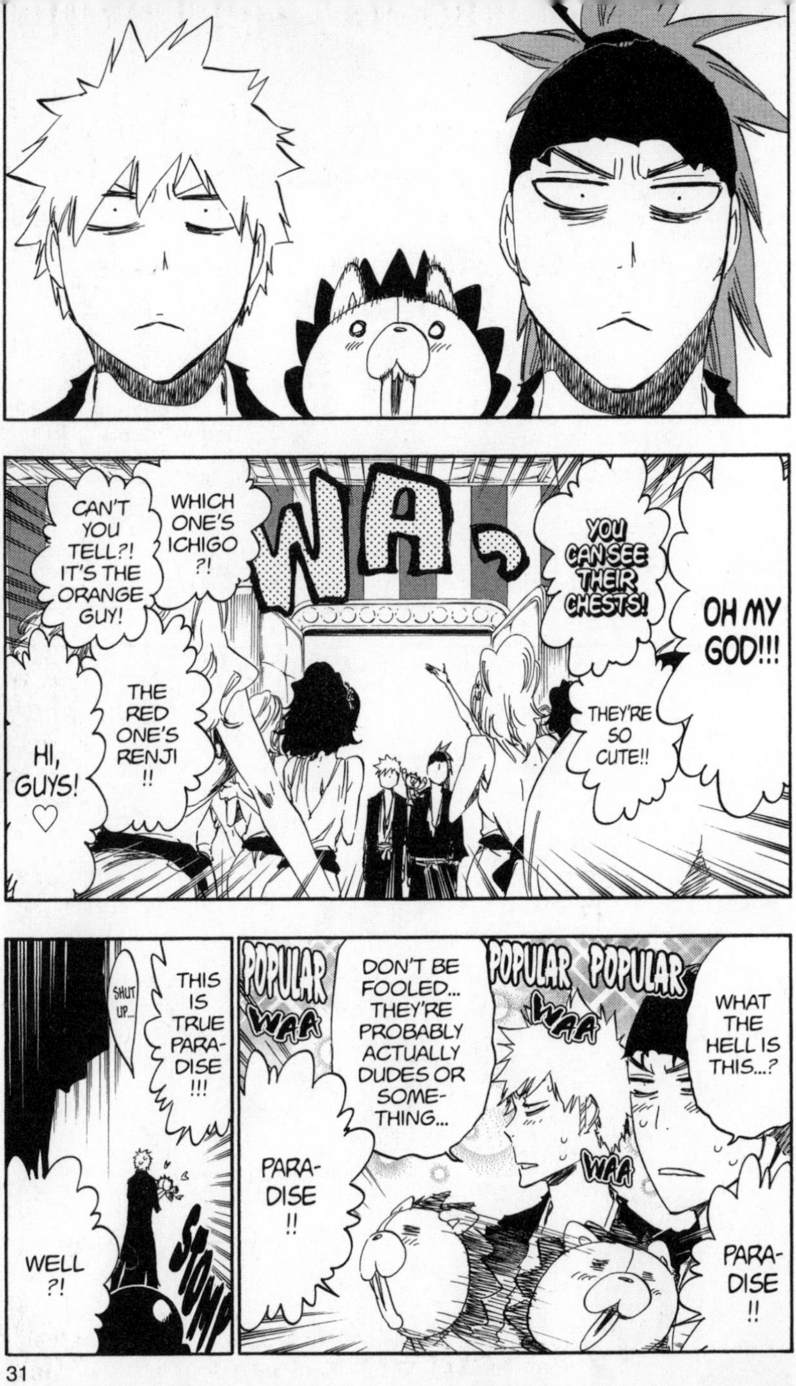
OH MY GOD!!!
YOU CAN SEE THEIR CHESTS!
THEY'RE SO CUTE!!
WA
WHICH ONE'S ICHIGO?!
CAN'T YOU TELL?! IT'S THE ORANGE GUY!
THE RED ONE'S RENJI!!
HI, GUYS! ♡
WHAT THE HELL IS THIS...?
POPULAR POPULAR
WAA
WAA
DON'T BE FOOLED... THEY'RE PROBABLY ACTUALLY DUDES OR SOME-THING...
POPULAR
WAA
PARA-DISE!!
PARA-DISE!!
THIS IS TRUE PARA-DISE!!!
SHUT UP...
WELL?!
STOMP

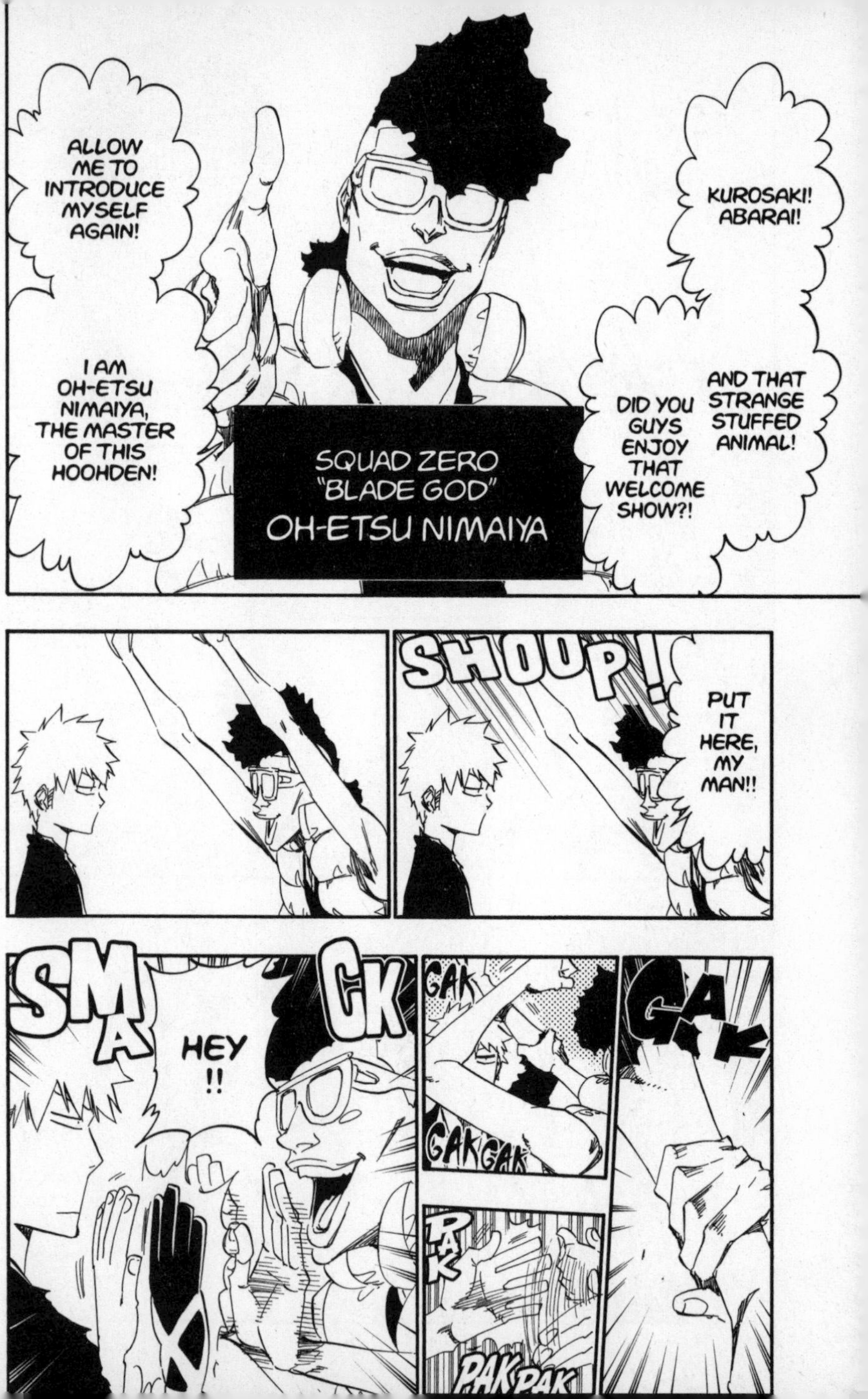
KUROSAKI! ABARAI!
AND THAT STRANGE STUFFED ANIMAL!
DID YOU GUYS ENJOY THAT WELCOME SHOW?!
ALLOW ME TO INTRODUCE MYSELF AGAIN!
I AM OH-ETSU NIMAIYA, THE MASTER OF THIS HOOHDEN!
SQUAD ZERO "BLADE GOD" OH-ETSU NIMAIYA
SHOOP!
PUT IT HERE, MY MAN!!
GAK
GAK
GAKGAK
PAK
PAK PAK
SMACK
HEY!!

READ THIS WAY

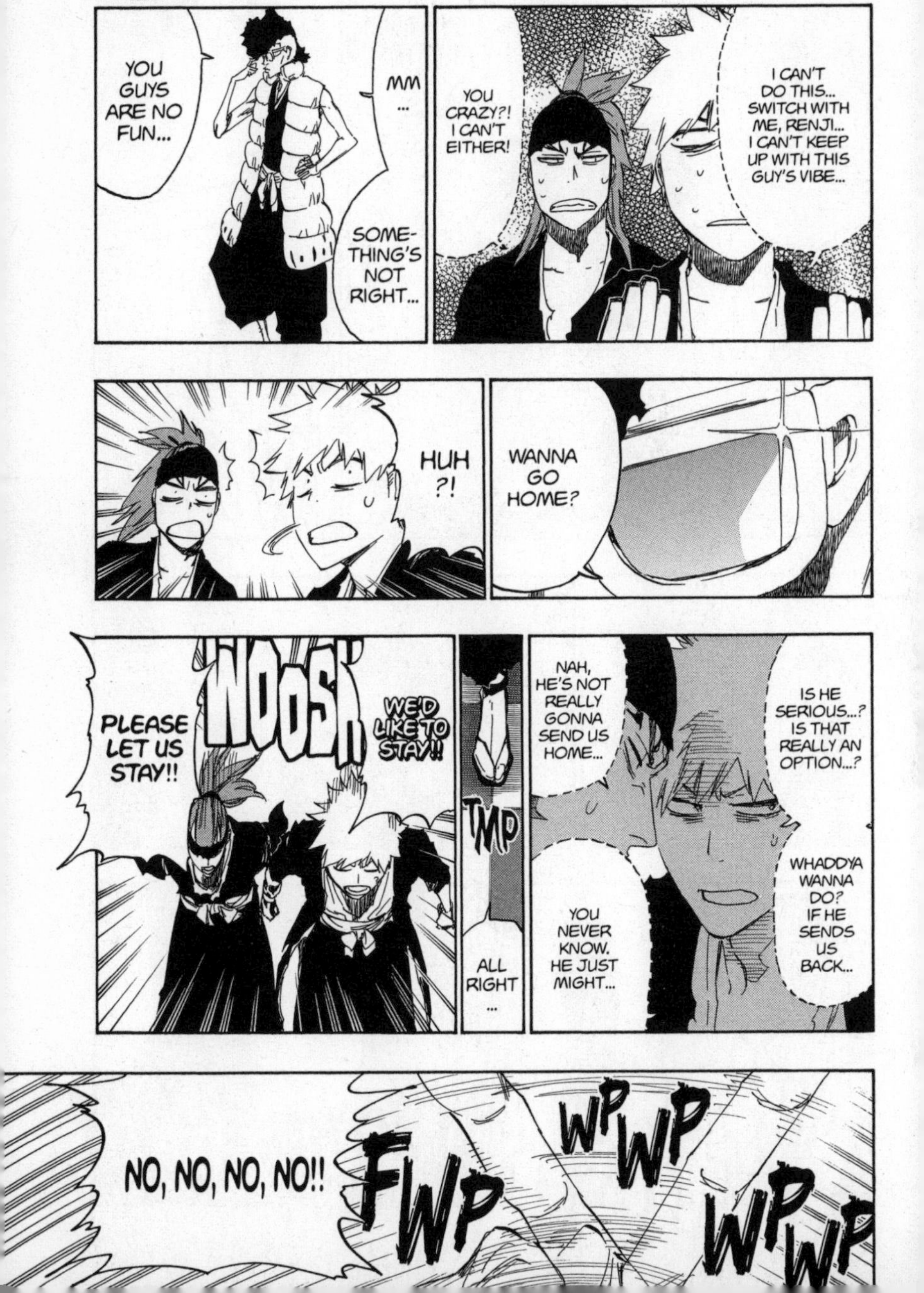
I CAN'T DO THIS... SWITCH WITH ME, RENJI... I CAN'T KEEP UP WITH THIS GUY'S VIBE...
YOU CRAZY?! I CAN'T EITHER!
MM ...
SOME-THING'S NOT RIGHT...
YOU GUYS ARE NO FUN...
WANNA GO HOME?
HUH ?!
IS HE SERIOUS...? IS THAT REALLY AN OPTION...?
NAH, HE'S NOT REALLY GONNA SEND US HOME...
WHADDYA WANNA DO? IF HE SENDS US BACK...
YOU NEVER KNOW. HE JUST MIGHT...
TMP
ALL RIGHT ...
WHOOSH
WE'D LIKE TO STAY!!
PLEASE LET US STAY!!
WP WP
WP WP WP
FWP
NO, NO, NO, NO!!

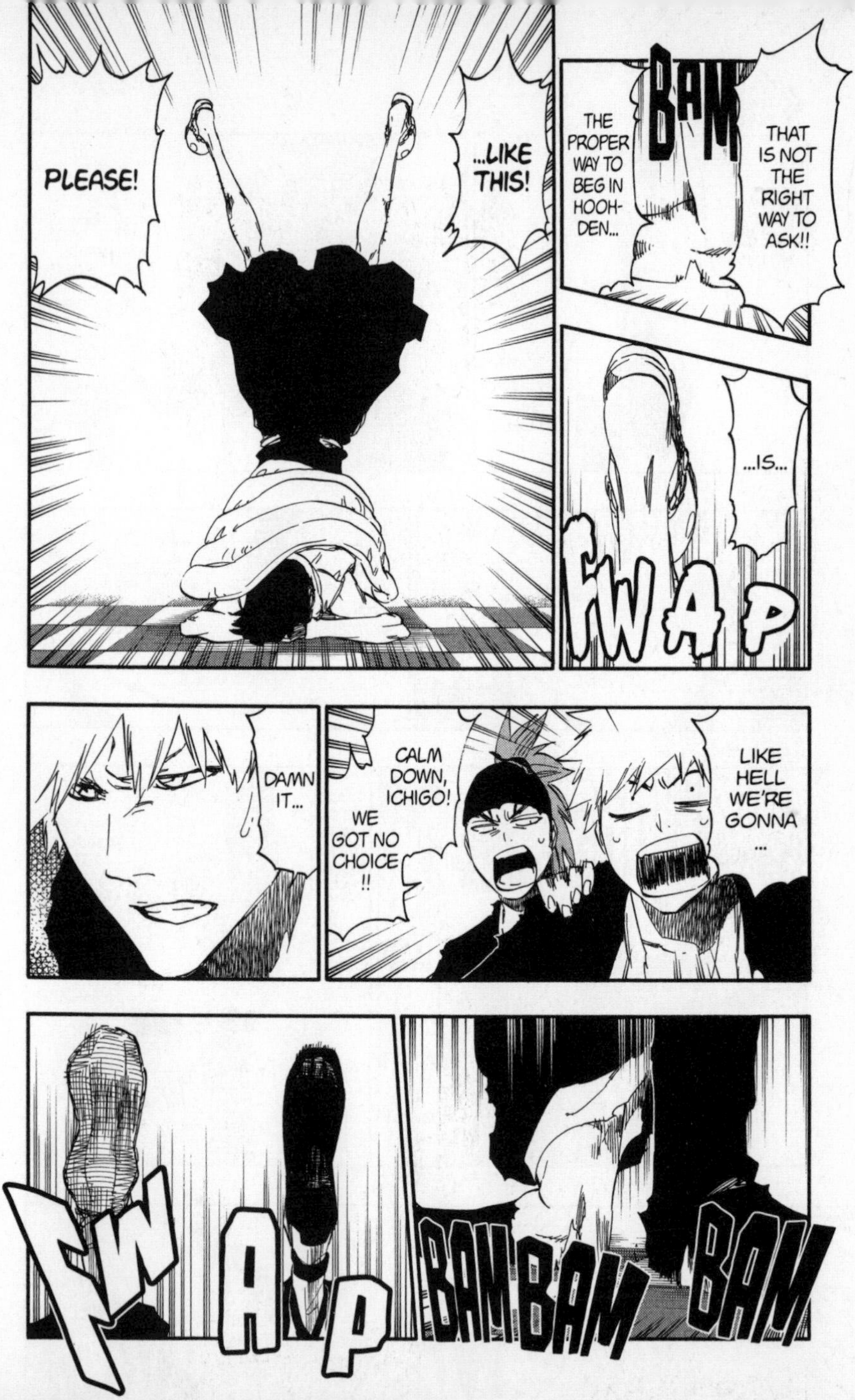
BAM
THAT IS NOT THE RIGHT WAY TO ASK!!
THE PROPER WAY TO BEG IN HOOH-DEN...
...IS...
FWAP
...LIKE THIS!
PLEASE!
LIKE HELL WE'RE GONNA ...
CALM DOWN, ICHIGO!
WE GOT NO CHOICE !!
DAMN IT...
BAM BAM BAM BAM
FWAP

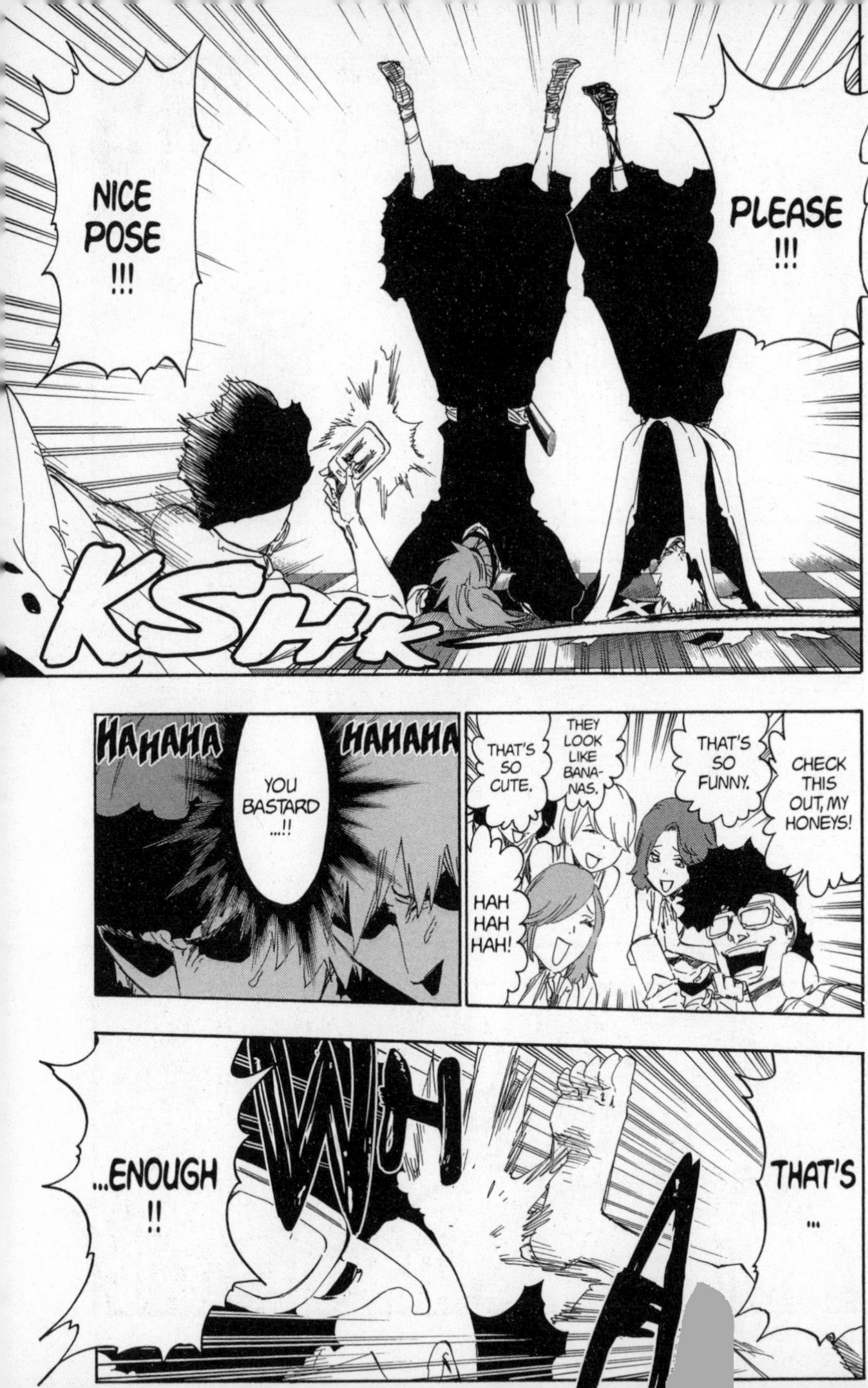
PLEASE !!!
NICE POSE !!!
KSHK
CHECK THIS OUT, MY HONEYS!
THAT'S SO FUNNY.
THEY LOOK LIKE BANA-NAS.
THAT'S SO CUTE.
HAH HAH HAH!
HAHAHA
YOU BASTARD ...!!
HAHAHA
THAT'S ...
WHA
...ENOUGH !!

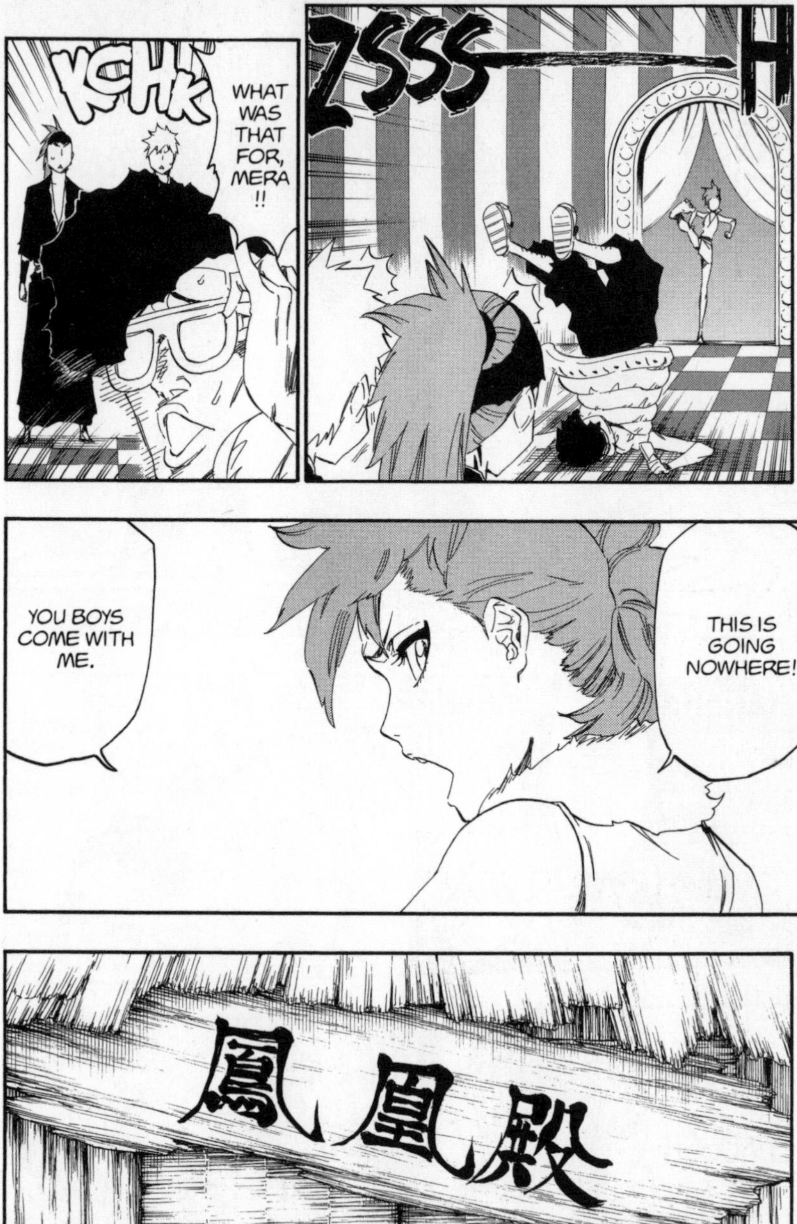
ZSSS—H
KCHK
WHAT WAS THAT FOR, MERA !!
THIS IS GOING NOWHERE!
YOU BOYS COME WITH ME.
鳳凰殿

*SIGN: HOOHDEN

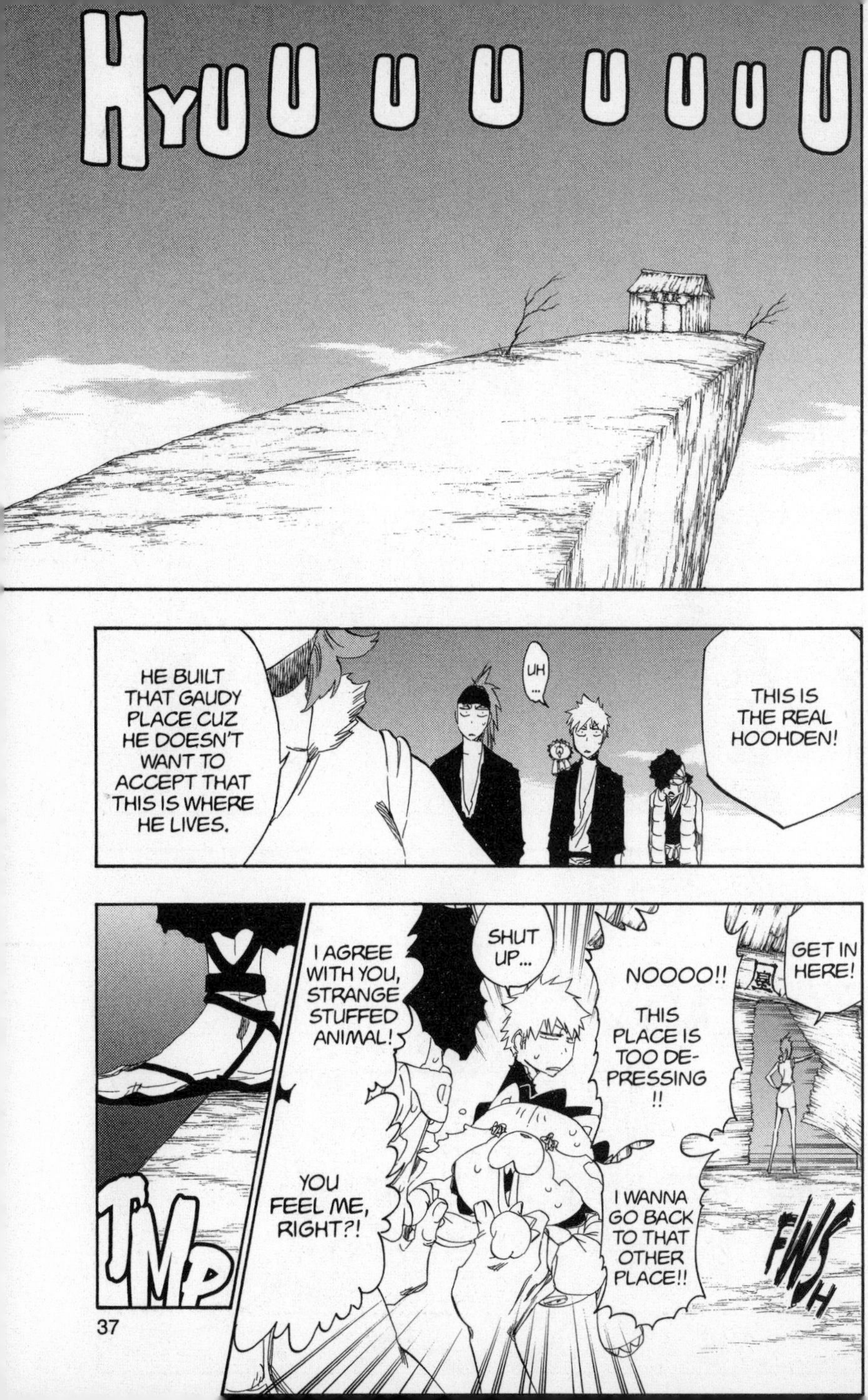
HYUUUUUUUUU
THIS IS THE REAL HOOHDEN!
UH ...
HE BUILT THAT GAUDY PLACE CUZ HE DOESN'T WANT TO ACCEPT THAT THIS IS WHERE HE LIVES.
GET IN HERE!
NOOOO!!
THIS PLACE IS TOO DE-PRESSING!!
I WANNA GO BACK TO THAT OTHER PLACE!!
FWSH
SHUT UP...
I AGREE WITH YOU, STRANGE STUFFED ANIMAL!
YOU FEEL ME, RIGHT?!
TMP

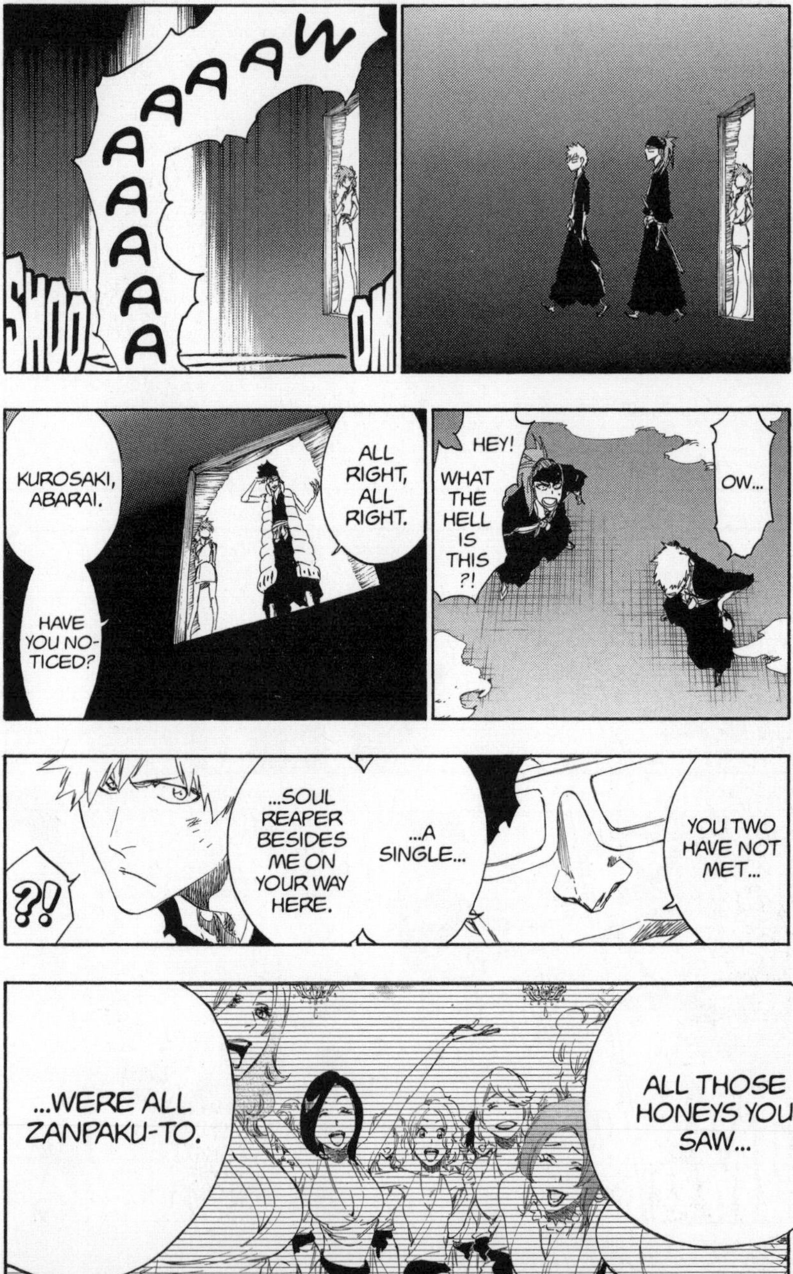
AAAAAAAAW
SHOO
OM
OW...
HEY!
WHAT THE HELL IS THIS?!
ALL RIGHT, ALL RIGHT.
KUROSAKI, ABARAI.
HAVE YOU NOTICED?
YOU TWO HAVE NOT MET...
...A SINGLE...
...SOUL REAPER BESIDES ME ON YOUR WAY HERE.
?!
ALL THOSE HONEYS YOU SAW...
...WERE ALL ZANPAKU-TO.

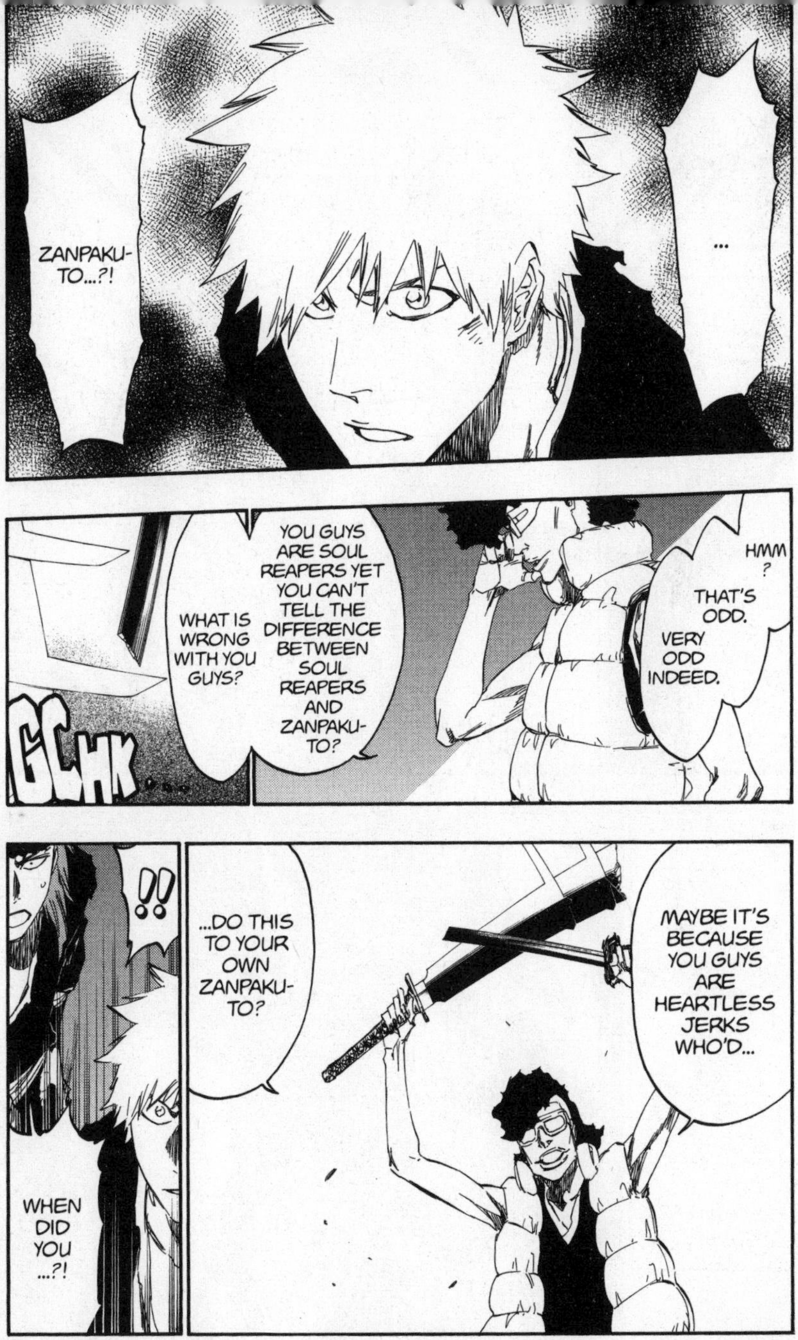
...
ZANPAKU-TO...?!
HMM?
THAT'S ODD.
VERY ODD INDEED.
YOU GUYS ARE SOUL REAPERS YET YOU CAN'T TELL THE DIFFERENCE BETWEEN SOUL REAPERS AND ZANPAKU-TO?
WHAT IS WRONG WITH YOU GUYS?
GCHK...
MAYBE IT'S BECAUSE YOU GUYS ARE HEARTLESS JERKS WHO'D...
...DO THIS TO YOUR OWN ZANPAKU-TO?
!!
WHEN DID YOU ...?!

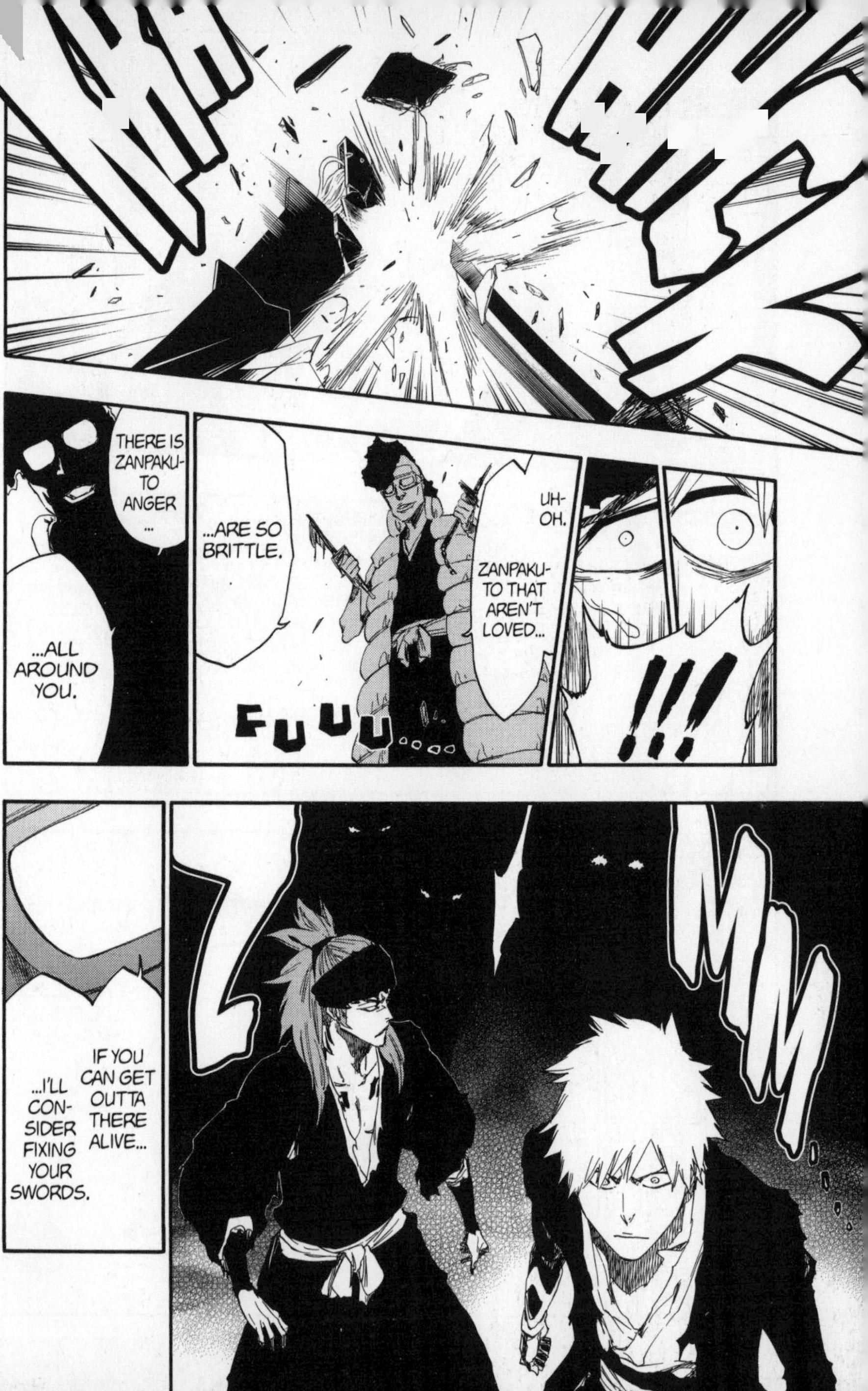
!!!
UH-OH.
ZANPAKU-TO THAT AREN'T LOVED...
...ARE SO BRITTLE.
FUUU
THERE IS ZANPAKU-TO ANGER ...
...ALL AROUND YOU.
IF YOU CAN GET OUTTA THERE ALIVE...
...I'LL CON-SIDER FIXING YOUR SWORDS.

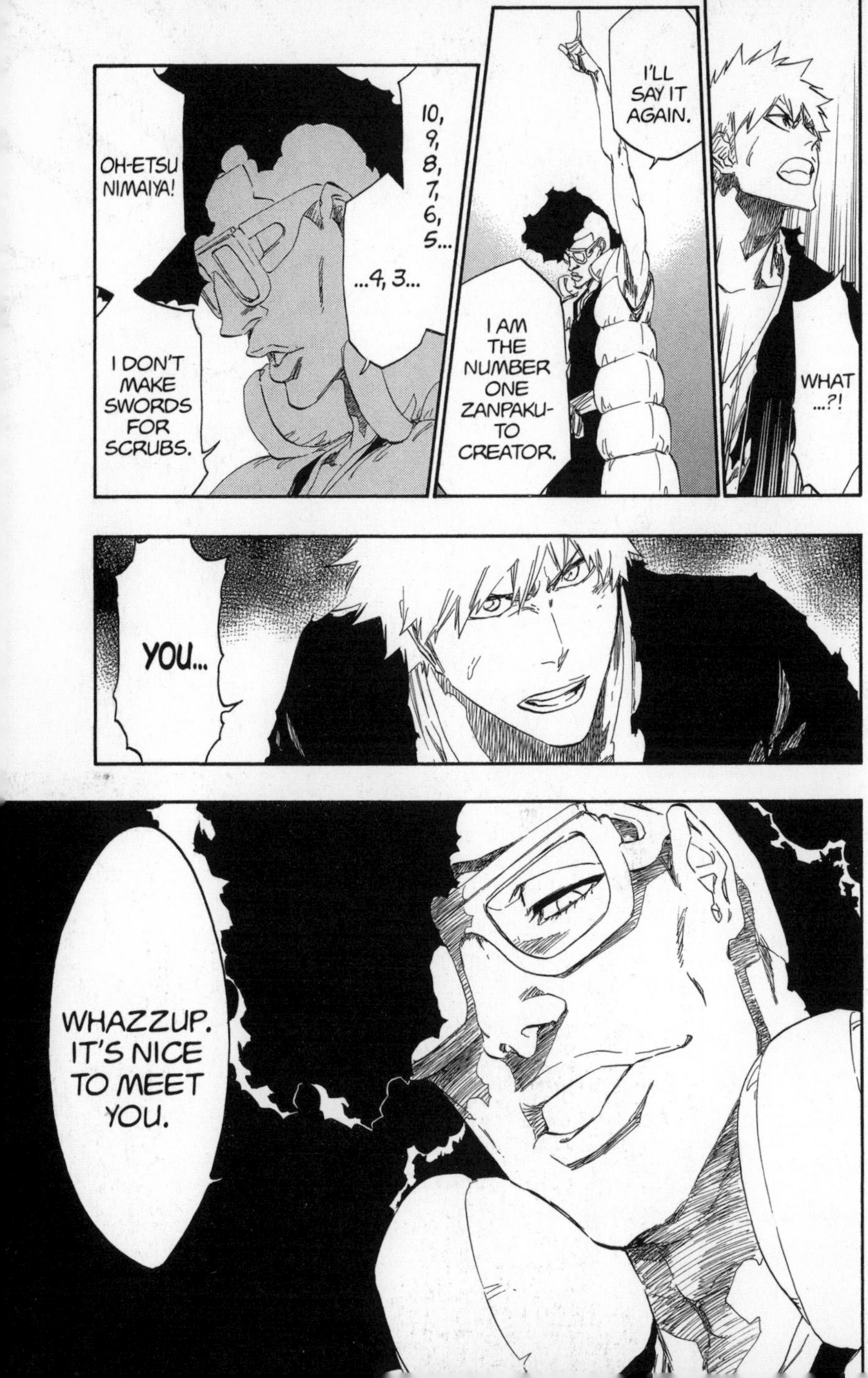
WHAT ...?!
I'LL SAY IT AGAIN.
I AM THE NUMBER ONE ZANPAKU-TO CREATOR.
10, 9, 8, 7, 6, 5...
...4, 3...
OH-ETSU NIMAIYA!
I DON'T MAKE SWORDS FOR SCRUBS.
YOU...
WHAZZUP. IT'S NICE TO MEET YOU.

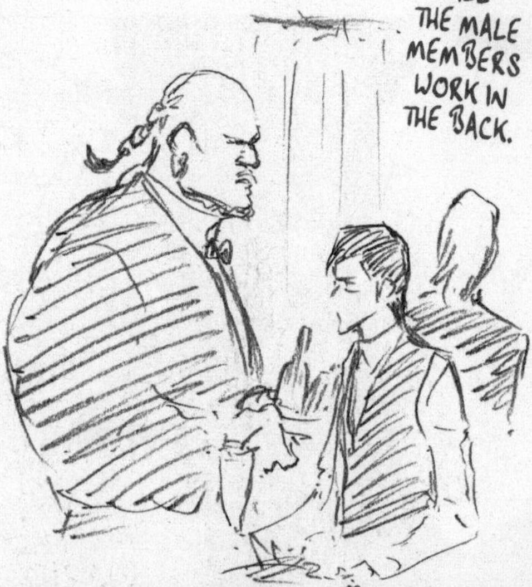
ALL THE MALE MEMBERS WORK IN THE BACK.

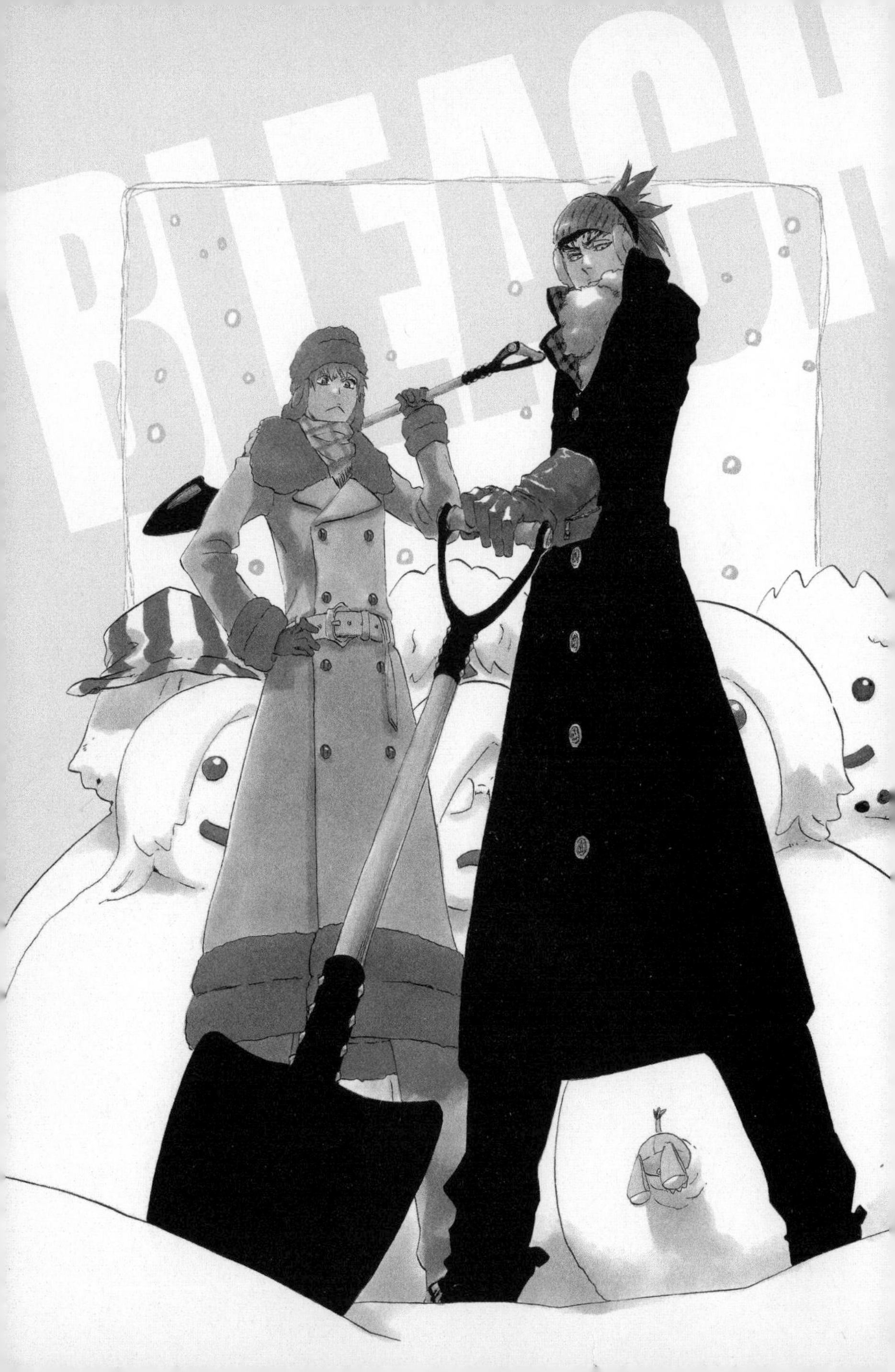
BLEACH

BLEACH
ブリーチ

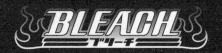

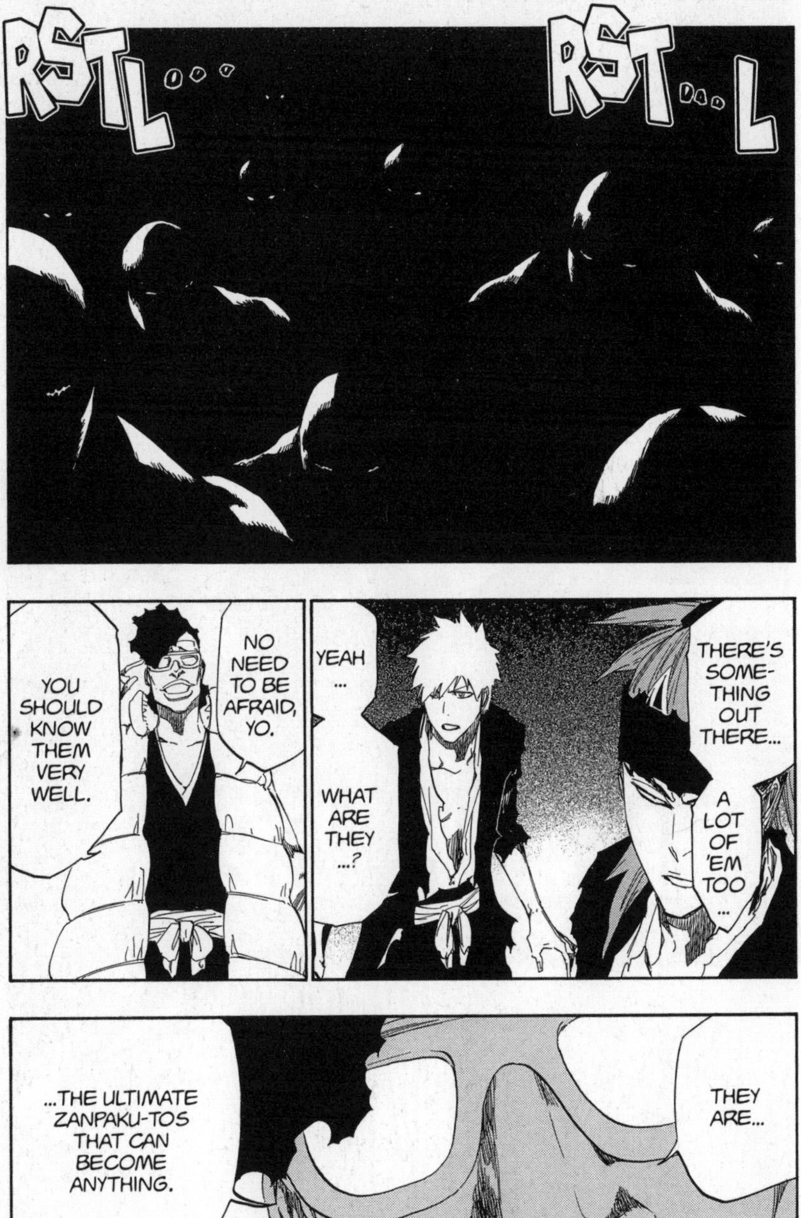
RST...L
RSTL...
THERE'S SOME-THING OUT THERE...
A LOT OF 'EM TOO...
YEAH...
WHAT ARE THEY...?
NO NEED TO BE AFRAID, YO.
YOU SHOULD KNOW THEM VERY WELL.
THEY ARE...
...THE ULTIMATE ZANPAKU-TOS THAT CAN BECOME ANYTHING.

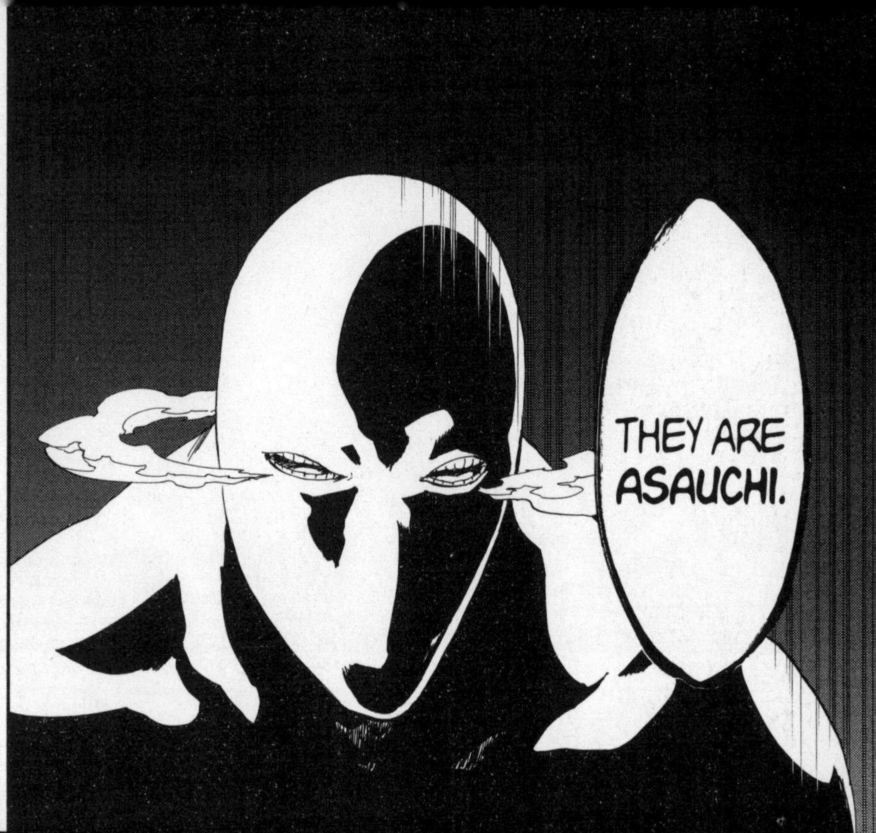
THEY ARE
ASAUCHI.

BLEACH 523

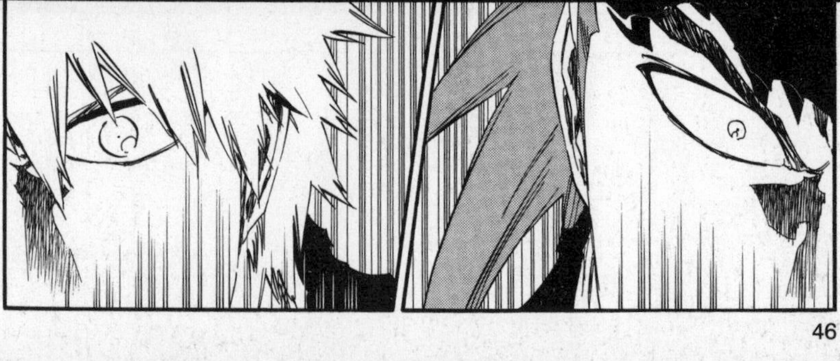

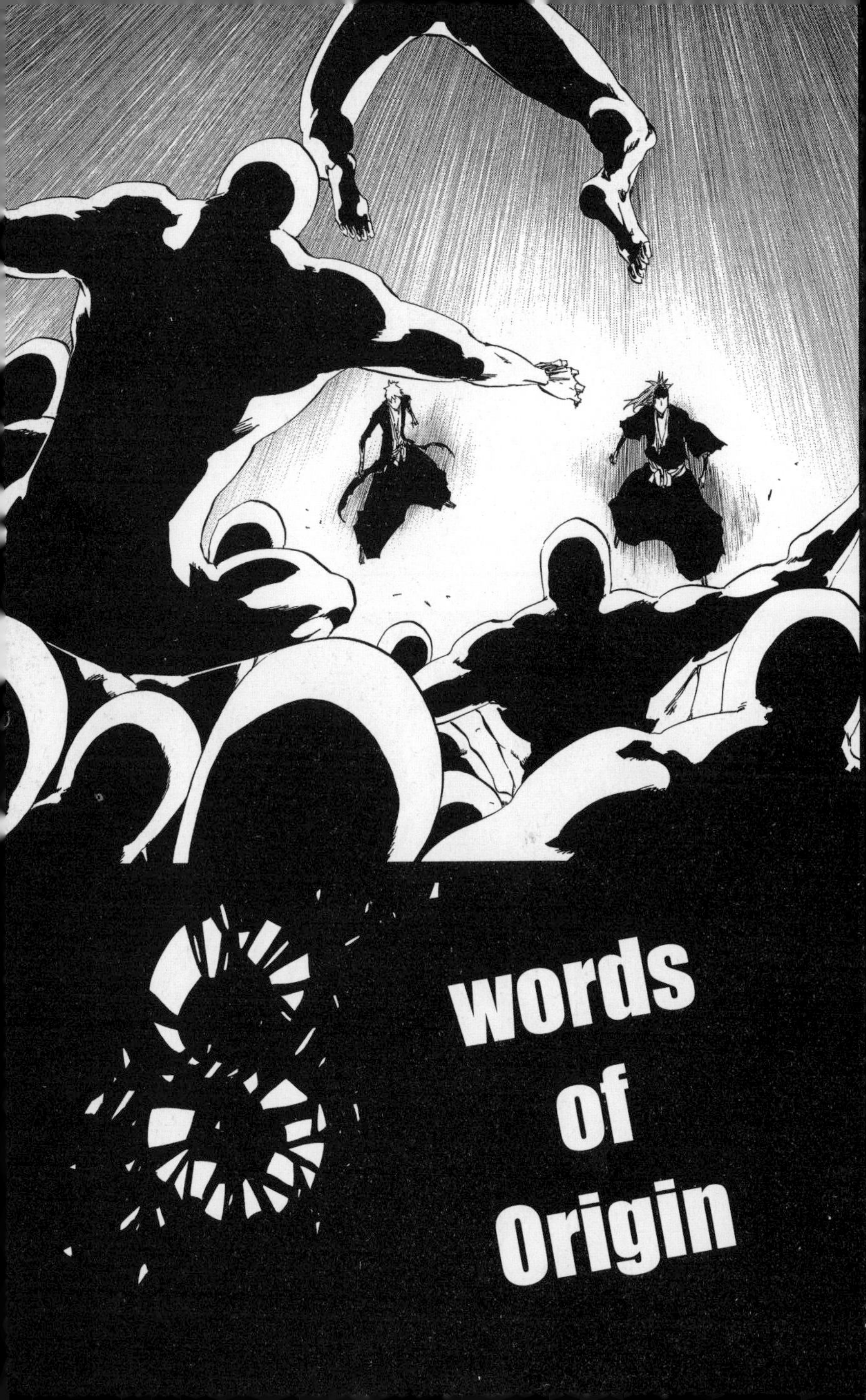
words of Origin

「浅打」(あさうち)

ASAUCHI

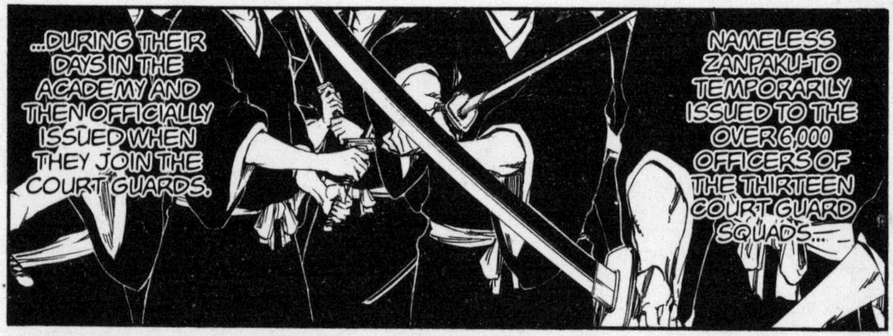
NAMELESS ZANPAKU-TO TEMPORARILY ISSUED TO THE OVER 6,000 OFFICERS OF THE THIRTEEN COURT GUARD SQUADS...
...DURING THEIR DAYS IN THE ACADEMY AND THEN OFFICIALLY ISSUED WHEN THEY JOIN THE COURT GUARDS.

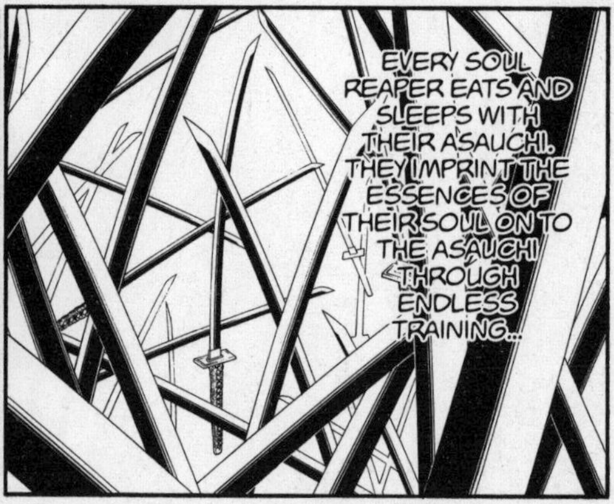
EVERY SOUL REAPER EATS AND SLEEPS WITH THEIR ASAUCHI. THEY IMPRINT THE ESSENCES OF THEIR SOUL ON TO THE ASAUCHI THROUGH ENDLESS TRAINING...

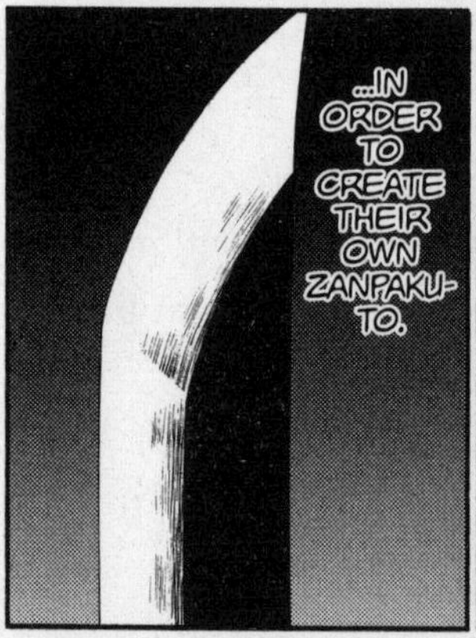
...IN ORDER TO CREATE THEIR OWN ZANPAKU-TO.

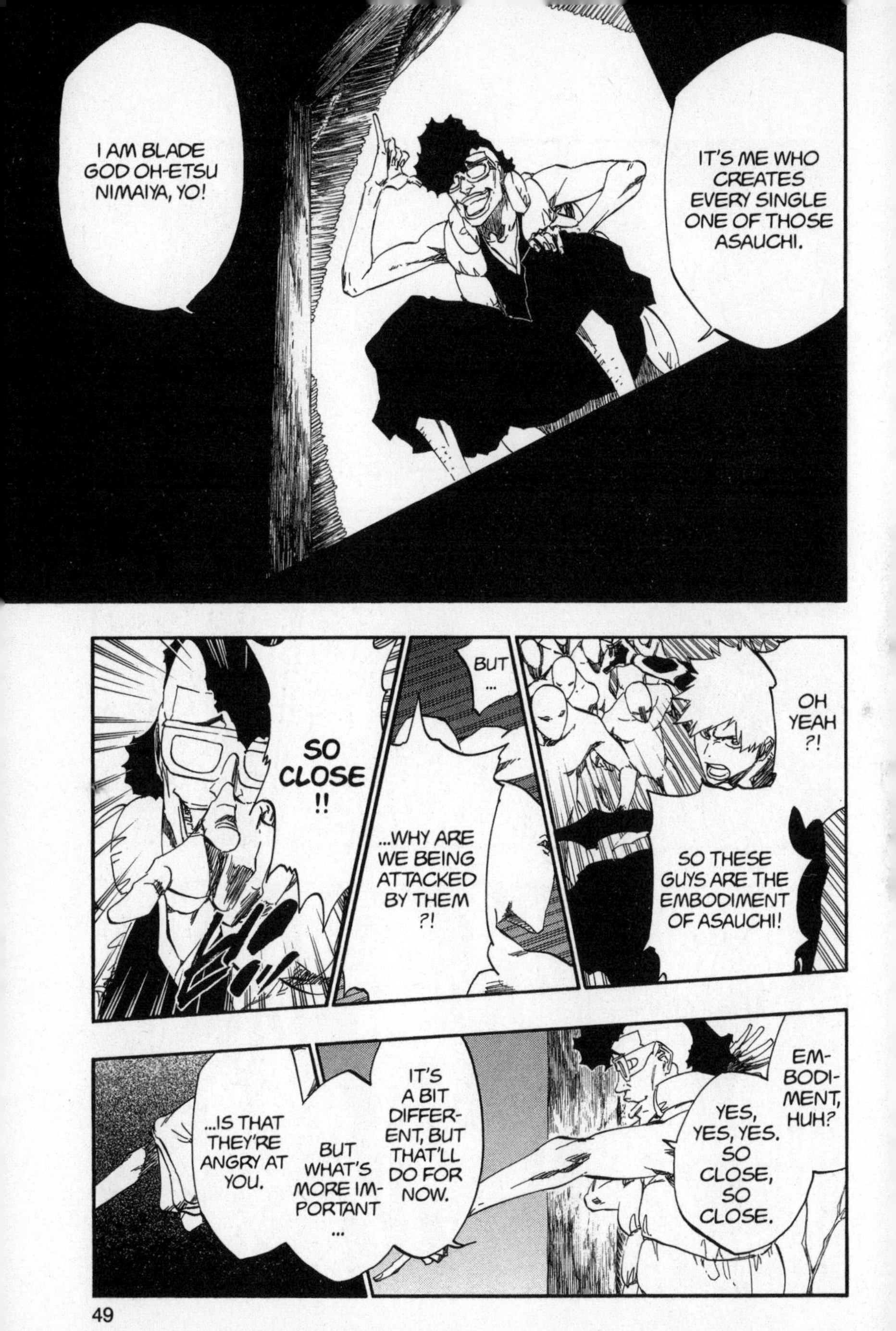
IT'S ME WHO CREATES EVERY SINGLE ONE OF THOSE ASAUCHI.
I AM BLADE GOD OH-ETSU NIMAIYA, YO!
OH YEAH?!
SO THESE GUYS ARE THE EMBODIMENT OF ASAUCHI!
BUT...
...WHY ARE WE BEING ATTACKED BY THEM?!
SO CLOSE!!
EMBODIMENT, HUH?
YES, YES, YES. SO CLOSE, SO CLOSE.
IT'S A BIT DIFFERENT, BUT THAT'LL DO FOR NOW.
BUT WHAT'S MORE IMPORTANT...
...IS THAT THEY'RE ANGRY AT YOU.

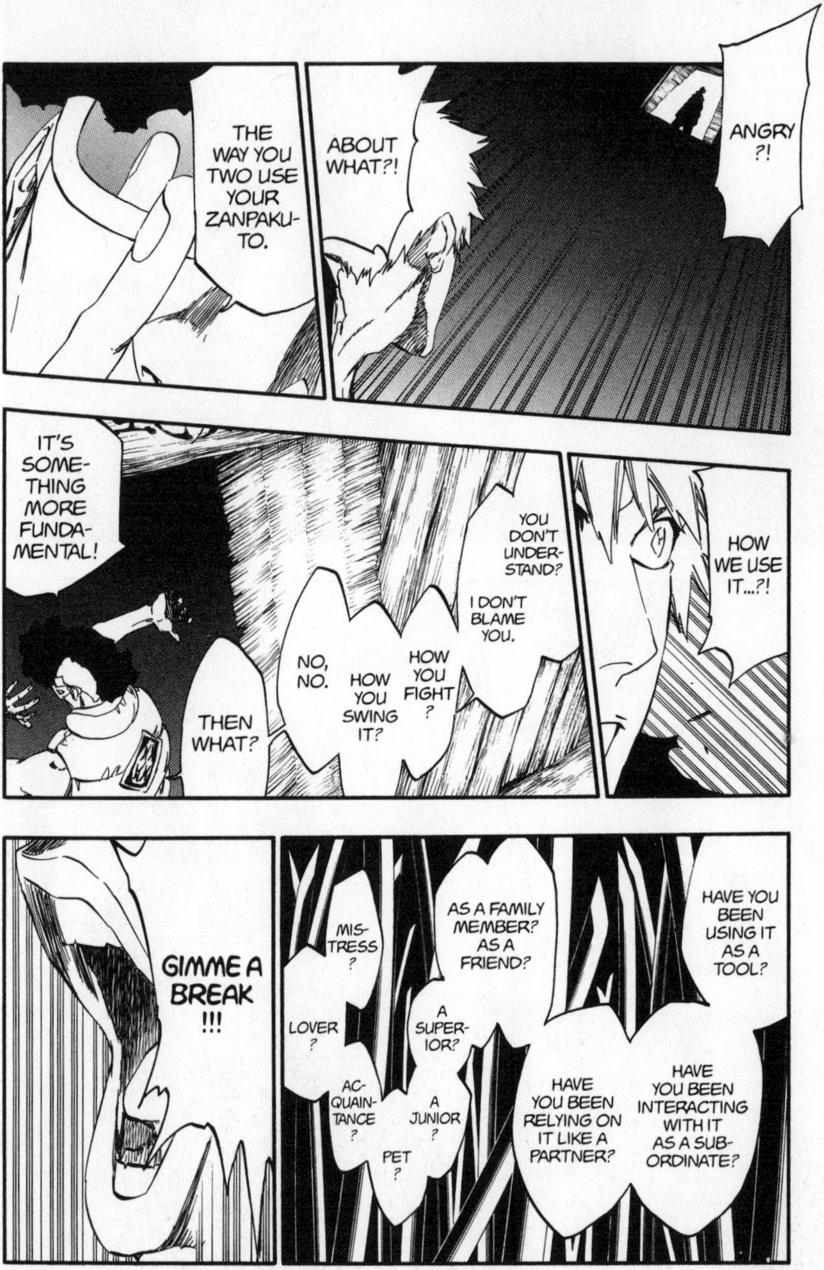
ANGRY?!
ABOUT WHAT?!
THE WAY YOU TWO USE YOUR ZANPAKU-TO.
HOW WE USE IT...?!
YOU DON'T UNDERSTAND?
I DON'T BLAME YOU.
HOW YOU FIGHT?
HOW YOU SWING IT?
NO, NO.
THEN WHAT?
IT'S SOMETHING MORE FUNDAMENTAL!
HAVE YOU BEEN USING IT AS A TOOL?
AS A FAMILY MEMBER? AS A FRIEND?
MISTRESS?
HAVE YOU BEEN INTERACTING WITH IT AS A SUBORDINATE?
HAVE YOU BEEN RELYING ON IT LIKE A PARTNER?
A SUPERIOR?
LOVER?
A JUNIOR?
ACQUAINTANCE?
PET?
GIMME A BREAK!!!

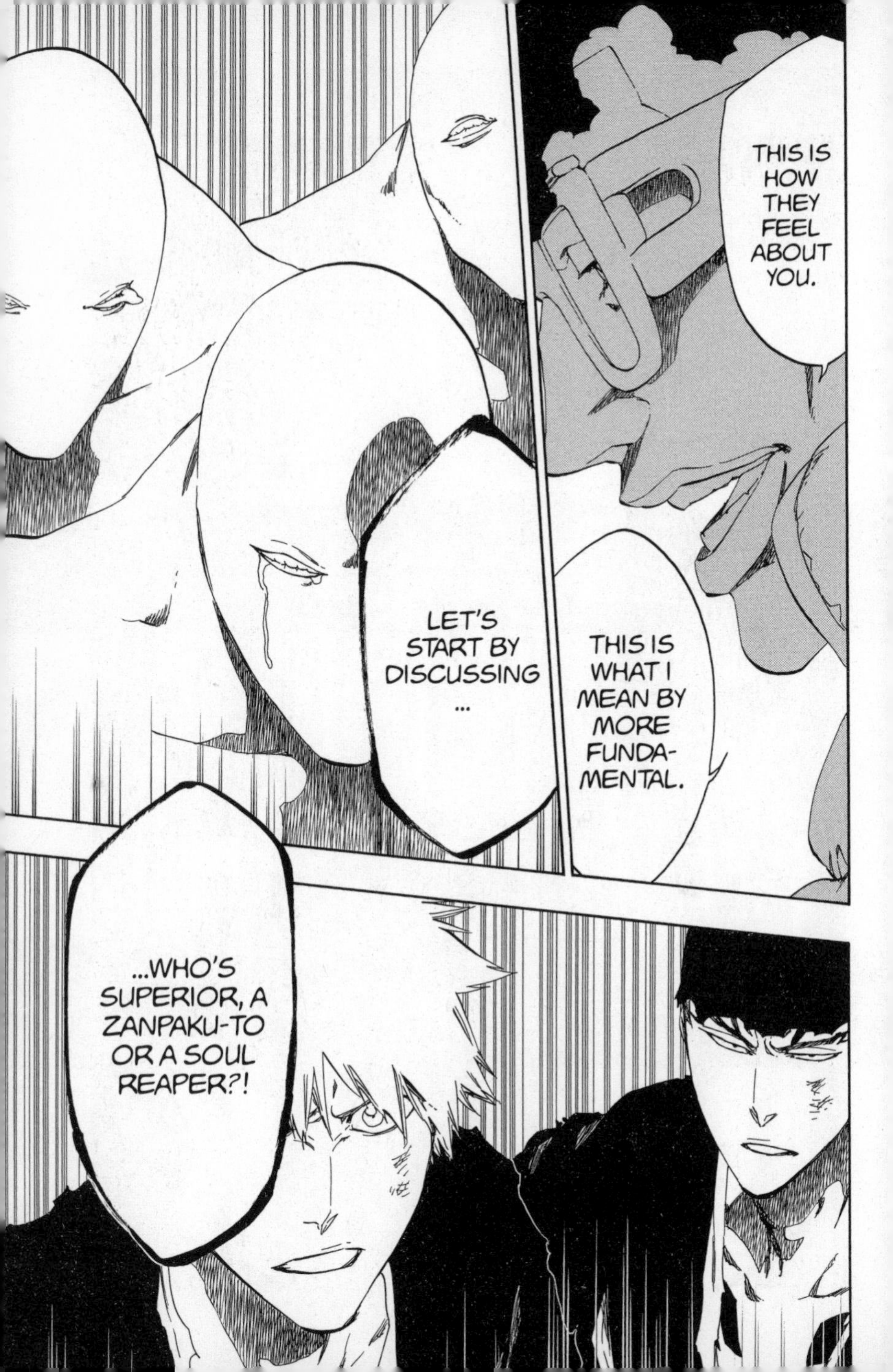
THIS IS HOW THEY FEEL ABOUT YOU.
THIS IS WHAT I MEAN BY MORE FUNDA-MENTAL.
LET'S START BY DISCUSSING ...
...WHO'S SUPERIOR, A ZANPAKU-TO OR A SOUL REAPER?!

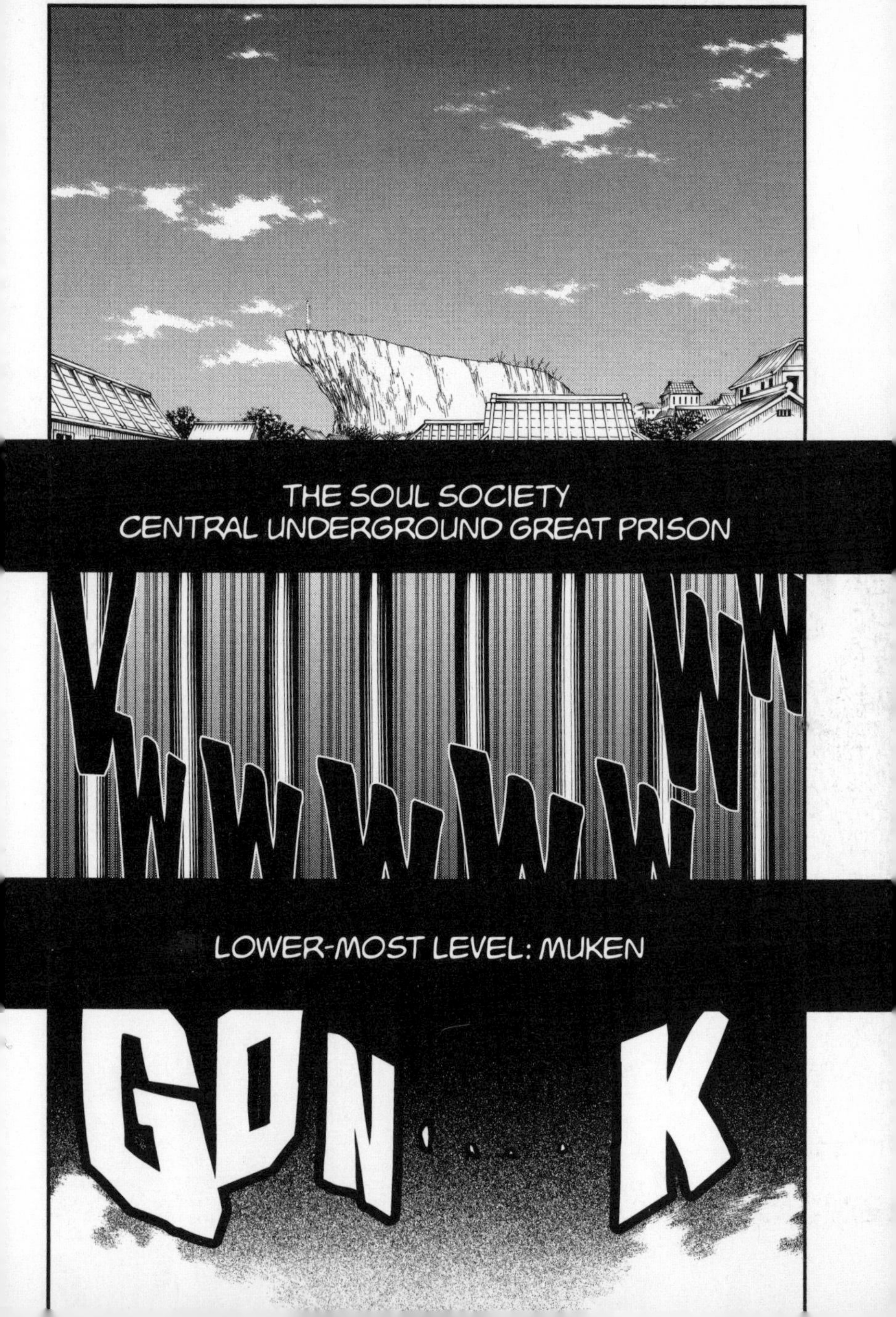
THE SOUL SOCIETY
CENTRAL UNDERGROUND GREAT PRISON
LOWER-MOST LEVEL: MUKEN
GON....K

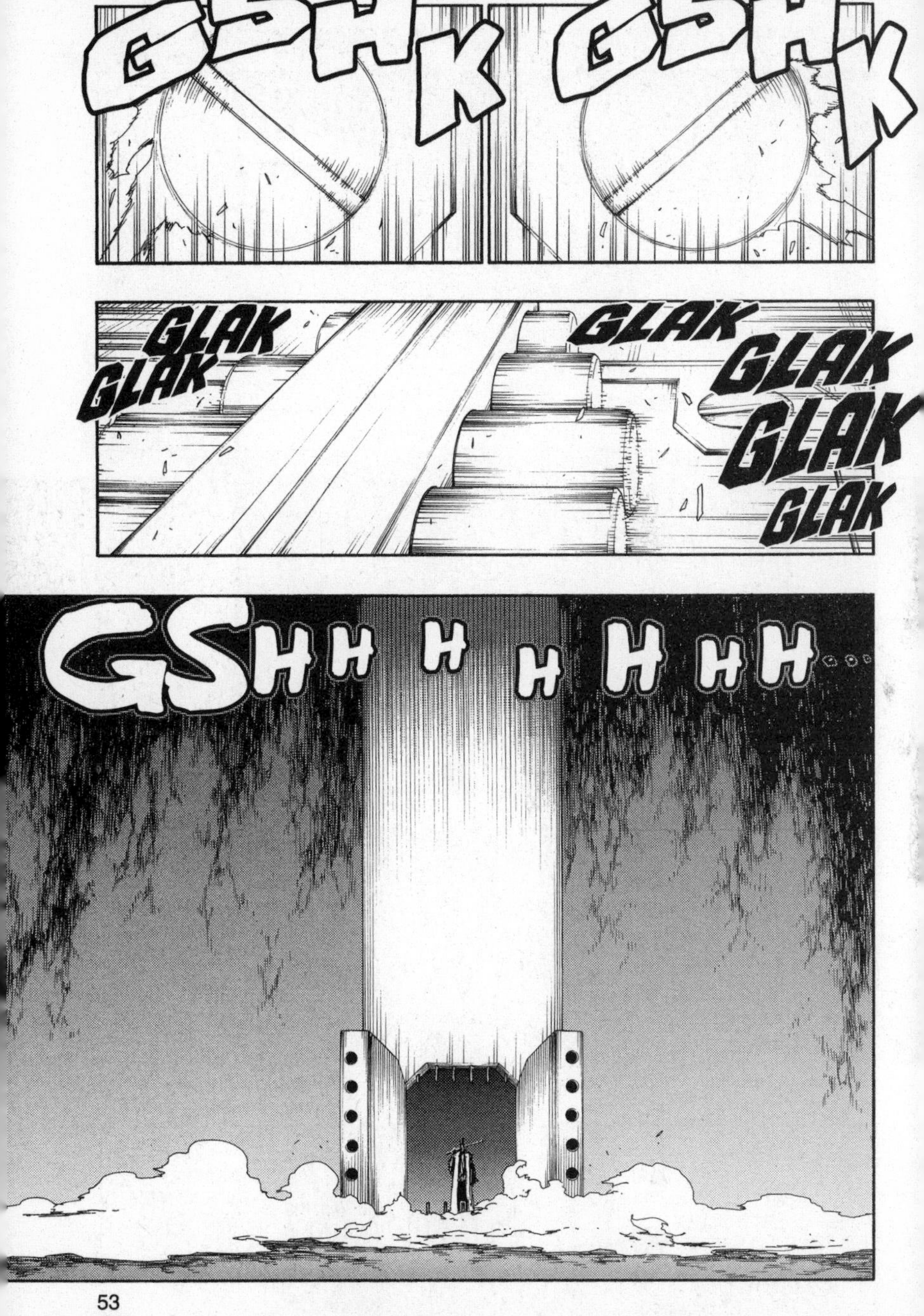
GSHK
GSHK
GLAK
GLAK
GLAK
GLAK
GLAK
GLAK
GSHHHHHHH...

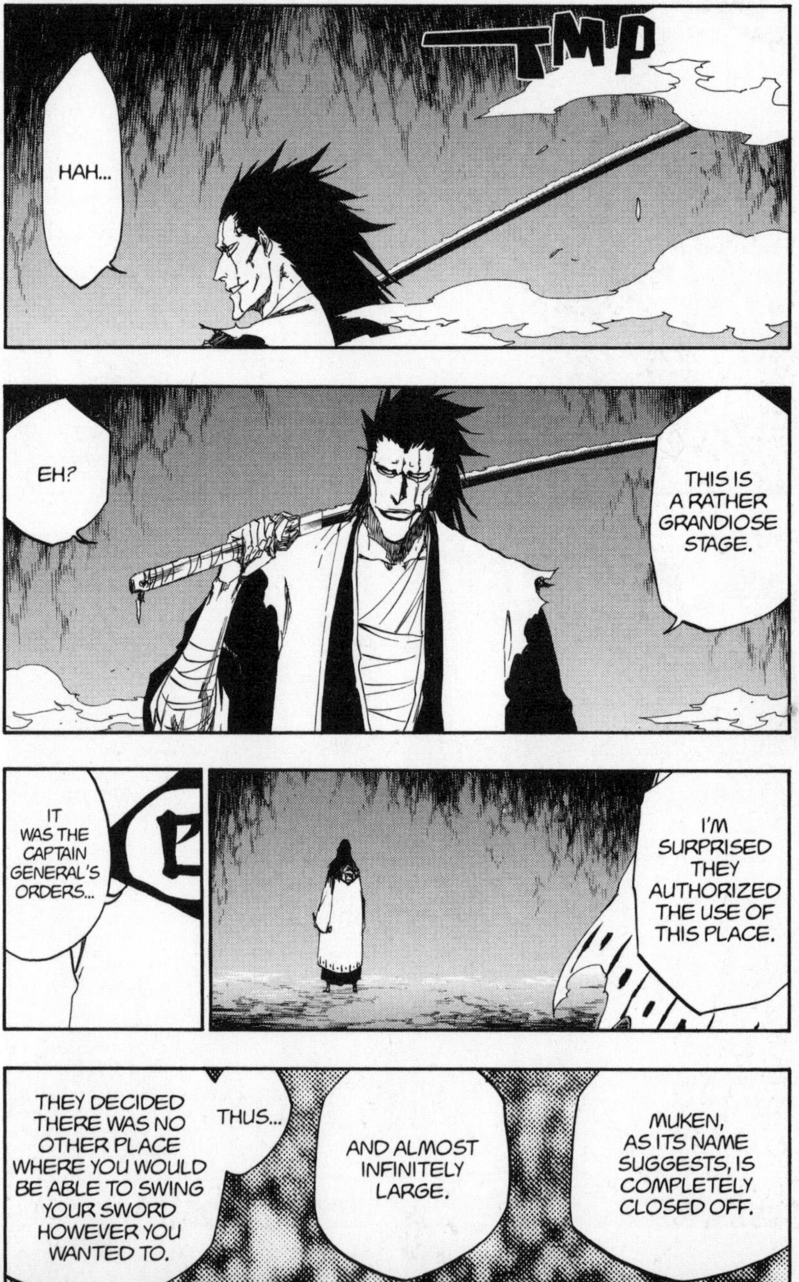
TMP
HAH...
THIS IS A RATHER GRANDIOSE STAGE.
EH?
I'M SURPRISED THEY AUTHORIZED THE USE OF THIS PLACE.
IT WAS THE CAPTAIN GENERAL'S ORDERS...
MUKEN, AS ITS NAME SUGGESTS, IS COMPLETELY CLOSED OFF.
AND ALMOST INFINITELY LARGE.
THUS...
THEY DECIDED THERE WAS NO OTHER PLACE WHERE YOU WOULD BE ABLE TO SWING YOUR SWORD HOWEVER YOU WANTED TO.

READ THIS WAY

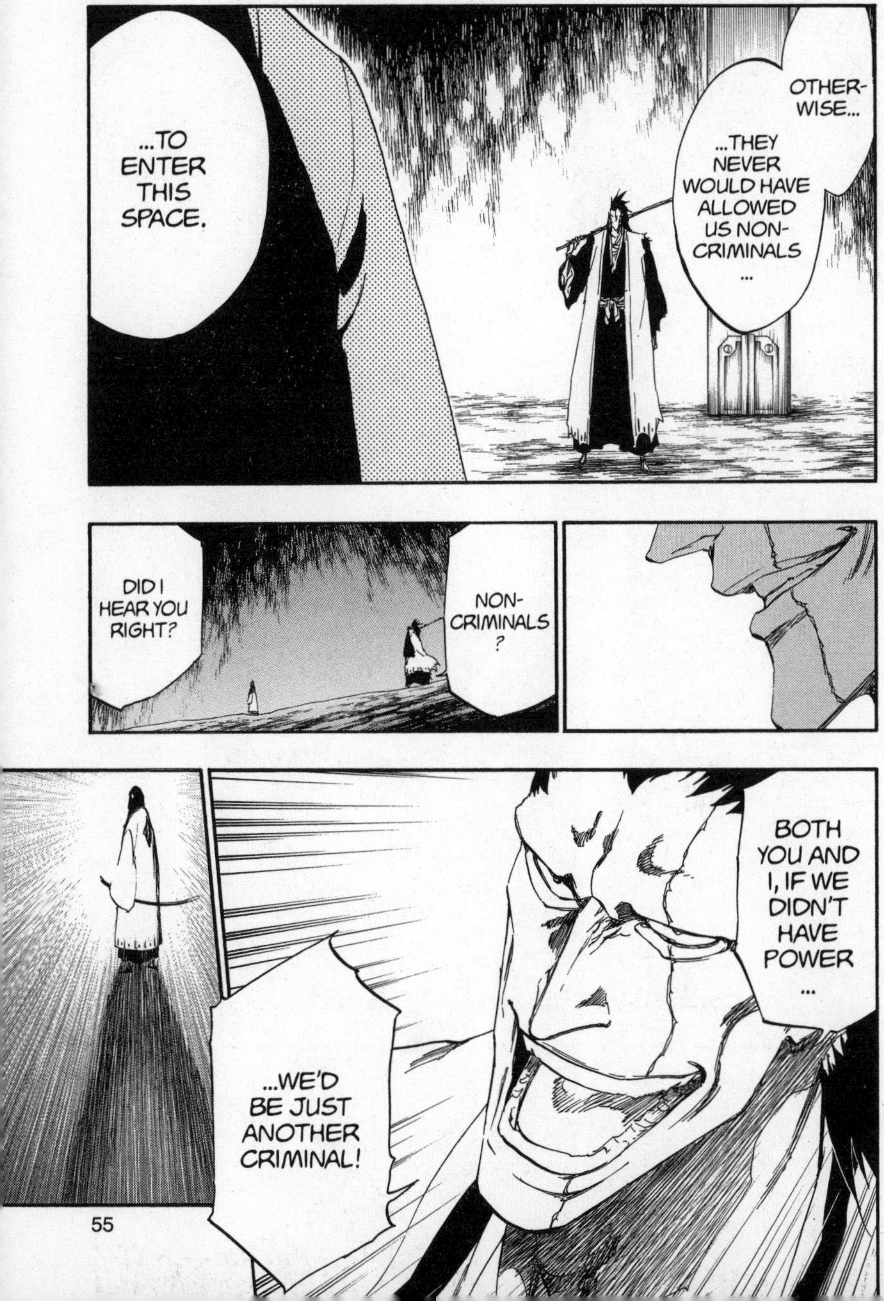
OTHER-WISE...
...THEY NEVER WOULD HAVE ALLOWED US NON-CRIMINALS ...
...TO ENTER THIS SPACE.
NON-CRIMINALS ?
DID I HEAR YOU RIGHT?
BOTH YOU AND I, IF WE DIDN'T HAVE POWER ...
...WE'D BE JUST ANOTHER CRIMINAL!

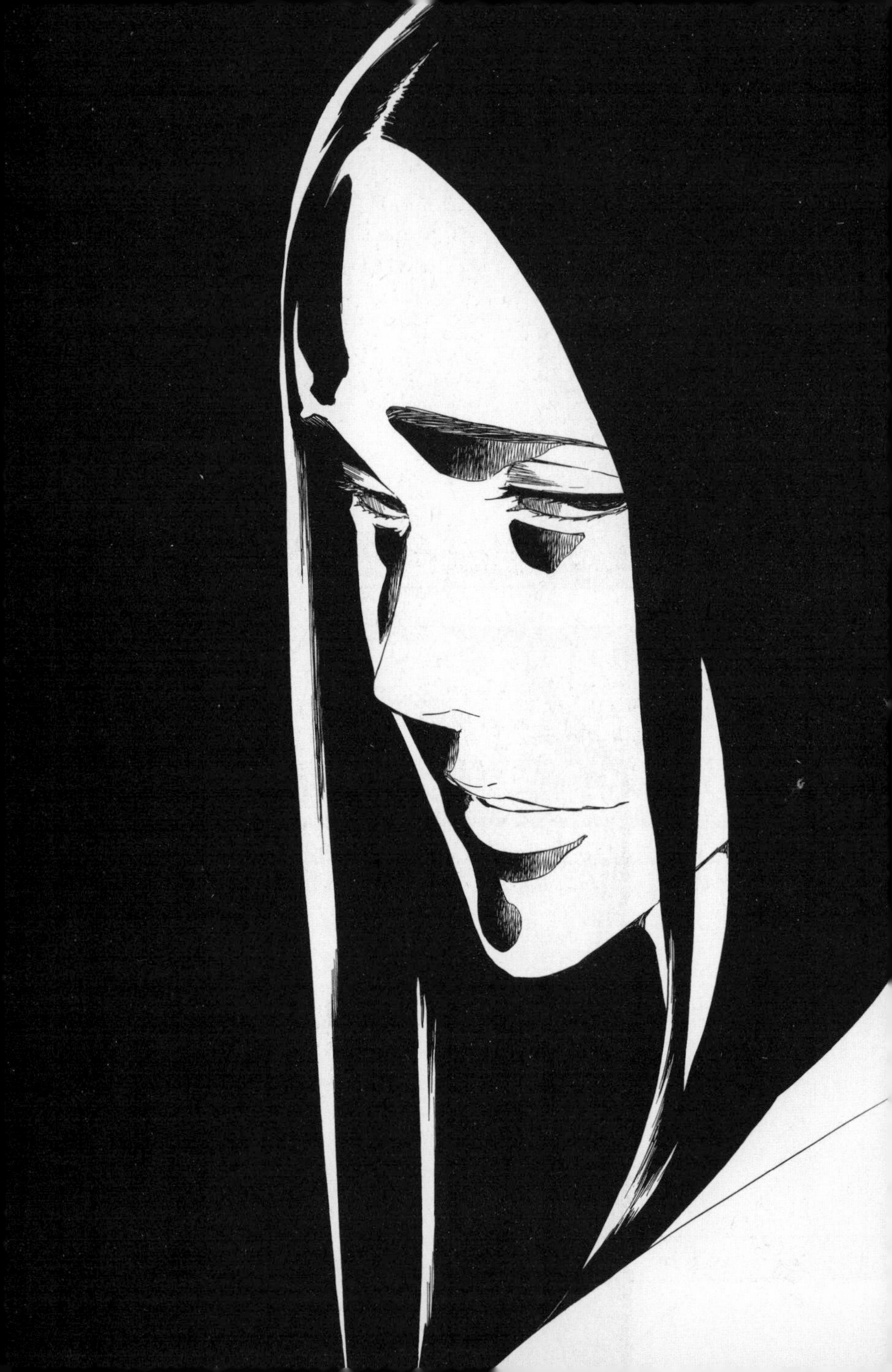

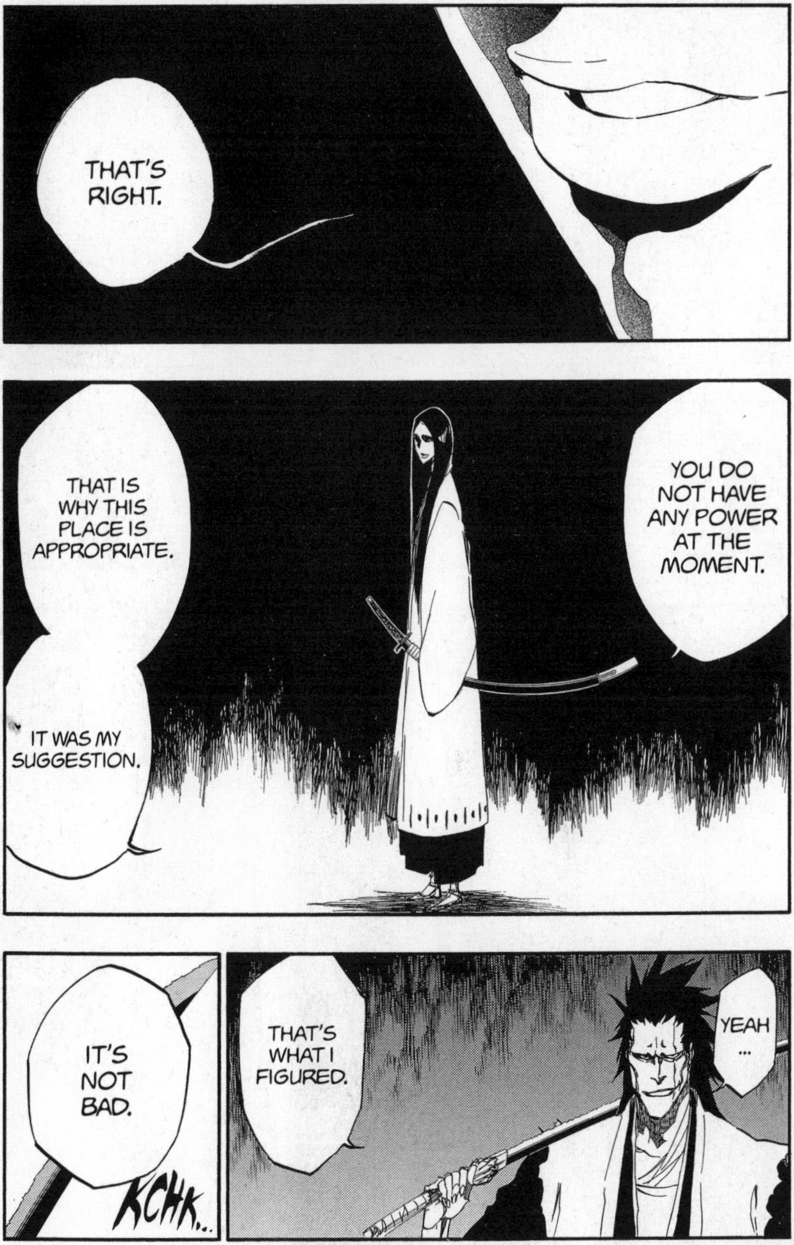
THAT'S RIGHT.
YOU DO NOT HAVE ANY POWER AT THE MOMENT.
THAT IS WHY THIS PLACE IS APPROPRIATE.
IT WAS MY SUGGESTION.
YEAH ...
THAT'S WHAT I FIGURED.
IT'S NOT BAD.
KCHK...

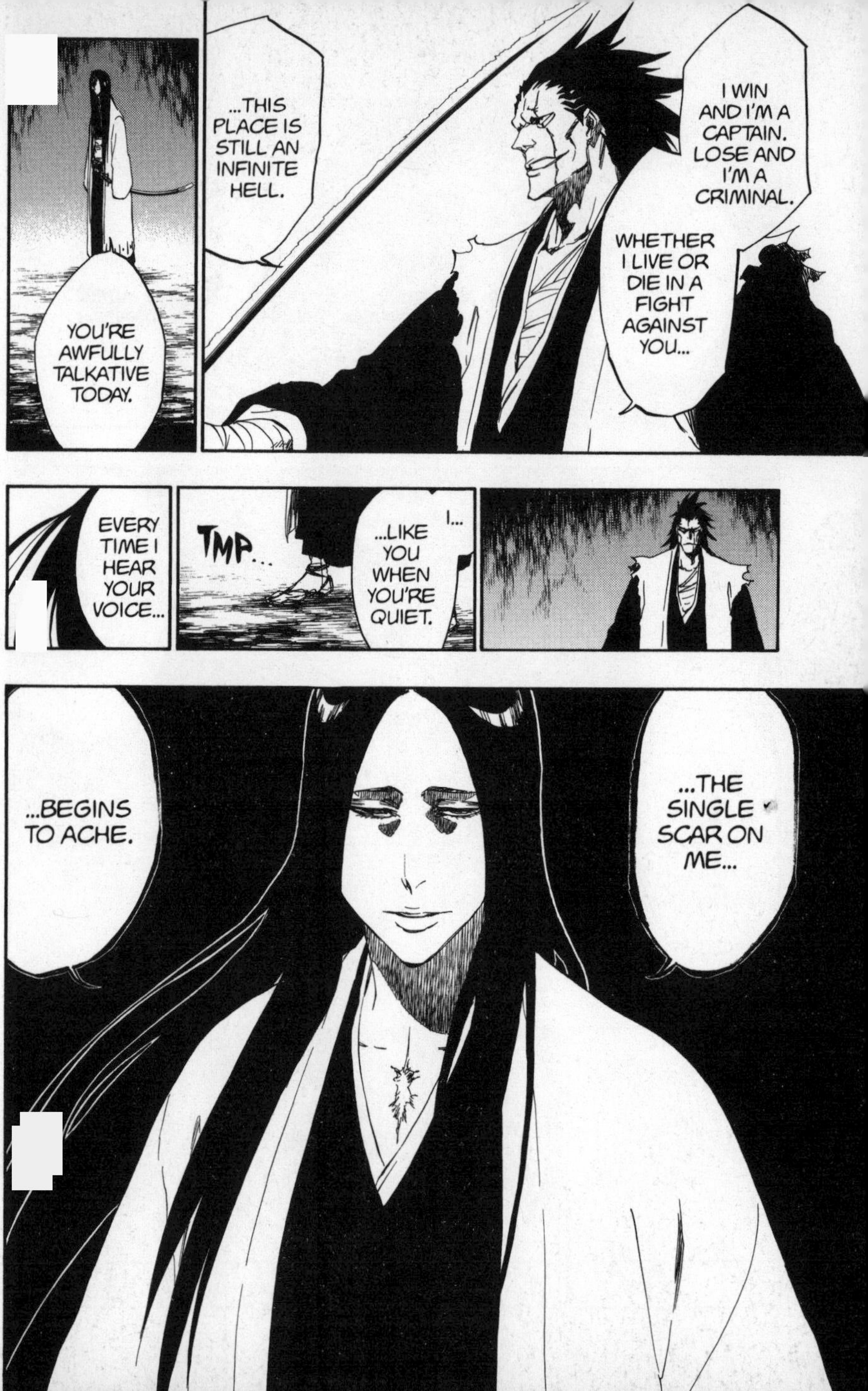
I WIN AND I'M A CAPTAIN. LOSE AND I'M A CRIMINAL.
WHETHER I LIVE OR DIE IN A FIGHT AGAINST YOU...
...THIS PLACE IS STILL AN INFINITE HELL.
YOU'RE AWFULLY TALKATIVE TODAY.
I...
...LIKE YOU WHEN YOU'RE QUIET.
TMP...
EVERY TIME I HEAR YOUR VOICE...
...THE SINGLE SCAR ON ME...
...BEGINS TO ACHE.

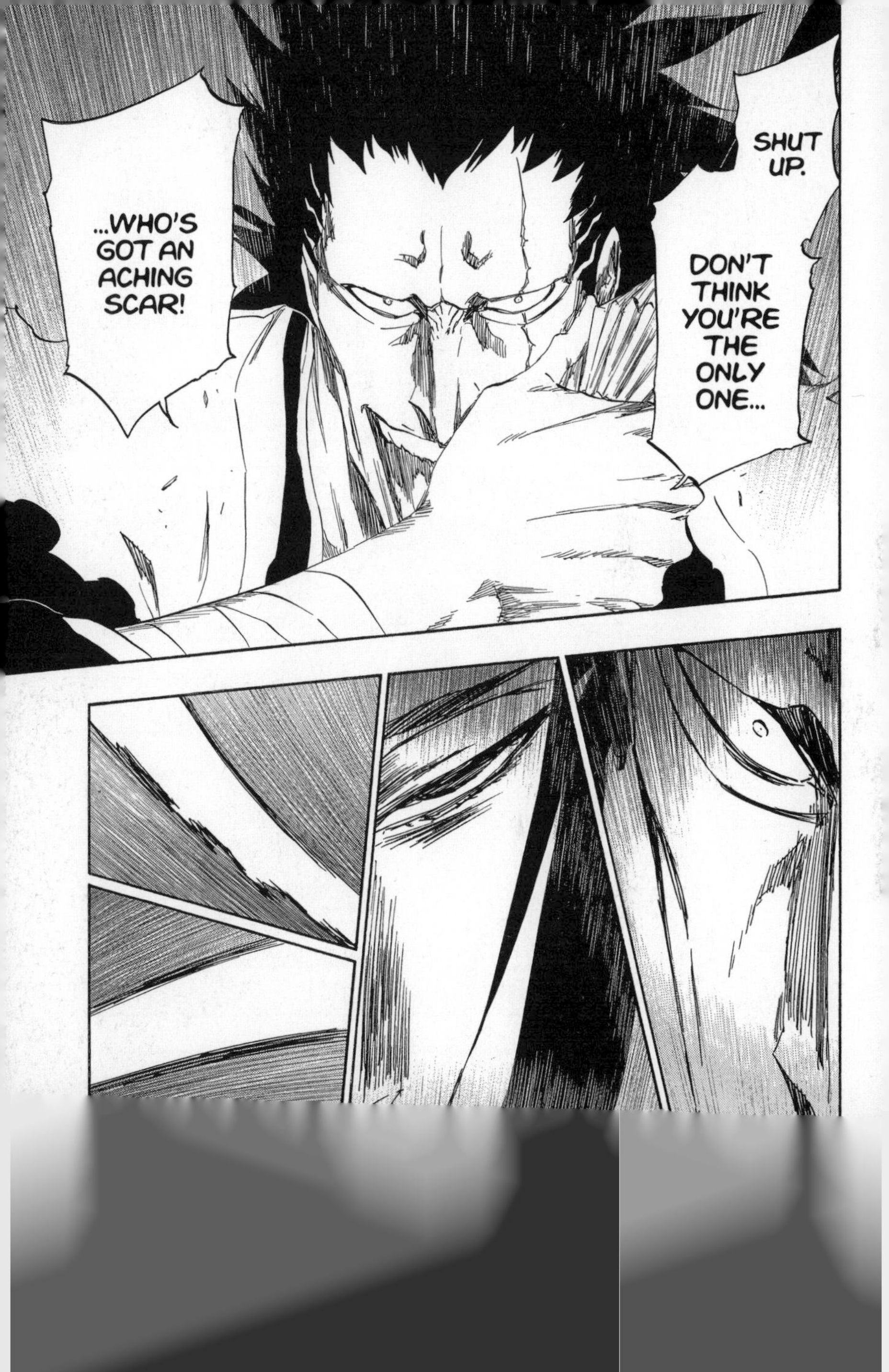
SHUT UP.
DON'T THINK YOU'RE THE ONLY ONE...
...WHO'S GOT AN ACHING SCAR!

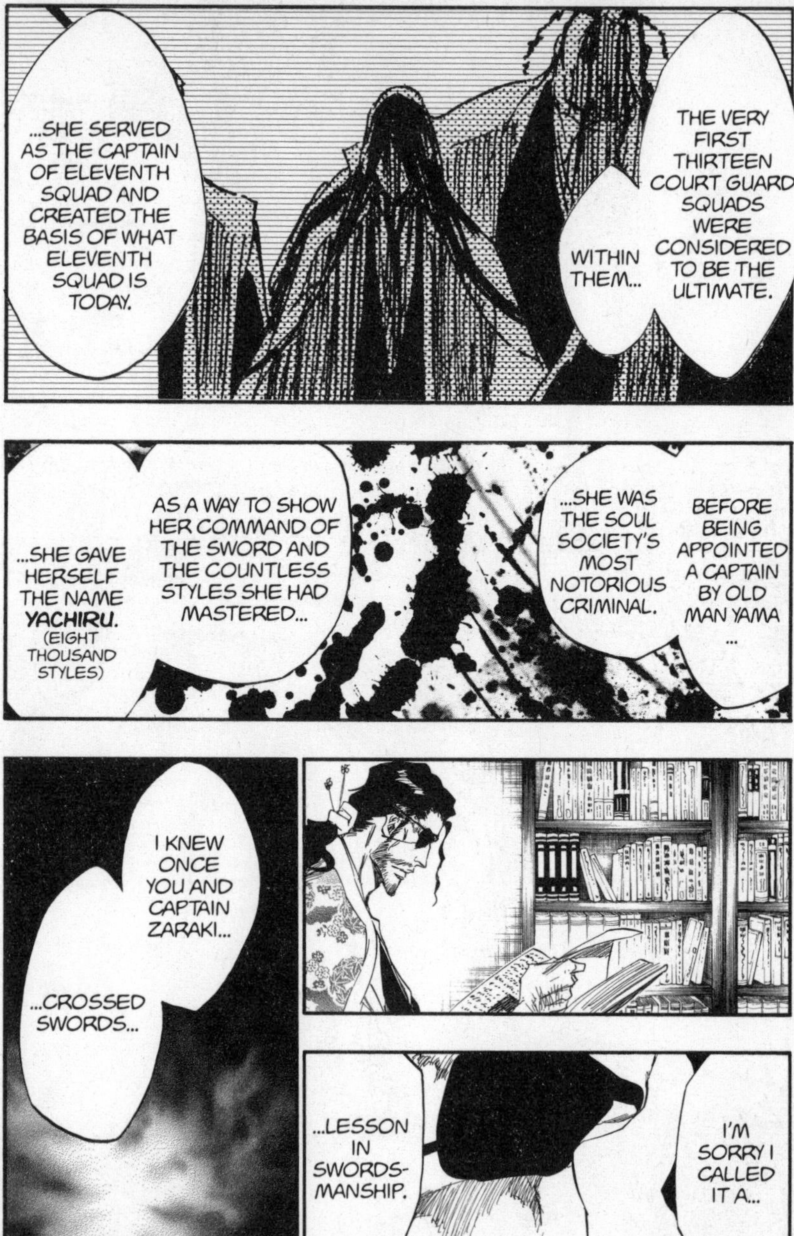
THE VERY FIRST THIRTEEN COURT GUARD SQUADS WERE CONSIDERED TO BE THE ULTIMATE.
WITHIN THEM...
...SHE SERVED AS THE CAPTAIN OF ELEVENTH SQUAD AND CREATED THE BASIS OF WHAT ELEVENTH SQUAD IS TODAY.
BEFORE BEING APPOINTED A CAPTAIN BY OLD MAN YAMA ...
...SHE WAS THE SOUL SOCIETY'S MOST NOTORIOUS CRIMINAL.
AS A WAY TO SHOW HER COMMAND OF THE SWORD AND THE COUNTLESS STYLES SHE HAD MASTERED...
...SHE GAVE HERSELF THE NAME YACHIRU. (EIGHT THOUSAND STYLES)
I'M SORRY I CALLED IT A...
...LESSON IN SWORDS-MANSHIP.
I KNEW ONCE YOU AND CAPTAIN ZARAKI...
...CROSSED SWORDS...

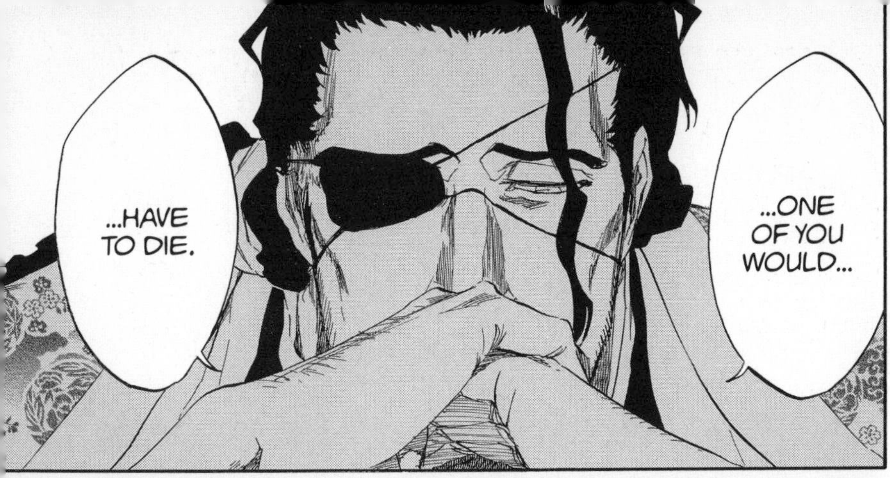
...ONE OF YOU WOULD...
...HAVE TO DIE.
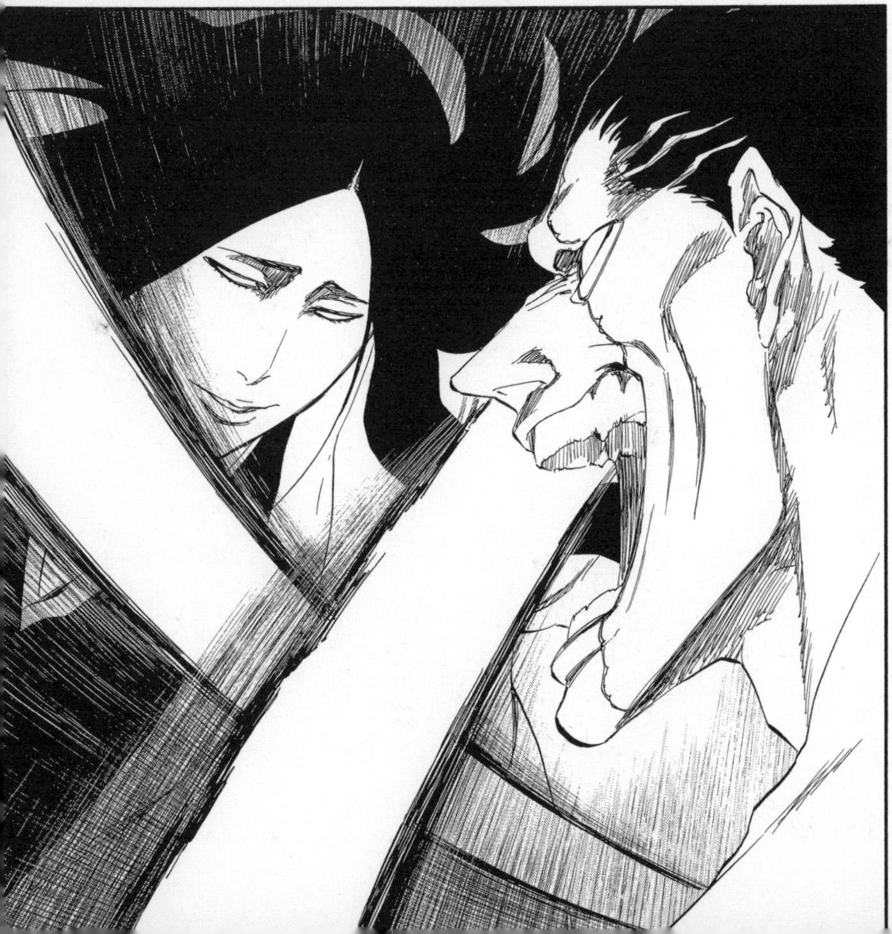

524. THE DROP

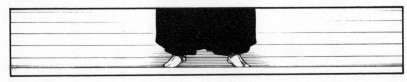

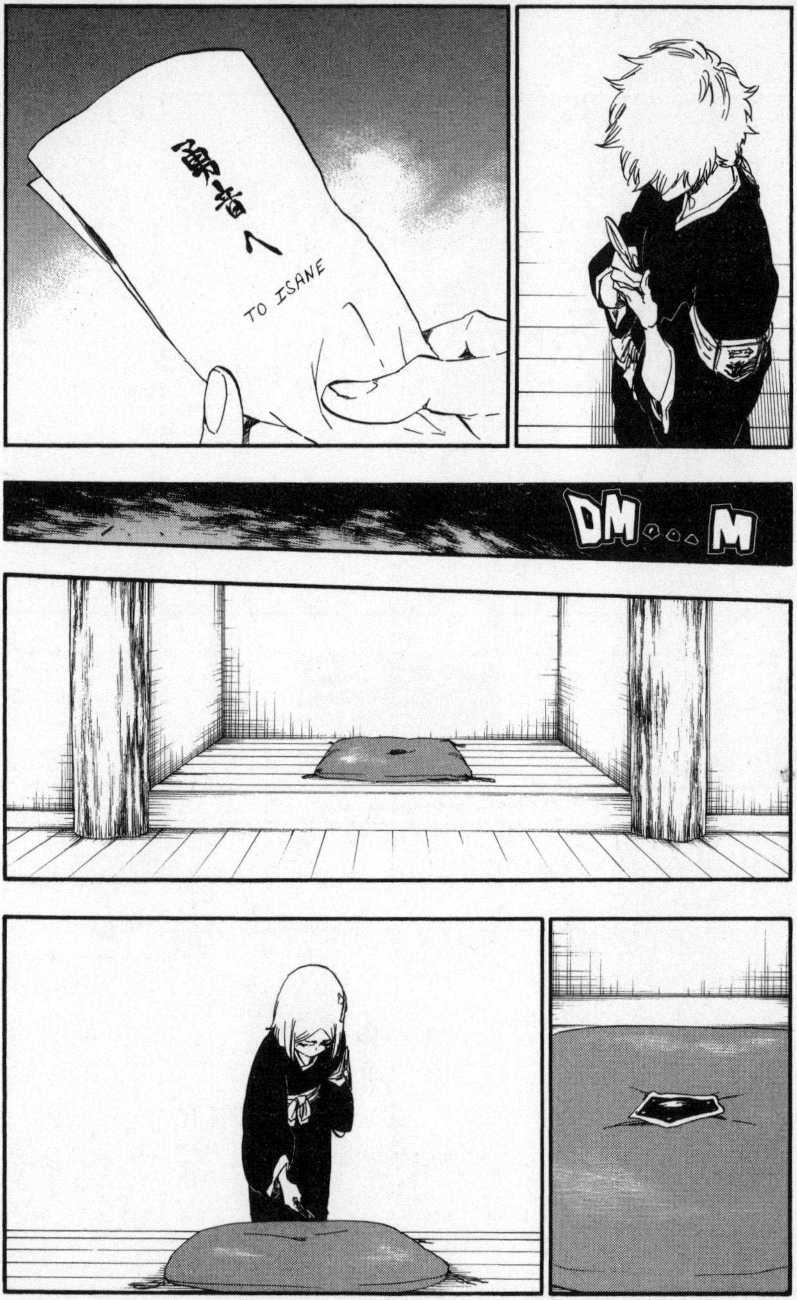
勇音へ
TO ISANE
DM...M

READ THIS WAY

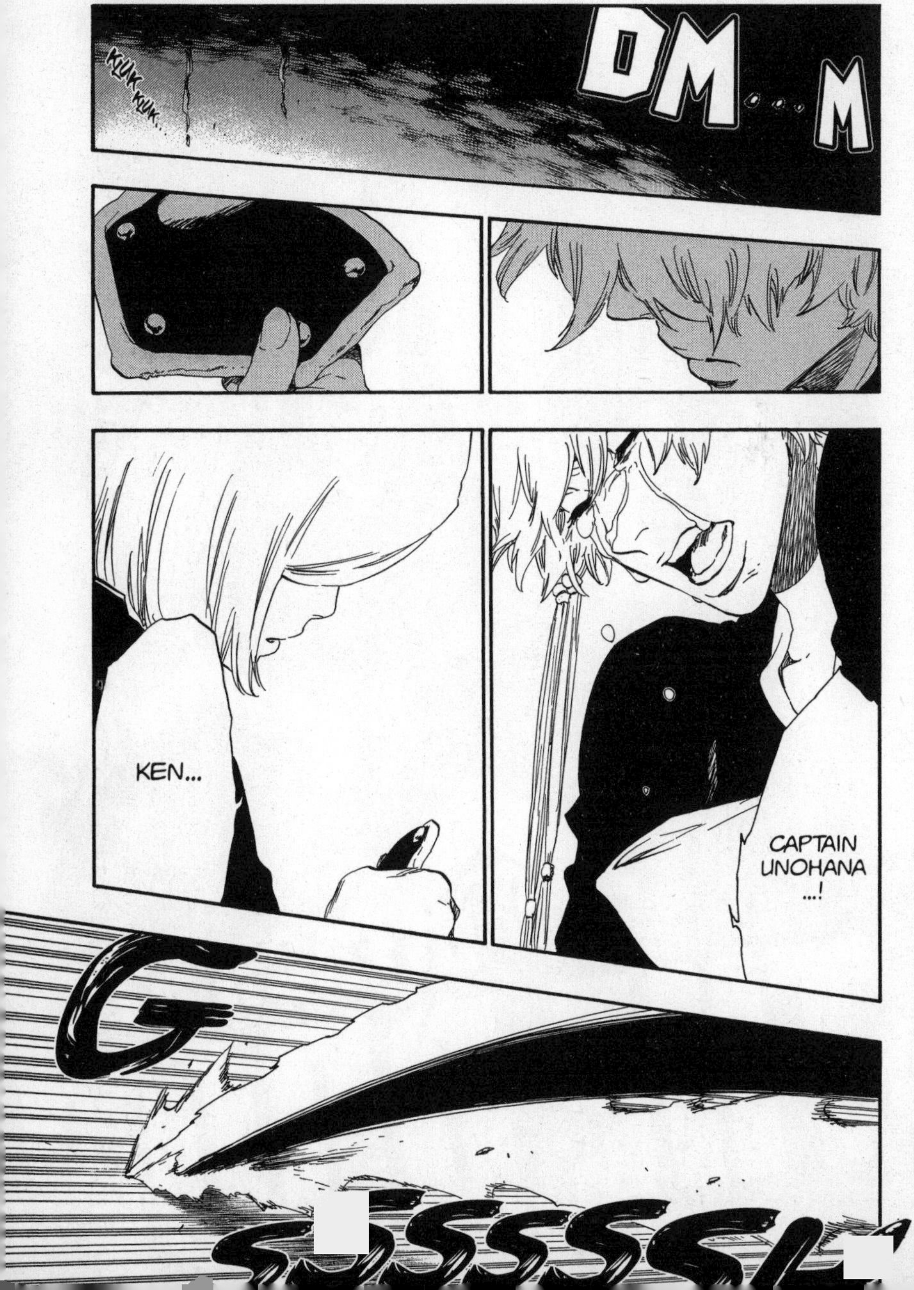
DM...M
KLUK KLUK...
CAPTAIN UNOHANA ...!
KEN...
G

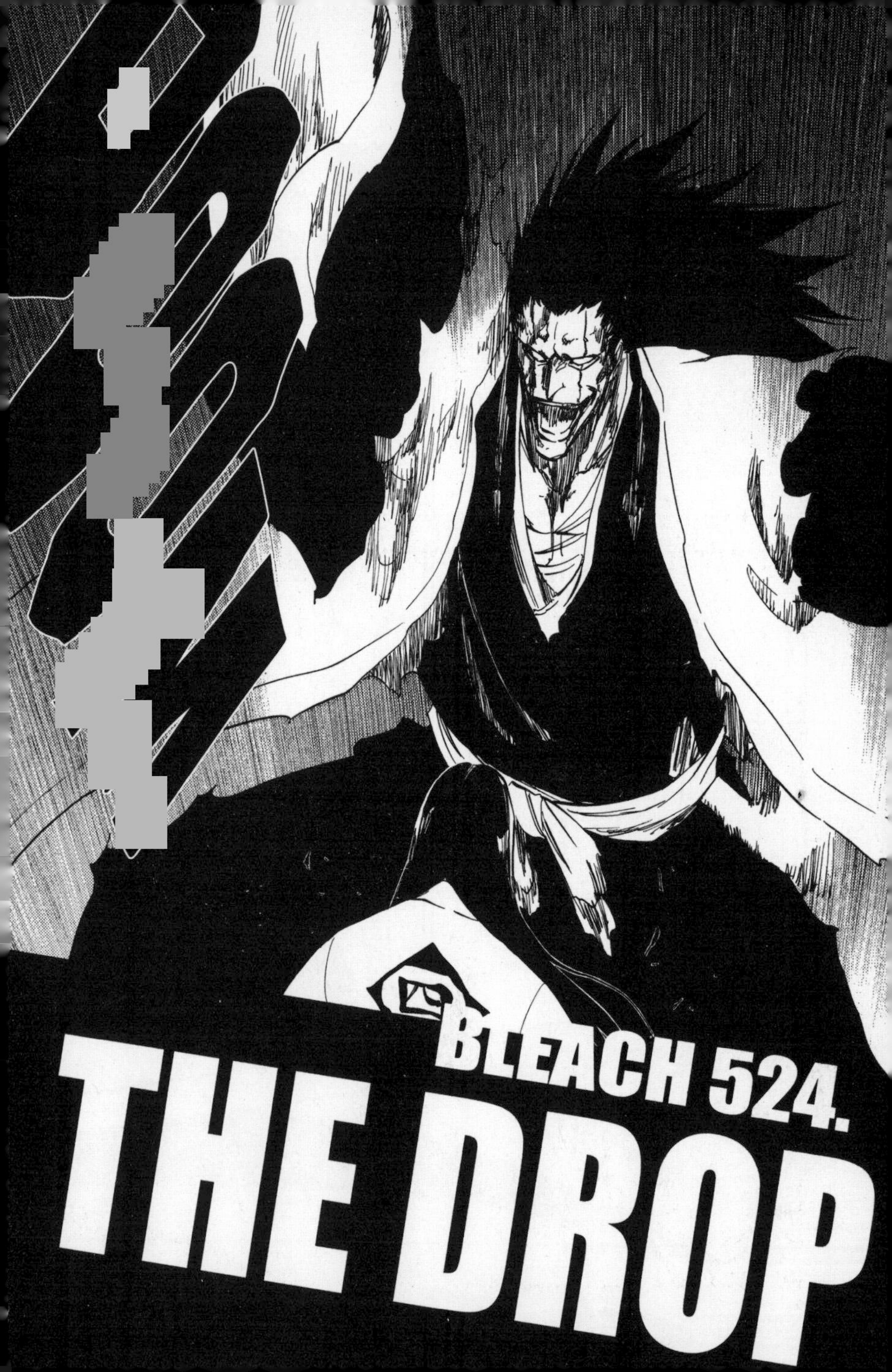
BLEACH 524.
THE DROP

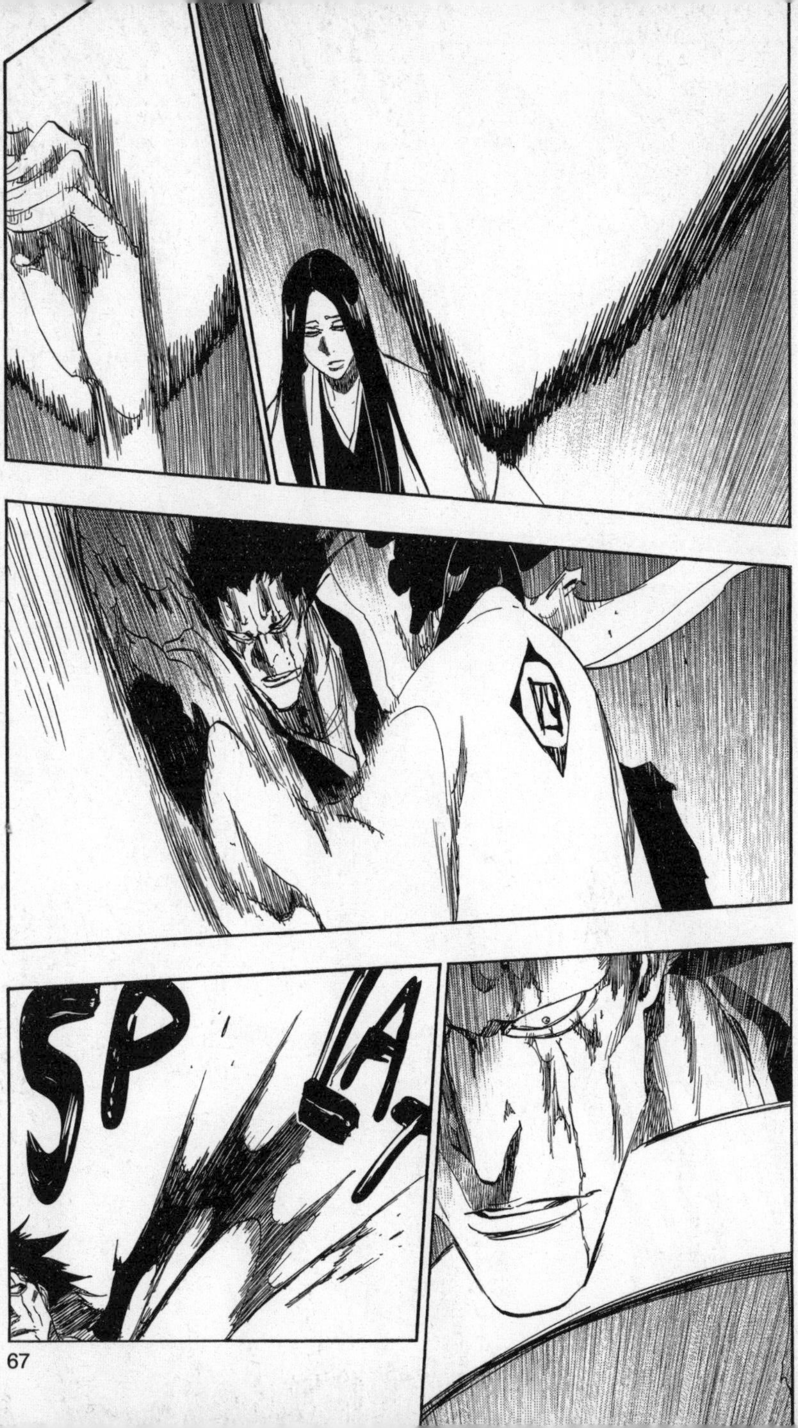
SPLAT

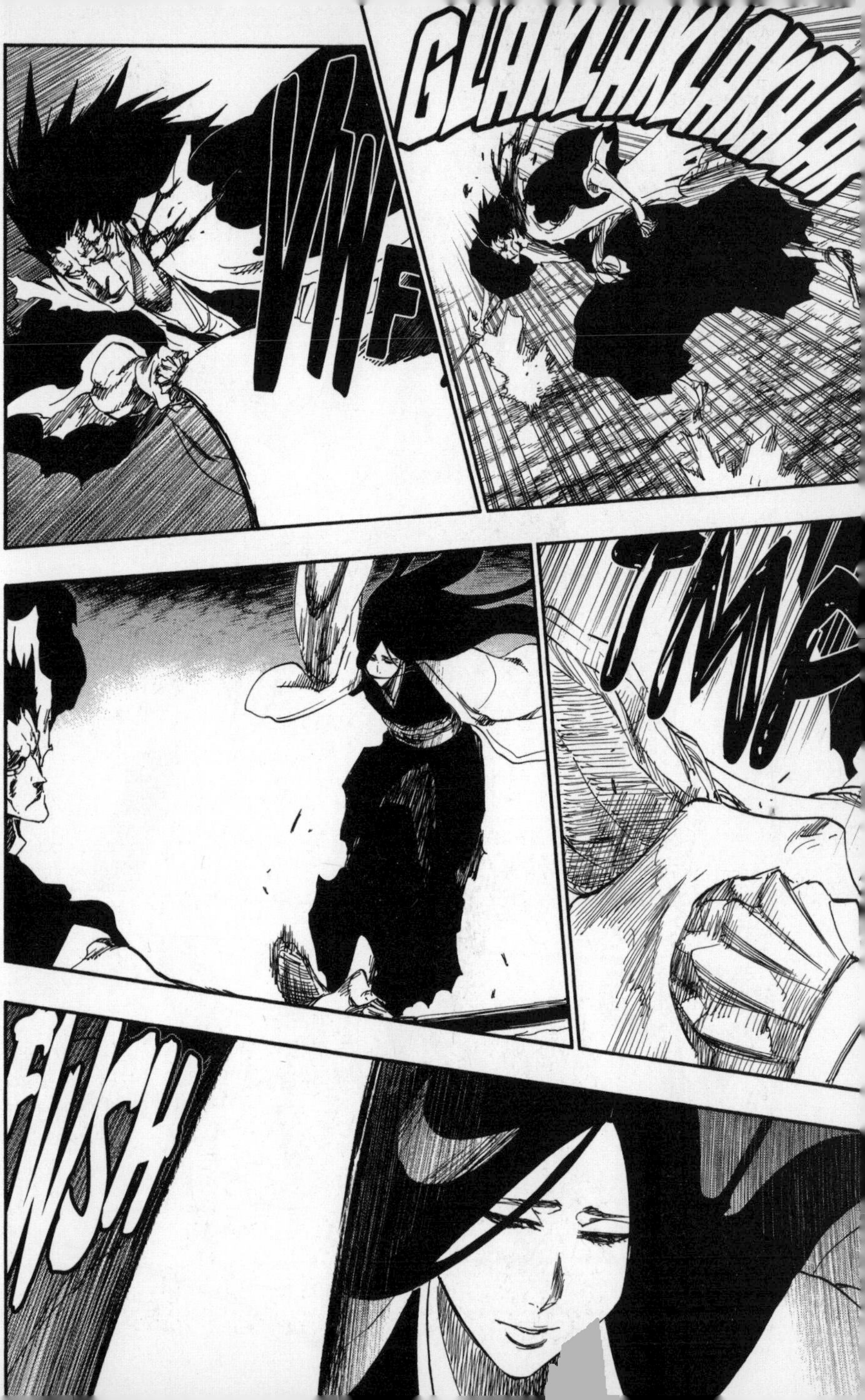
VWF
TMP
FWSH

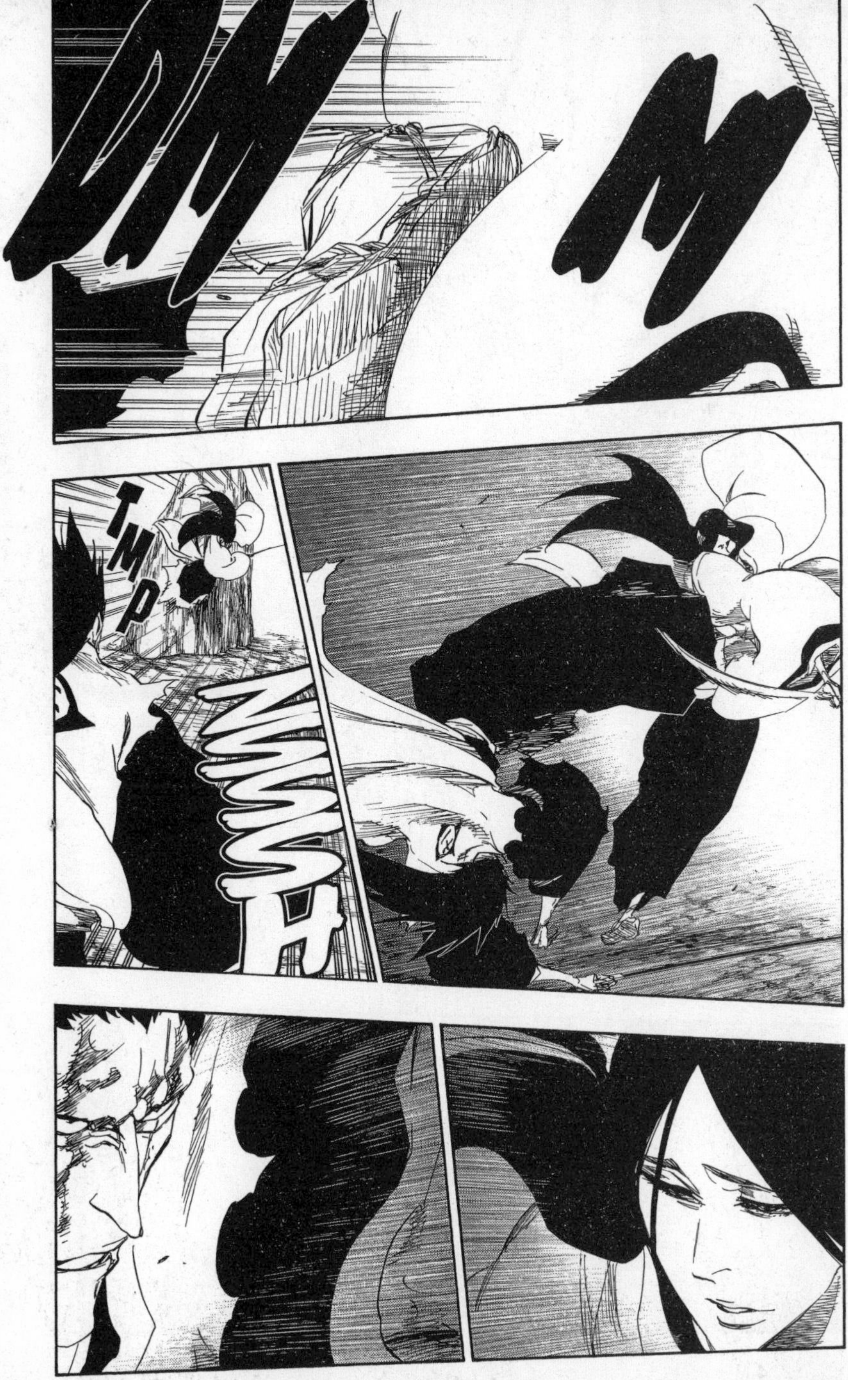
DMM
TMP

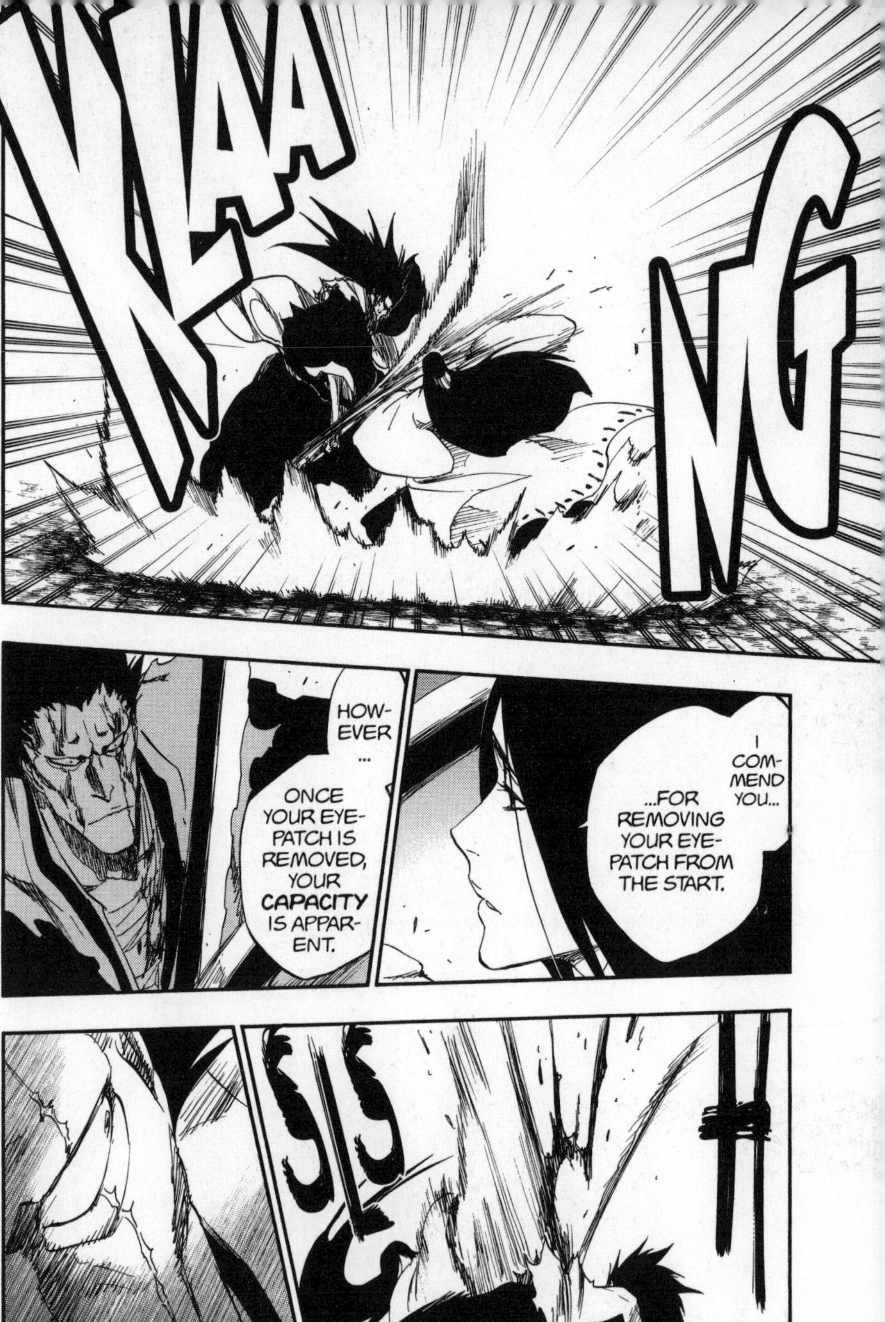
VLAANNG
I COMMEND YOU...
...FOR REMOVING YOUR EYE-PATCH FROM THE START.
HOWEVER...
ONCE YOUR EYE-PATCH IS REMOVED, YOUR **CAPACITY** IS APPARENT.
SLS

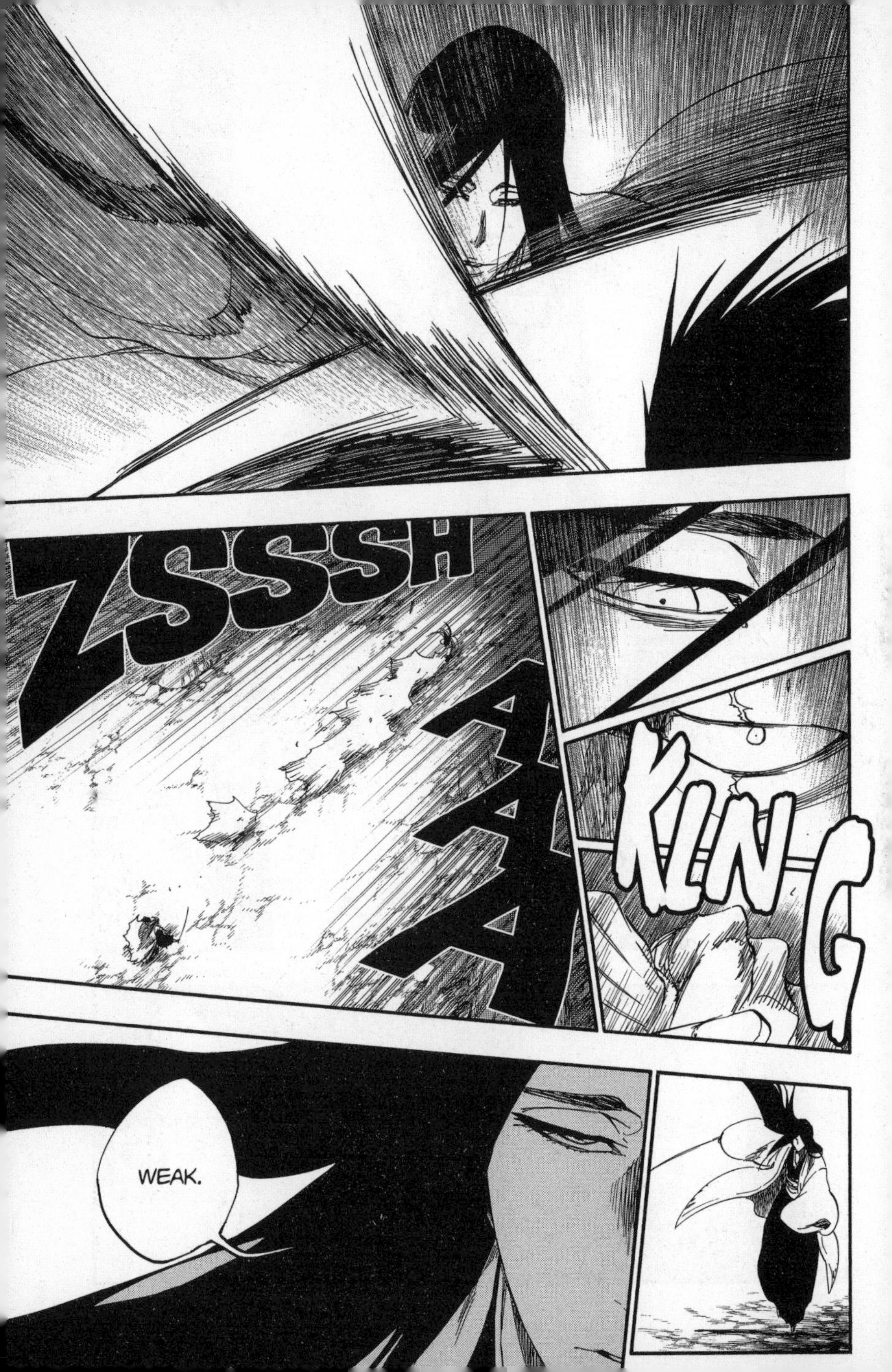
KLIN G
ZSSSH
WEAK.

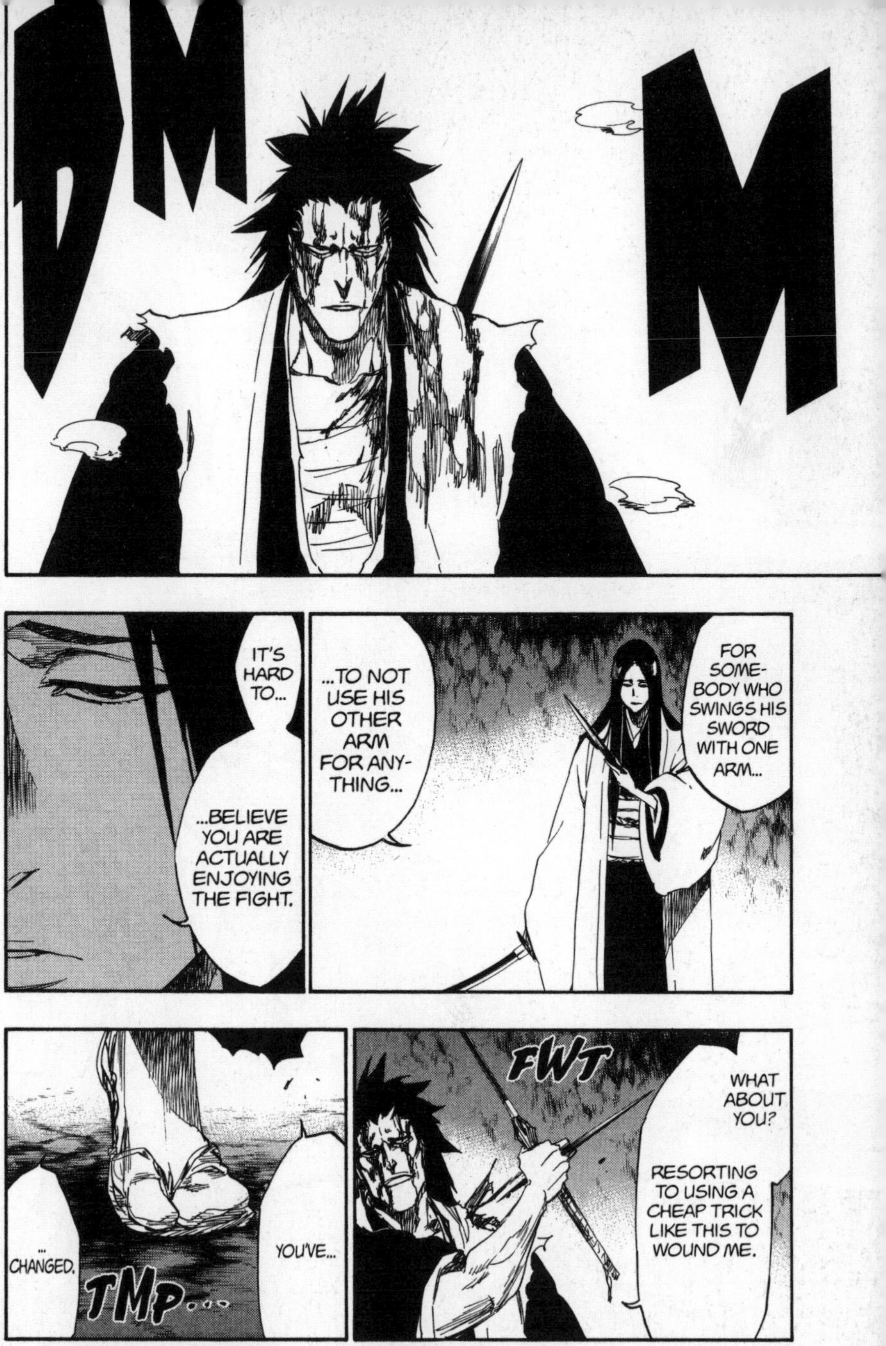
DM
M
FOR SOMEBODY WHO SWINGS HIS SWORD WITH ONE ARM...
...TO NOT USE HIS OTHER ARM FOR ANYTHING...
IT'S HARD TO...
...BELIEVE YOU ARE ACTUALLY ENJOYING THE FIGHT.
FWT
WHAT ABOUT YOU?
RESORTING TO USING A CHEAP TRICK LIKE THIS TO WOUND ME.
YOU'VE...
...CHANGED.
TMP...

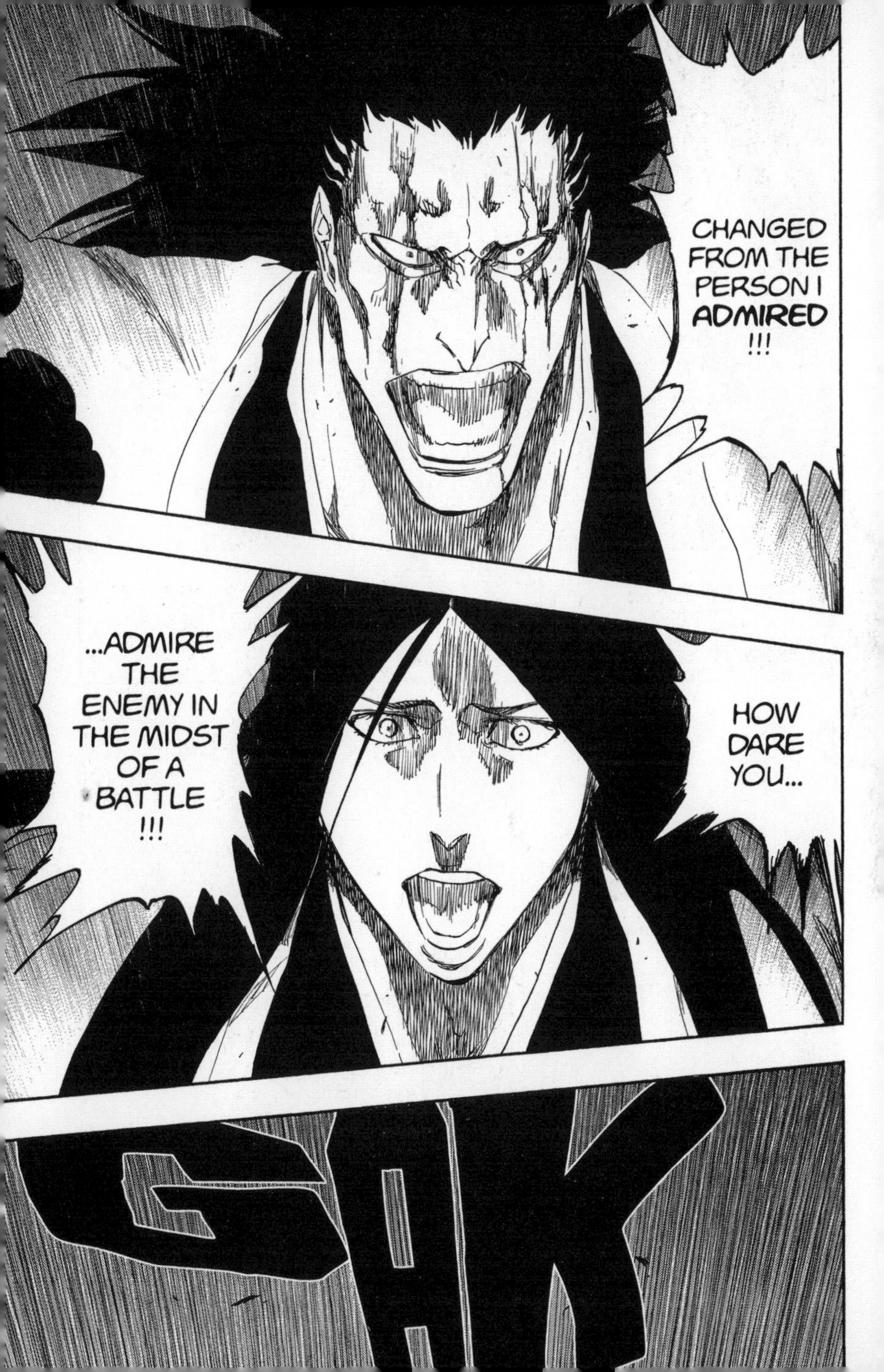
CHANGED FROM THE PERSON I ADMIRED !!!
HOW DARE YOU...
...ADMIRE THE ENEMY IN THE MIDST OF A BATTLE !!!
GAK

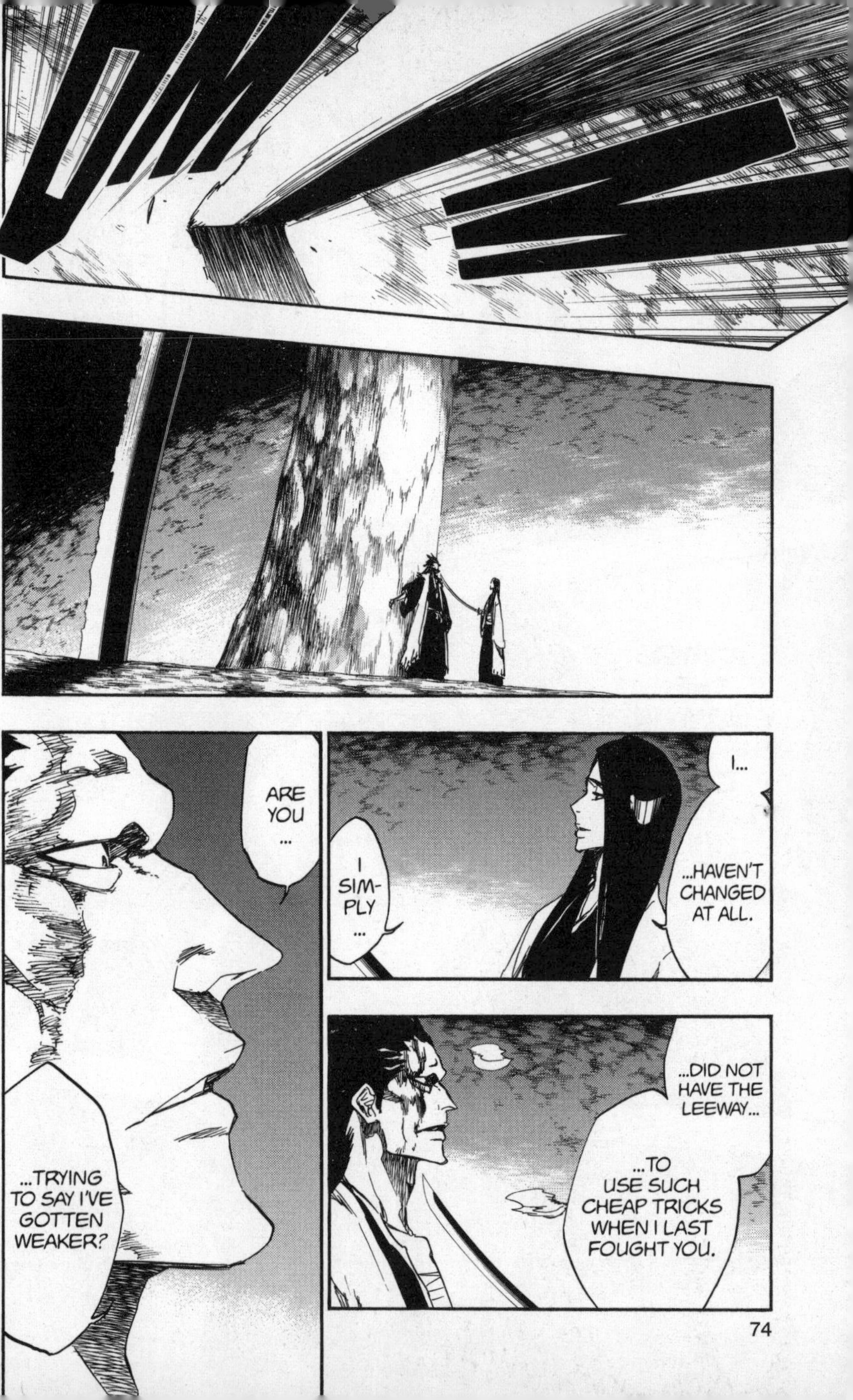

I...
...HAVEN'T CHANGED AT ALL.
I SIM-PLY ...
...DID NOT HAVE THE LEEWAY...
...TO USE SUCH CHEAP TRICKS WHEN I LAST FOUGHT YOU.
ARE YOU ...
...TRYING TO SAY I'VE GOTTEN WEAKER?

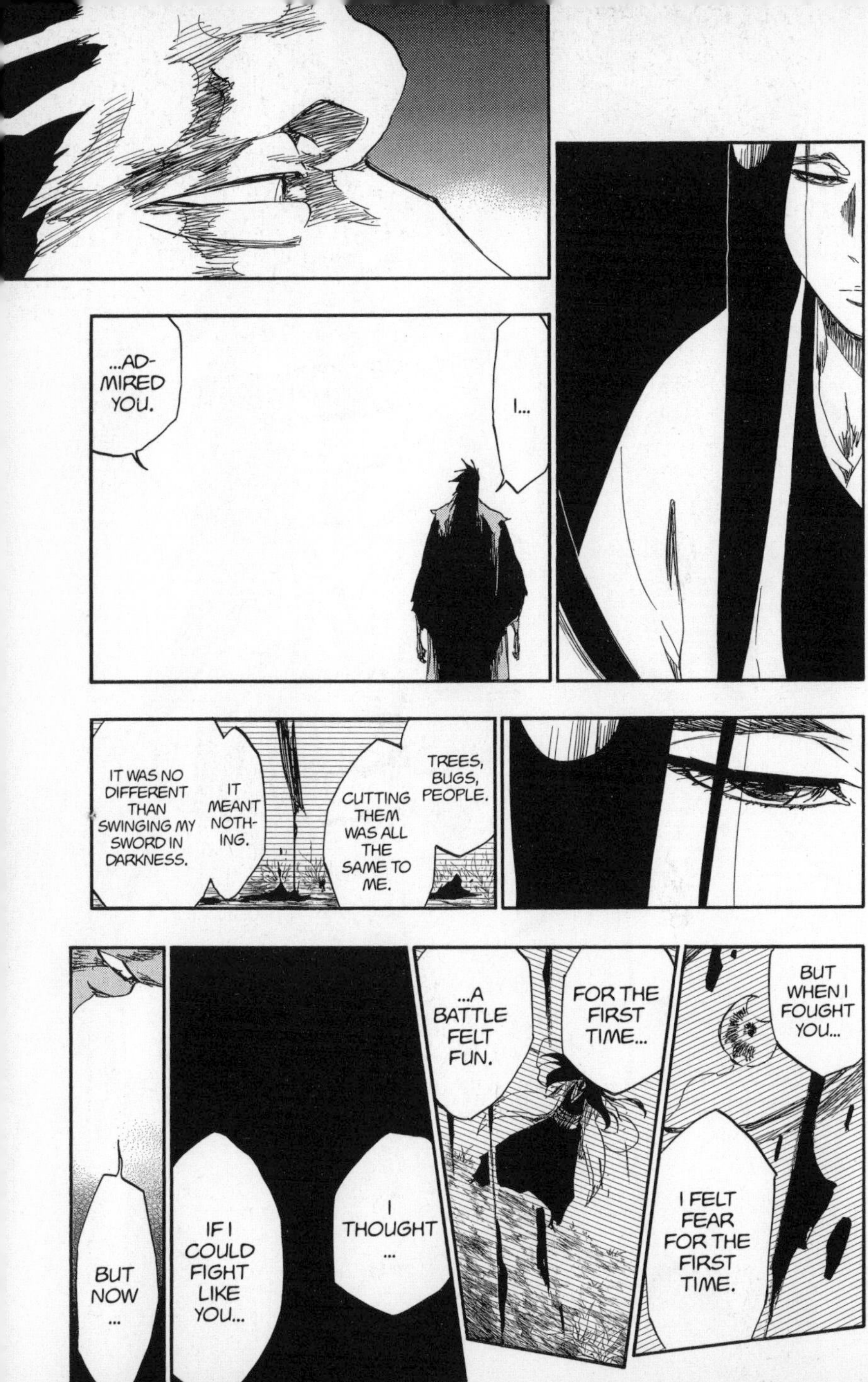
I...
...ADMIRED YOU.
TREES, BUGS, PEOPLE.
CUTTING THEM WAS ALL THE SAME TO ME.
IT MEANT NOTHING.
IT WAS NO DIFFERENT THAN SWINGING MY SWORD IN DARKNESS.
BUT WHEN I FOUGHT YOU...
I FELT FEAR FOR THE FIRST TIME.
FOR THE FIRST TIME...
...A BATTLE FELT FUN.
I THOUGHT...
IF I COULD FIGHT LIKE YOU...
BUT NOW...

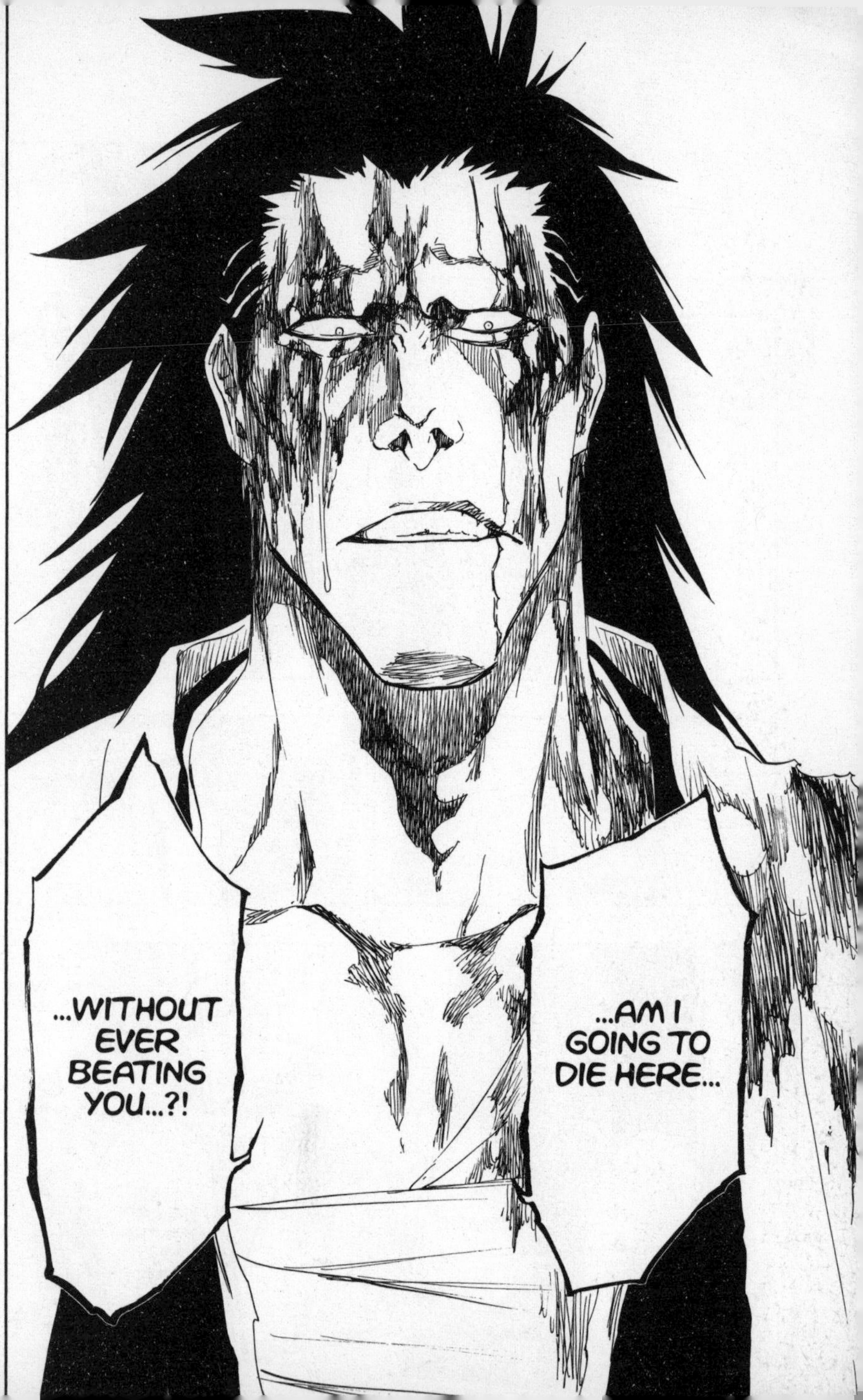
...AM I GOING TO DIE HERE...
...WITHOUT EVER BEATING YOU...?!

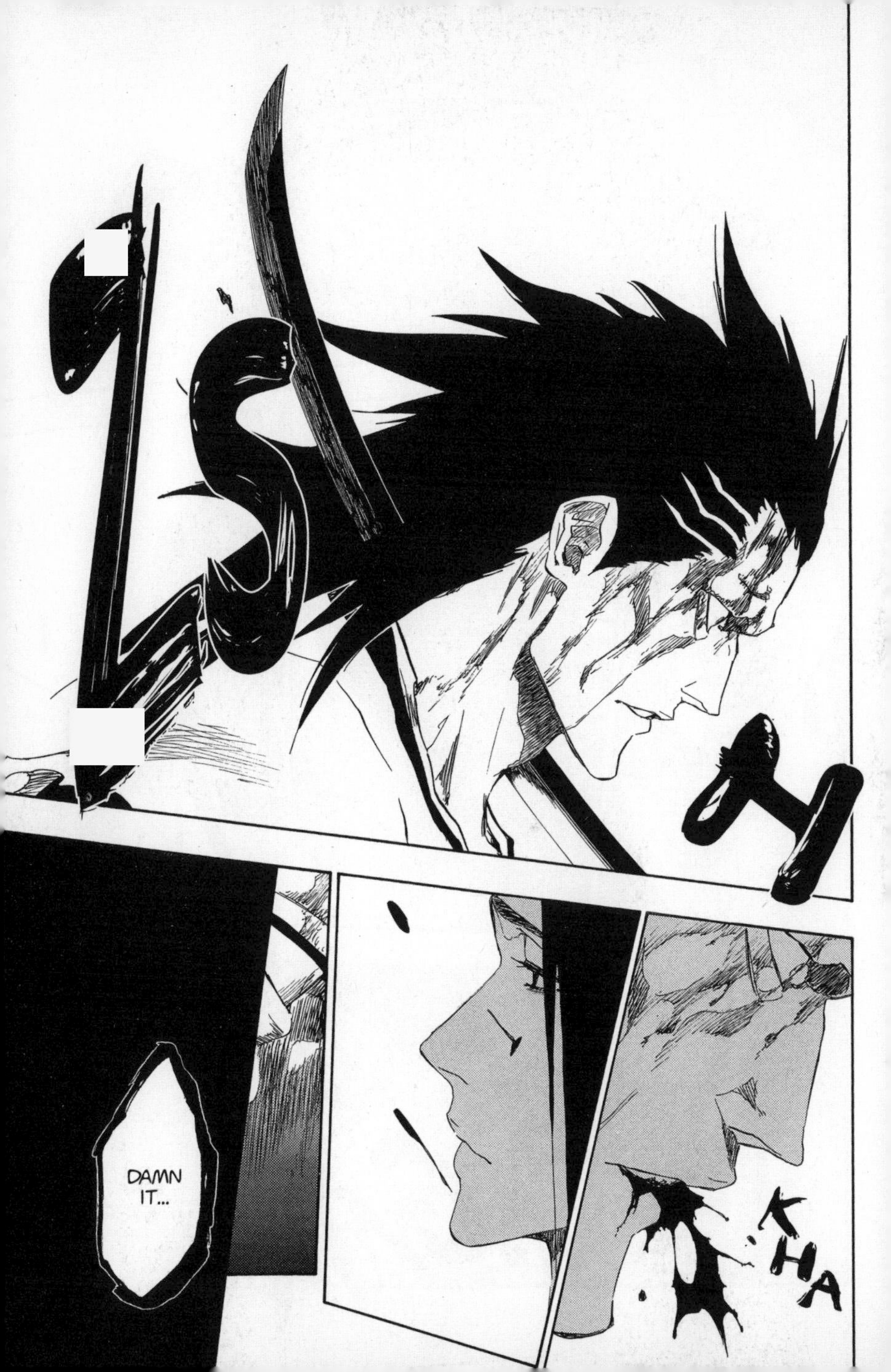
KHA
DAMN IT...

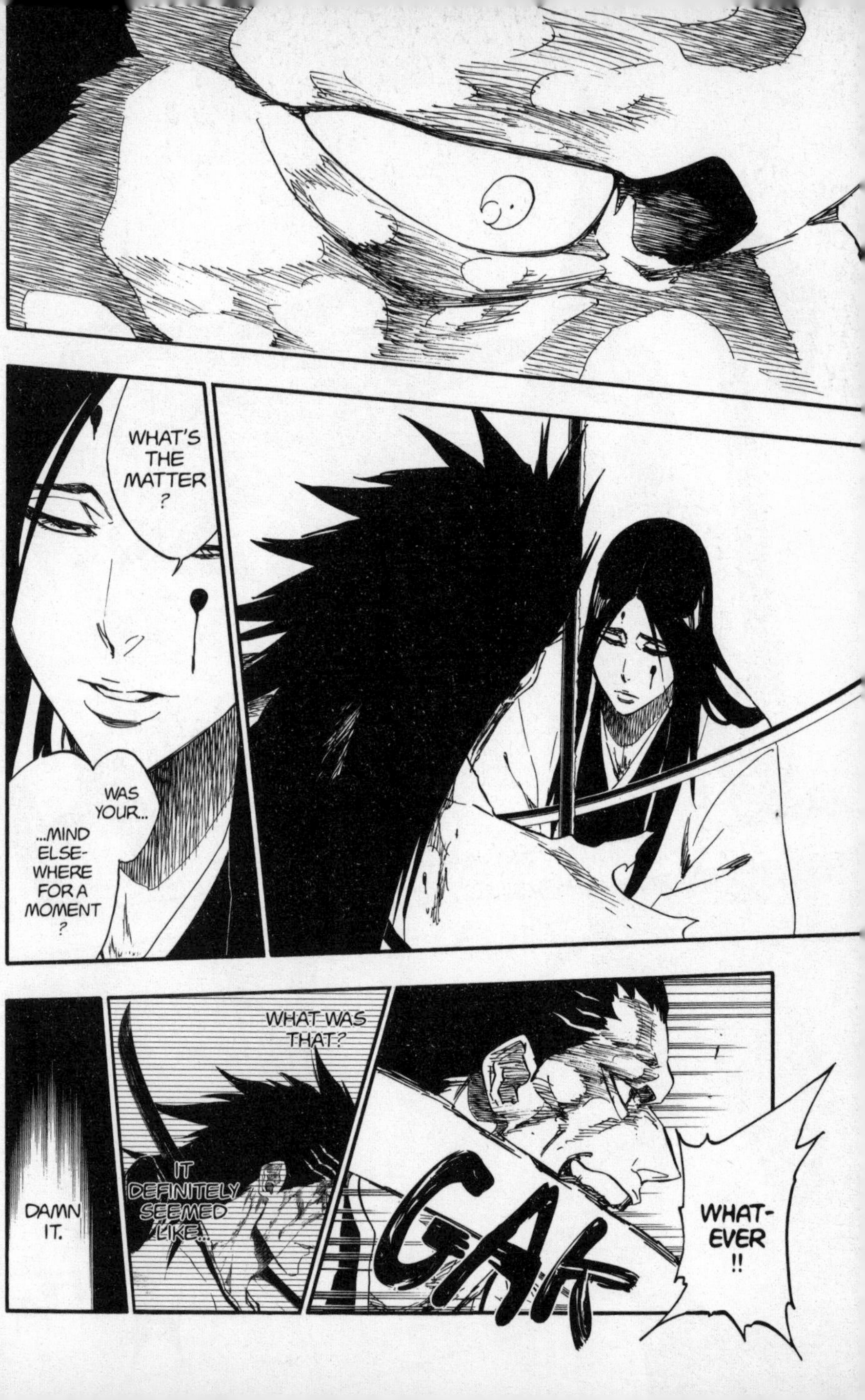
WHAT'S THE MATTER?
WAS YOUR...
...MIND ELSEWHERE FOR A MOMENT?
WHAT-EVER!!
GAH
WHAT WAS THAT?
IT DEFINITELY SEEMED LIKE...
DAMN IT.

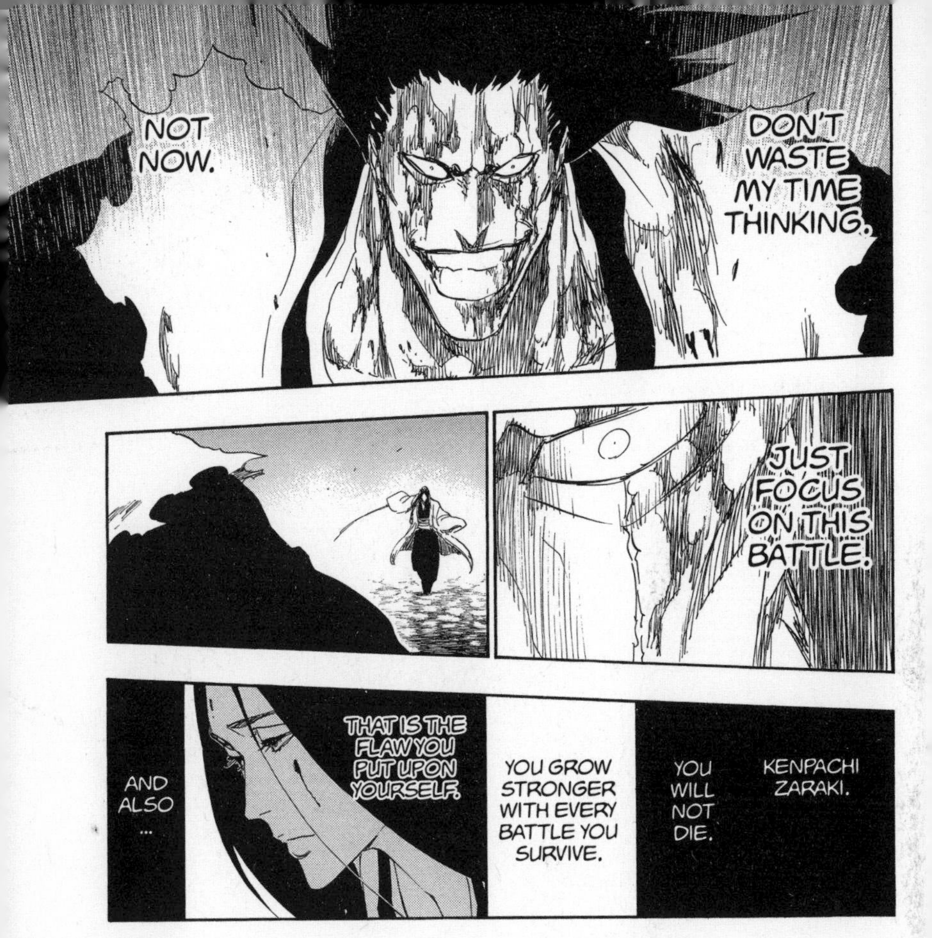
DON'T WASTE MY TIME THINKING.
NOT NOW.
JUST FOCUS ON THIS BATTLE.
KENPACHI ZARAKI.
YOU WILL NOT DIE.
YOU GROW STRONGER WITH EVERY BATTLE YOU SURVIVE.
THAT IS THE FLAW YOU PUT UPON YOURSELF.
AND ALSO ...

...MY SIN.

525. EDGES

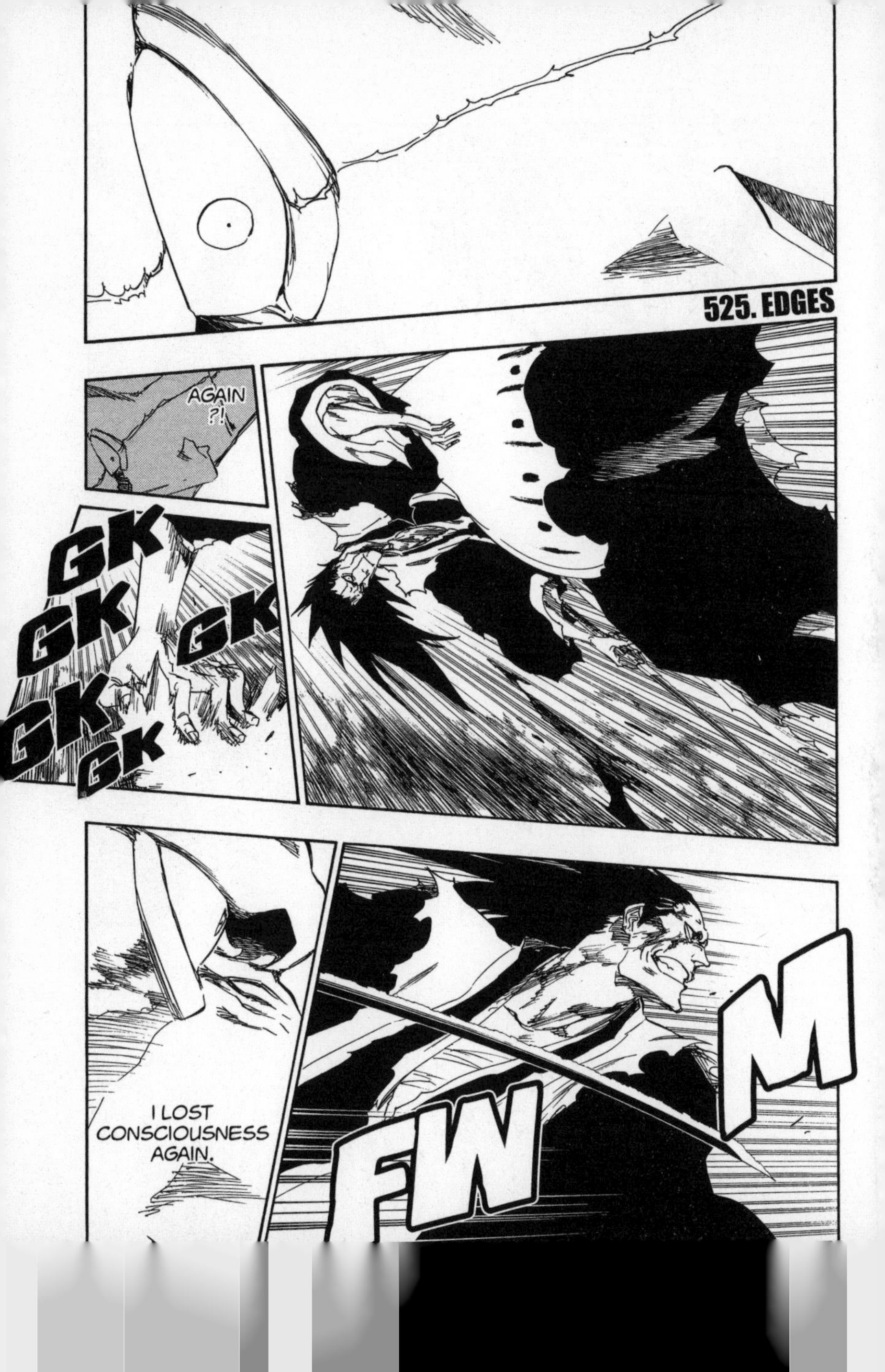
AGAIN ?!
GK GK GK GK GK GK
FWM
I LOST CONSCIOUSNESS AGAIN.

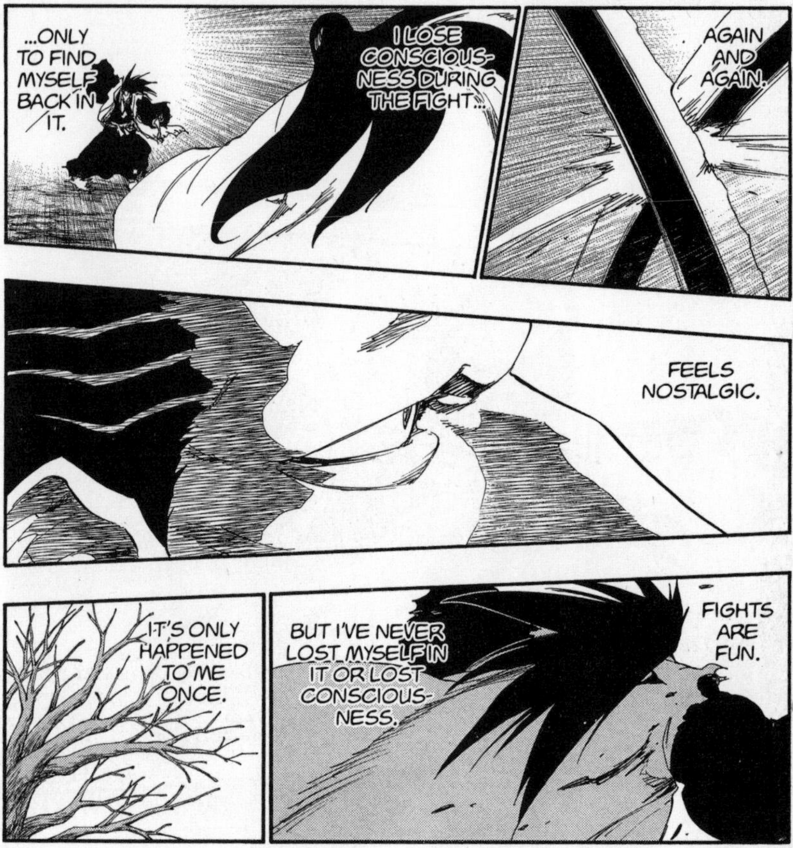
AGAIN AND AGAIN.
I LOSE CONSCIOUSNESS DURING THE FIGHT...
...ONLY TO FIND MYSELF BACK IN IT.
FEELS NOSTALGIC.
FIGHTS ARE FUN.
BUT I'VE NEVER LOST MYSELF IN IT OR LOST CONSCIOUSNESS.
IT'S ONLY HAPPENED TO ME ONCE.

THAT DAY I FOUGHT YOU.

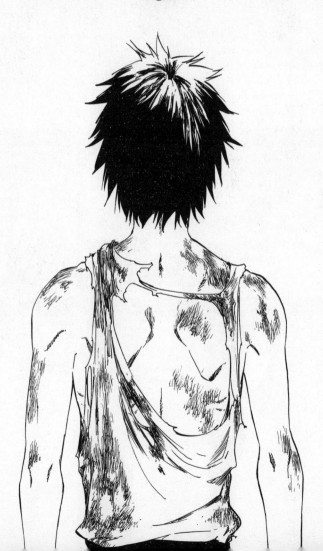

BLEACH 525.

Edges

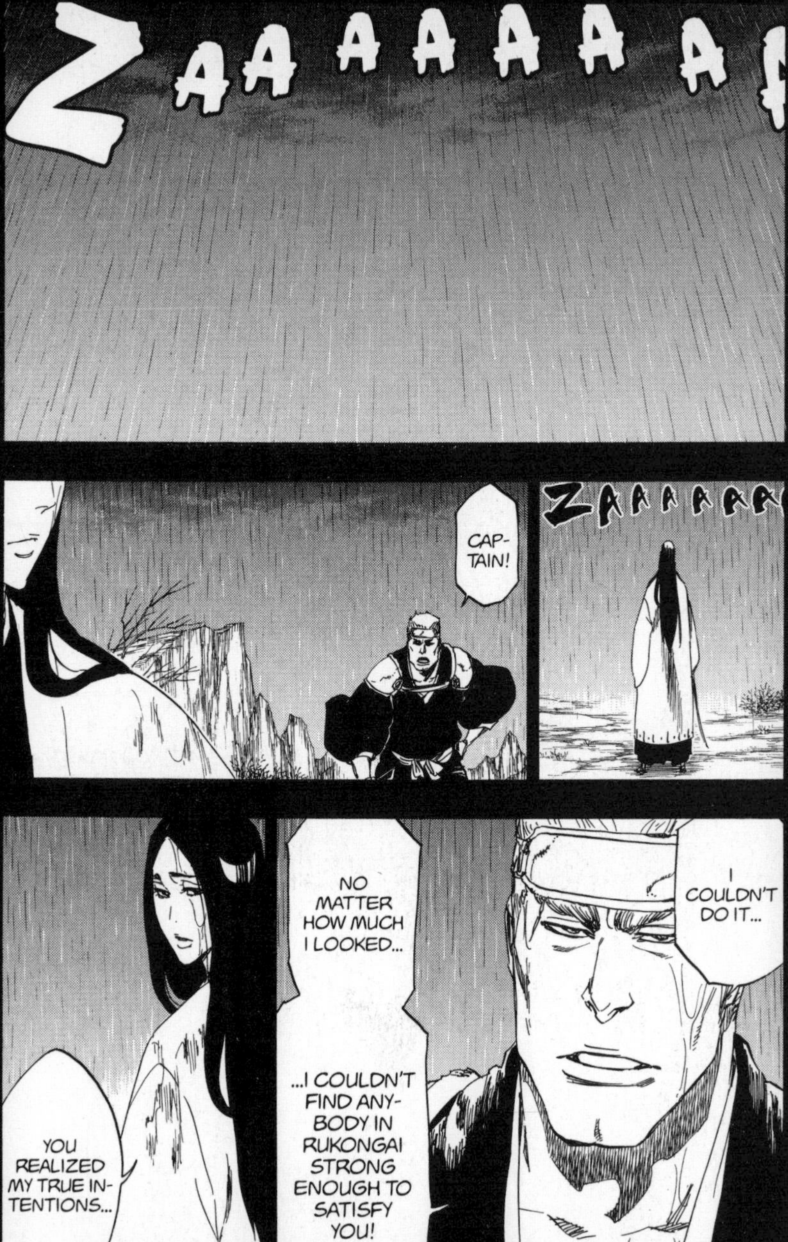
ZAAAAAAA
ZAAAAAAA
CAPTAIN!
I COULDN'T DO IT...
NO MATTER HOW MUCH I LOOKED...
...I COULDN'T FIND ANYBODY IN RUKONGAI STRONG ENOUGH TO SATISFY YOU!
YOU REALIZED MY TRUE INTENTIONS...

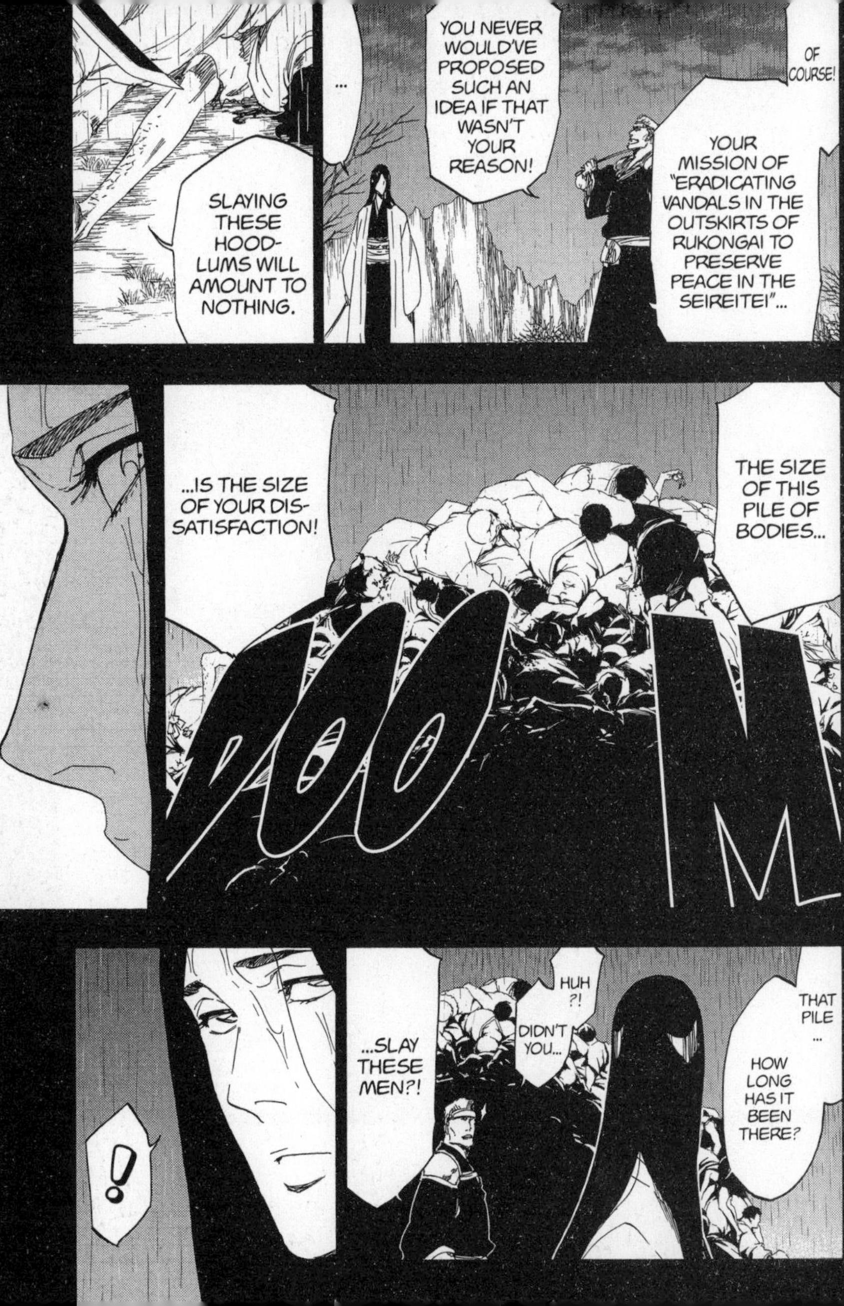
OF COURSE!
YOUR MISSION OF "ERADICATING VANDALS IN THE OUTSKIRTS OF RUKONGAI TO PRESERVE PEACE IN THE SEIREITEI"...
YOU NEVER WOULD'VE PROPOSED SUCH AN IDEA IF THAT WASN'T YOUR REASON!
...
SLAYING THESE HOOD-LUMS WILL AMOUNT TO NOTHING.
THE SIZE OF THIS PILE OF BODIES...
...IS THE SIZE OF YOUR DIS-SATISFACTION!
DOOM
THAT PILE...
HOW LONG HAS IT BEEN THERE?
HUH?!
DIDN'T YOU...
...SLAY THESE MEN?!
!

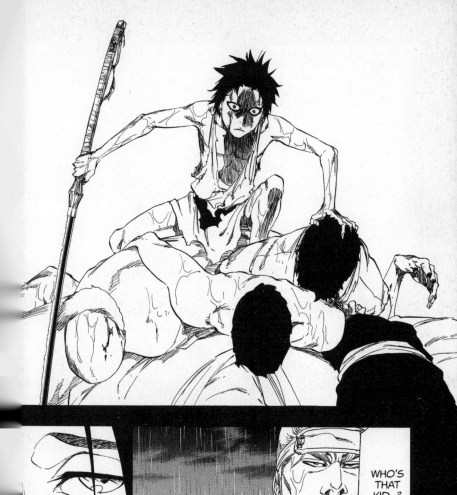

WHO'S THAT KID...?

WE WERE BORED.

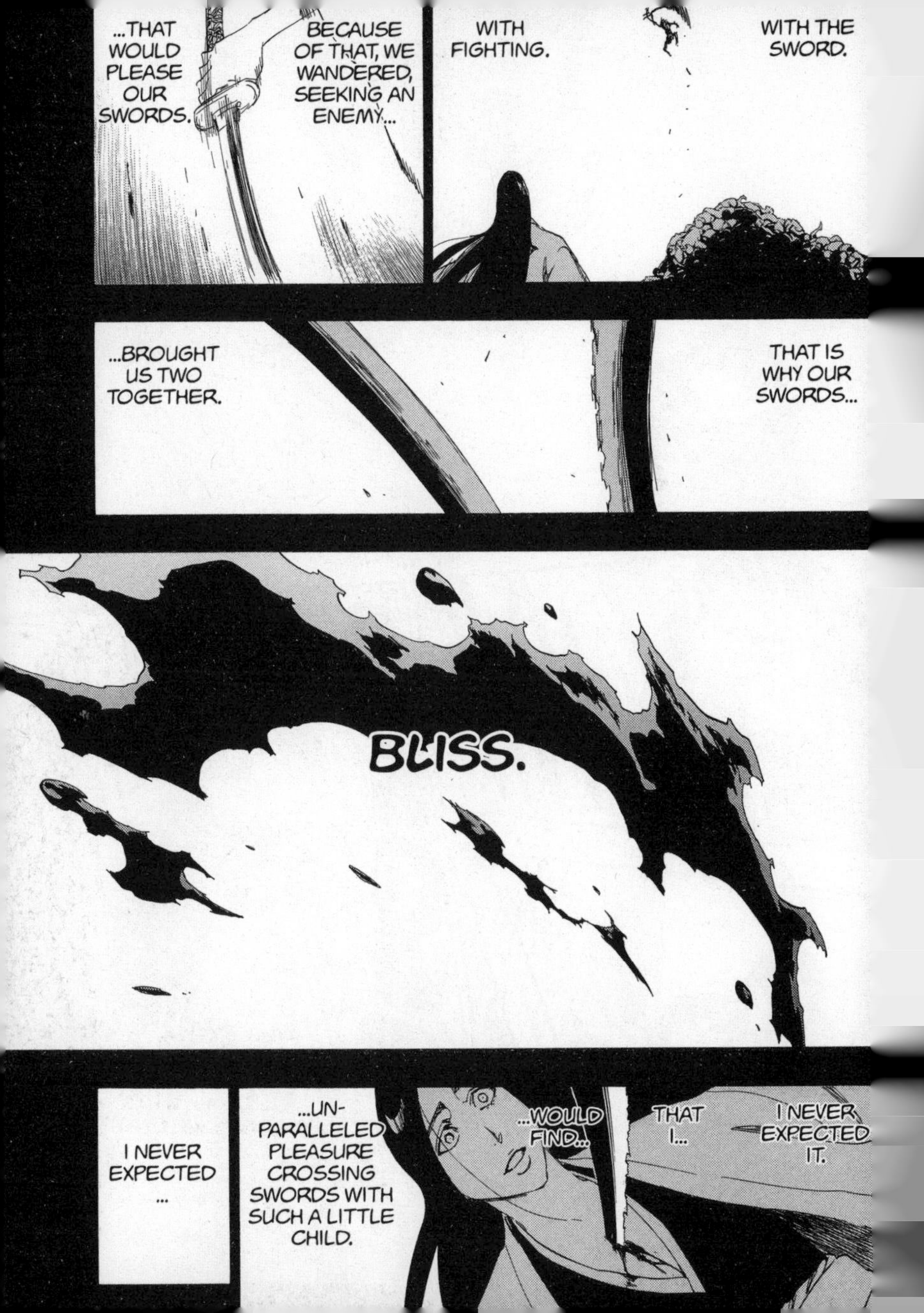
WITH THE SWORD.
WITH FIGHTING.
BECAUSE OF THAT, WE WANDERED, SEEKING AN ENEMY...
...THAT WOULD PLEASE OUR SWORDS.
THAT IS WHY OUR SWORDS...
...BROUGHT US TWO TOGETHER.
BLISS.
I NEVER EXPECTED IT.
THAT I...
...WOULD FIND...
...UN-PARALLELED PLEASURE CROSSING SWORDS WITH SUCH A LITTLE CHILD.
I NEVER EXPECTED ...

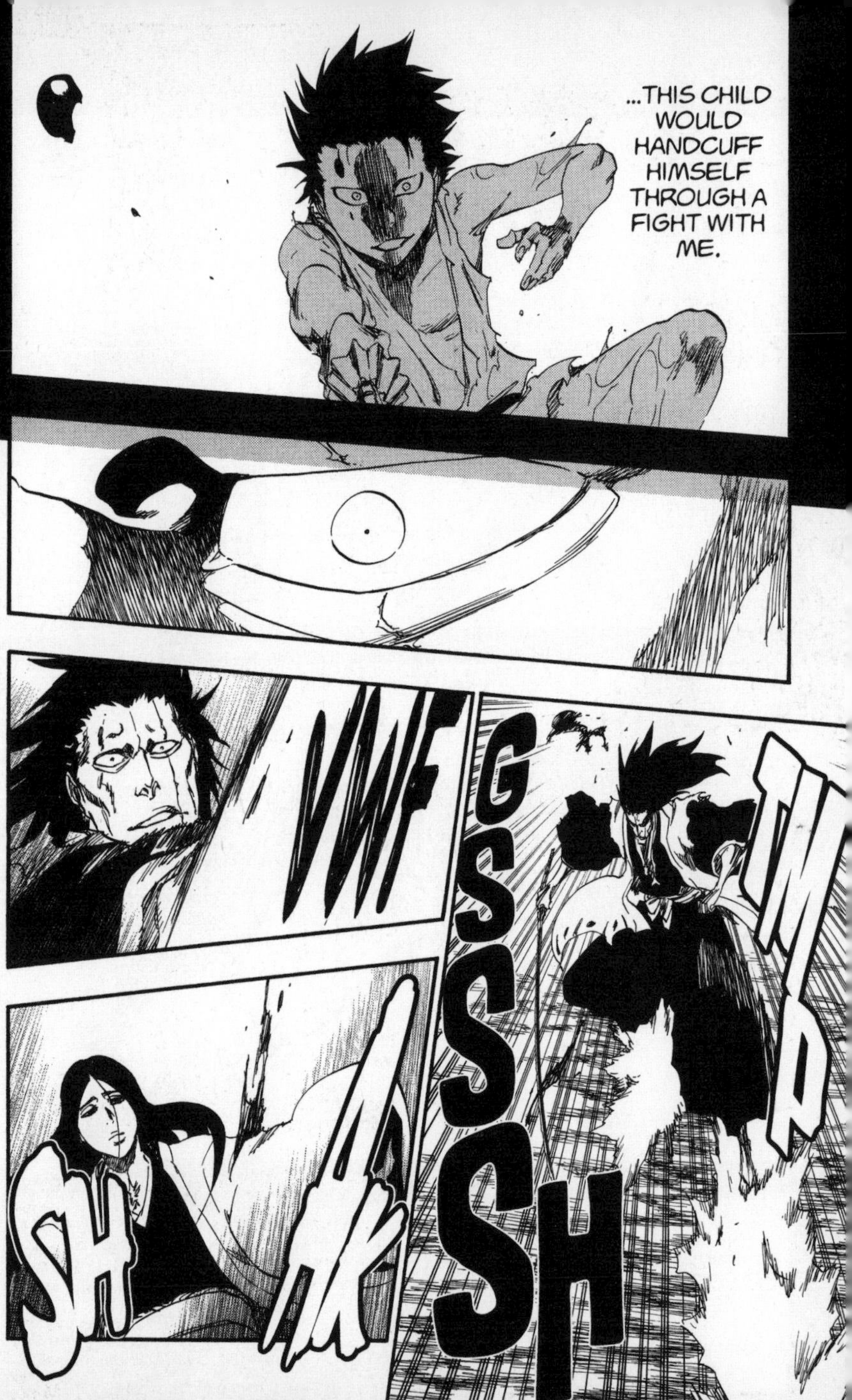
...THIS CHILD WOULD HANDCUFF HIMSELF THROUGH A FIGHT WITH ME.
VWF
GSSSH
THMP

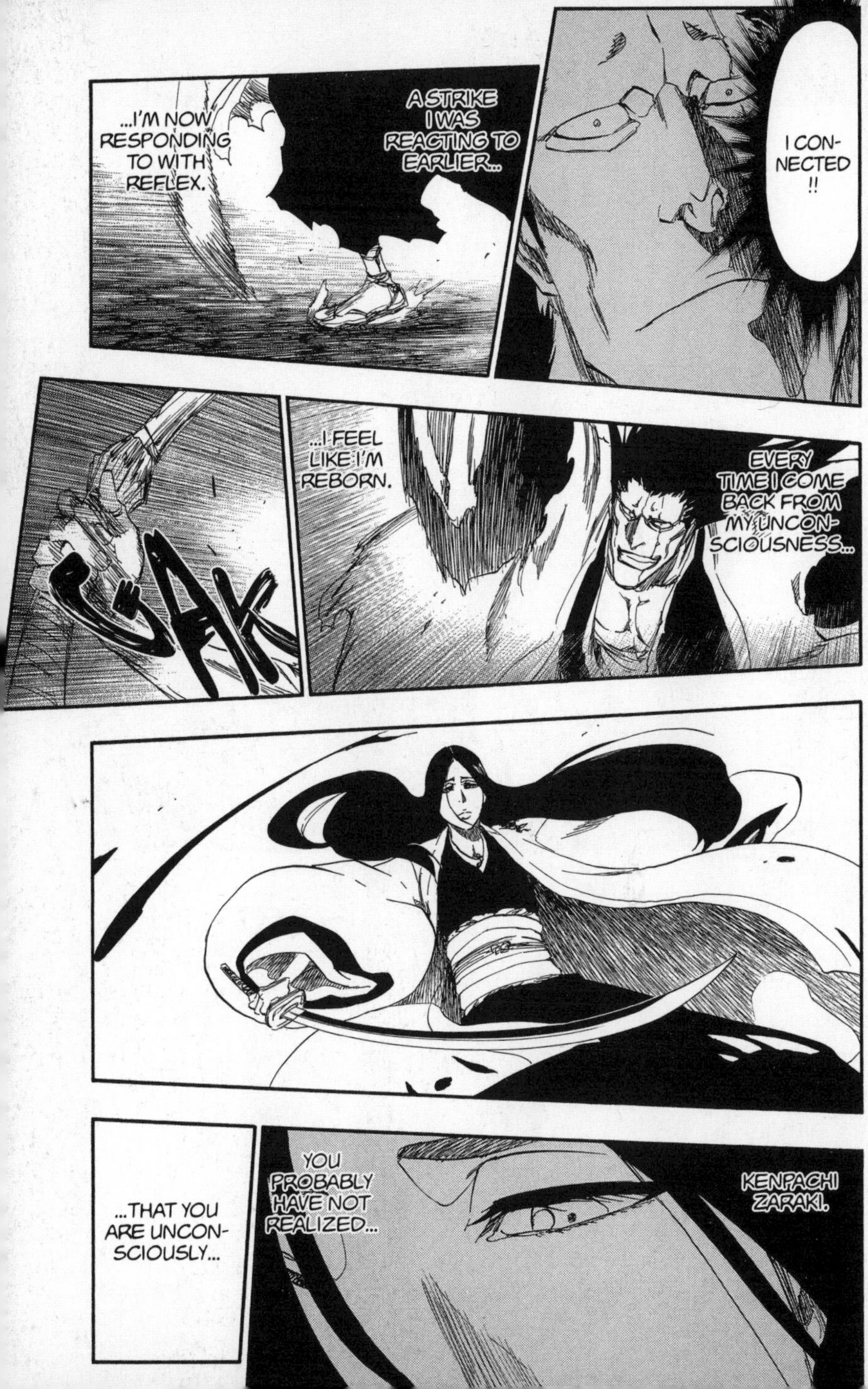
I CONNECTED!!
A STRIKE I WAS REACTING TO EARLIER...
...I'M NOW RESPONDING TO WITH REFLEX.
EVERY TIME I COME BACK FROM MY UNCONSCIOUSNESS...
...I FEEL LIKE I'M REBORN.
GAK
KENPACHI ZARAKI.
YOU PROBABLY HAVE NOT REALIZED...
...THAT YOU ARE UNCONSCIOUSLY...

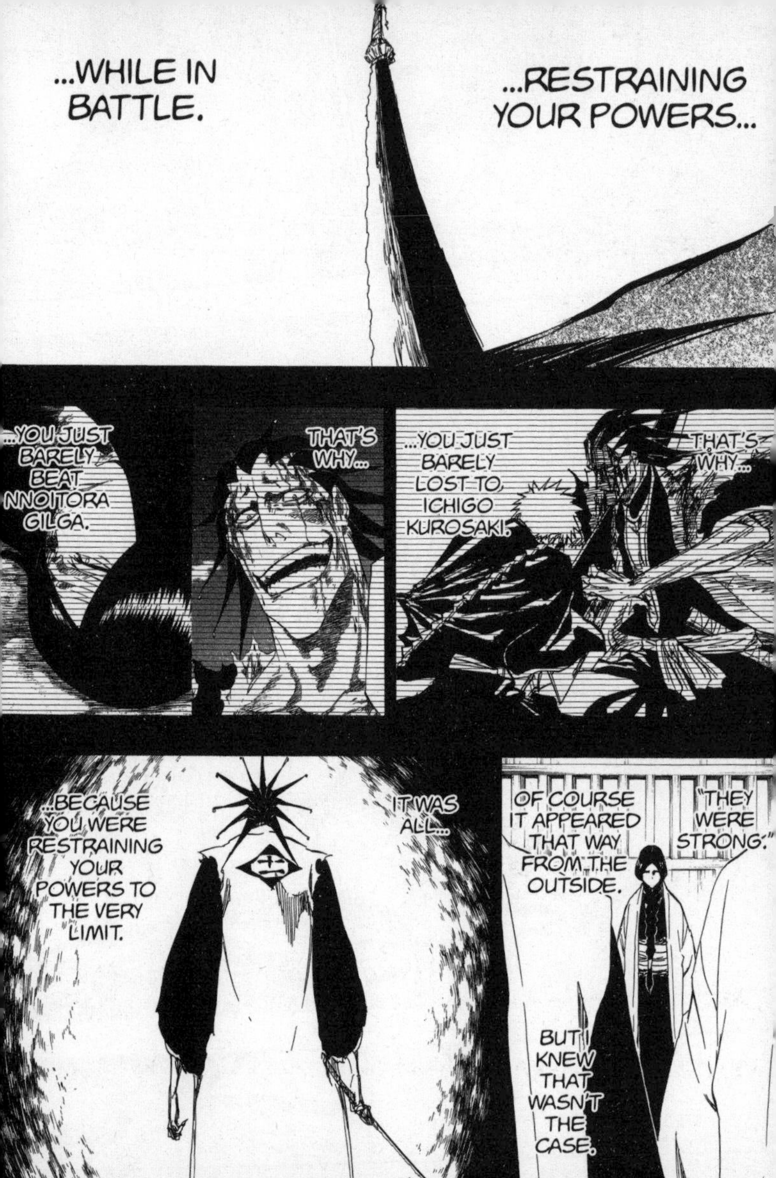
...RESTRAINING YOUR POWERS...
...WHILE IN BATTLE.
THAT'S WHY...
...YOU JUST BARELY LOST TO ICHIGO KUROSAKI.
THAT'S WHY...
...YOU JUST BARELY BEAT NNOITORA GILGA.
"THEY WERE STRONG."
OF COURSE IT APPEARED THAT WAY FROM THE OUTSIDE.
BUT I KNEW THAT WASN'T THE CASE.
IT WAS ALL...
...BECAUSE YOU WERE RESTRAINING YOUR POWERS TO THE VERY LIMIT.

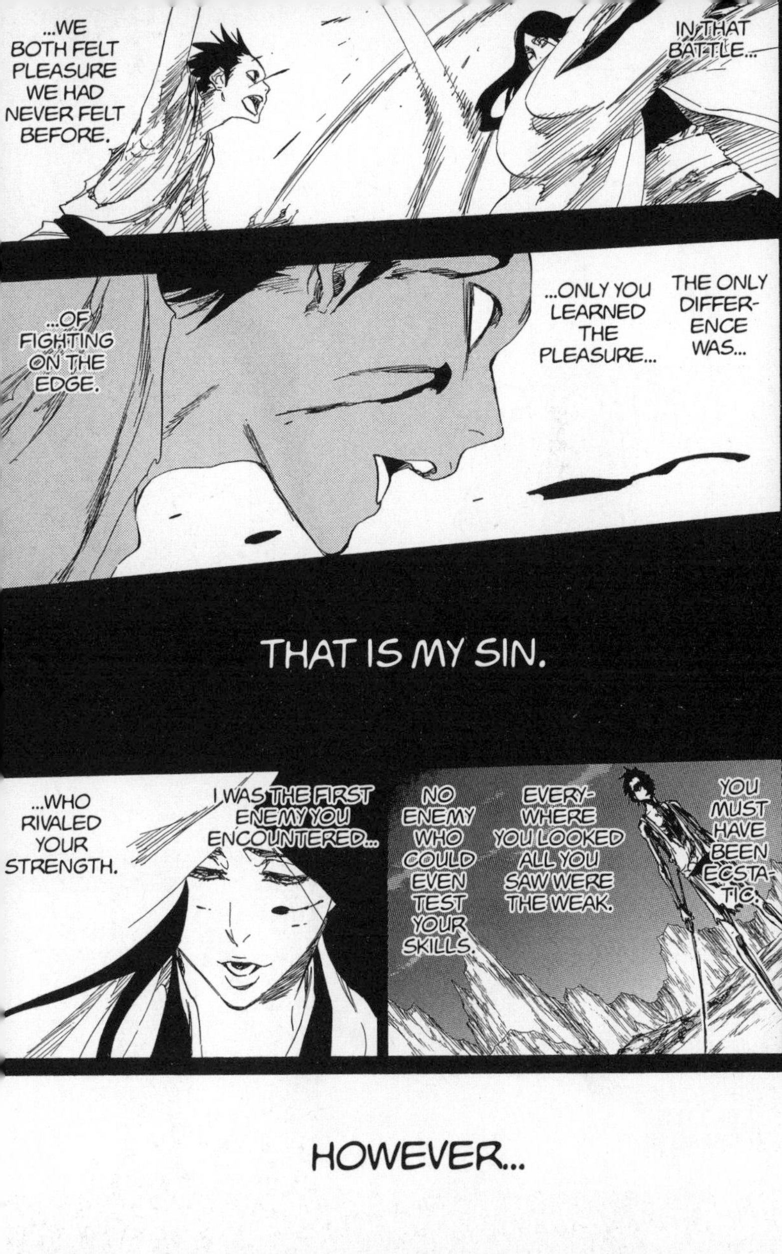
IN THAT BATTLE...
...WE BOTH FELT PLEASURE WE HAD NEVER FELT BEFORE.
THE ONLY DIFFERENCE WAS...
...ONLY YOU LEARNED THE PLEASURE...
...OF FIGHTING ON THE EDGE.
THAT IS MY SIN.
YOU MUST HAVE BEEN ECSTATIC.
EVERYWHERE YOU LOOKED ALL YOU SAW WERE THE WEAK.
NO ENEMY WHO COULD EVEN TEST YOUR SKILLS.
I WAS THE FIRST ENEMY YOU ENCOUNTERED...
...WHO RIVALED YOUR STRENGTH.
HOWEVER...

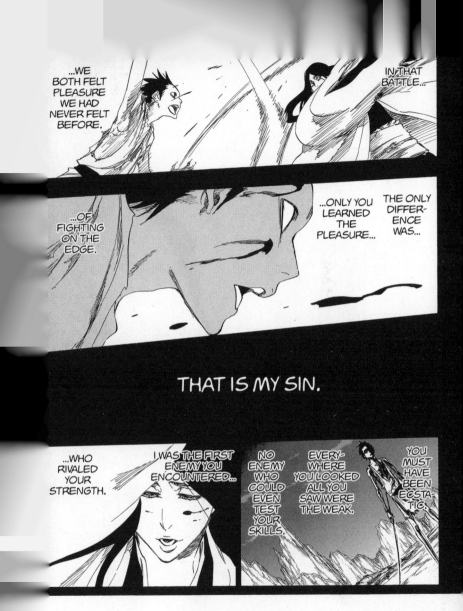

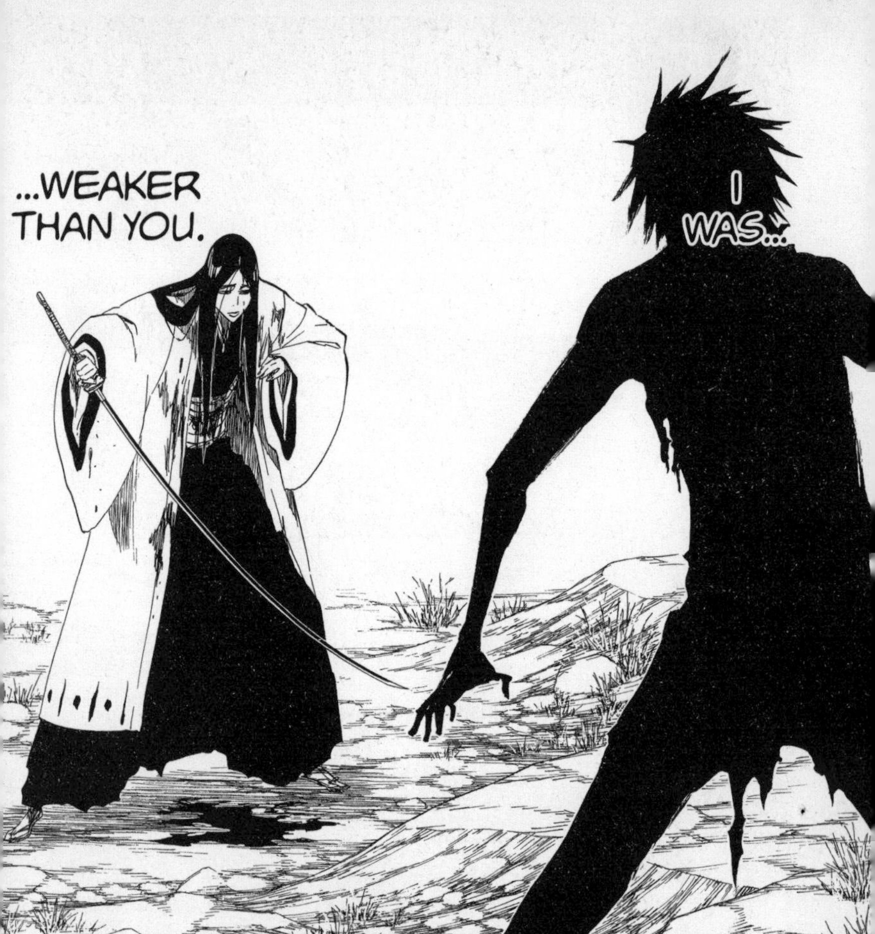
I WAS...
...WEAKER THAN YOU.
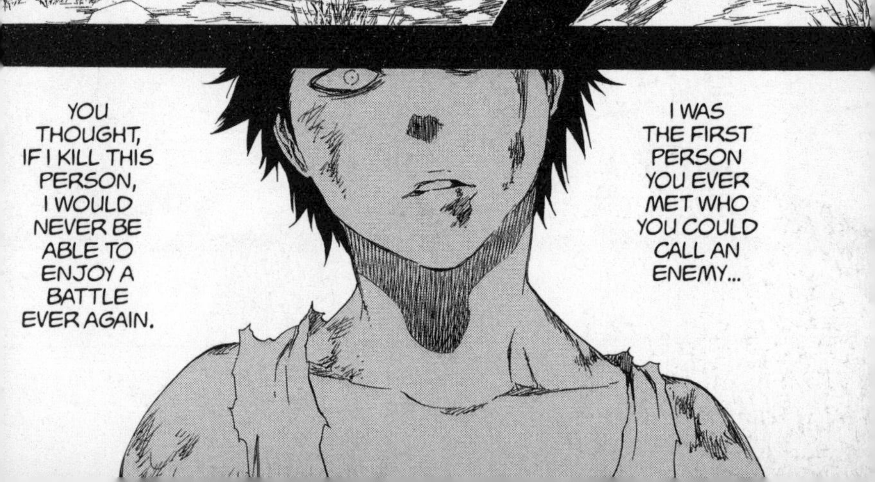
I WAS THE FIRST PERSON YOU EVER MET WHO YOU COULD CALL AN ENEMY...
YOU THOUGHT, IF I KILL THIS PERSON, I WOULD NEVER BE ABLE TO ENJOY A BATTLE EVER AGAIN.

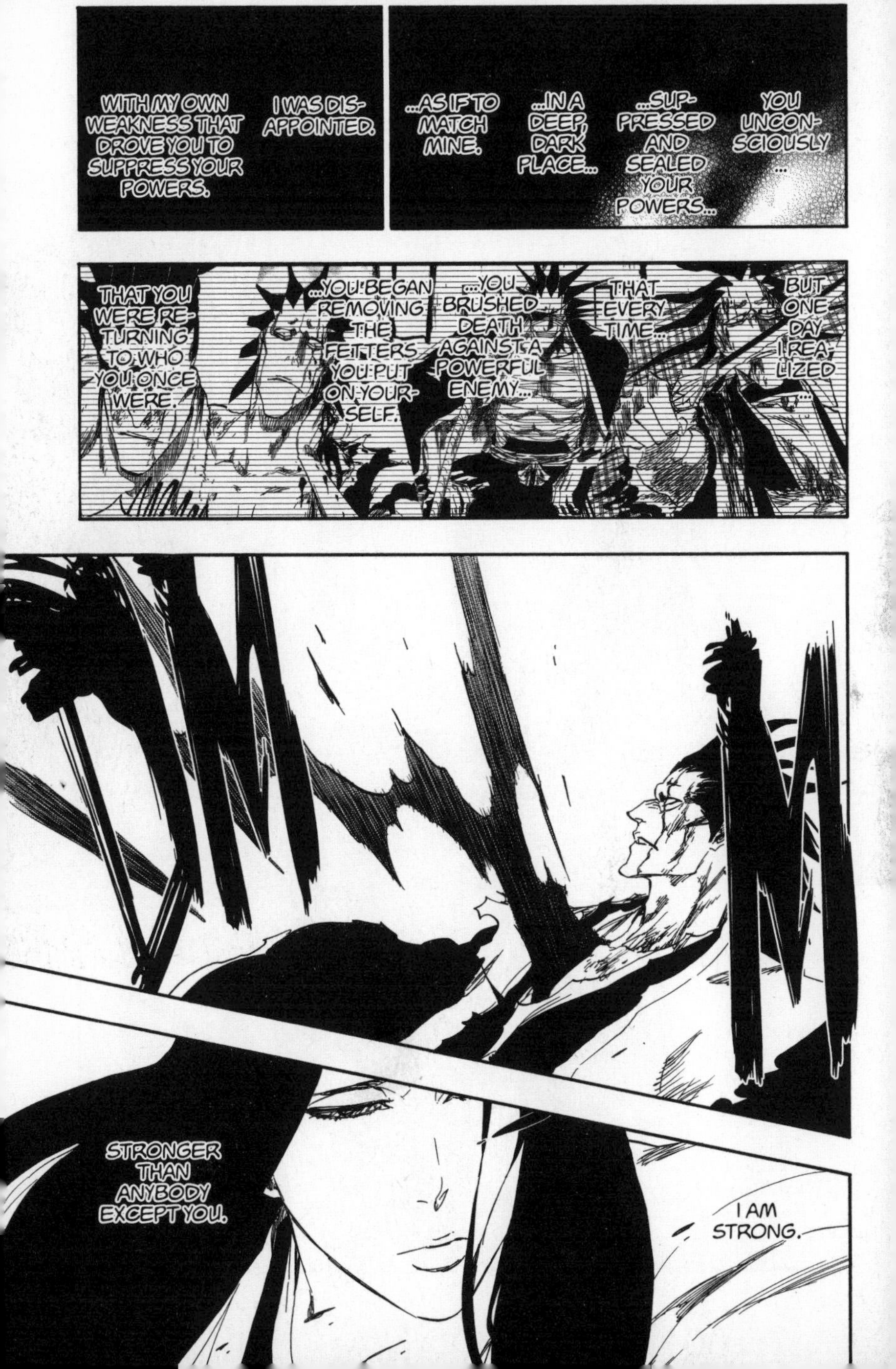
YOU UNCONSCIOUSLY...
...SUPPRESSED AND SEALED YOUR POWERS...
...IN A DEEP, DARK PLACE...
...AS IF TO MATCH MINE.
I WAS DISAPPOINTED.
WITH MY OWN WEAKNESS THAT DROVE YOU TO SUPPRESS YOUR POWERS.
BUT ONE DAY I REALIZED...
THAT EVERY TIME...
...YOU BRUSHED DEATH AGAINST A POWERFUL ENEMY...
...YOU BEGAN REMOVING THE FETTERS YOU PUT ON YOURSELF.
THAT YOU WERE RETURNING TO WHO YOU ONCE WERE.
I AM STRONG.
STRONGER THAN ANYBODY EXCEPT YOU.

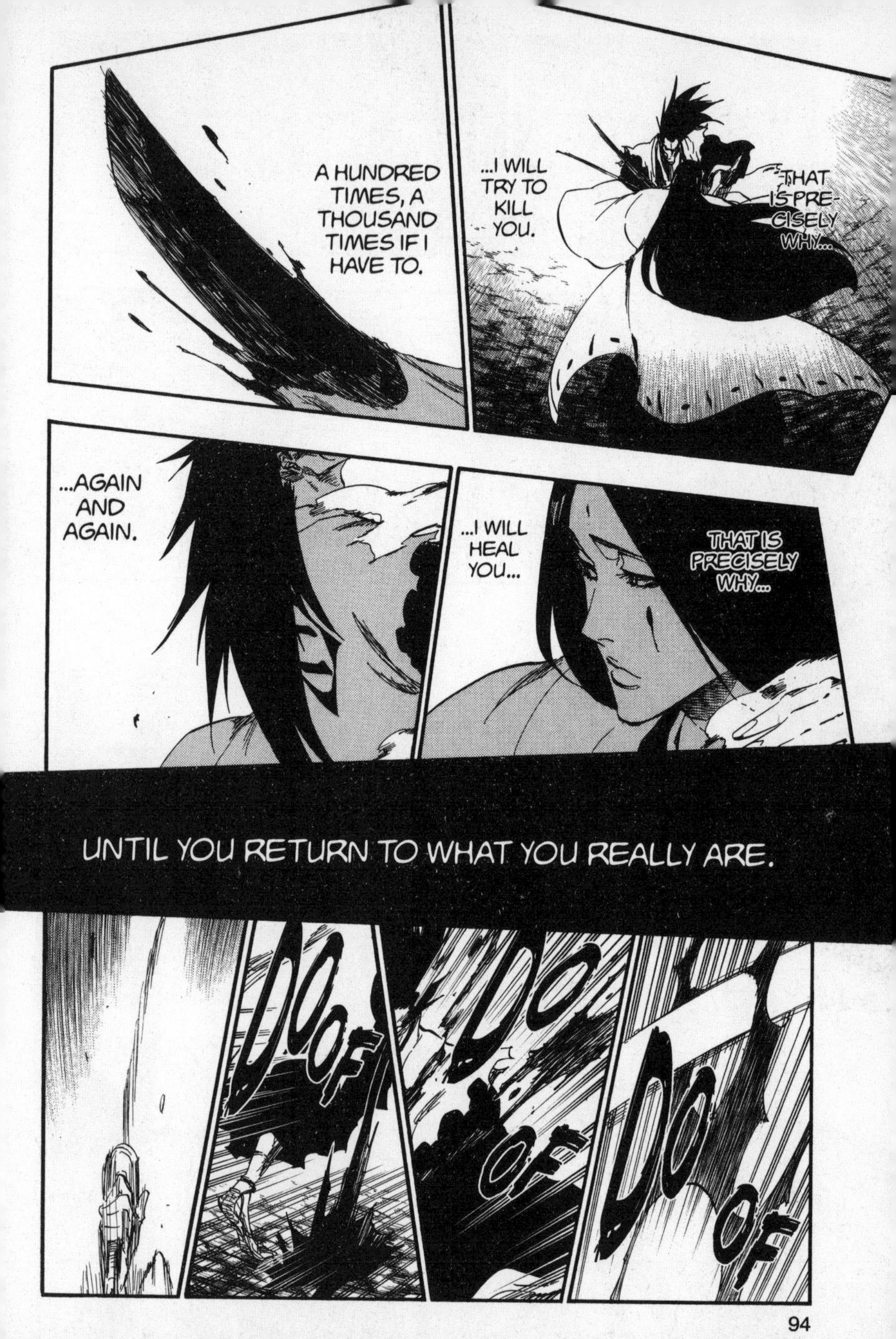
THAT IS PRECISELY WHY...
...I WILL TRY TO KILL YOU.
A HUNDRED TIMES, A THOUSAND TIMES IF I HAVE TO.
THAT IS PRECISELY WHY...
...I WILL HEAL YOU...
...AGAIN AND AGAIN.
UNTIL YOU RETURN TO WHAT YOU REALLY ARE.
DOOF
DOOF
DOOF

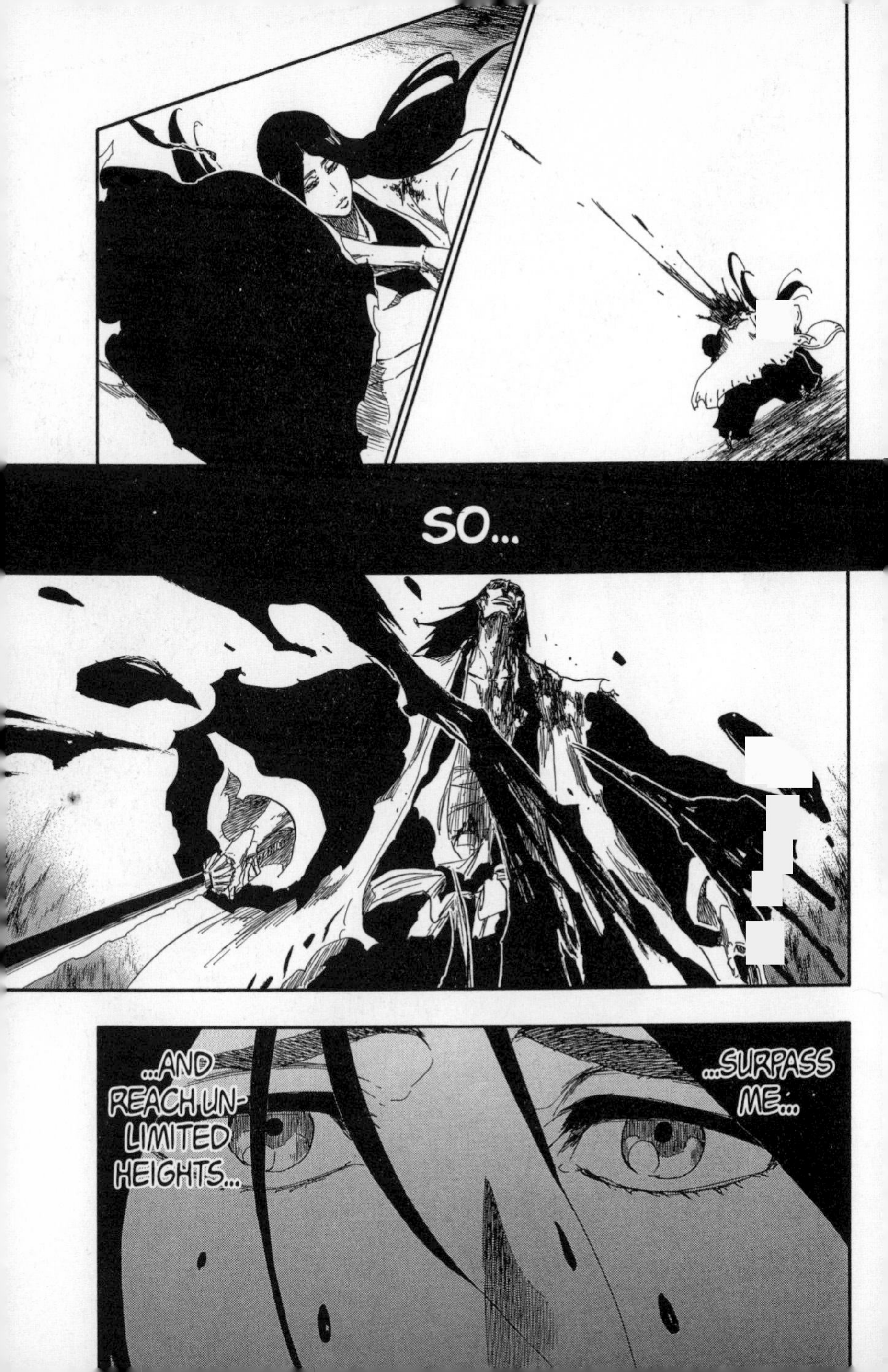
SO...
...SURPASS ME...
...AND REACH UN-LIMITED HEIGHTS...

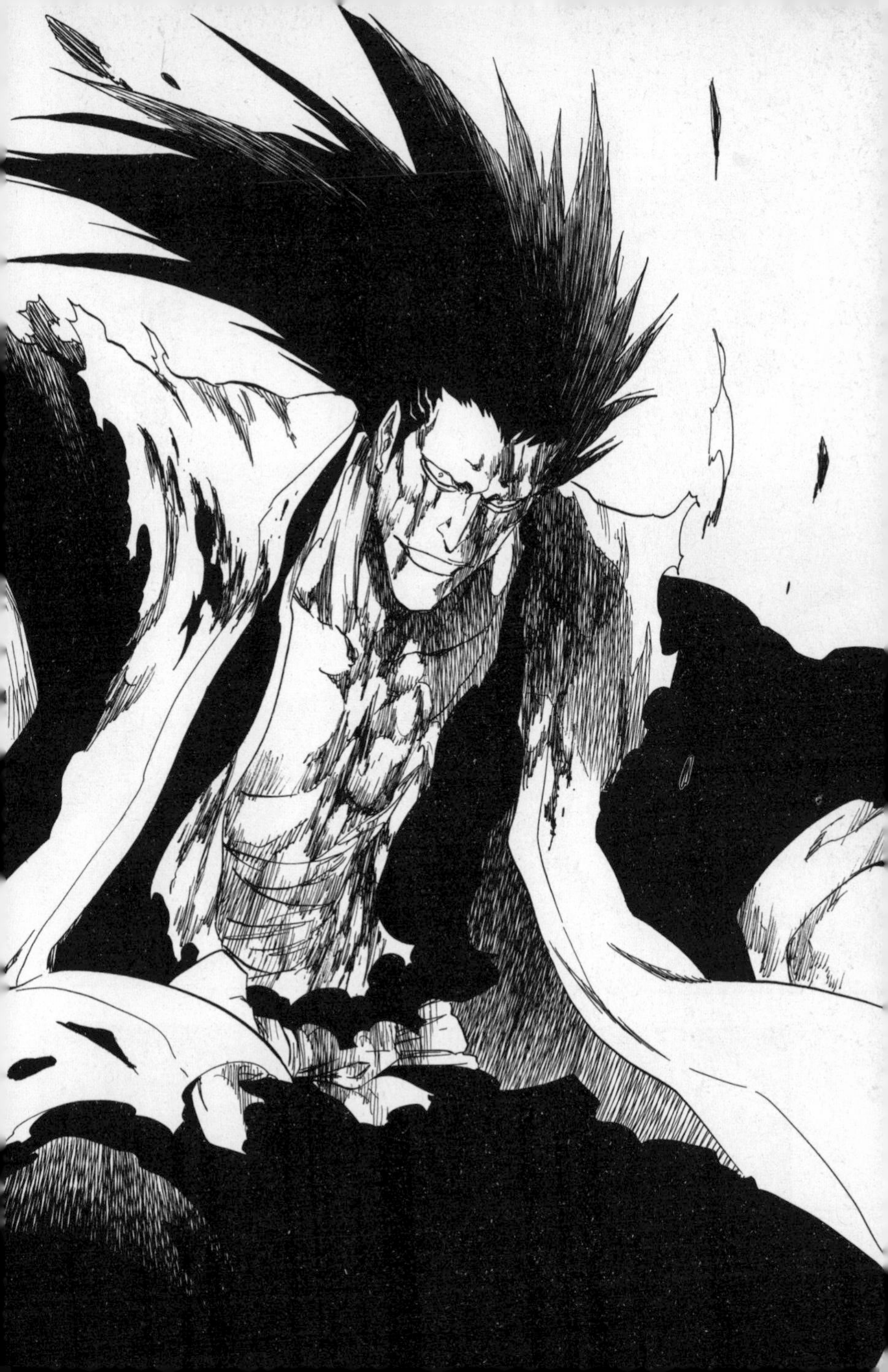

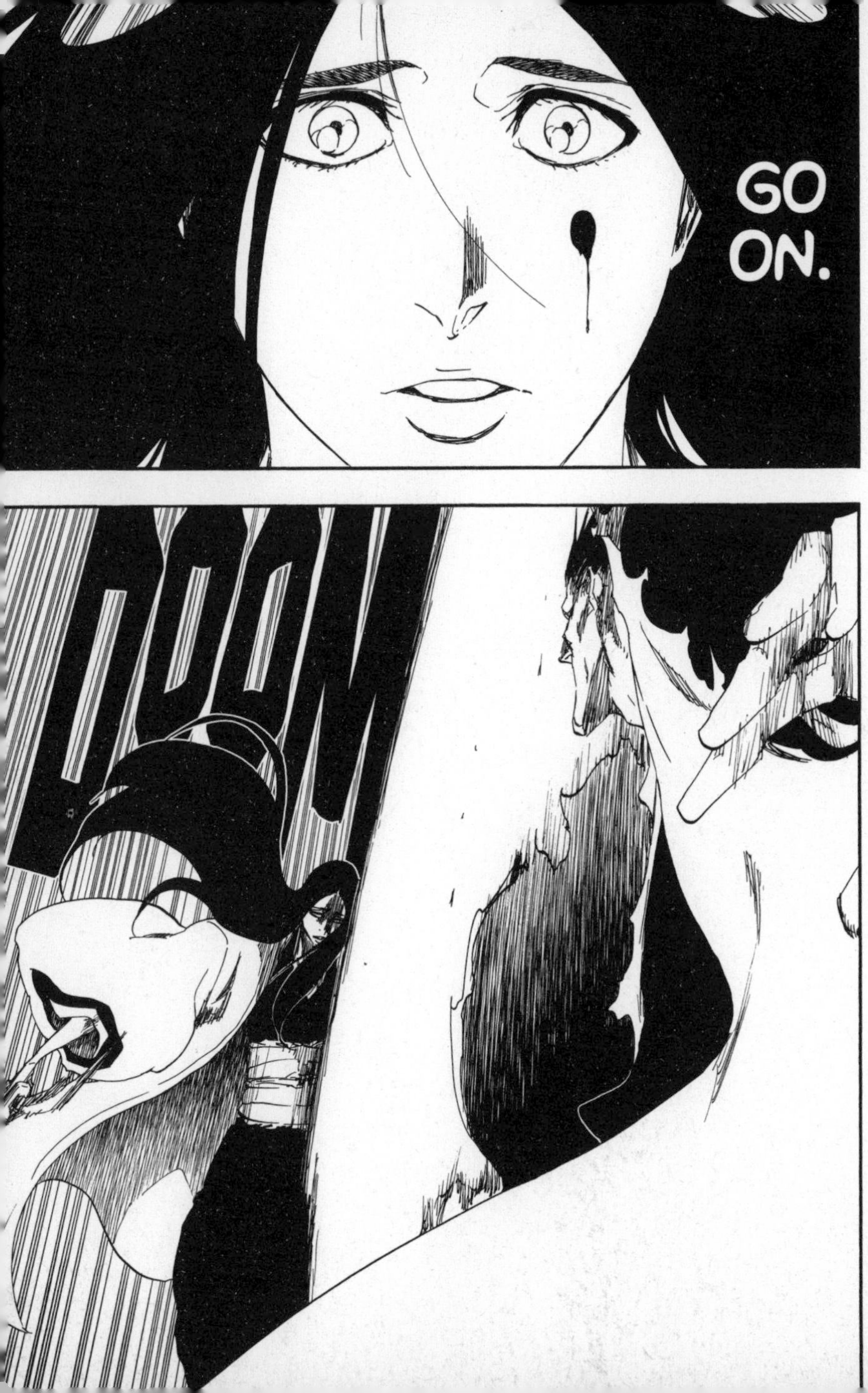
GO ON.
DOOM

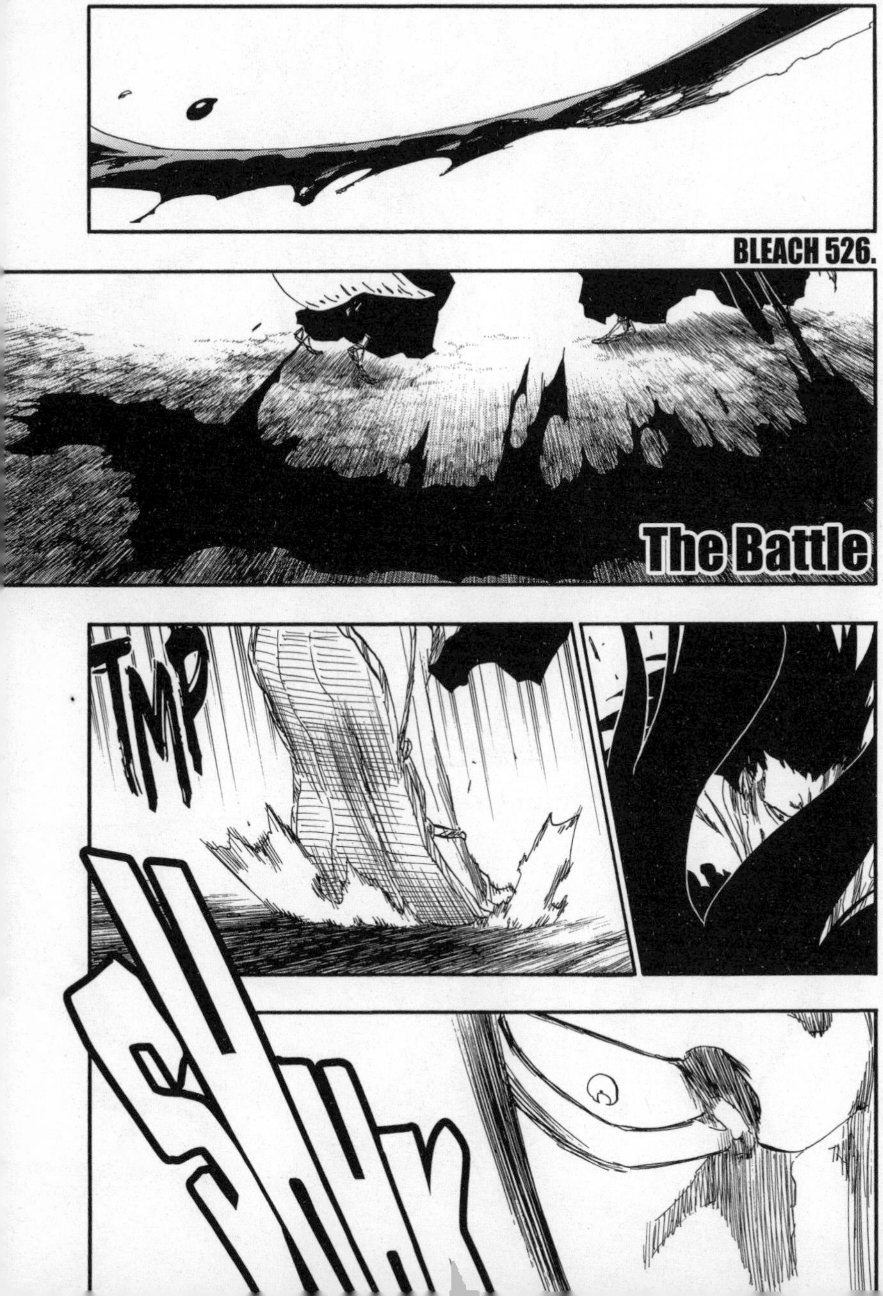

BLEACH 526.
The Battle
TMP
SHHH

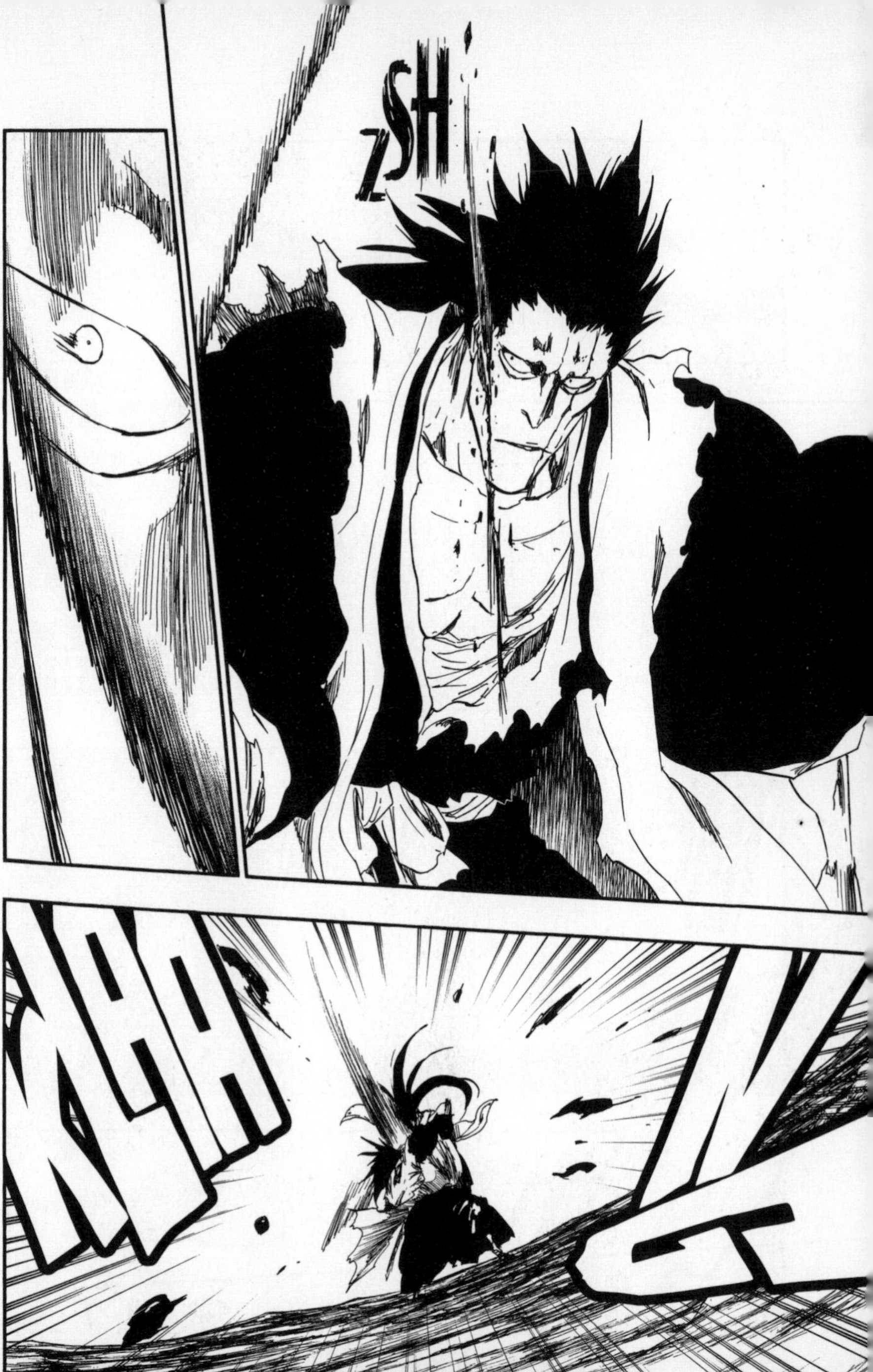
ZSH

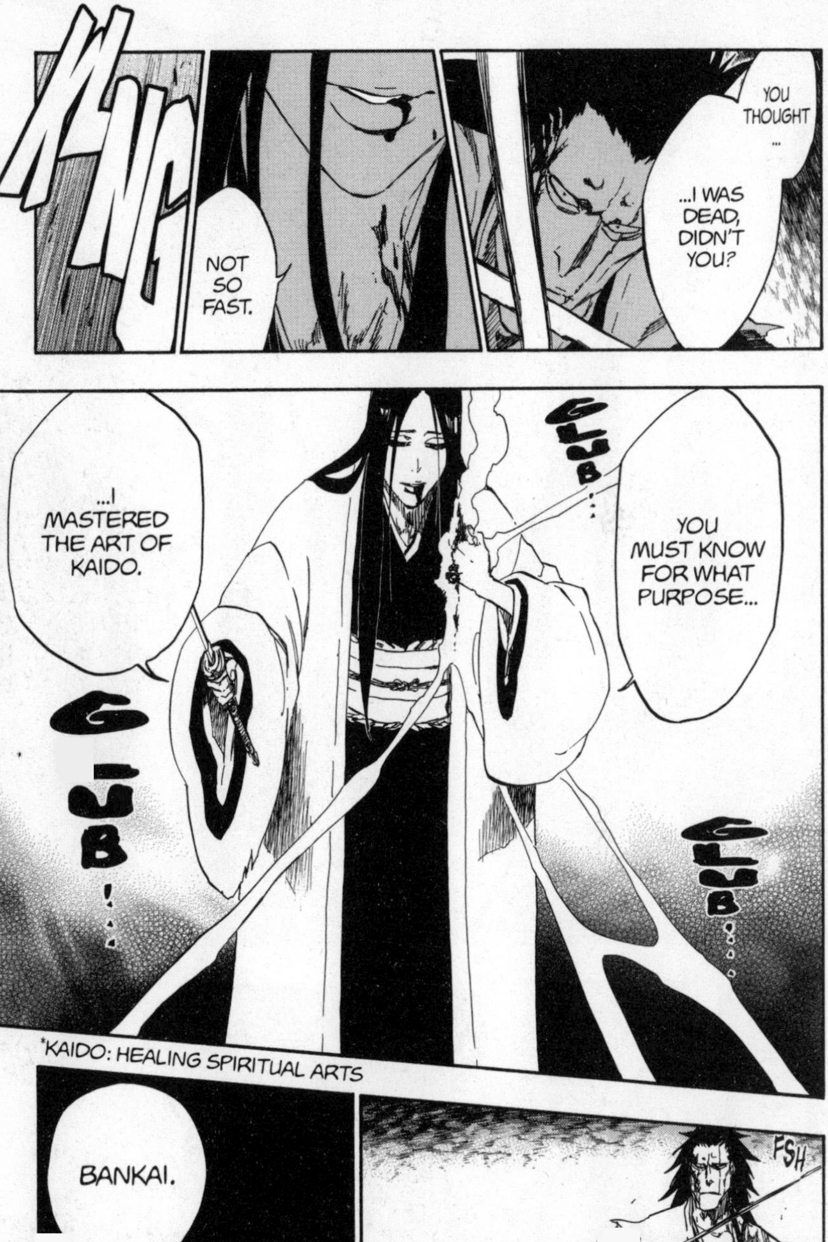
YOU THOUGHT ...
...I WAS DEAD, DIDN'T YOU?
NOT SO FAST.
GLUB...
YOU MUST KNOW FOR WHAT PURPOSE...
...I MASTERED THE ART OF KAIDO.
GLUB...
GLUB...
*KAIDO: HEALING SPIRITUAL ARTS
FSH
BANKAI.

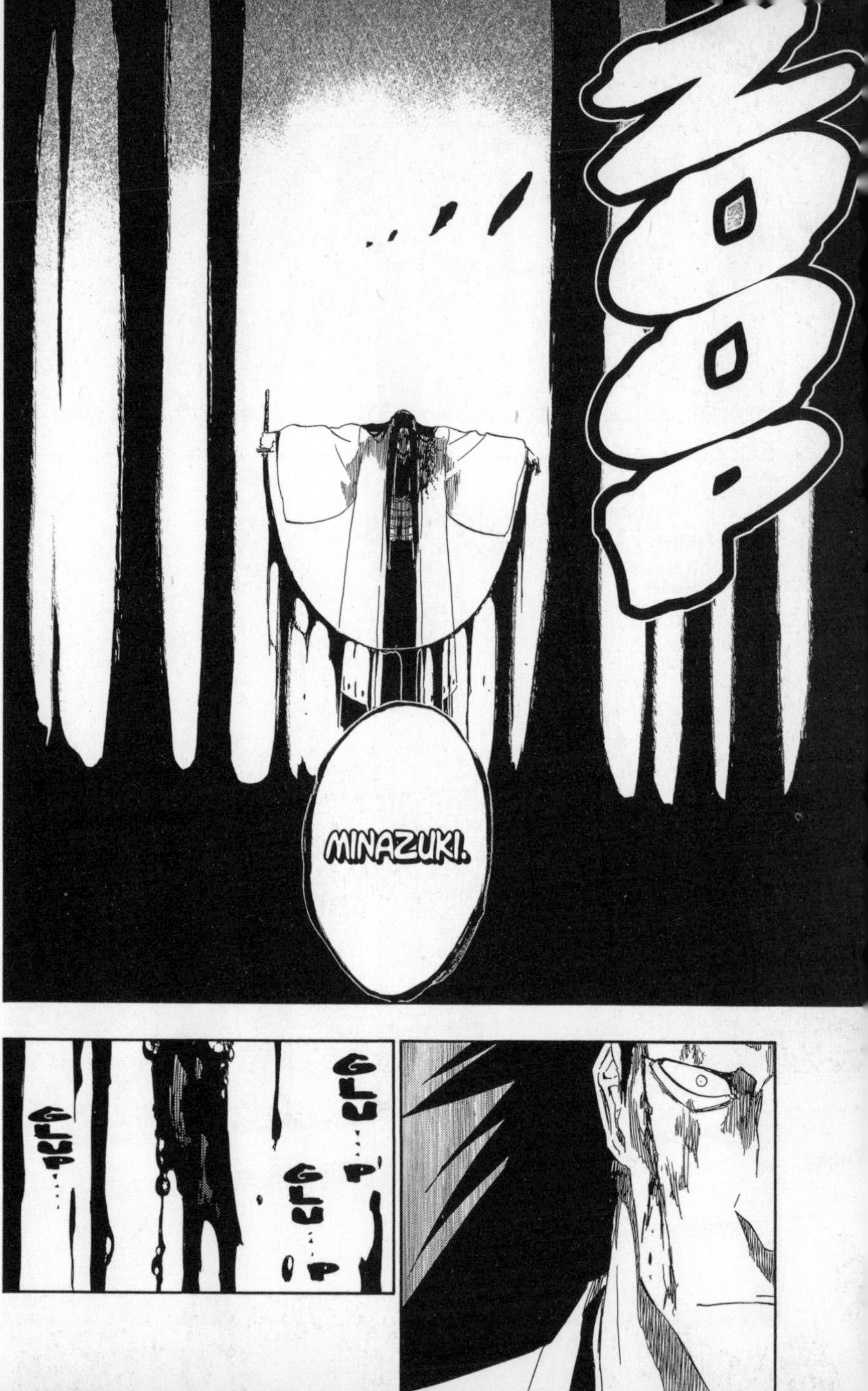
ZOOP
MINAZUKI.
GLU...P
GLU...P
GLUP...

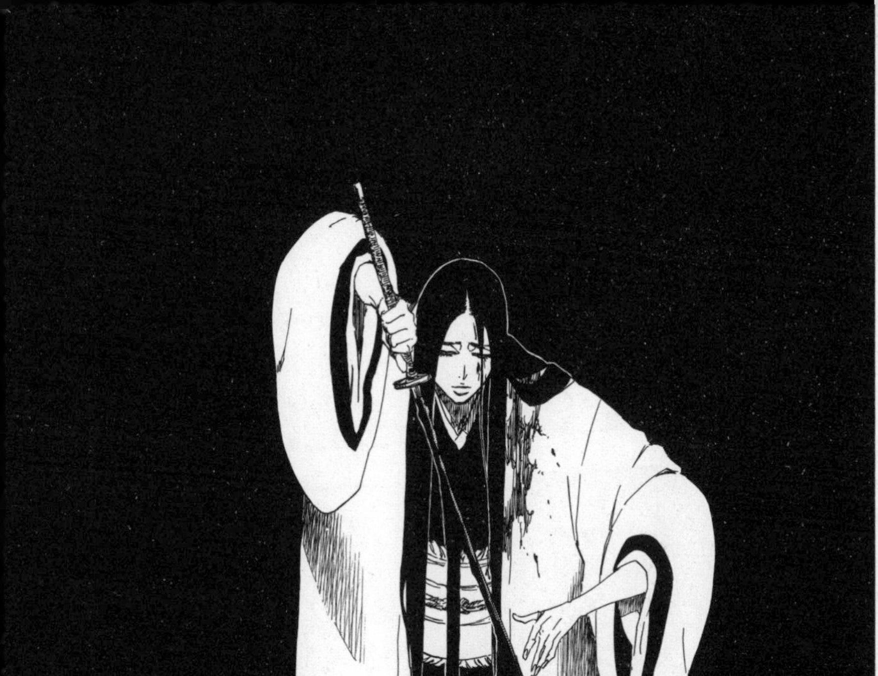
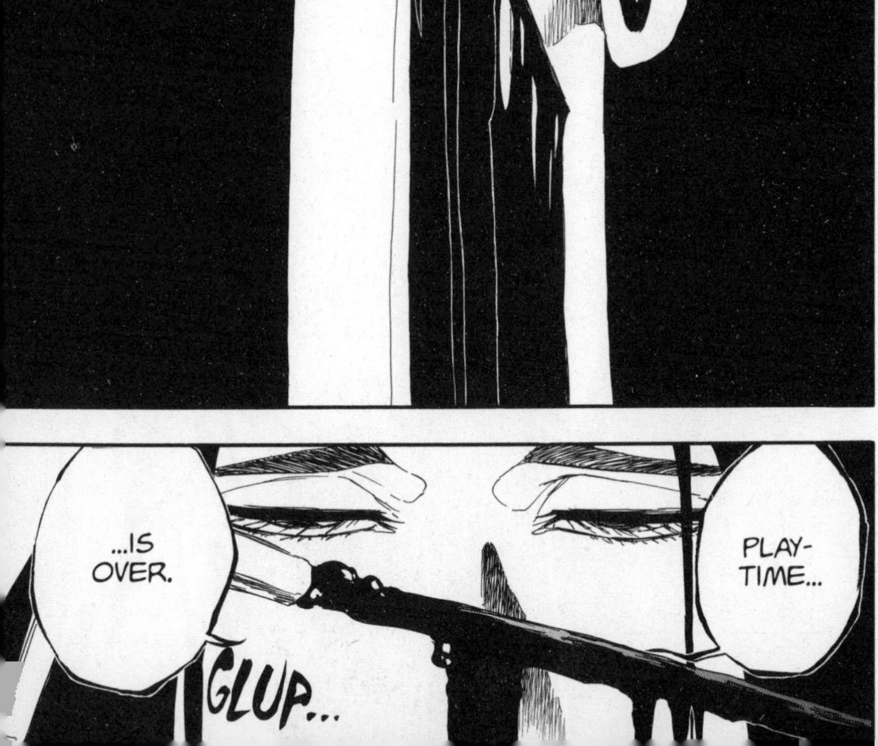
PLAY-TIME...
...IS OVER.
GLUP...

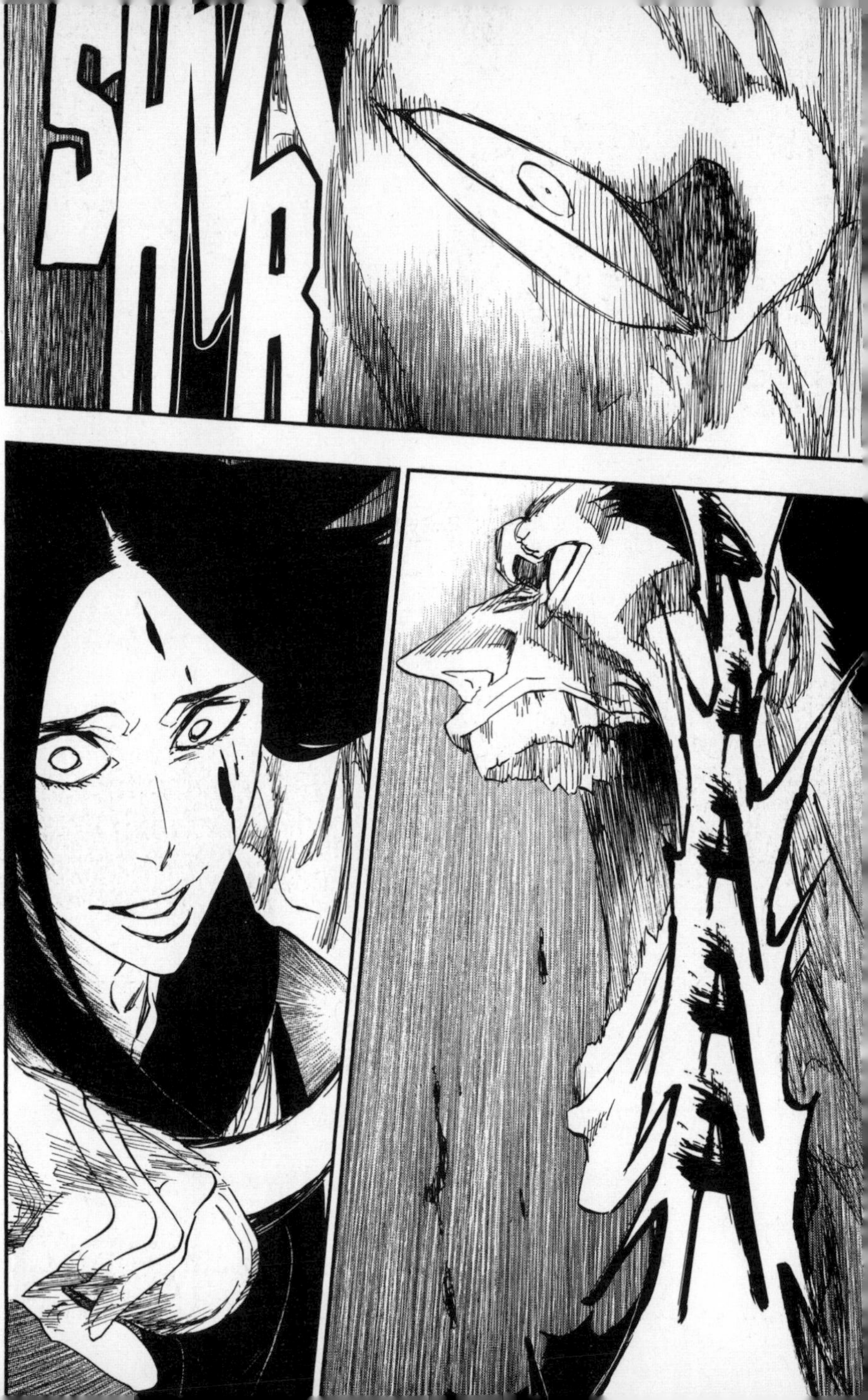
SHWA
RAAAA

OH...

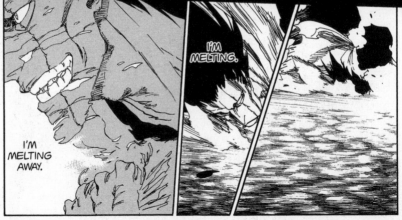

I'M
MELTING.

I'M
MELTING
AWAY.

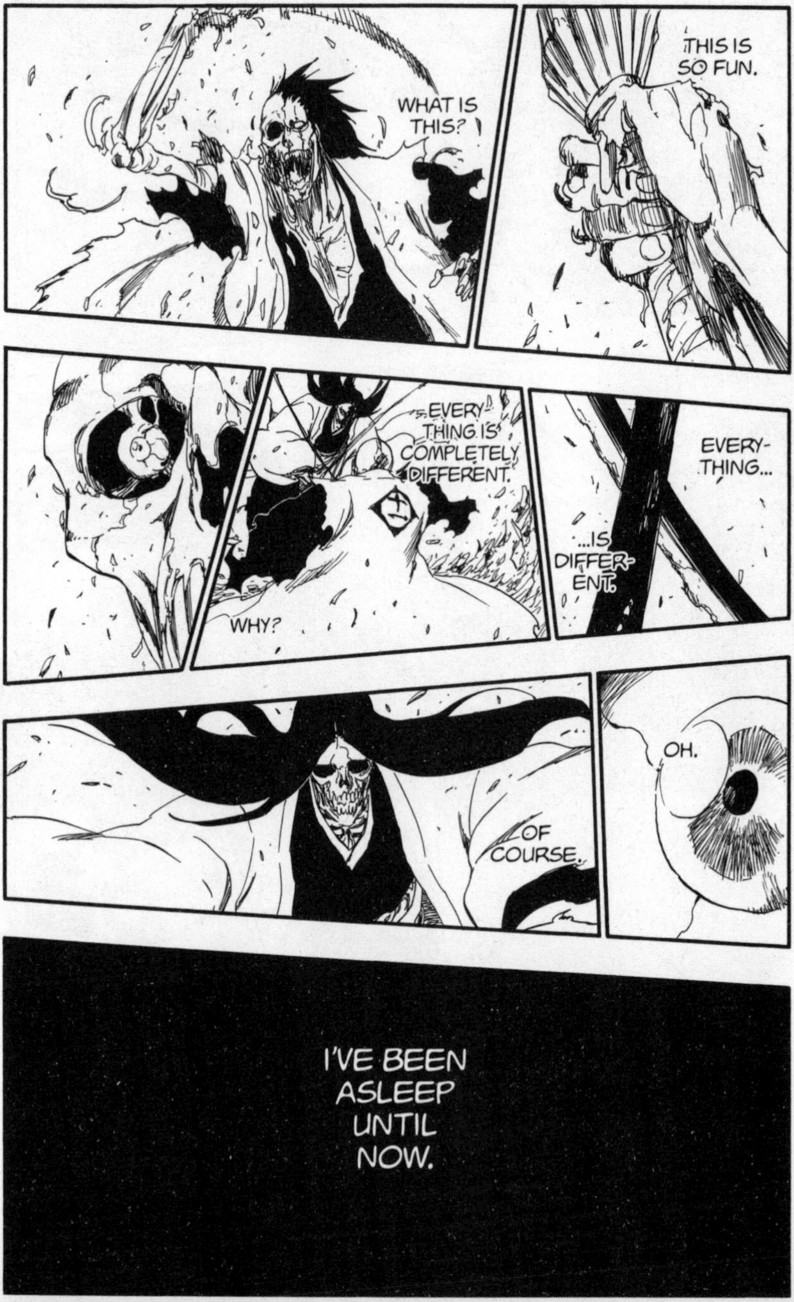
THIS IS SO FUN.
WHAT IS THIS?
EVERYTHING...
...IS DIFFERENT.
EVERYTHING IS COMPLETELY DIFFERENT.
WHY?
OH.
OF COURSE.
I'VE BEEN ASLEEP UNTIL NOW.

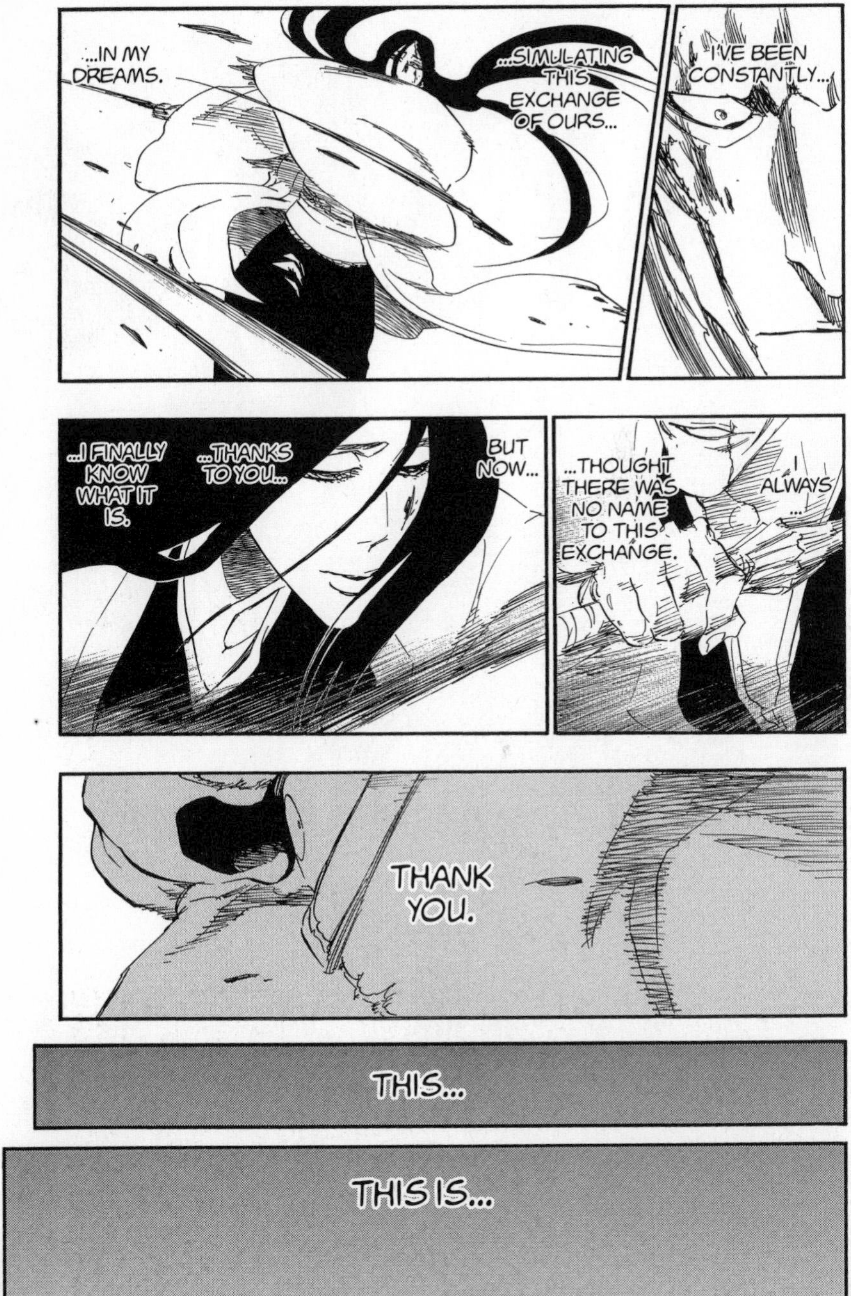
I'VE BEEN CONSTANTLY...
...SIMULATING THIS EXCHANGE OF OURS...
...IN MY DREAMS.
I ALWAYS...
...THOUGHT THERE WAS NO NAME TO THIS EXCHANGE.
BUT NOW...
...THANKS TO YOU...
...I FINALLY KNOW WHAT IT IS.
THANK YOU.
THIS...
THIS IS...

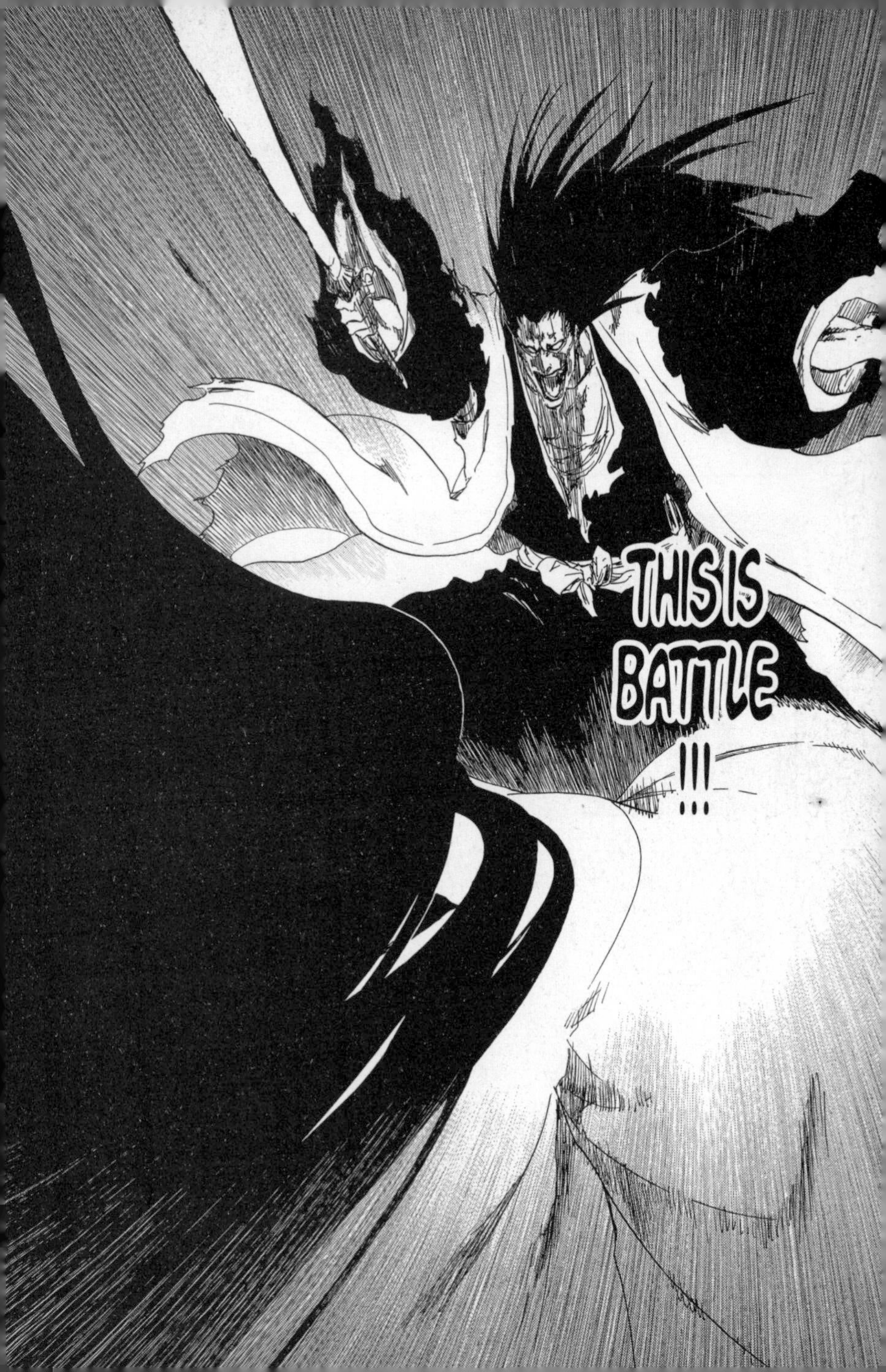
THIS IS BATTLE !!!

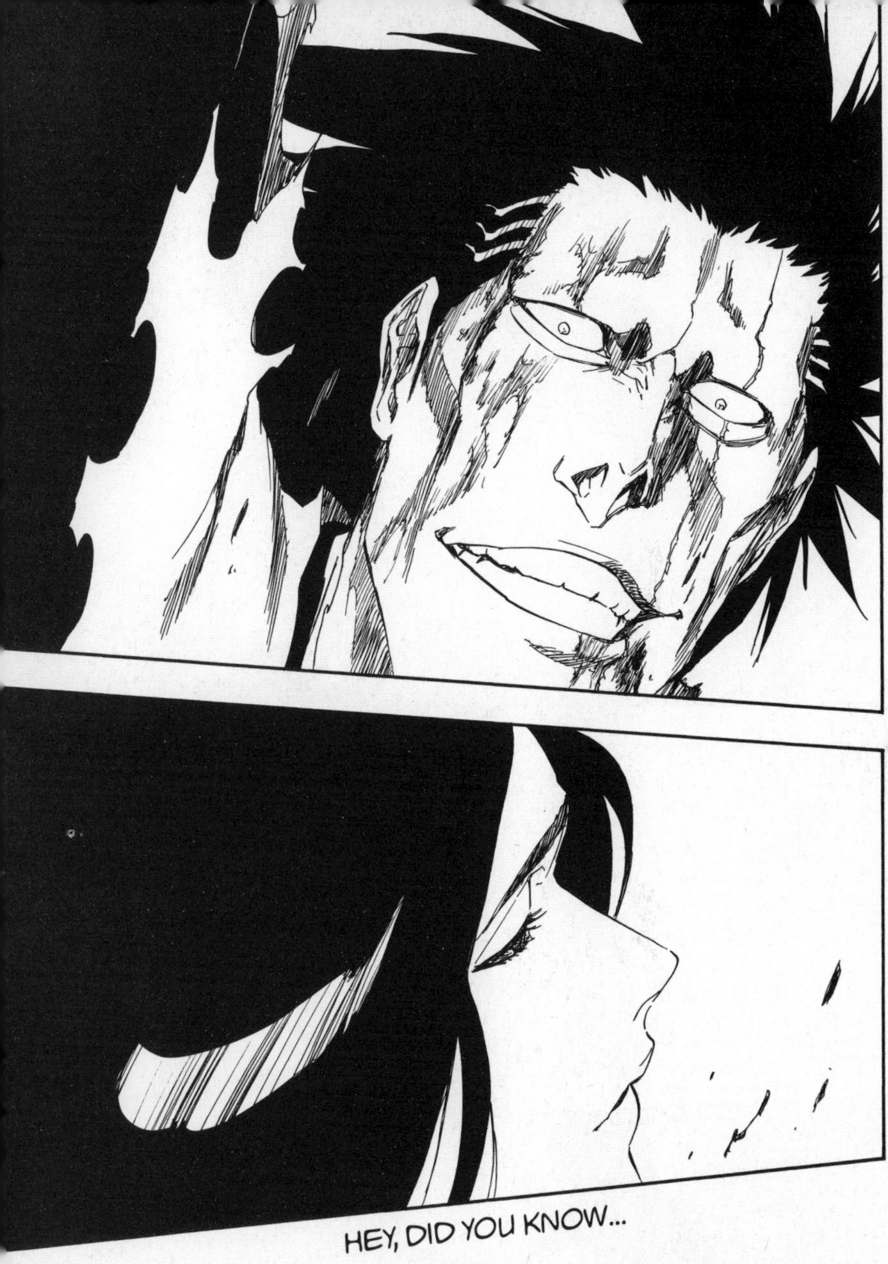

HEY, DID YOU KNOW...

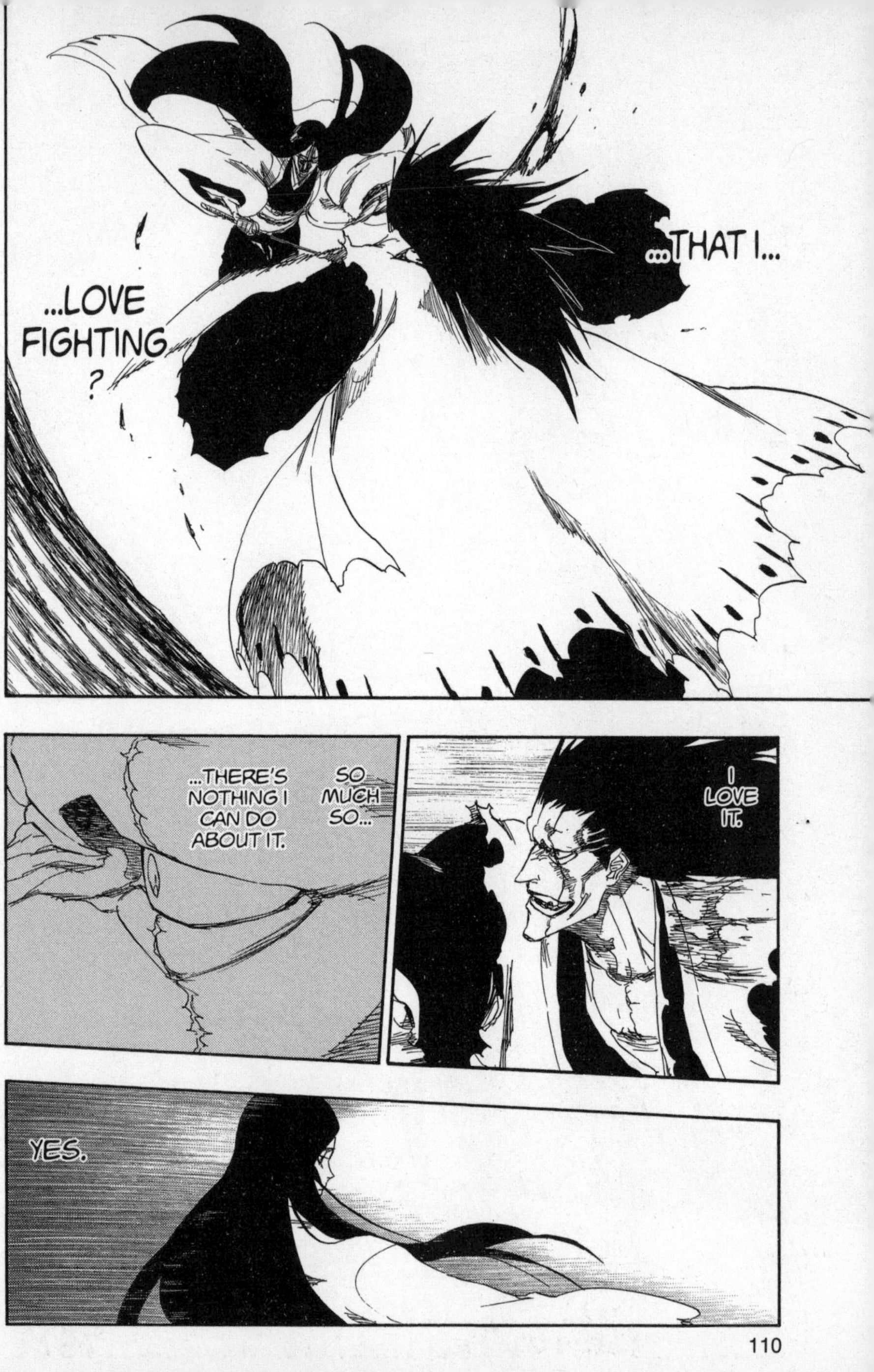
...THAT I...
...LOVE FIGHTING?
I LOVE IT.
SO MUCH SO...
...THERE'S NOTHING I CAN DO ABOUT IT.
YES.

READ THIS WAY
I KNEW.
PROBABLY...
...LONG BEFORE YOU EVER DID.
HEY, KENPACHI ZARAKI.
YOU...
...LEARNED TO RESTRAIN YOURSELF IN ORDER TO FOREVER ENJOY FIGHTING.
I...
...LEARNED TO HEAL MYSELF IN ORDER TO FOREVER ENJOY FIGHTING.
BUT...
...I AM FIRMLY CONVINCED...
...THAT THIS POWER I GAINED...
...WAS FOR THIS PARTICULAR MOMENT.
THERE CAN BE ONLY ONE KENPACHI IN ANY ERA.

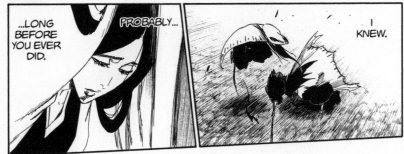

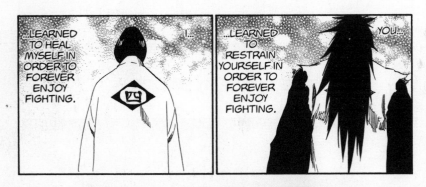

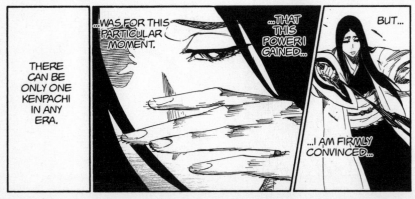

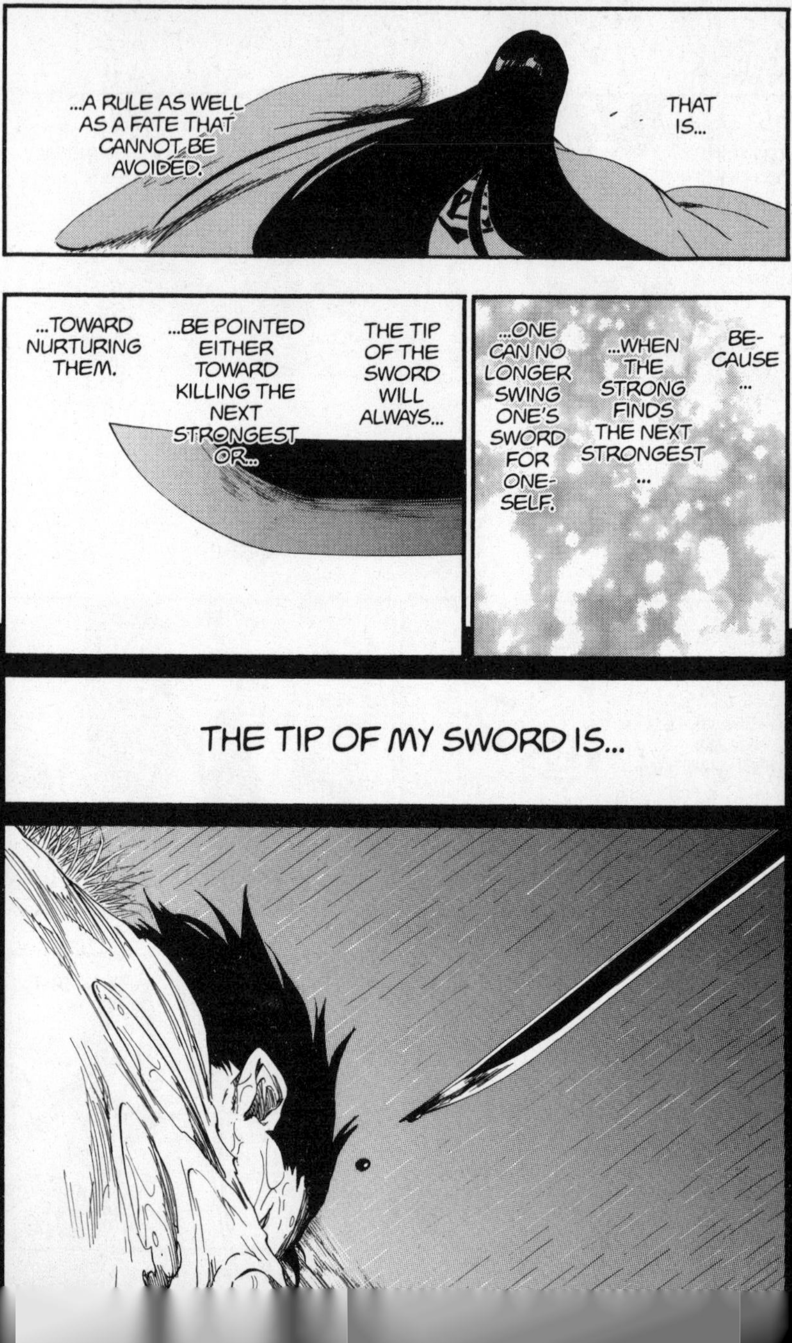
THAT IS...
...A RULE AS WELL AS A FATE THAT CANNOT BE AVOIDED.
BE-CAUSE...
...WHEN THE STRONG FINDS THE NEXT STRONGEST...
...ONE CAN NO LONGER SWING ONE'S SWORD FOR ONE-SELF.
THE TIP OF THE SWORD WILL ALWAYS...
...BE POINTED EITHER TOWARD KILLING THE NEXT STRONGEST OR...
...TOWARD NURTURING THEM.
THE TIP OF MY SWORD IS...

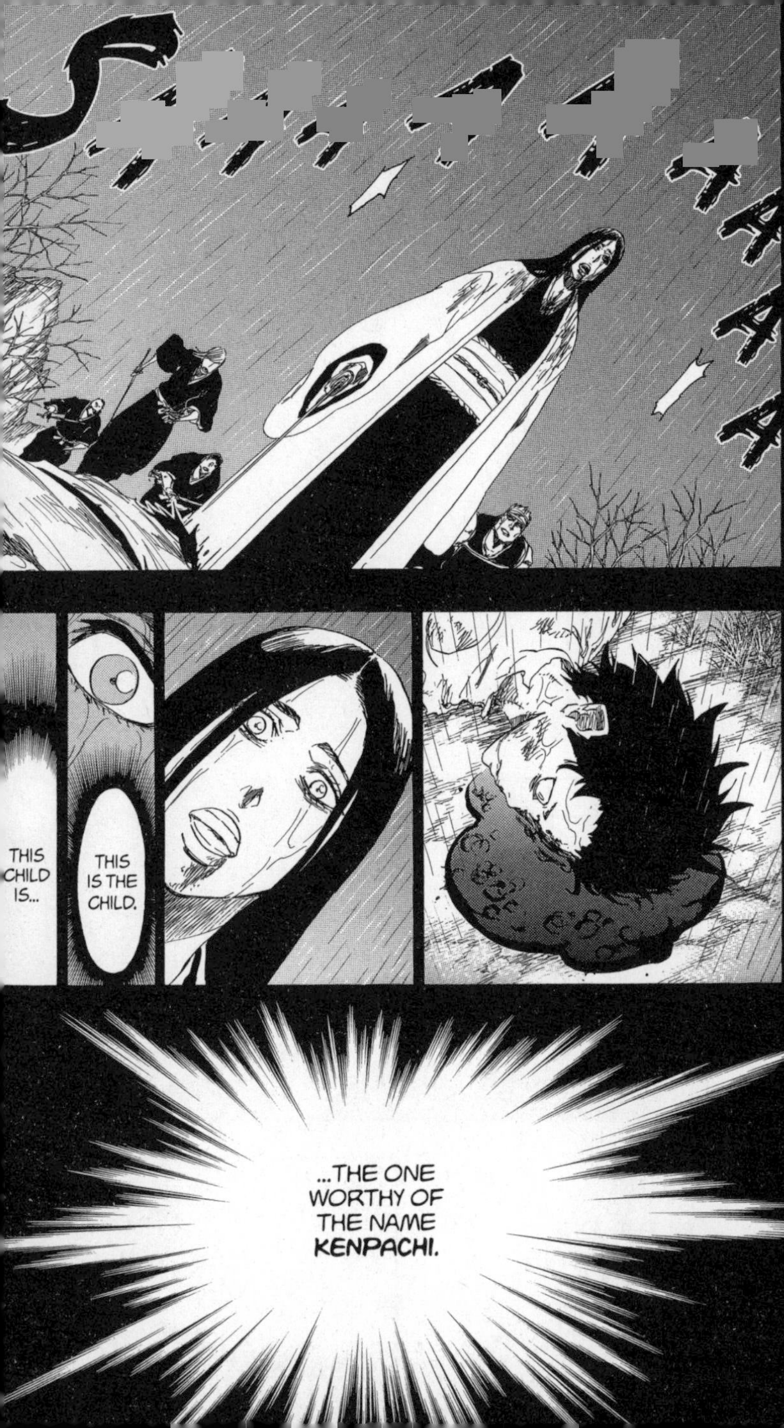
THIS IS THE CHILD.
THIS CHILD IS...
...THE ONE WORTHY OF THE NAME **KENPACHI.**

THE ONE
MAN IN THIS
WORLD...

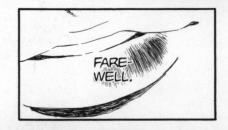

FARE-
WELL.

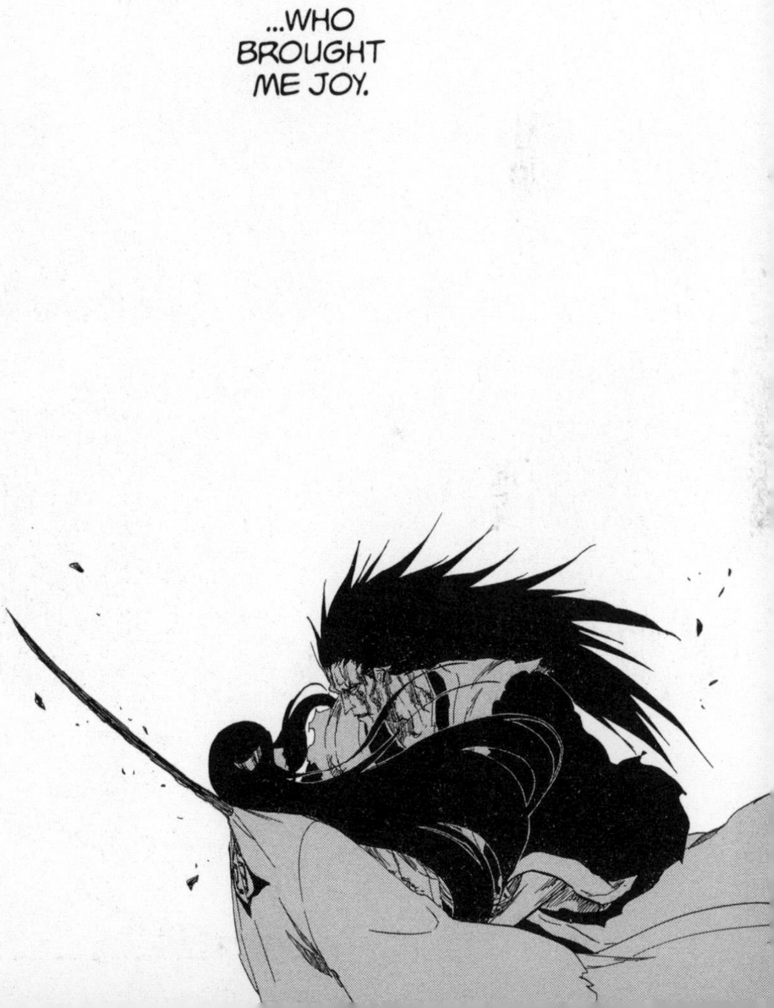
...WHO BROUGHT ME JOY.

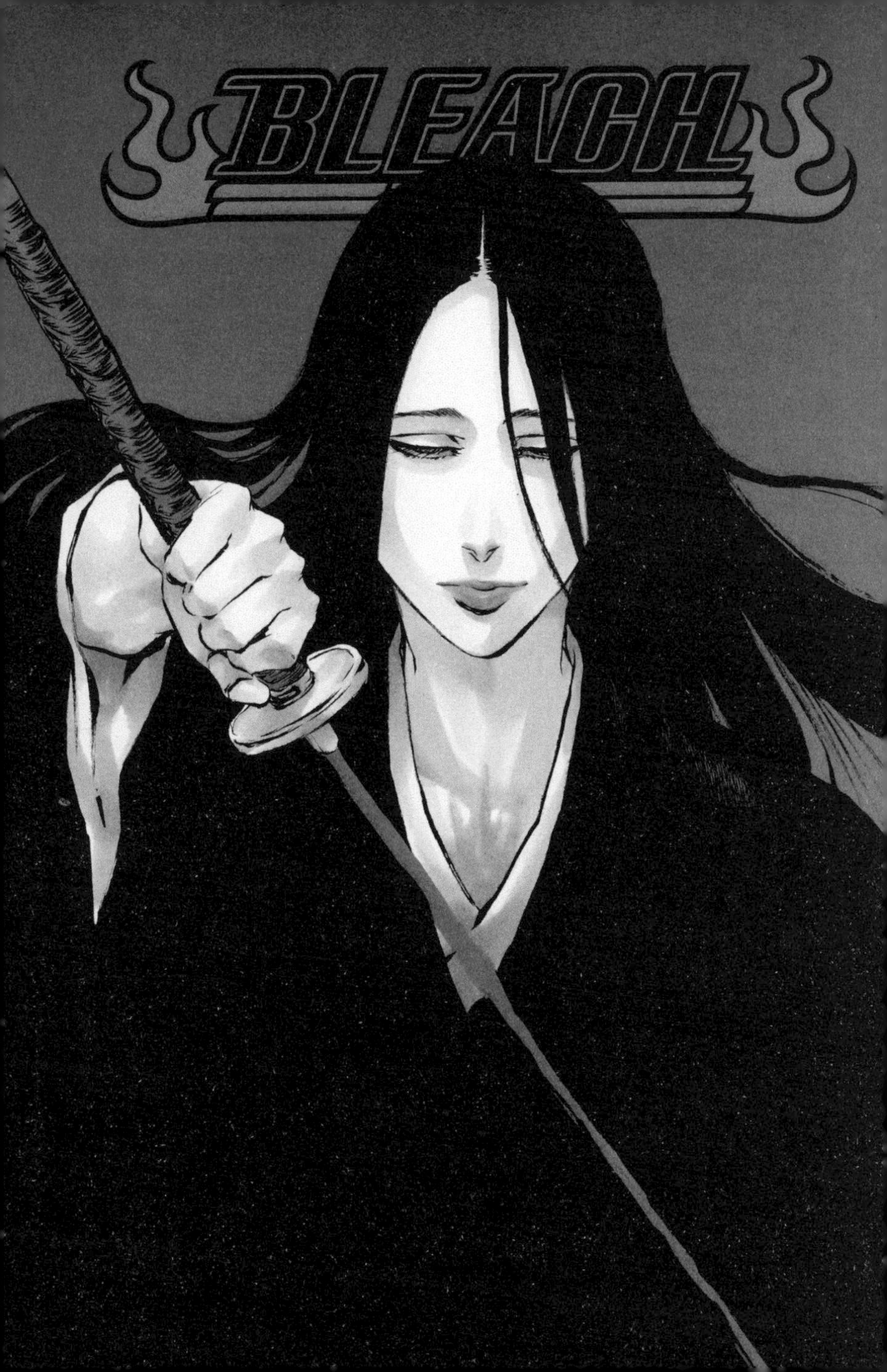
BLEACH

BLEACH
ブリーチ

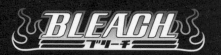

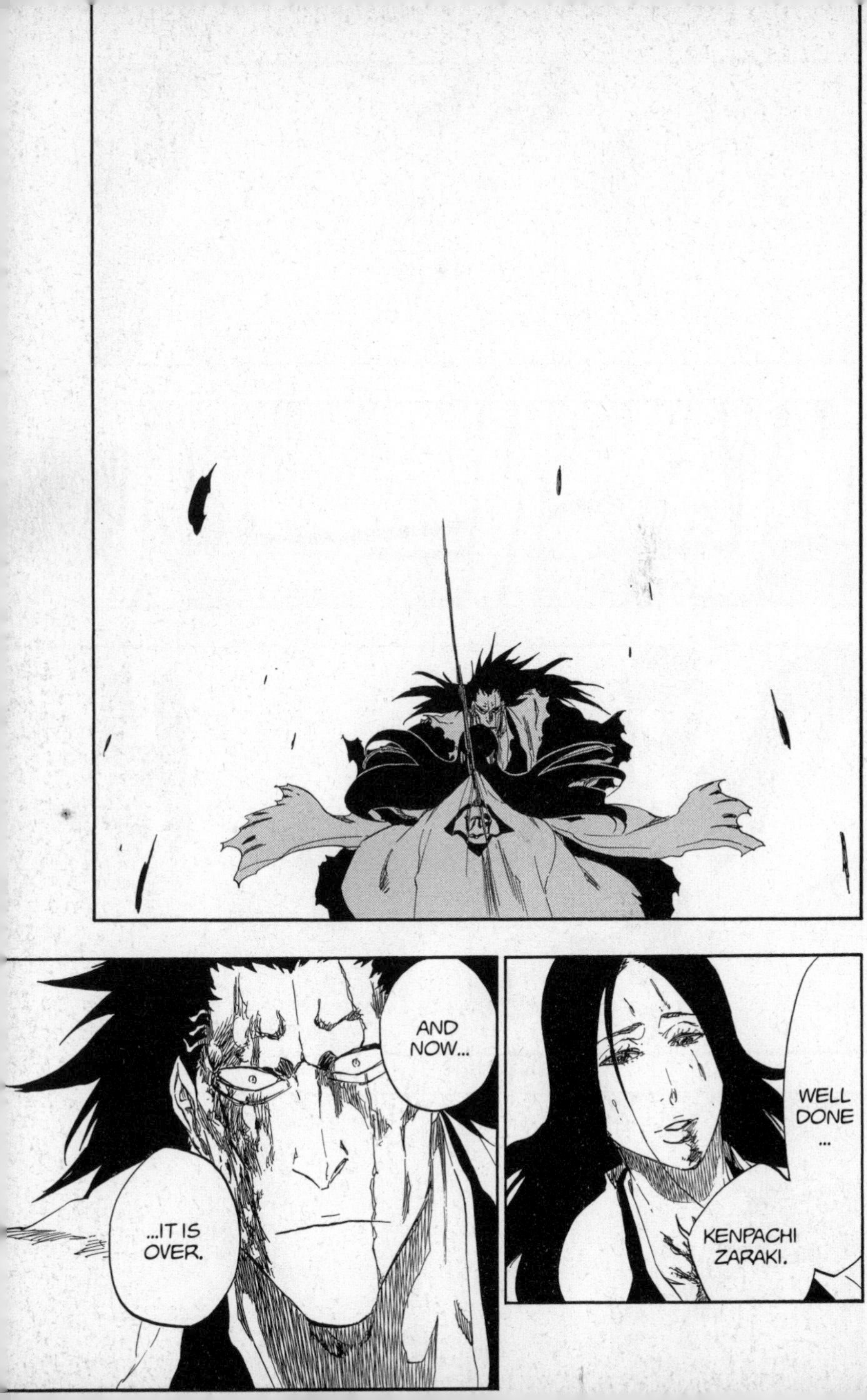
WELL DONE ...
KENPACHI ZARAKI.
AND NOW...
...IT IS OVER.

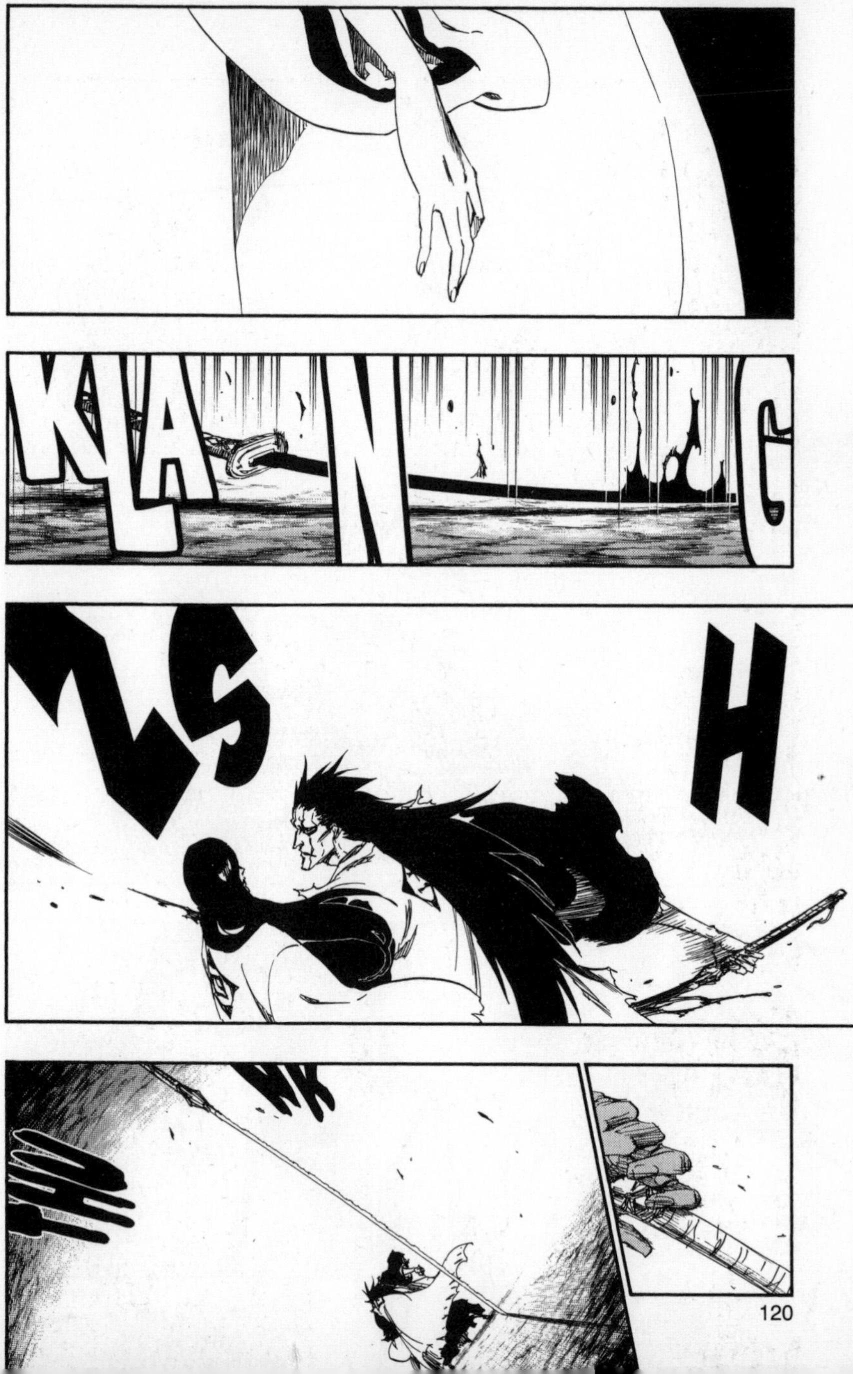
KLANG
ZLSH

READ THIS WAY

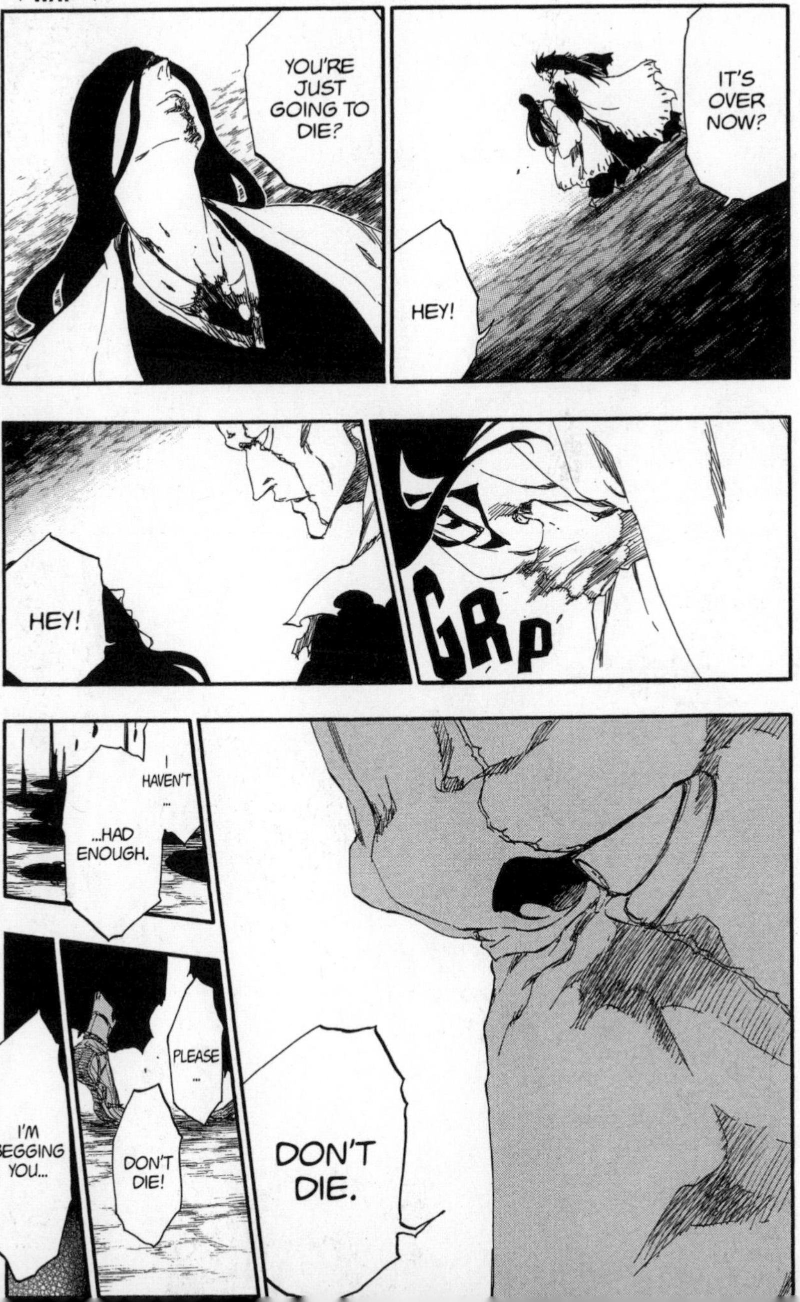
IT'S OVER NOW?
HEY!
YOU'RE JUST GOING TO DIE?
GRP
HEY!
I HAVEN'T ...
...HAD ENOUGH.
PLEASE ...
DON'T DIE!
I'M BEGGING YOU...
DON'T DIE.

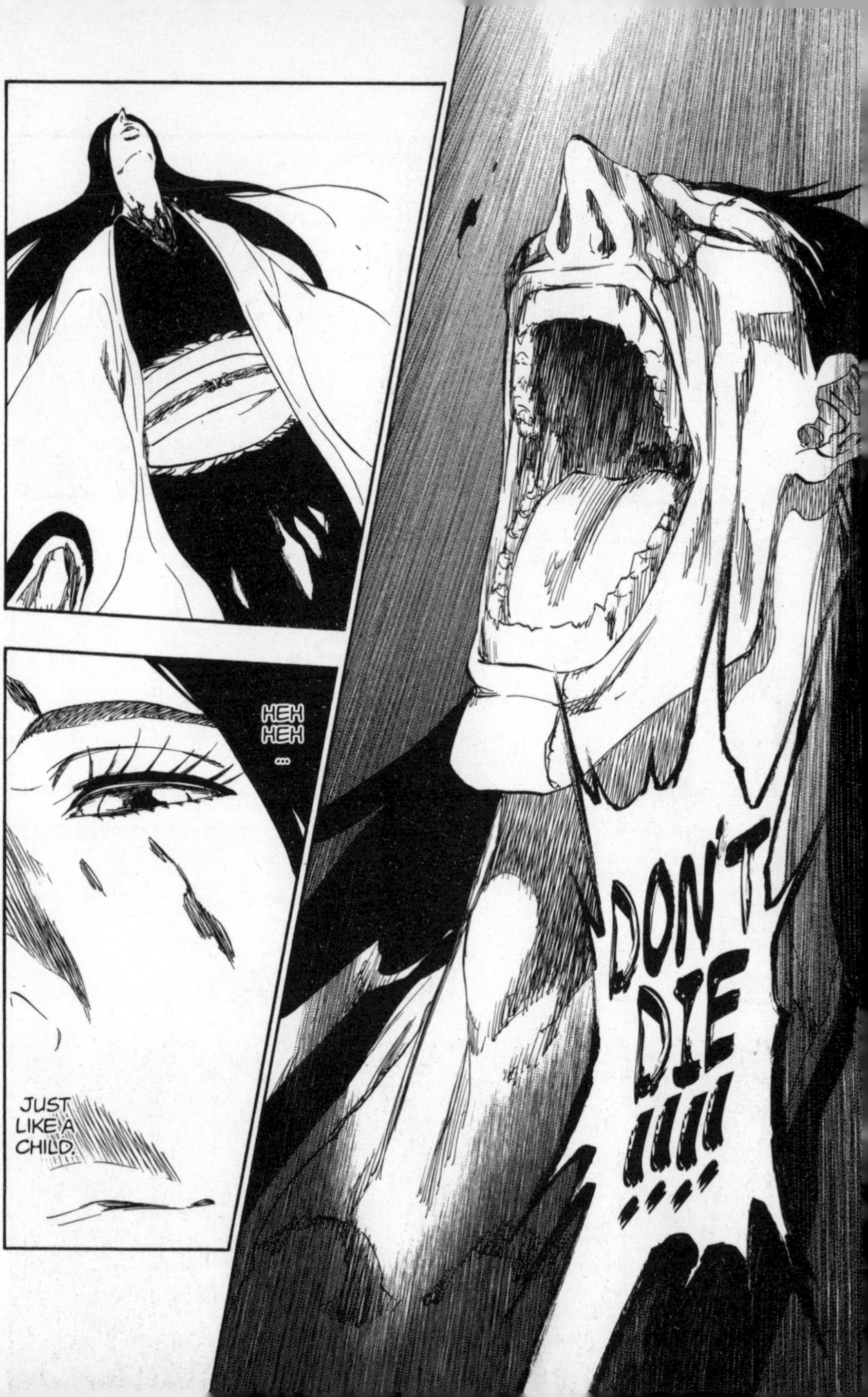
DON'T DIE!!!!
HEH HEH...
JUST LIKE A CHILD.

READ THIS WAY

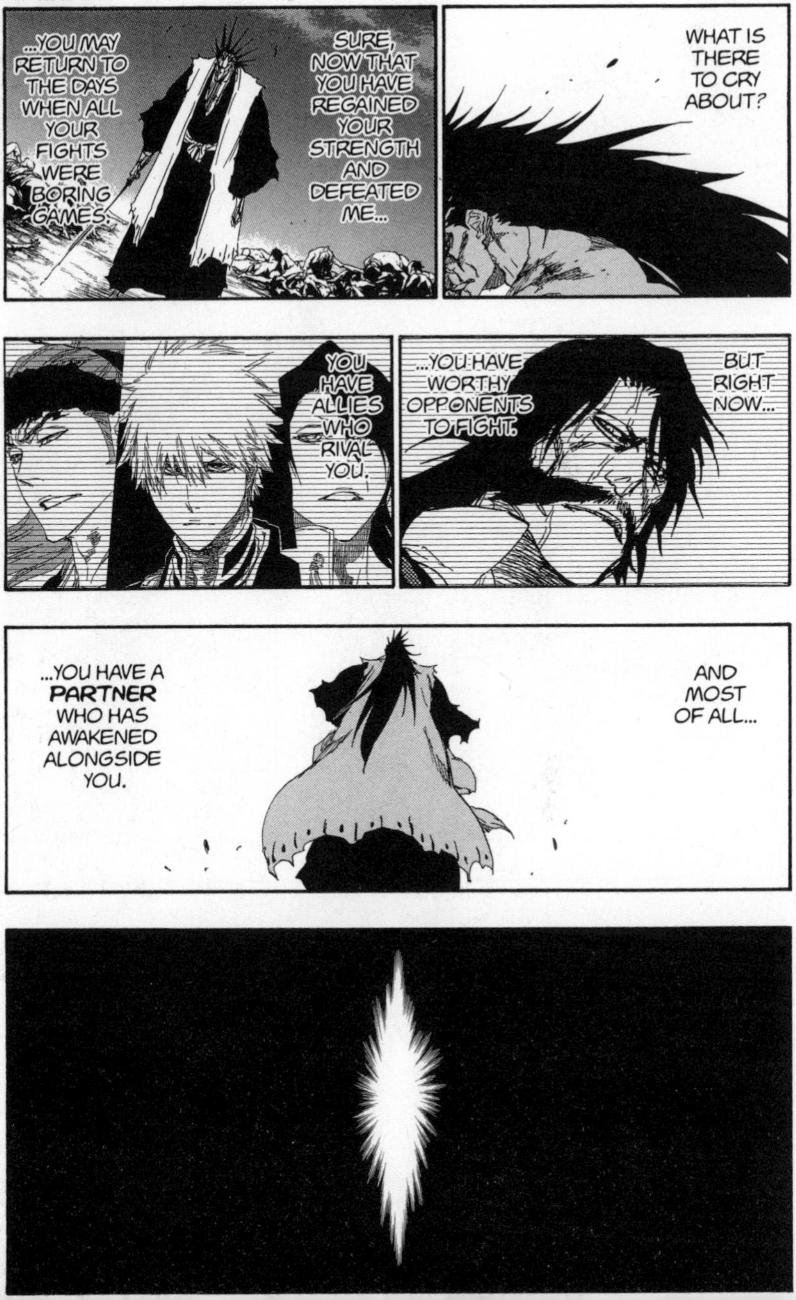
WHAT IS THERE TO CRY ABOUT?
SURE, NOW THAT YOU HAVE REGAINED YOUR STRENGTH AND DEFEATED ME...
...YOU MAY RETURN TO THE DAYS WHEN ALL YOUR FIGHTS WERE BORING GAMES.
BUT RIGHT NOW...
...YOU HAVE WORTHY OPPONENTS TO FIGHT.
YOU HAVE ALLIES WHO RIVAL YOU.
AND MOST OF ALL...
...YOU HAVE A **PARTNER** WHO HAS AWAKENED ALONGSIDE YOU.

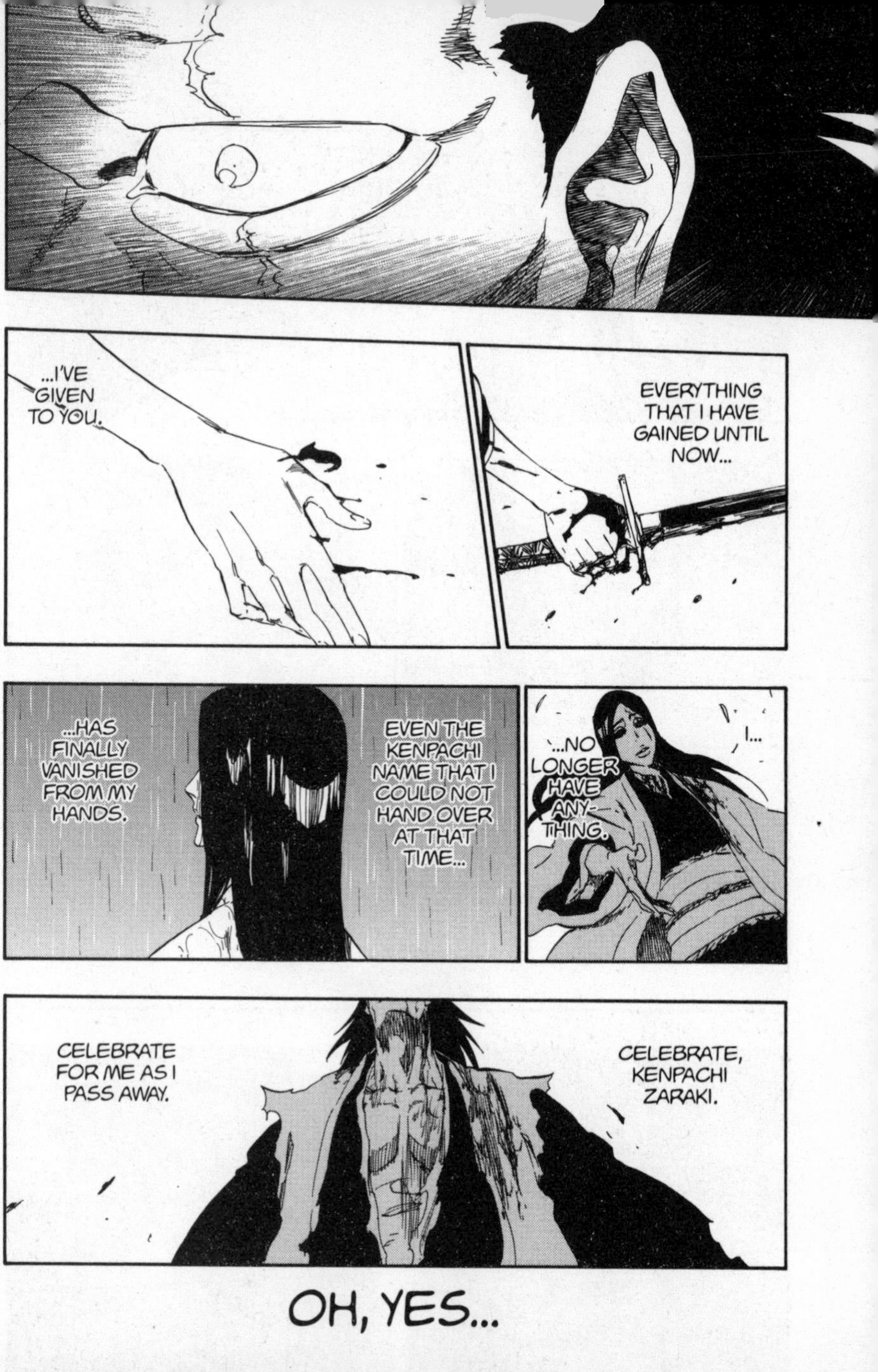
EVERYTHING THAT I HAVE GAINED UNTIL NOW...
...I'VE GIVEN TO YOU.
I...
...NO LONGER HAVE ANY-THING.
EVEN THE KENPACHI NAME THAT I COULD NOT HAND OVER AT THAT TIME...
...HAS FINALLY VANISHED FROM MY HANDS.
CELEBRATE, KENPACHI ZARAKI.
CELEBRATE FOR ME AS I PASS AWAY.
OH, YES...

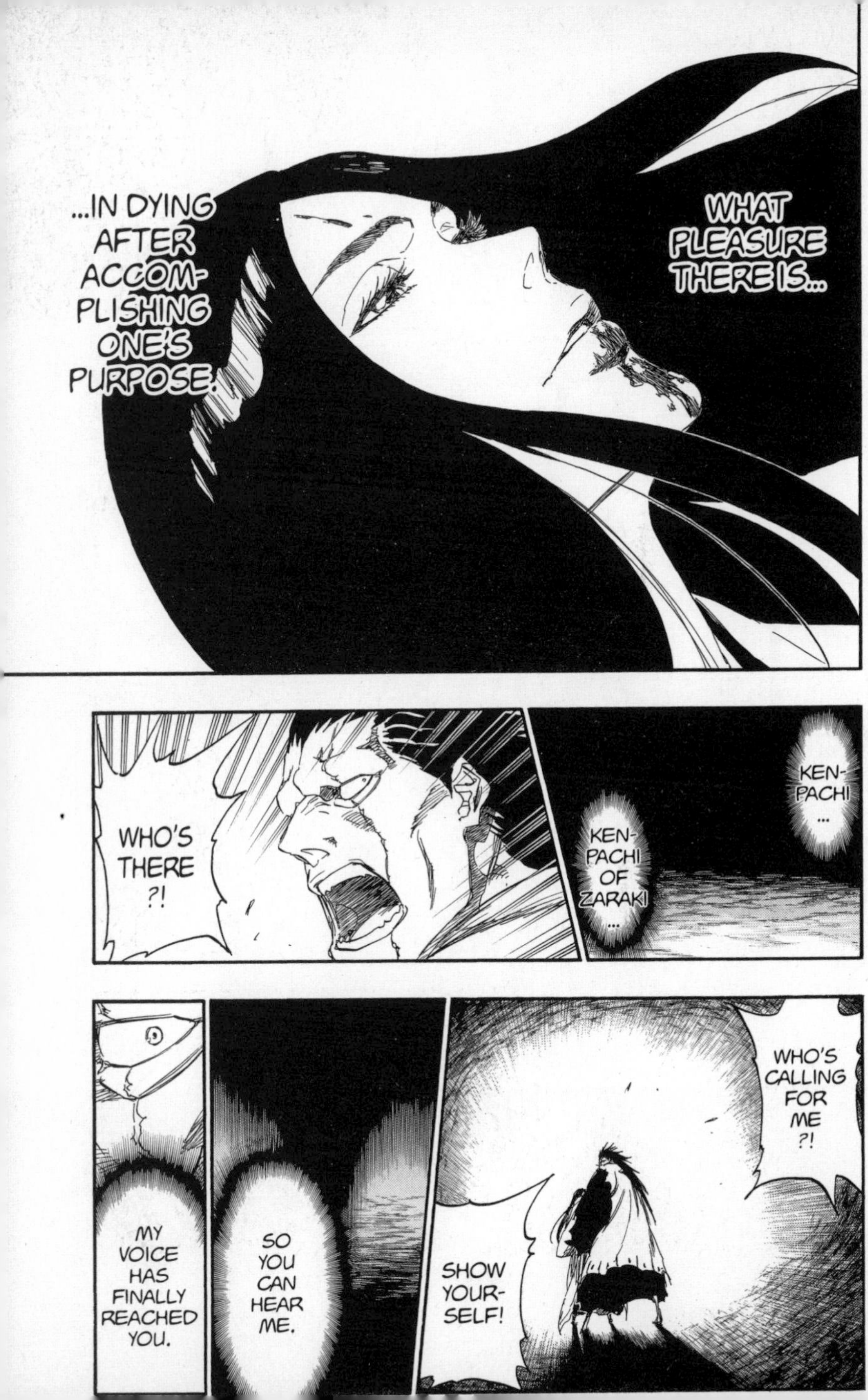
WHAT PLEASURE THERE IS...
...IN DYING AFTER ACCOMPLISHING ONE'S PURPOSE.
KENPACHI...
KENPACHI OF ZARAKI...
WHO'S THERE?!
WHO'S CALLING FOR ME?!
SHOW YOURSELF!
SO YOU CAN HEAR ME.
MY VOICE HAS FINALLY REACHED YOU.

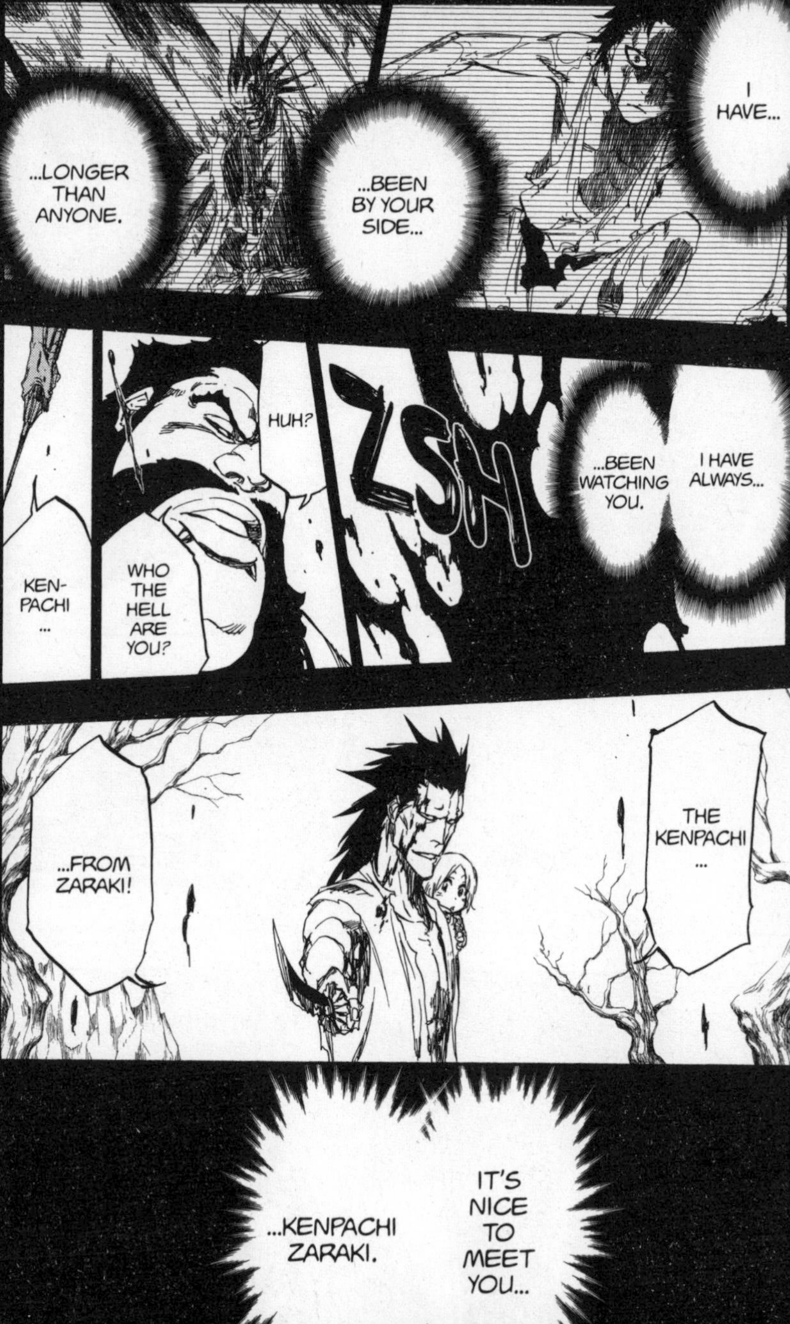
I HAVE...
...BEEN BY YOUR SIDE...
...LONGER THAN ANYONE.
I HAVE ALWAYS...
...BEEN WATCHING YOU.
ZSH
HUH?
WHO THE HELL ARE YOU?
KEN-PACHI ...
THE KENPACHI ...
...FROM ZARAKI!
IT'S NICE TO MEET YOU...
...KENPACHI ZARAKI.

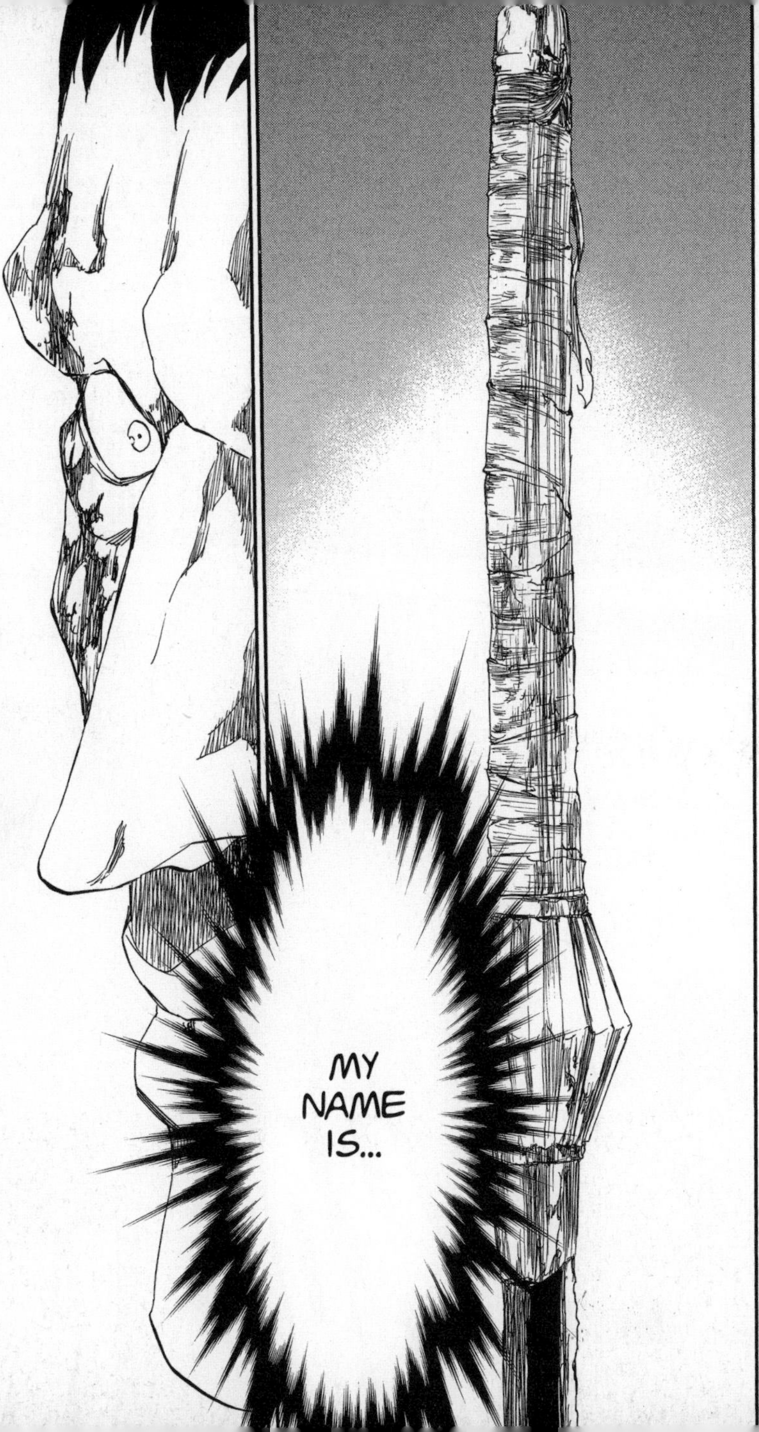
MY NAME IS...

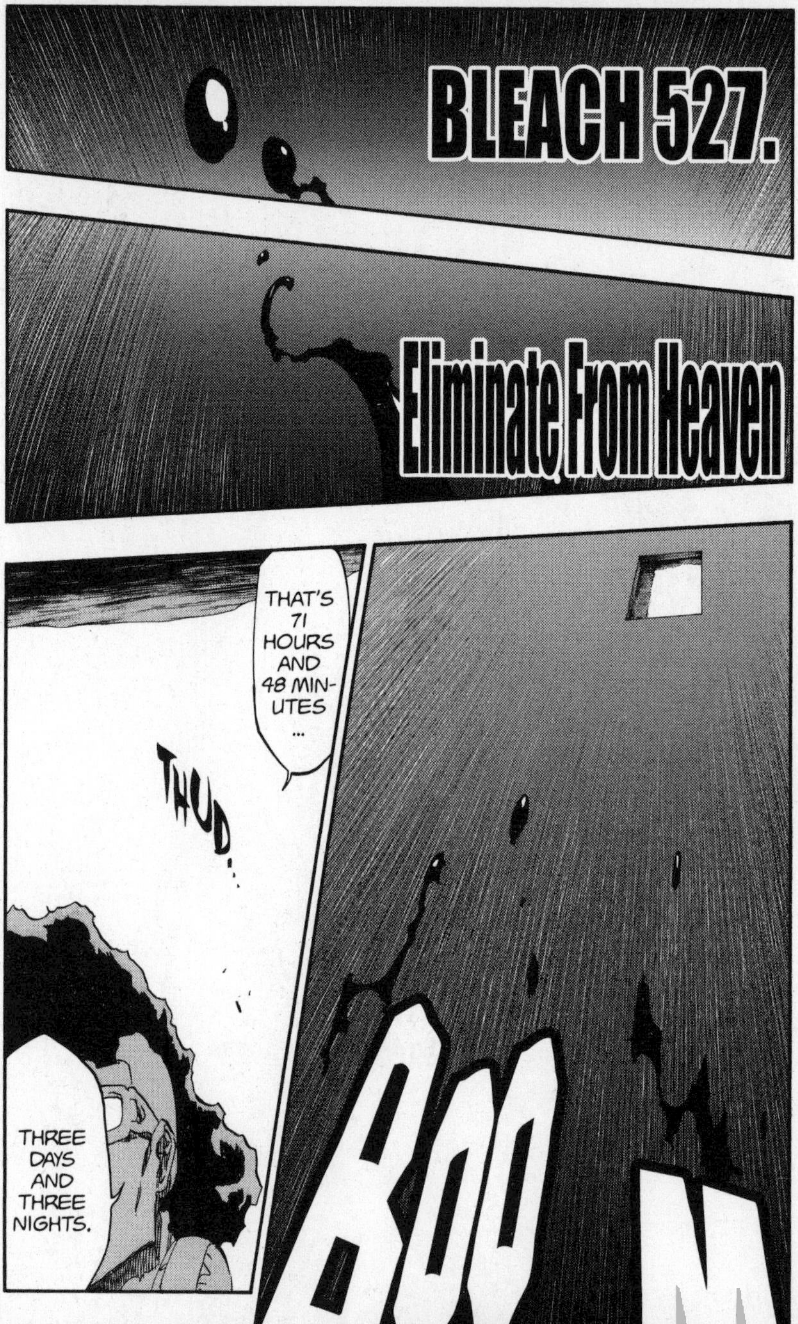
BLEACH 527.
Eliminate From Heaven
BOOM
THAT'S 71 HOURS AND 48 MIN-UTES...
THUD...
THREE DAYS AND THREE NIGHTS.

READ THIS WAY

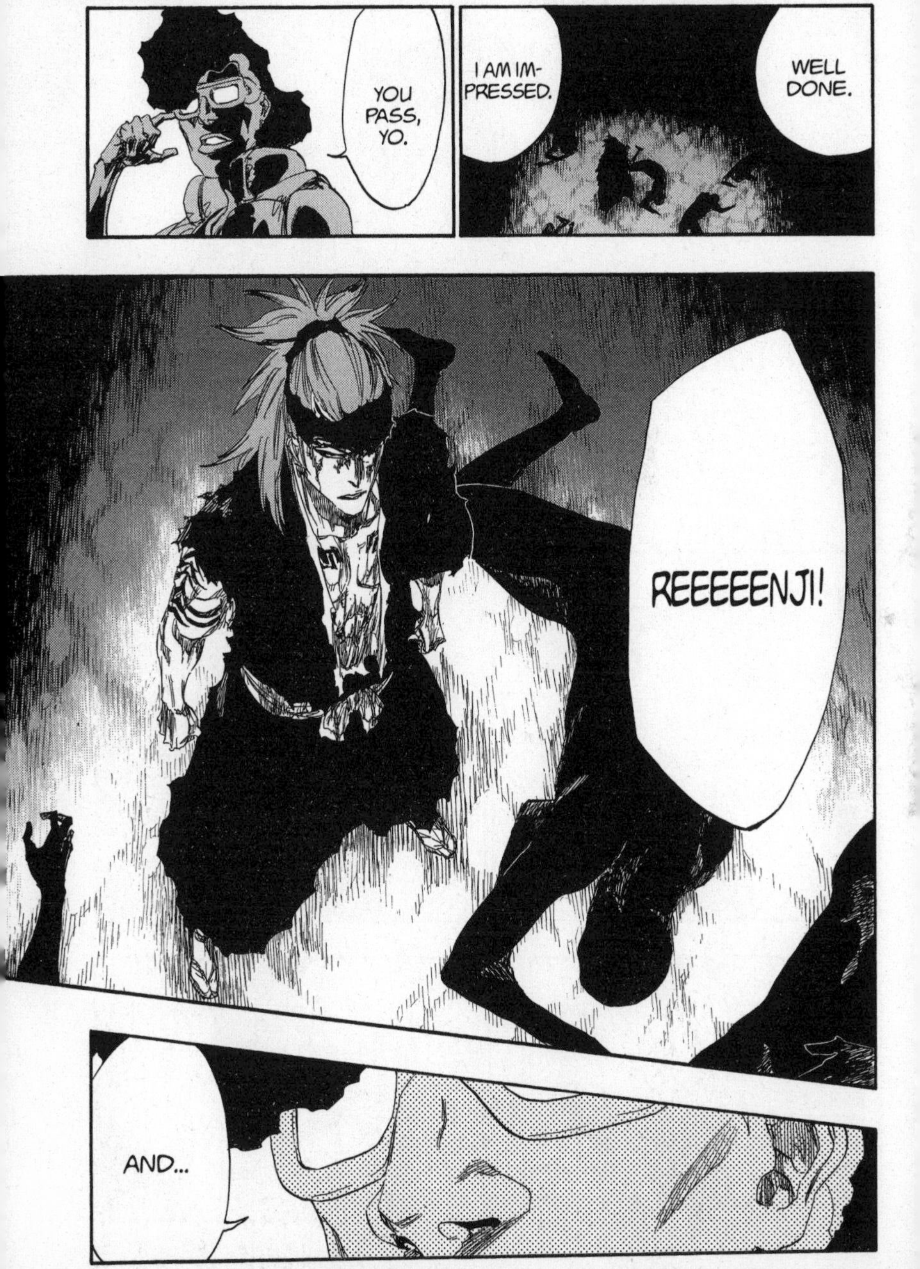
WELL DONE.
I AM IM-PRESSED.
YOU PASS, YO.
REEEEEENJI!
AND...

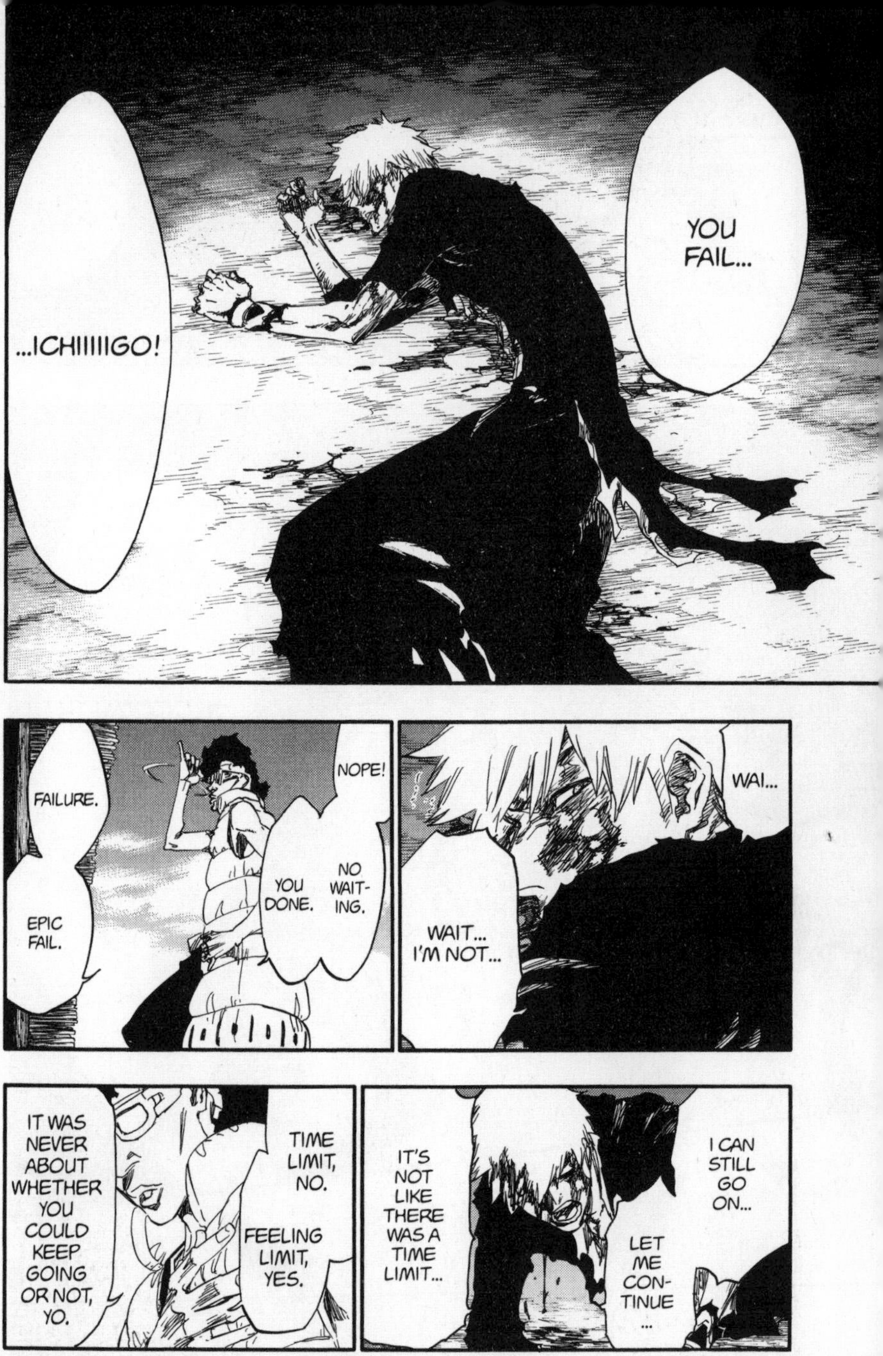
YOU FAIL...
...ICHIIIIIGO!
WAI...
WAIT... I'M NOT...
NOPE!
NO WAITING.
YOU DONE.
FAILURE.
EPIC FAIL.
I CAN STILL GO ON...
LET ME CONTINUE...
IT'S NOT LIKE THERE WAS A TIME LIMIT...
TIME LIMIT, NO.
FEELING LIMIT, YES.
IT WAS NEVER ABOUT WHETHER YOU COULD KEEP GOING OR NOT, YO.

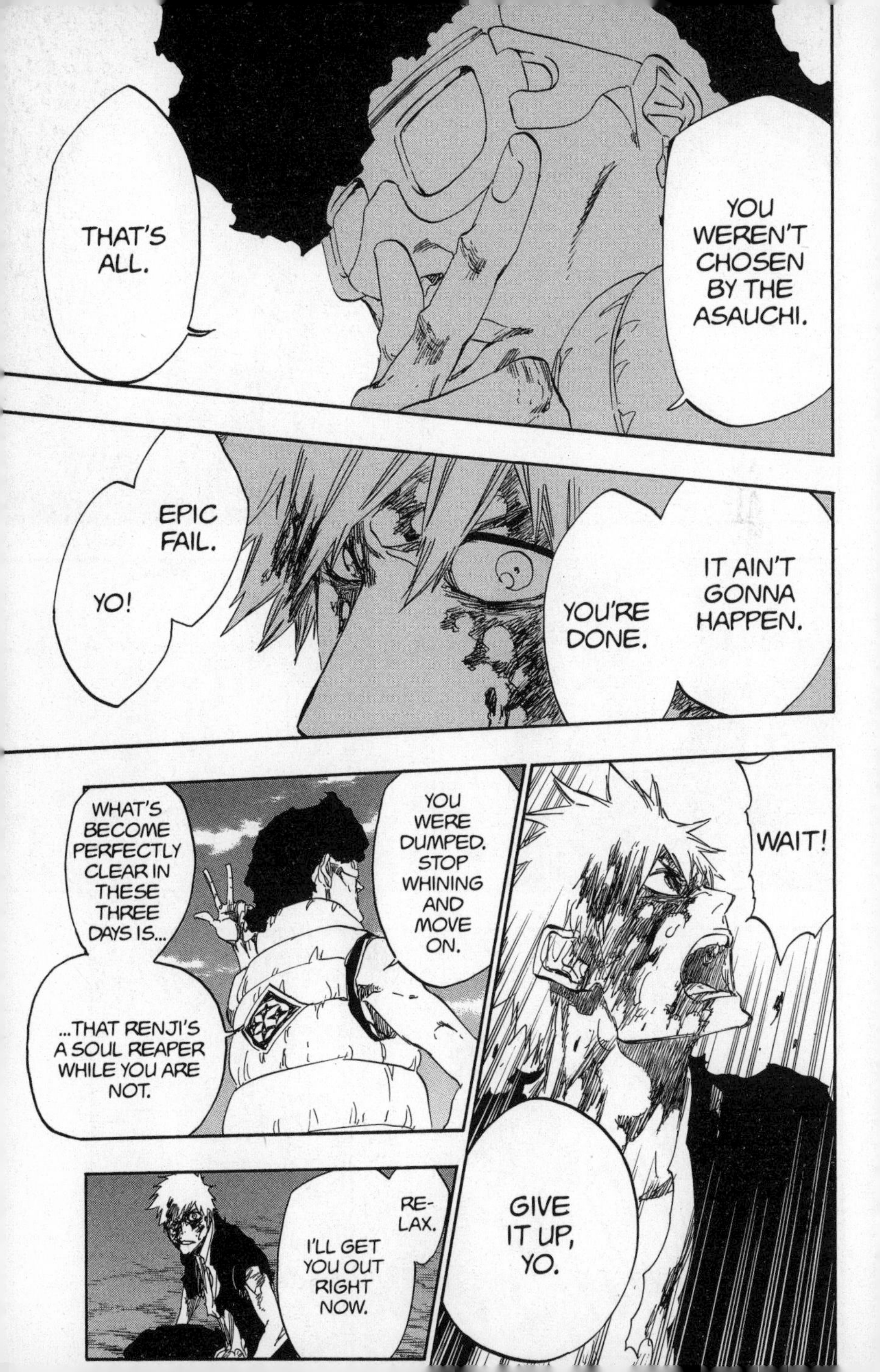
YOU WEREN'T CHOSEN BY THE ASAUCHI.
THAT'S ALL.
IT AIN'T GONNA HAPPEN.
YOU'RE DONE.
EPIC FAIL.
YO!
WAIT!
GIVE IT UP, YO.
YOU WERE DUMPED. STOP WHINING AND MOVE ON.
WHAT'S BECOME PERFECTLY CLEAR IN THESE THREE DAYS IS...
...THAT RENJI'S A SOUL REAPER WHILE YOU ARE NOT.
RE-LAX.
I'LL GET YOU OUT RIGHT NOW.

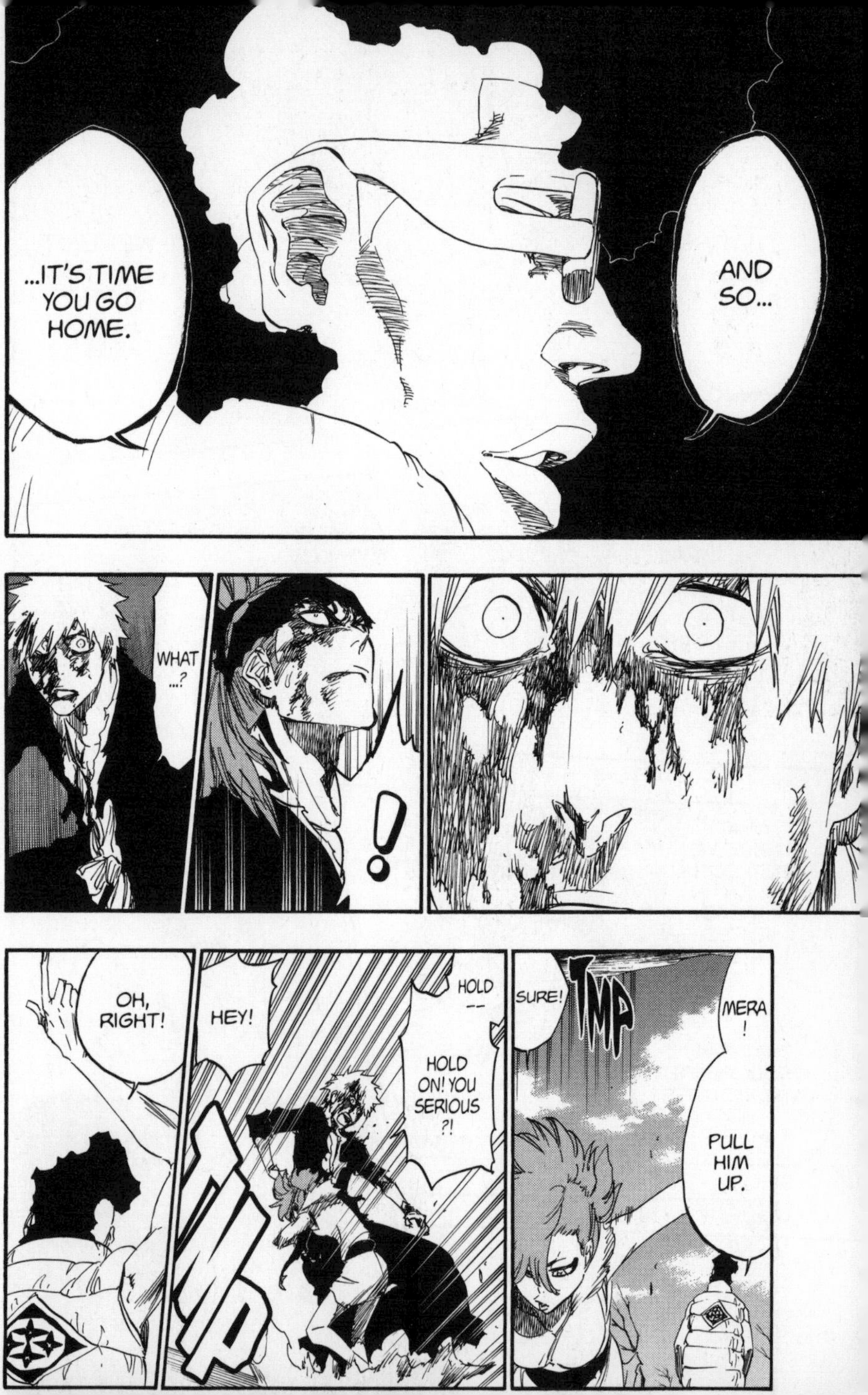
AND SO...
...IT'S TIME YOU GO HOME.
!
WHAT ...?
MERA!
PULL HIM UP.
SURE!
TMP
HOLD --
HOLD ON! YOU SERIOUS ?!
HEY!
TMP
OH, RIGHT!

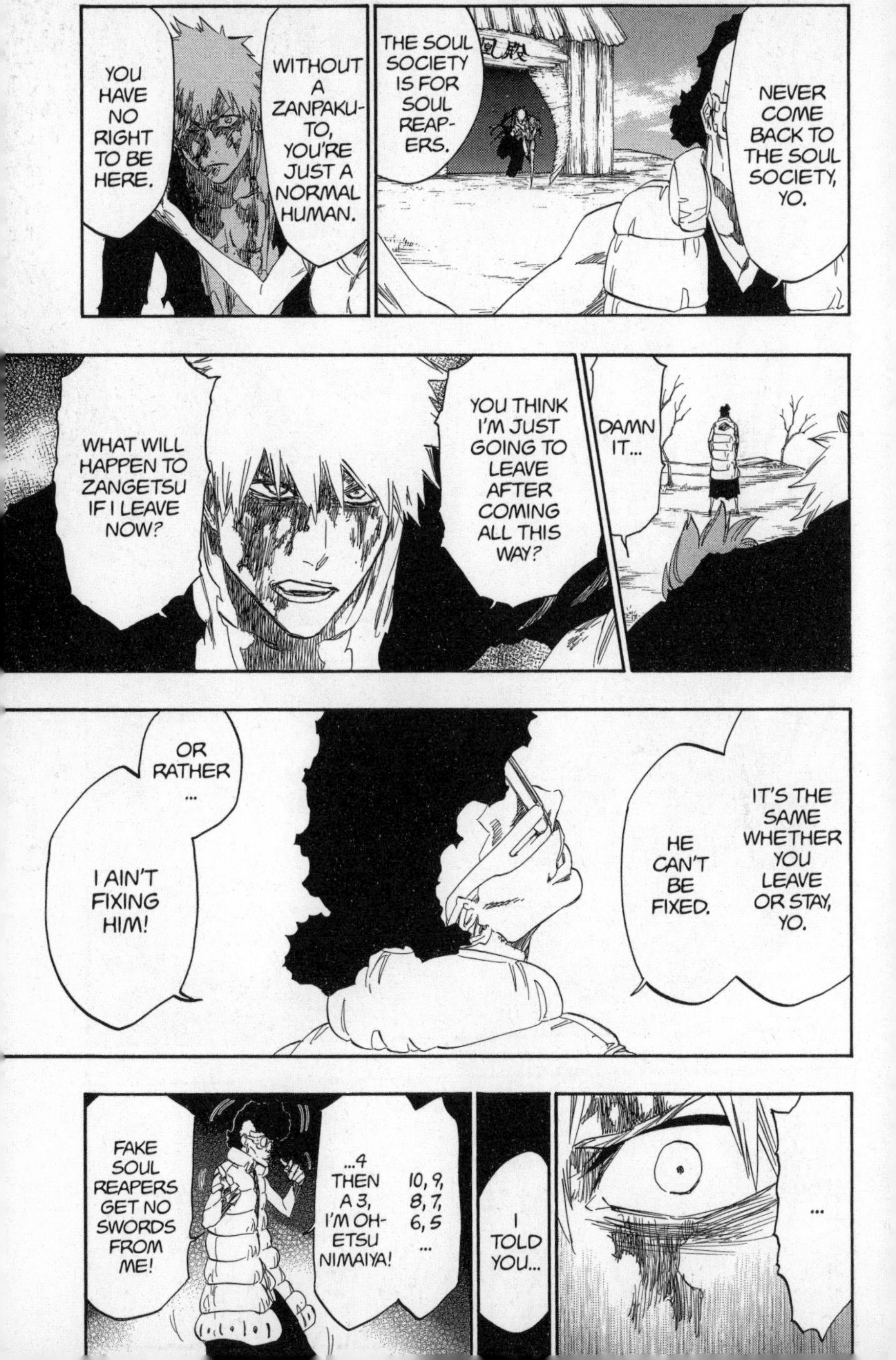
NEVER COME BACK TO THE SOUL SOCIETY, YO.
THE SOUL SOCIETY IS FOR SOUL REAPERS.
WITHOUT A ZANPAKU-TO, YOU'RE JUST A NORMAL HUMAN.
YOU HAVE NO RIGHT TO BE HERE.
DAMN IT...
YOU THINK I'M JUST GOING TO LEAVE AFTER COMING ALL THIS WAY?
WHAT WILL HAPPEN TO ZANGETSU IF I LEAVE NOW?
IT'S THE SAME WHETHER YOU LEAVE OR STAY, YO.
HE CAN'T BE FIXED.
OR RATHER...
I AIN'T FIXING HIM!
...
I TOLD YOU...
10, 9, 8, 7, 6, 5 ...
...4 THEN A 3, I'M OH-ETSU NIMAIYA!
FAKE SOUL REAPERS GET NO SWORDS FROM ME!

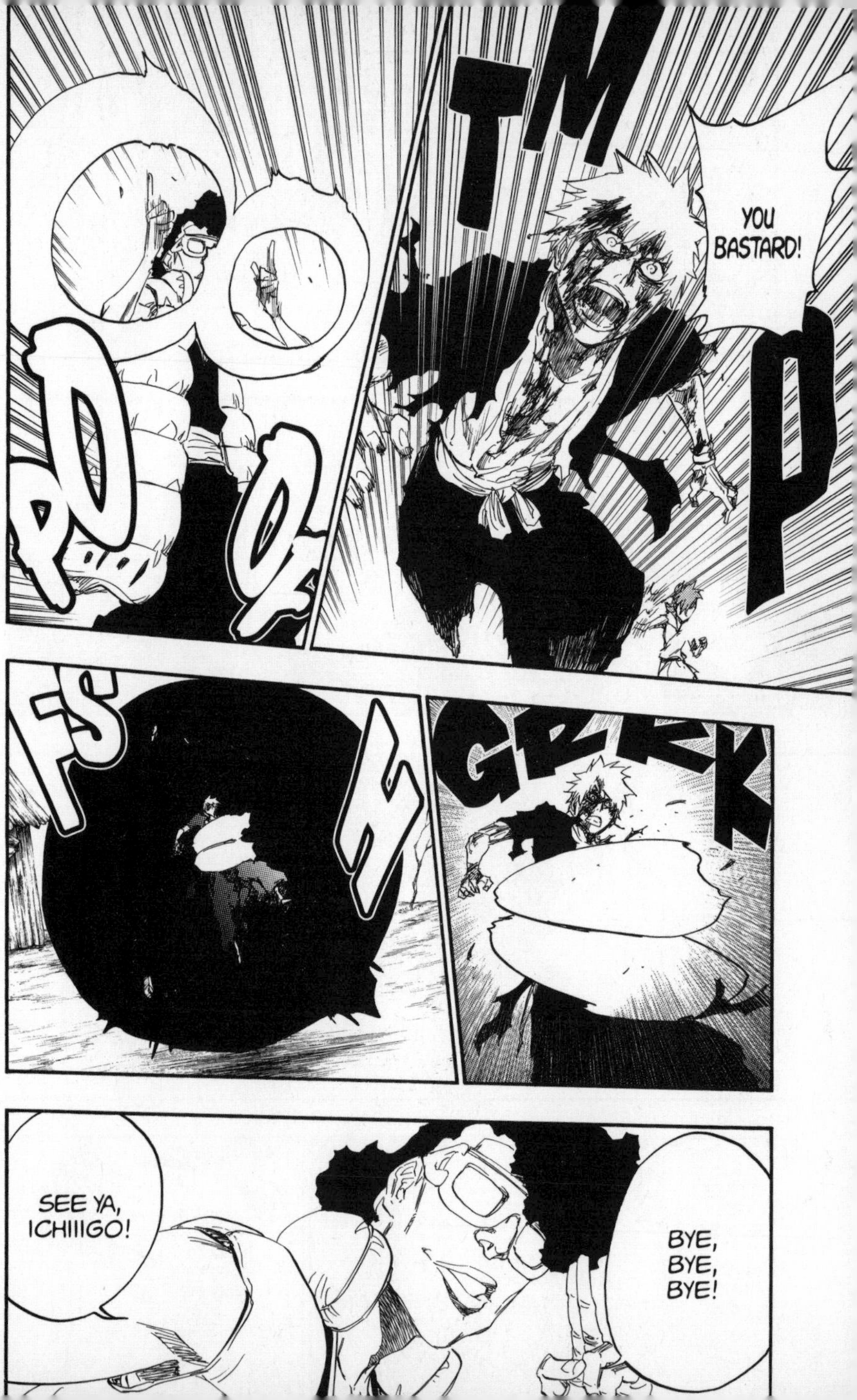
TMP
YOU BASTARD!
GRRK
BYE, BYE, BYE!
SEE YA, ICHIIIGO!

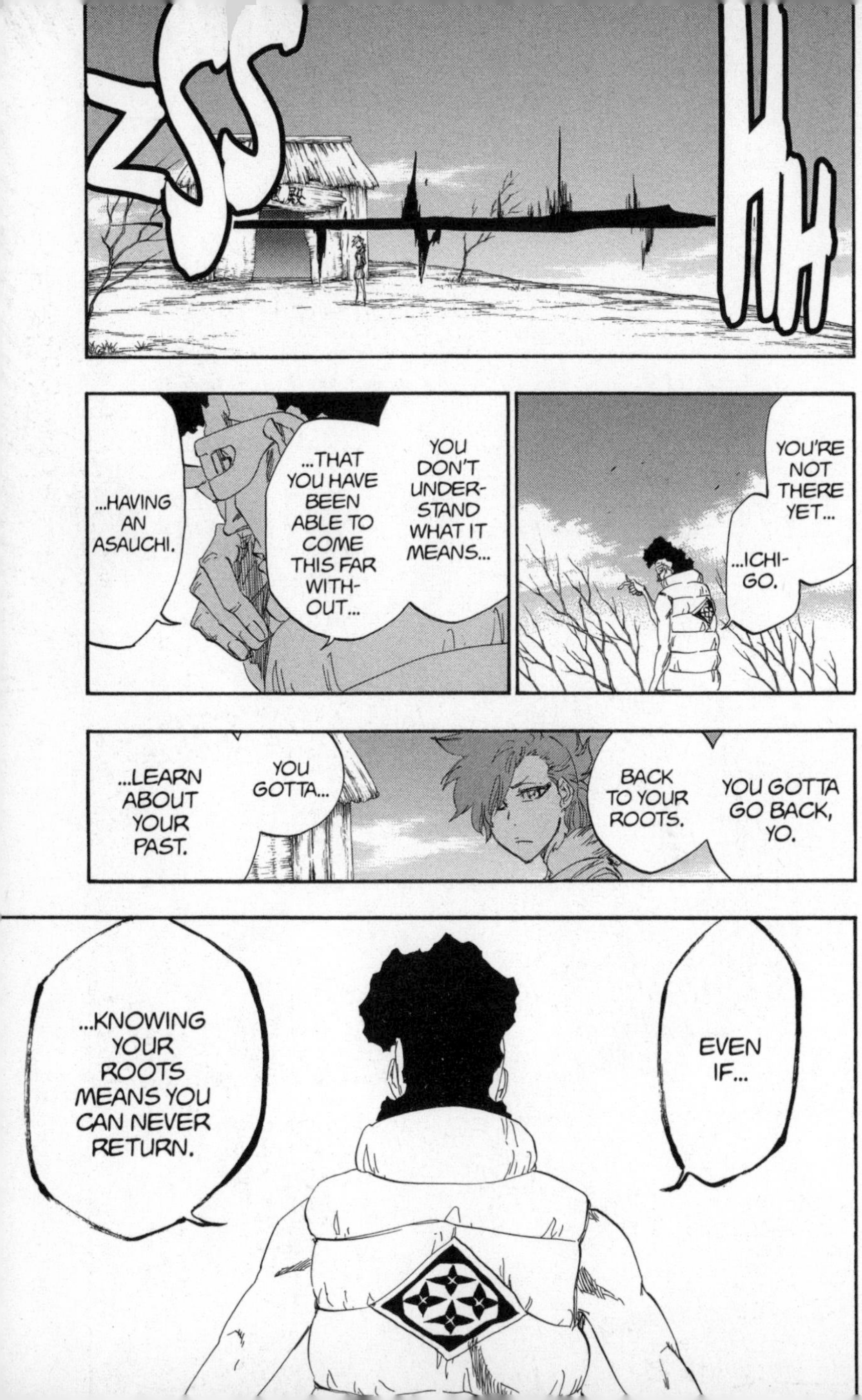
ZSSHH
YOU'RE NOT THERE YET...
...ICHIGO.
YOU DON'T UNDERSTAND WHAT IT MEANS...
...THAT YOU HAVE BEEN ABLE TO COME THIS FAR WITHOUT...
...HAVING AN ASAUCHI.
YOU GOTTA GO BACK, YO.
BACK TO YOUR ROOTS.
YOU GOTTA...
...LEARN ABOUT YOUR PAST.
EVEN IF...
...KNOWING YOUR ROOTS MEANS YOU CAN NEVER RETURN.

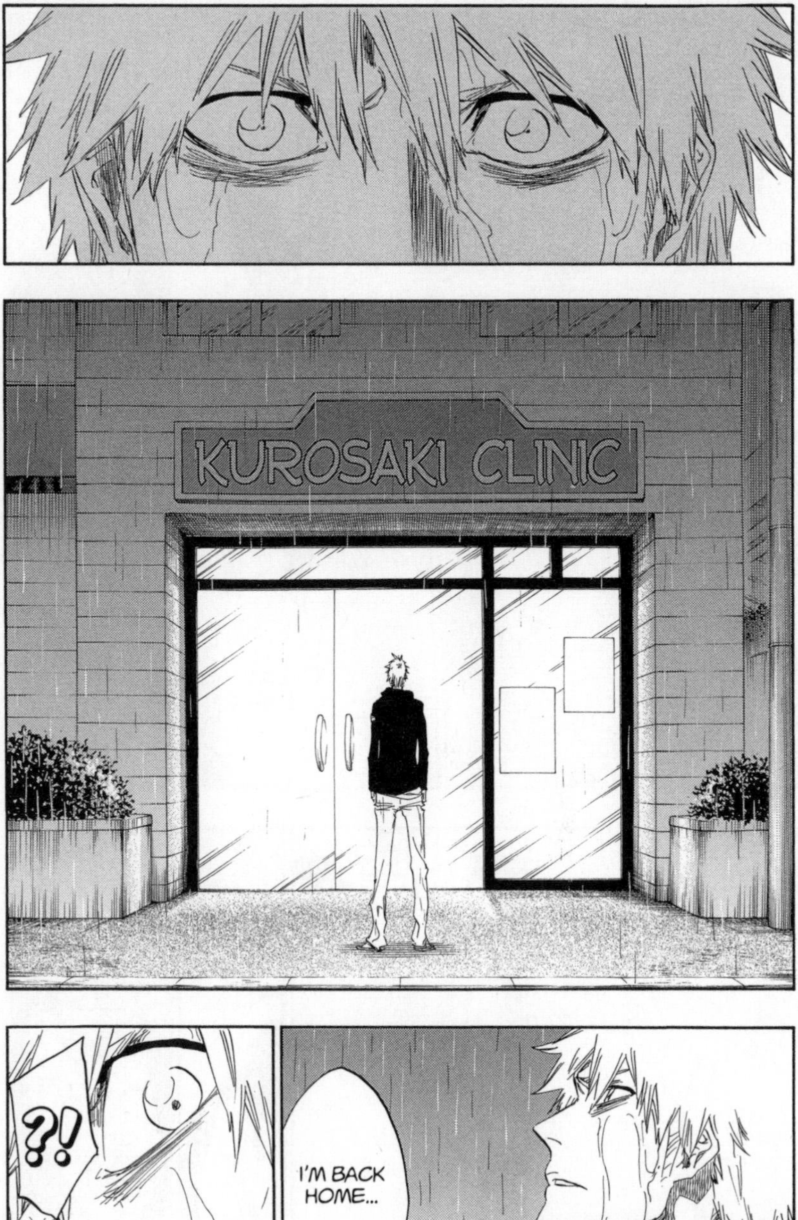
KUROSAKI CLINIC
I'M BACK HOME...
?!

528. EVERYTHING BUT THE RAIN

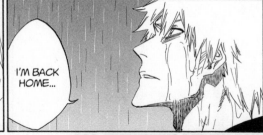

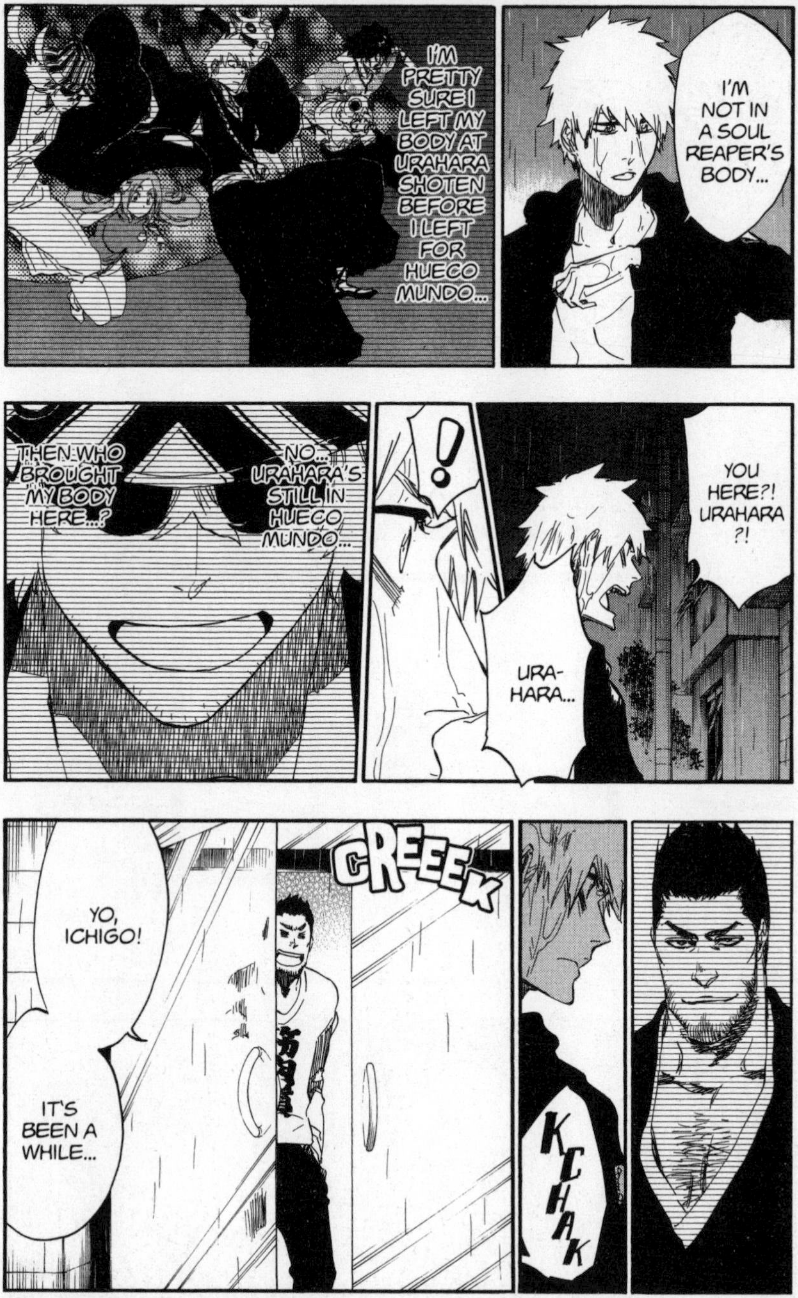
I'M NOT IN A SOUL REAPER'S BODY...
I'M PRETTY SURE I LEFT MY BODY AT URAHARA SHOTEN BEFORE I LEFT FOR HUECO MUNDO...
YOU HERE?! URAHARA ?!
!
URA-HARA...
NO... URAHARA'S STILL IN HUECO MUNDO...
THEN WHO BROUGHT MY BODY HERE...?
KCHAK
CREEEK
YO, ICHIGO!
IT'S BEEN A WHILE...

READ THIS WAY

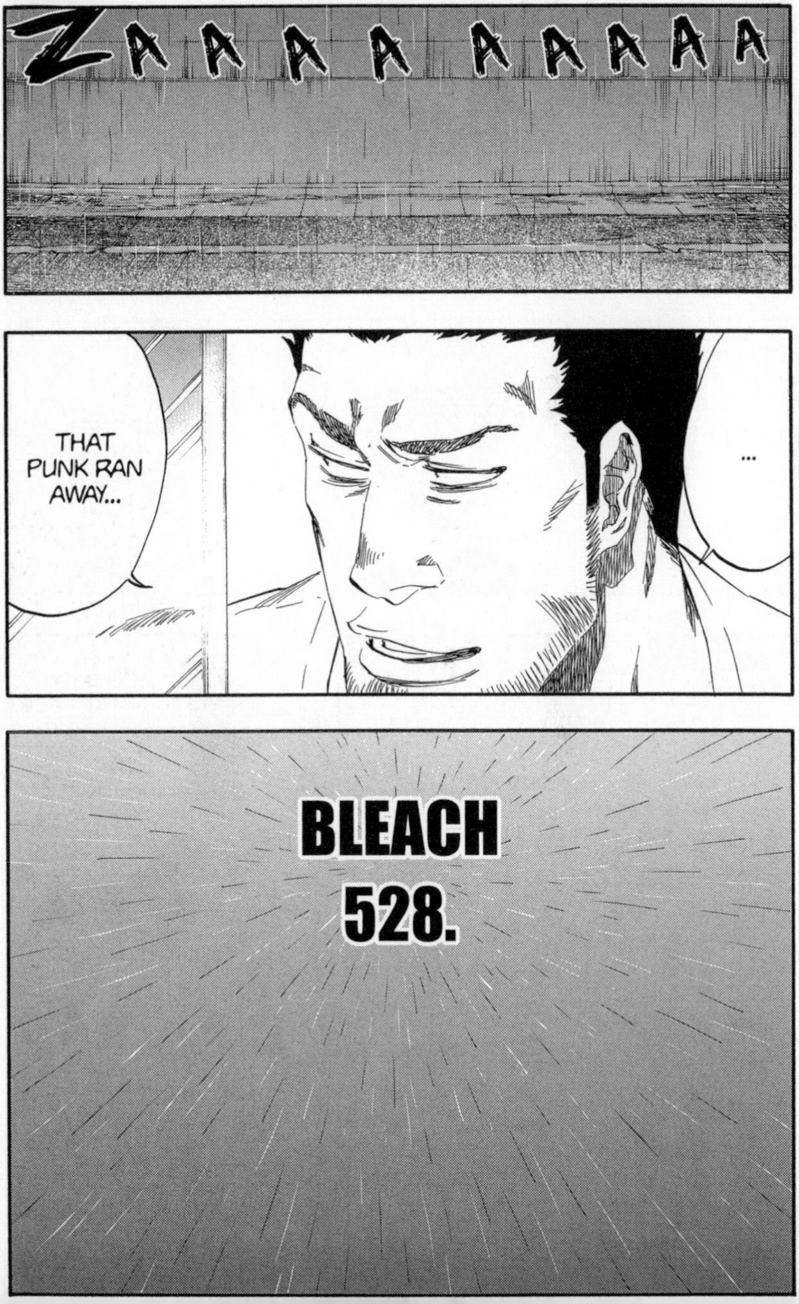
ZAAAAAAAAA
...
THAT PUNK RAN AWAY...
BLEACH
528.

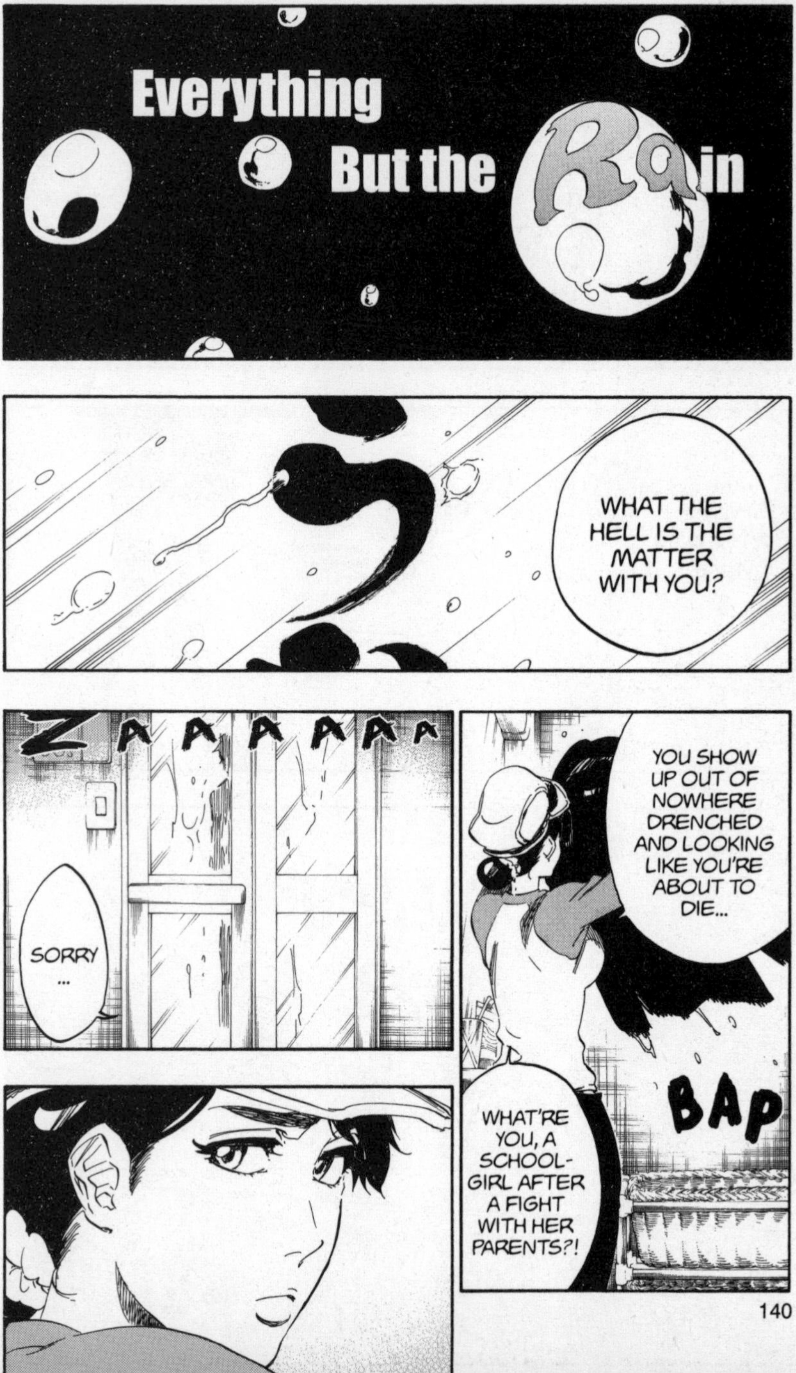
Everything But the Rain
WHAT THE HELL IS THE MATTER WITH YOU?
YOU SHOW UP OUT OF NOWHERE DRENCHED AND LOOKING LIKE YOU'RE ABOUT TO DIE...
BAP
WHAT'RE YOU, A SCHOOL-GIRL AFTER A FIGHT WITH HER PARENTS?!
ZAAAAAAA
SORRY ...

READ THIS WAY

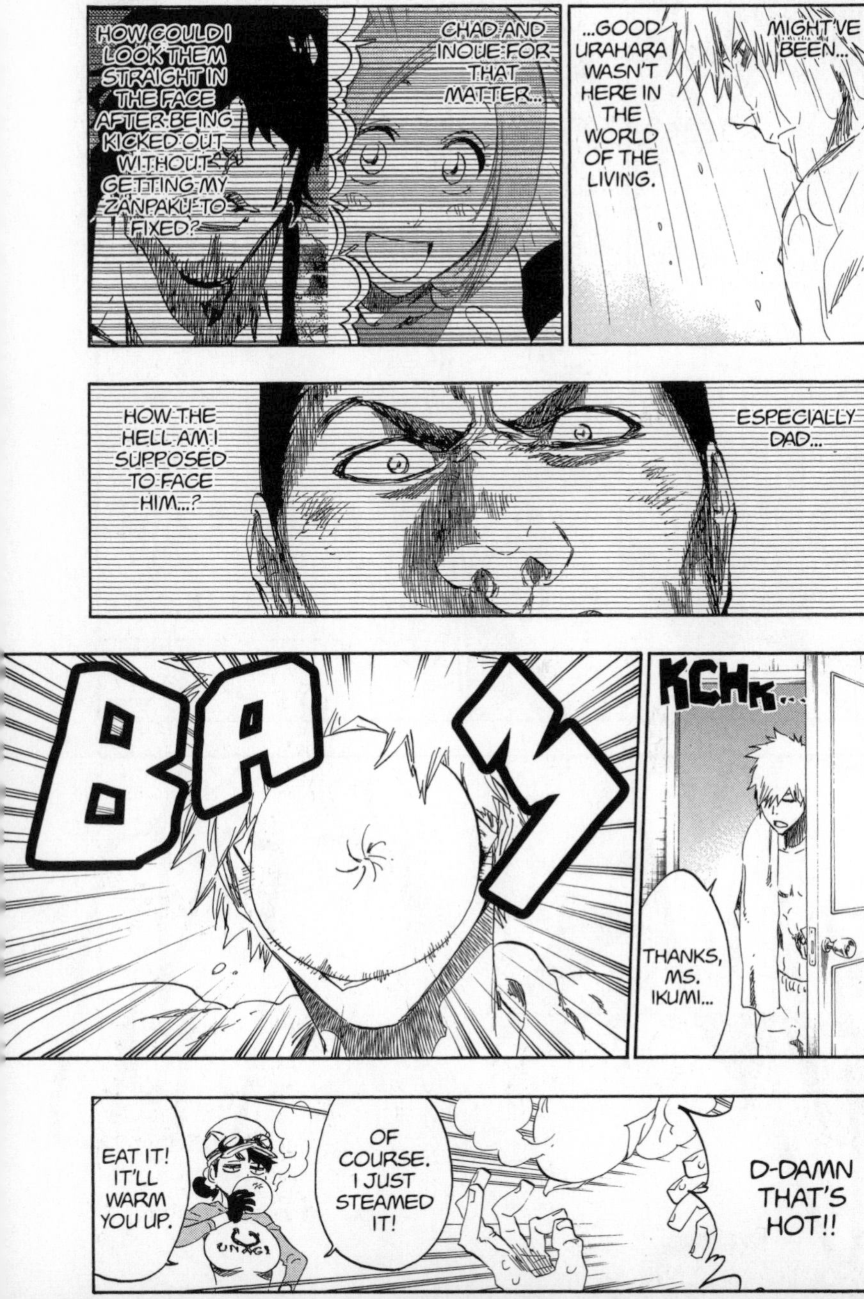
MIGHT'VE BEEN...
...GOOD URAHARA WASN'T HERE IN THE WORLD OF THE LIVING.
CHAD AND INOUE FOR THAT MATTER...
HOW COULD I LOOK THEM STRAIGHT IN THE FACE AFTER BEING KICKED OUT WITHOUT GETTING MY ZANPAKU-TO FIXED?
ESPECIALLY DAD...
HOW THE HELL AM I SUPPOSED TO FACE HIM...?
KCHK...
THANKS, MS. IKUMI...
BAM
D-DAMN THAT'S HOT!!
OF COURSE. I JUST STEAMED IT!
EAT IT! IT'LL WARM YOU UP.
UNAGI

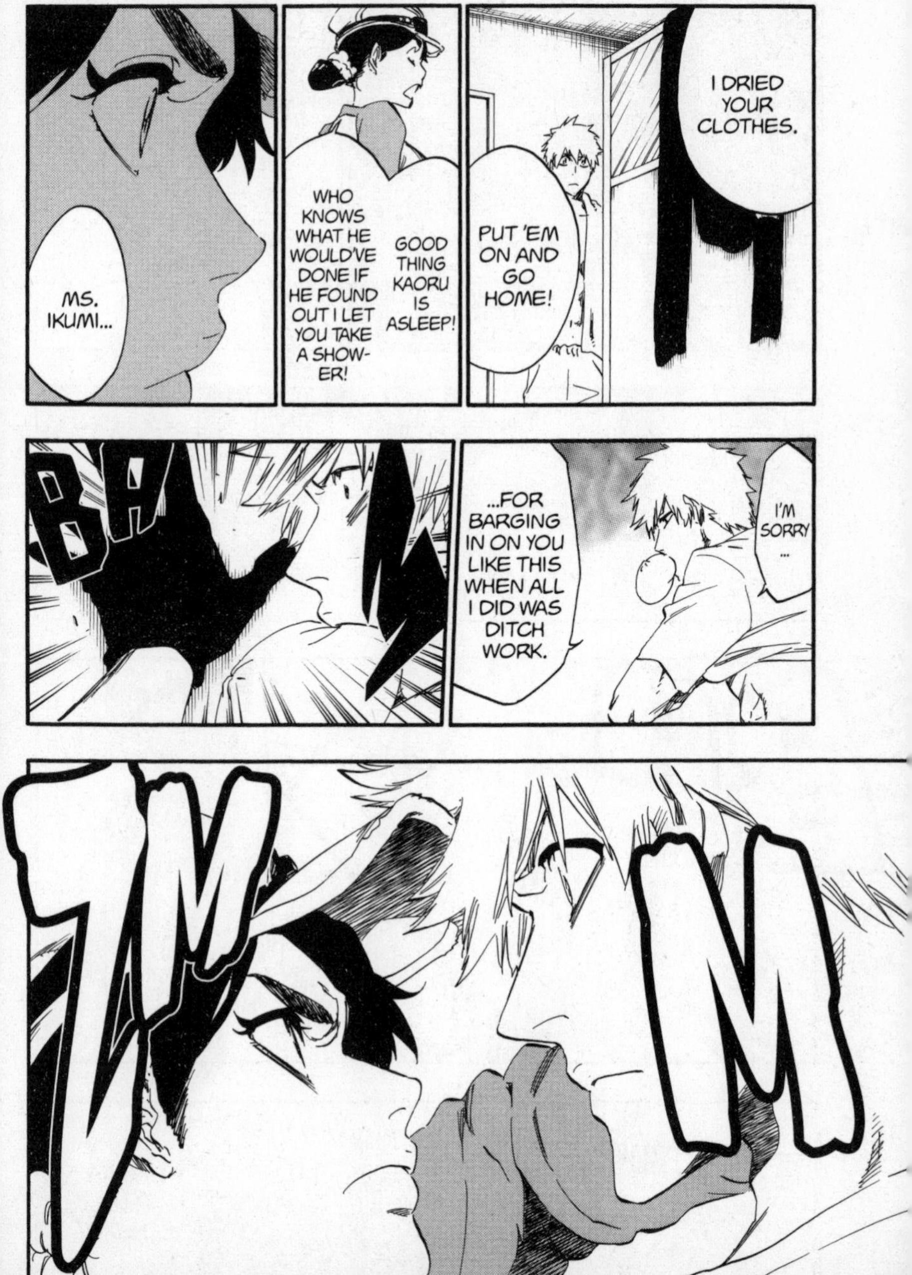
I DRIED YOUR CLOTHES.
PUT 'EM ON AND GO HOME!
GOOD THING KAORU IS ASLEEP!
WHO KNOWS WHAT HE WOULD'VE DONE IF HE FOUND OUT I LET YOU TAKE A SHOWER!
MS. IKUMI...
I'M SORRY ...
...FOR BARGING IN ON YOU LIKE THIS WHEN ALL I DID WAS DITCH WORK.
BA

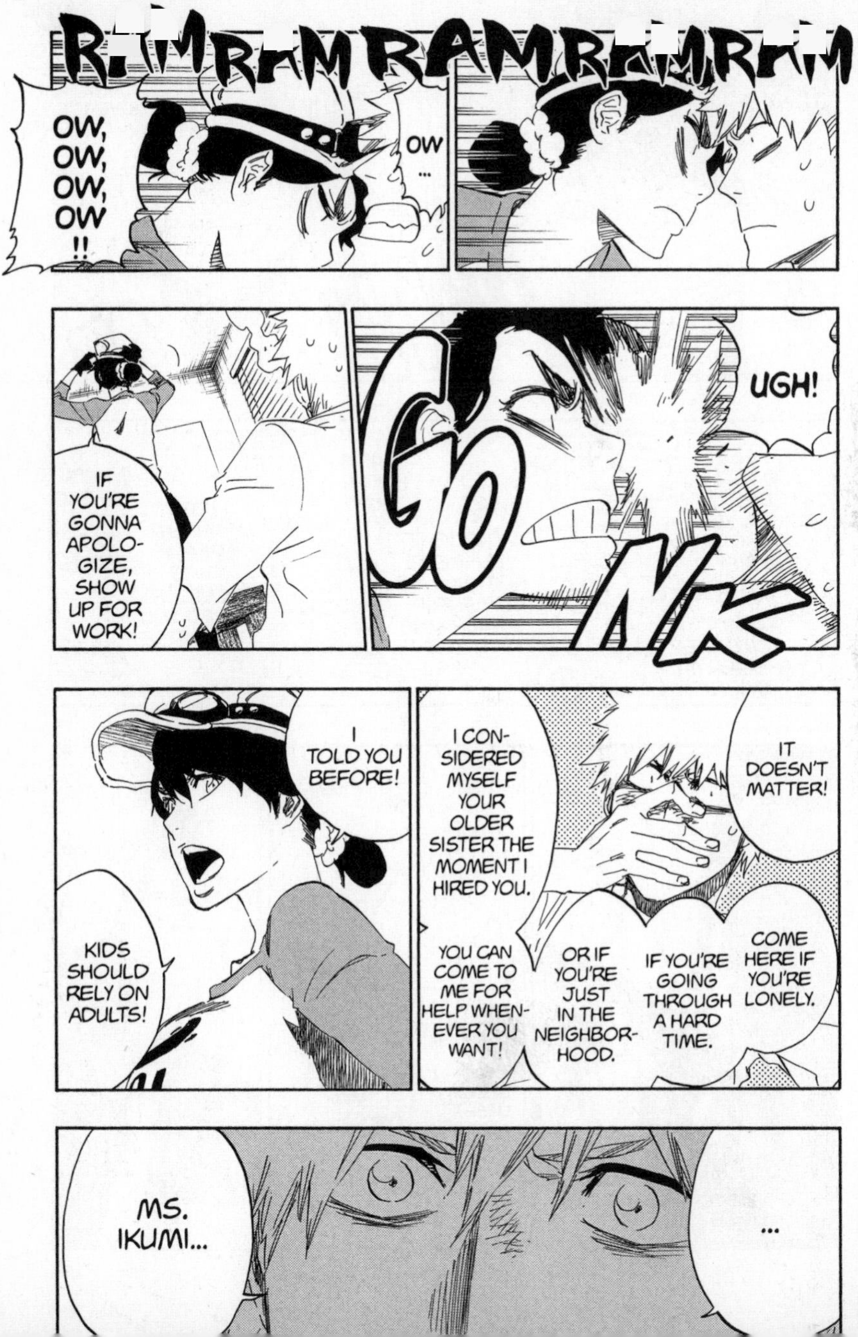
RAMRAMRAMRAMRAM
OW ...
OW, OW, OW, OW!!
UGH!
GONK
IF YOU'RE GONNA APOLO-GIZE, SHOW UP FOR WORK!
IT DOESN'T MATTER!
I CON-SIDERED MYSELF YOUR OLDER SISTER THE MOMENT I HIRED YOU.
COME HERE IF YOU'RE LONELY.
IF YOU'RE GOING THROUGH A HARD TIME.
OR IF YOU'RE JUST IN THE NEIGHBOR-HOOD.
YOU CAN COME TO ME FOR HELP WHEN-EVER YOU WANT!
I TOLD YOU BEFORE!
KIDS SHOULD RELY ON ADULTS!
...
MS. IKUMI...

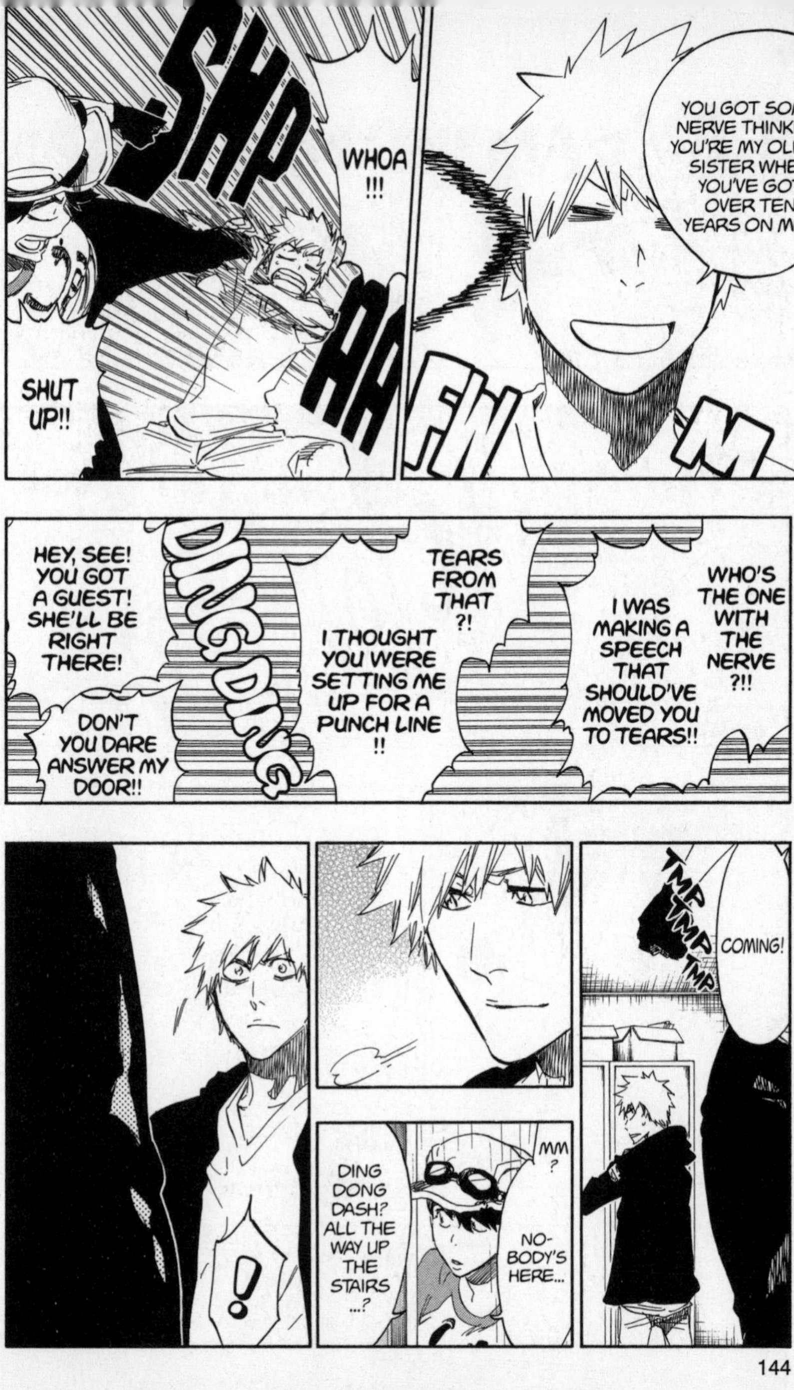
YOU GOT SOME NERVE THINKING YOU'RE MY OLDER SISTER WHEN YOU'VE GOT OVER TEN YEARS ON ME...
WHOA!!!
SHP
SHUT UP!!
WHO'S THE ONE WITH THE NERVE?!!
I WAS MAKING A SPEECH THAT SHOULD'VE MOVED YOU TO TEARS!!
TEARS FROM THAT?!
I THOUGHT YOU WERE SETTING ME UP FOR A PUNCH LINE!!
DING DING DING
HEY, SEE! YOU GOT A GUEST! SHE'LL BE RIGHT THERE!
DON'T YOU DARE ANSWER MY DOOR!!
TMP TMP TMP TMP
COMING!
MM?
NO-BODY'S HERE...
DING DONG DASH? ALL THE WAY UP THE STAIRS...?
!

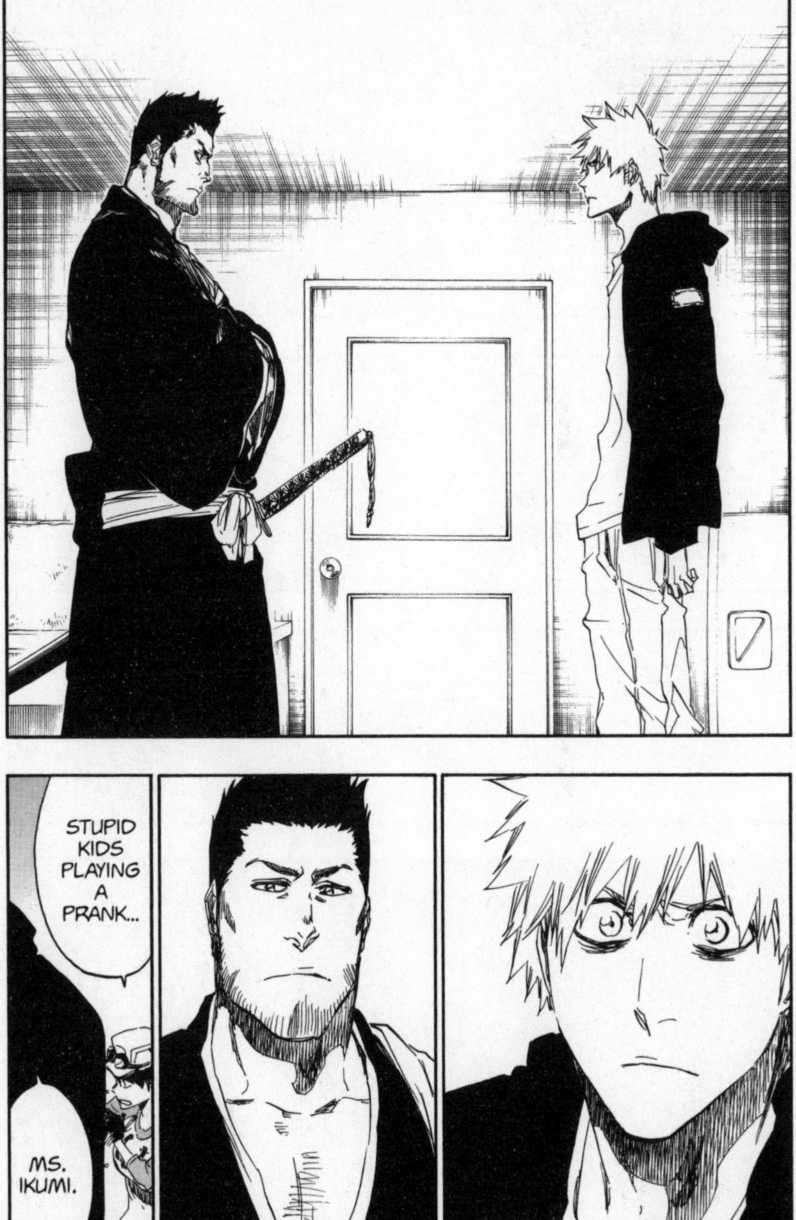
STUPID KIDS PLAYING A PRANK...
MS. IKUMI.

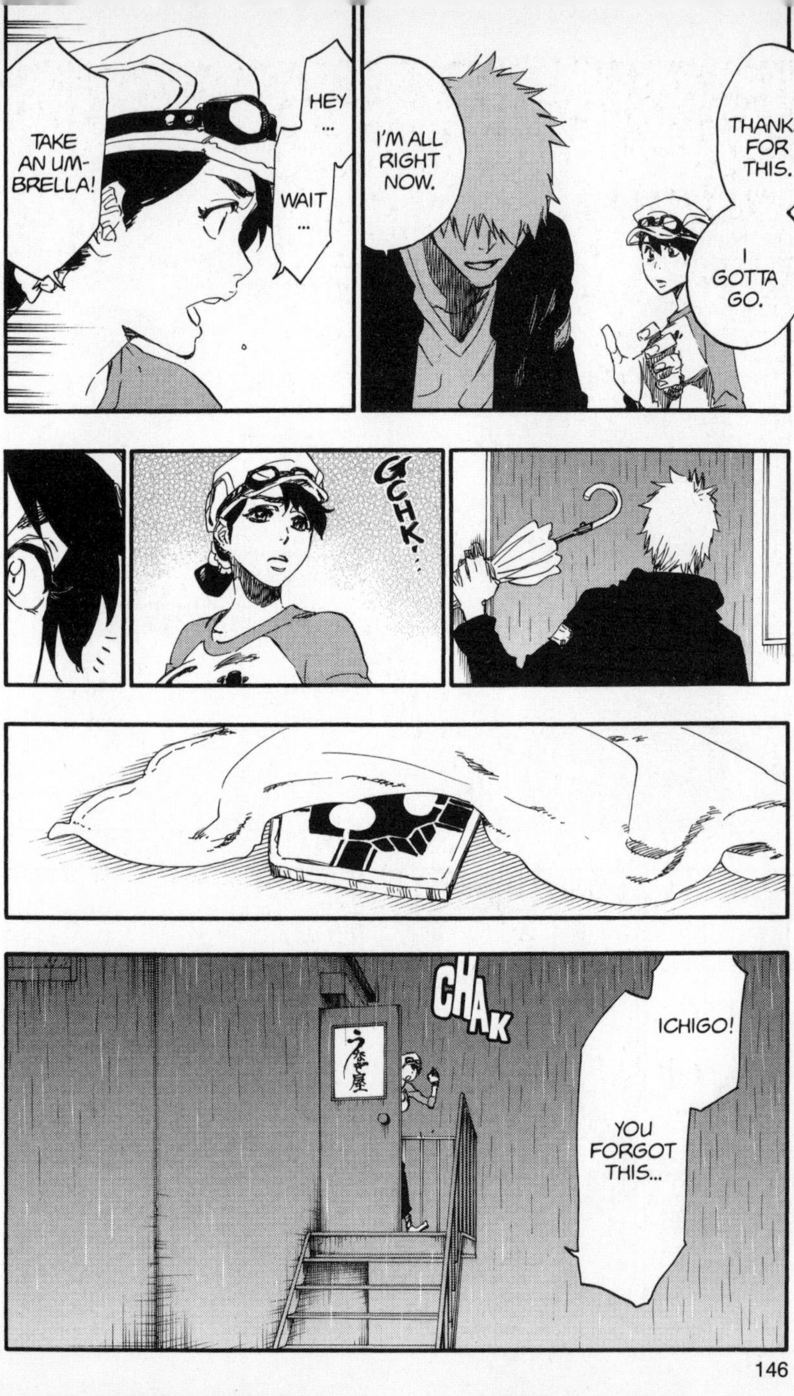
I'M ALL RIGHT NOW.
THANKS FOR THIS.
I GOTTA GO.
HEY ...
WAIT ...
TAKE AN UM-BRELLA!
GCHK
CHAK
ICHIGO!
YOU FORGOT THIS...

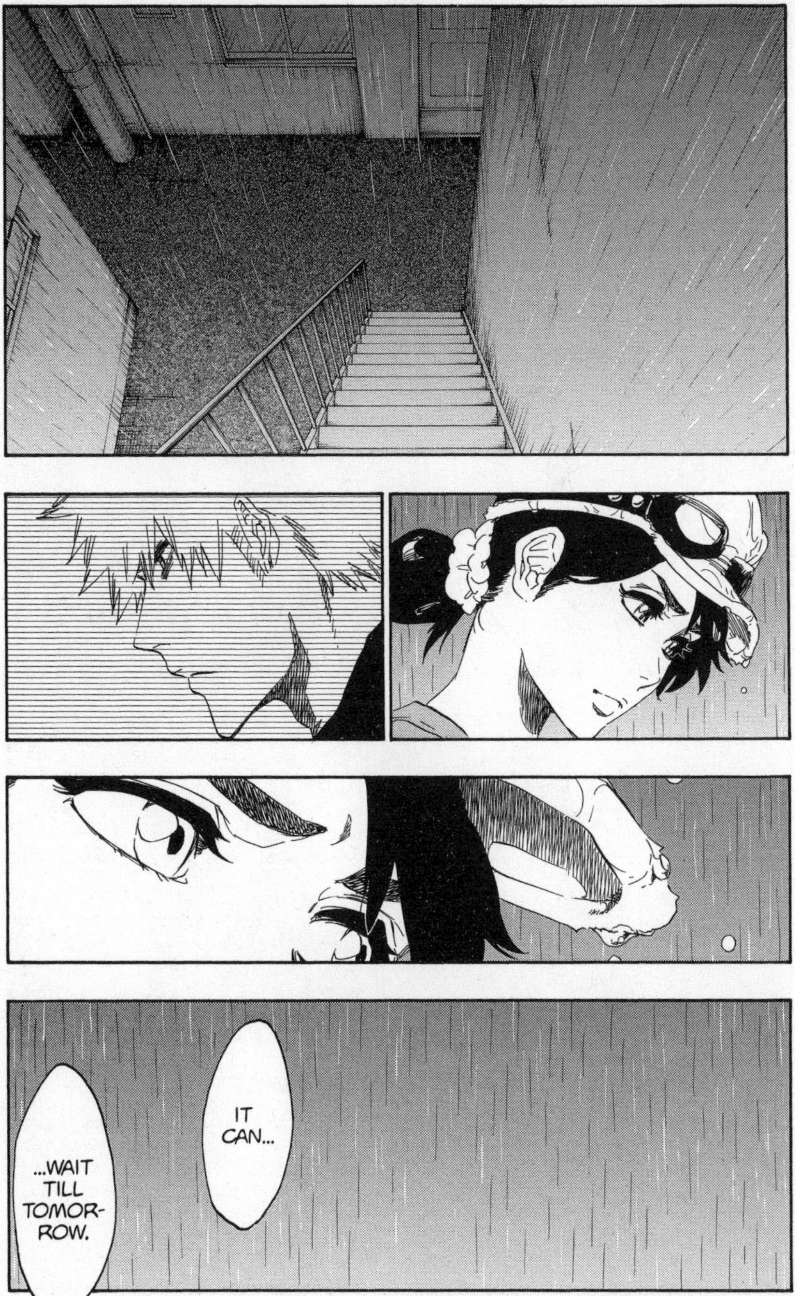
IT CAN...
...WAIT TILL TOMOR-ROW.

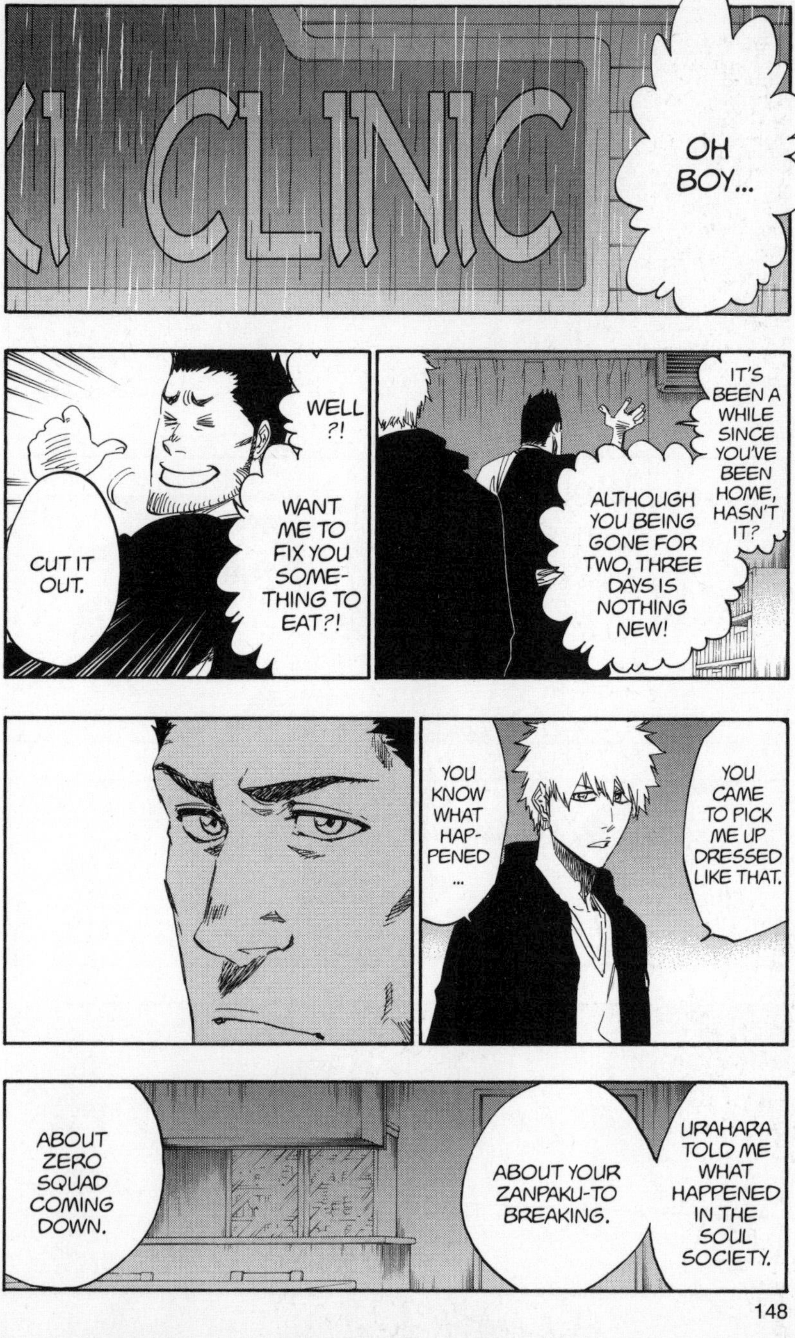
CLINIC
OH BOY...
IT'S BEEN A WHILE SINCE YOU'VE BEEN HOME, HASN'T IT?
ALTHOUGH YOU BEING GONE FOR TWO, THREE DAYS IS NOTHING NEW!
WELL ?!
WANT ME TO FIX YOU SOME-THING TO EAT?!
CUT IT OUT.
YOU CAME TO PICK ME UP DRESSED LIKE THAT.
YOU KNOW WHAT HAP-PENED ...
URAHARA TOLD ME WHAT HAPPENED IN THE SOUL SOCIETY.
ABOUT YOUR ZANPAKU-TO BREAKING.
ABOUT ZERO SQUAD COMING DOWN.

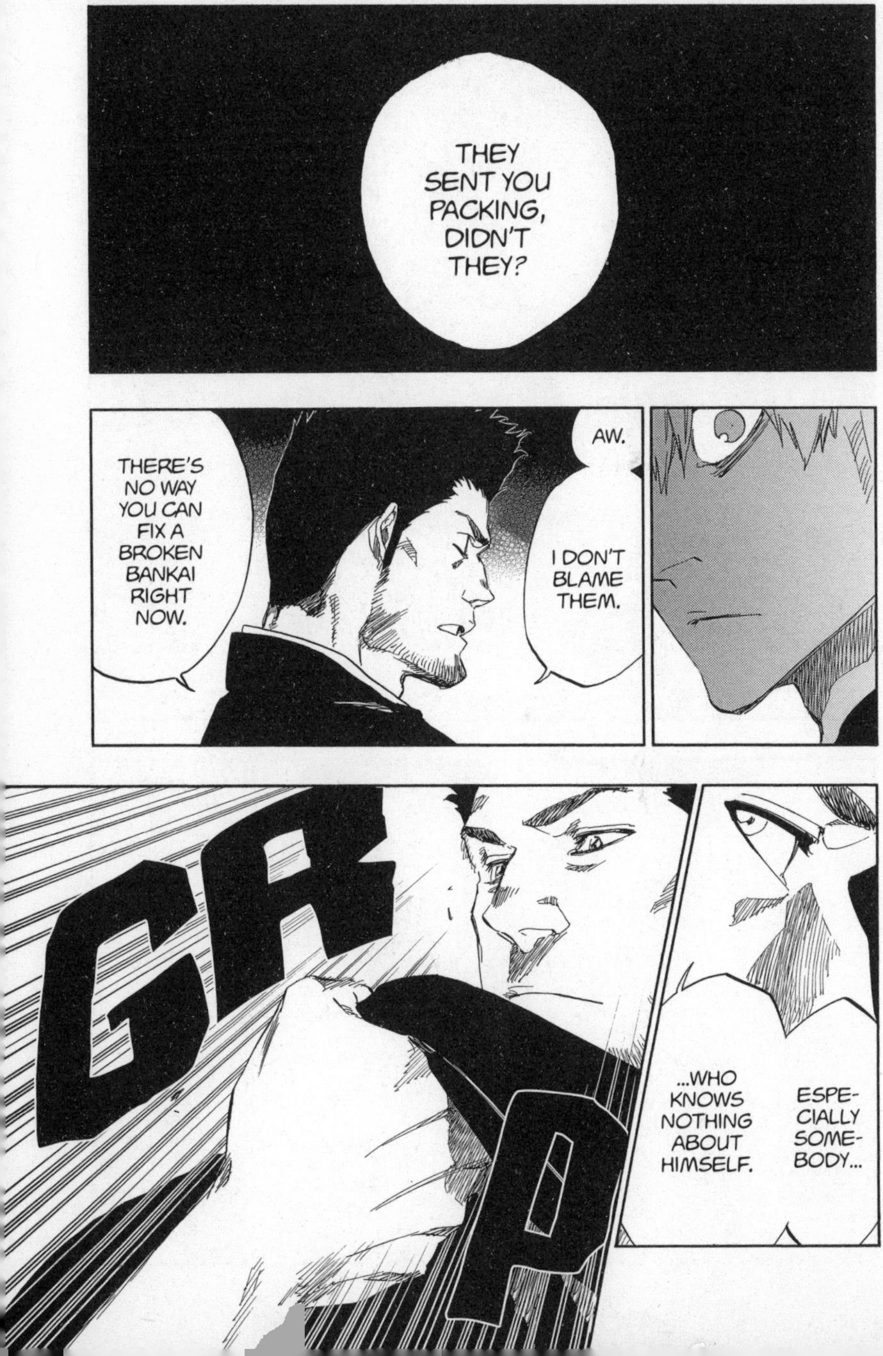
THEY SENT YOU PACKING, DIDN'T THEY?
AW.
I DON'T BLAME THEM.
THERE'S NO WAY YOU CAN FIX A BROKEN BANKAI RIGHT NOW.
ESPE-CIALLY SOME-BODY...
...WHO KNOWS NOTHING ABOUT HIMSELF.
GR

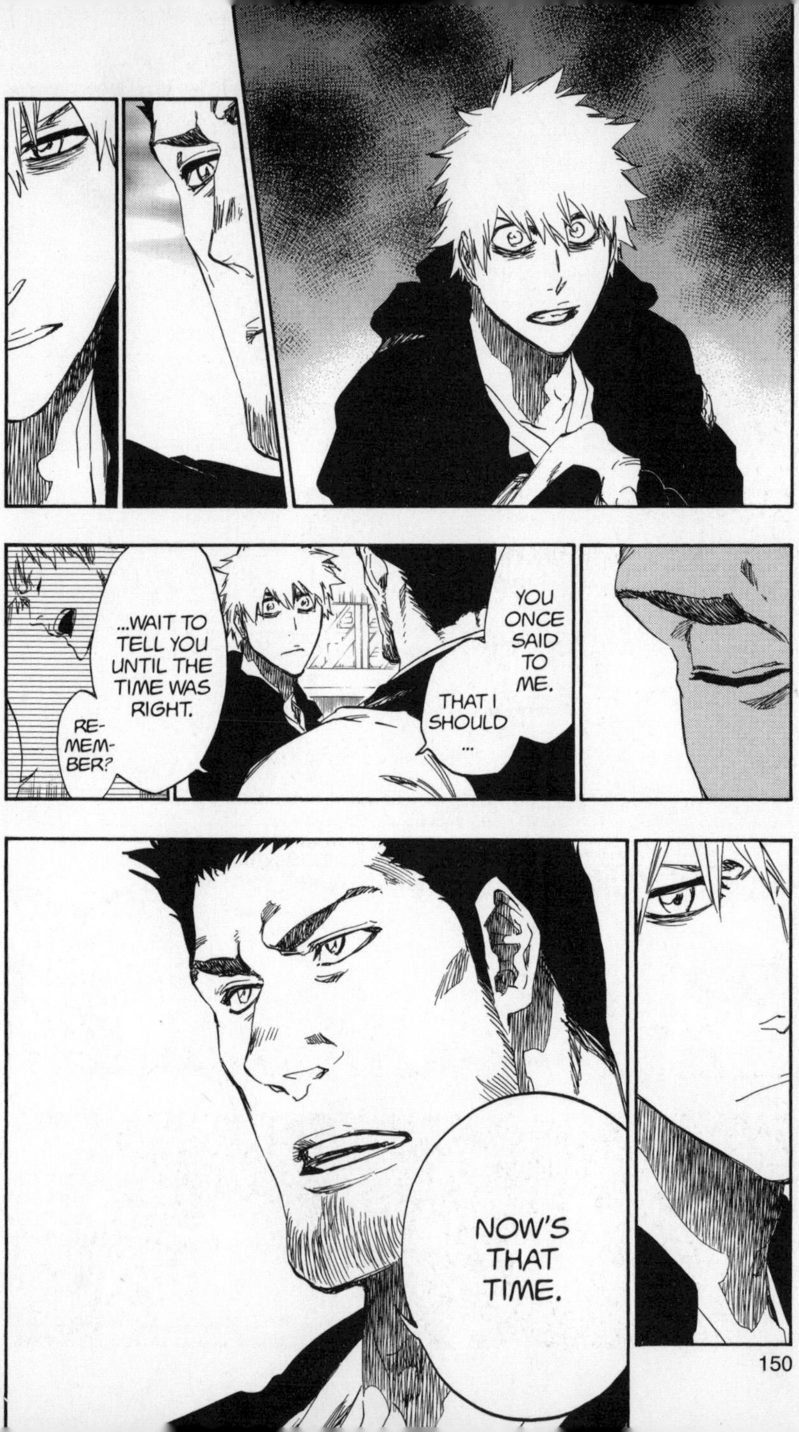
YOU ONCE SAID TO ME.
THAT I SHOULD ...
...WAIT TO TELL YOU UNTIL THE TIME WAS RIGHT.
RE-MEM-BER?
NOW'S THAT TIME.

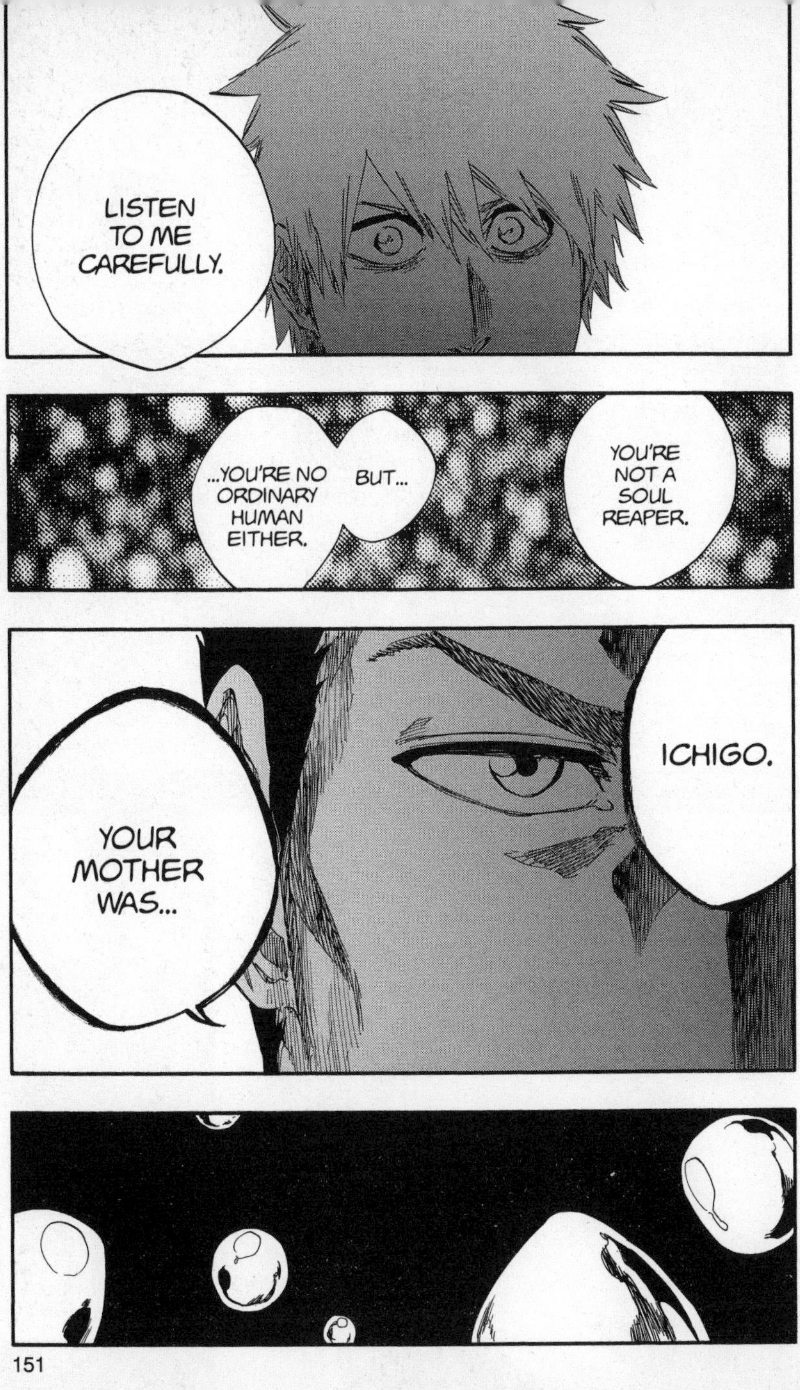
LISTEN TO ME CAREFULLY.
YOU'RE NOT A SOUL REAPER.
BUT...
...YOU'RE NO ORDINARY HUMAN EITHER.
ICHIGO.
YOUR MOTHER WAS...

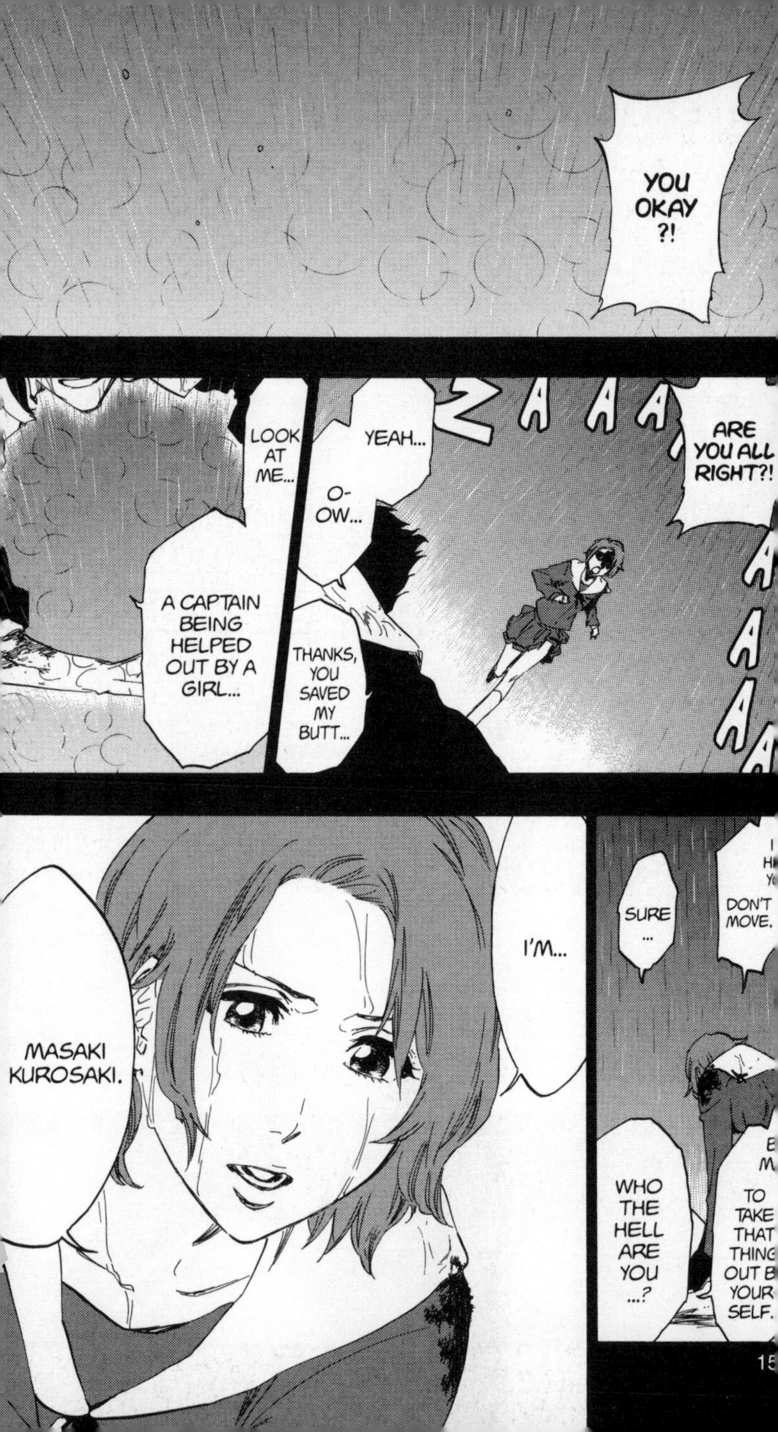
YOU OKAY ?!
ZAAAA
ARE YOU ALL RIGHT?!
AAAAA
YEAH...
O- OW...
THANKS, YOU SAVED MY BUTT...
LOOK AT ME...
A CAPTAIN BEING HELPED OUT BY A GIRL...
DON'T MOVE.
SURE ...
TO TAKE THAT THING OUT B YOUR SELF.
WHO THE HELL ARE YOU ...?
I'M...
MASAKI KUROSAKI.

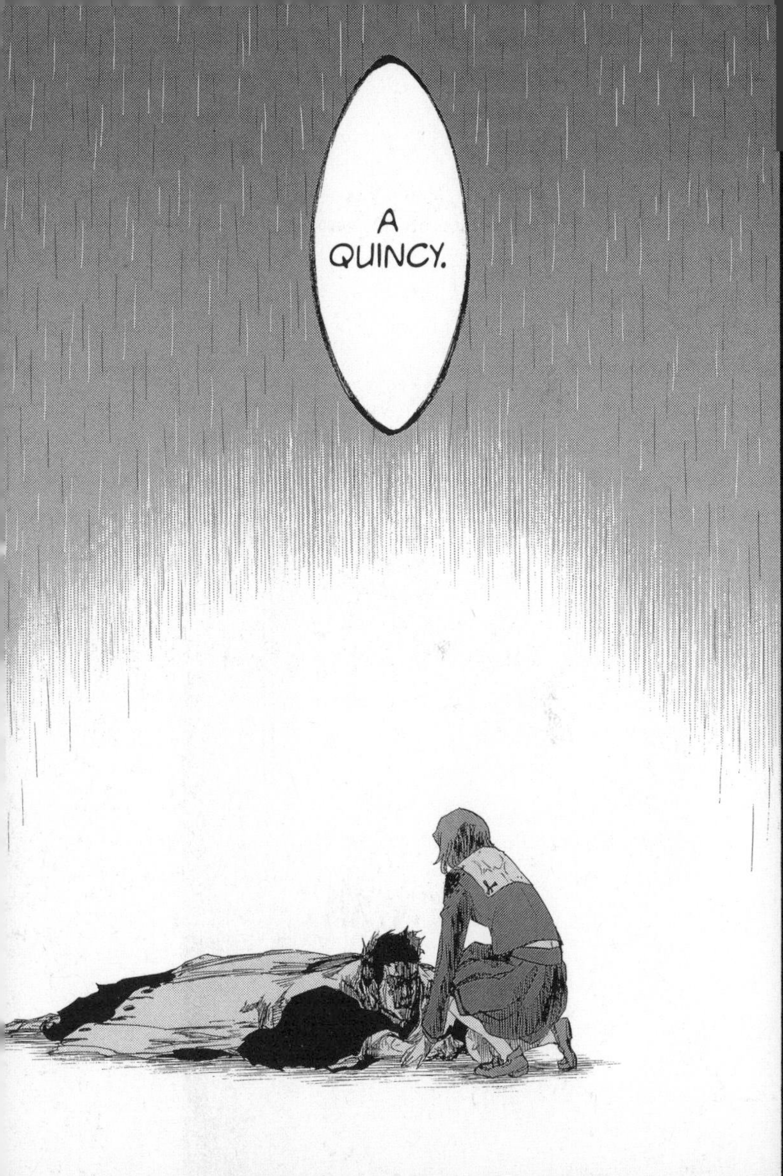
A QUINCY.

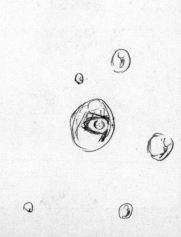

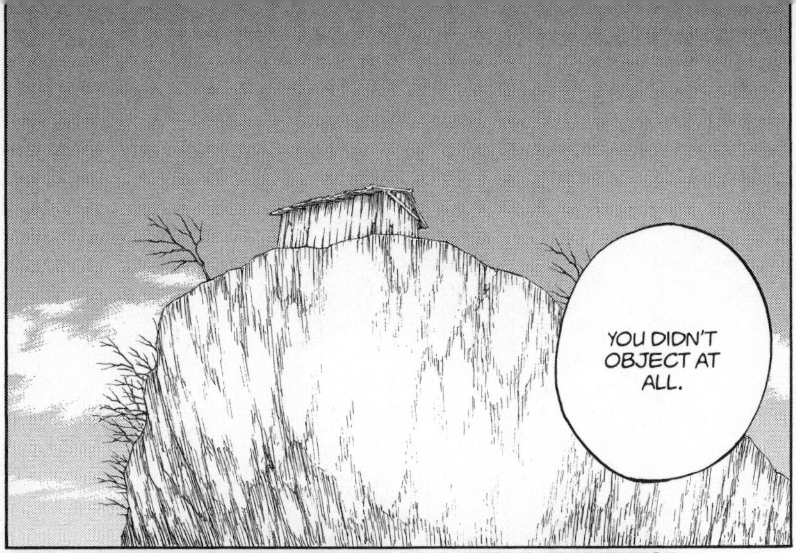
YOU DIDN'T OBJECT AT ALL.

529. EVERYTHING BUT THE RAIN OP. 2 "THE RUDIMENTS"

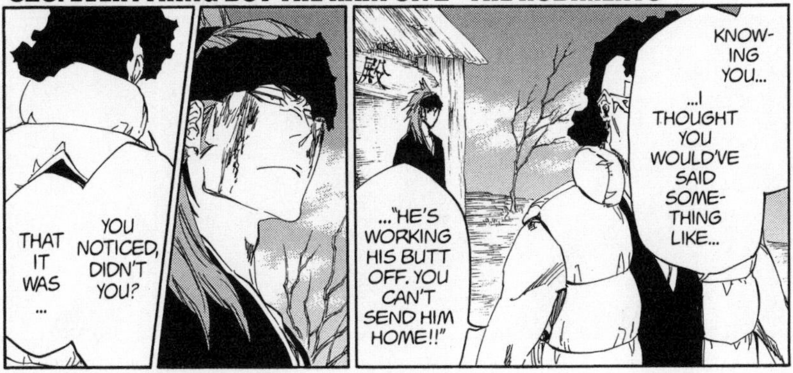
KNOWING YOU...
...I THOUGHT YOU WOULD'VE SAID SOMETHING LIKE...
..."HE'S WORKING HIS BUTT OFF. YOU CAN'T SEND HIM HOME!!"
YOU NOTICED, DIDN'T YOU?
THAT IT WAS ...

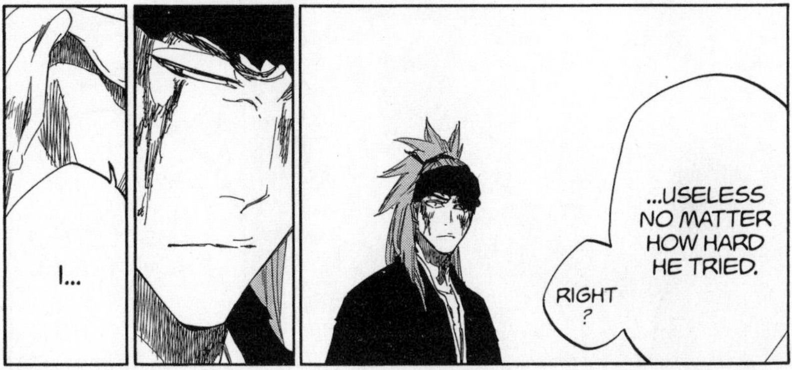
...USELESS NO MATTER HOW HARD HE TRIED.
RIGHT ?
I...

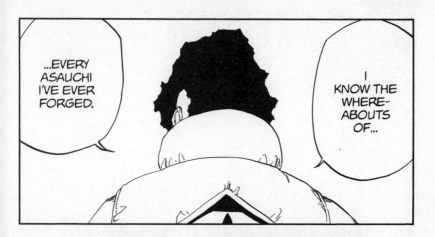

I KNOW THE WHERE-ABOUTS OF...
...EVERY ASAUCHI I'VE EVER FORGED.
ALL SOUL REAPERS...
...ARE GIVEN AN ASAUCHI.
WE THEN SHAPE IT INTO OUR OWN ZANPAKU-TO THROUGH CONTINUOUS TRAINING.
THAT IS THE CORE AND BASIS OF THE RELATIONSHIP BETWEEN A SOUL REAPER AND HIS ZANPAKU-TO.
ABSOLUTE PROVIDENCE.
OFFICERS.
AND OF COURSE CAPTAINS TOO.

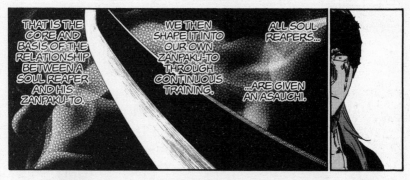

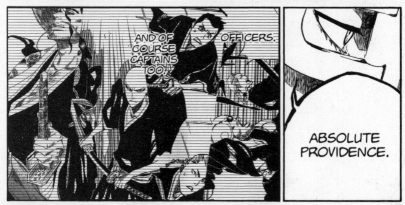

READ THIS WAY

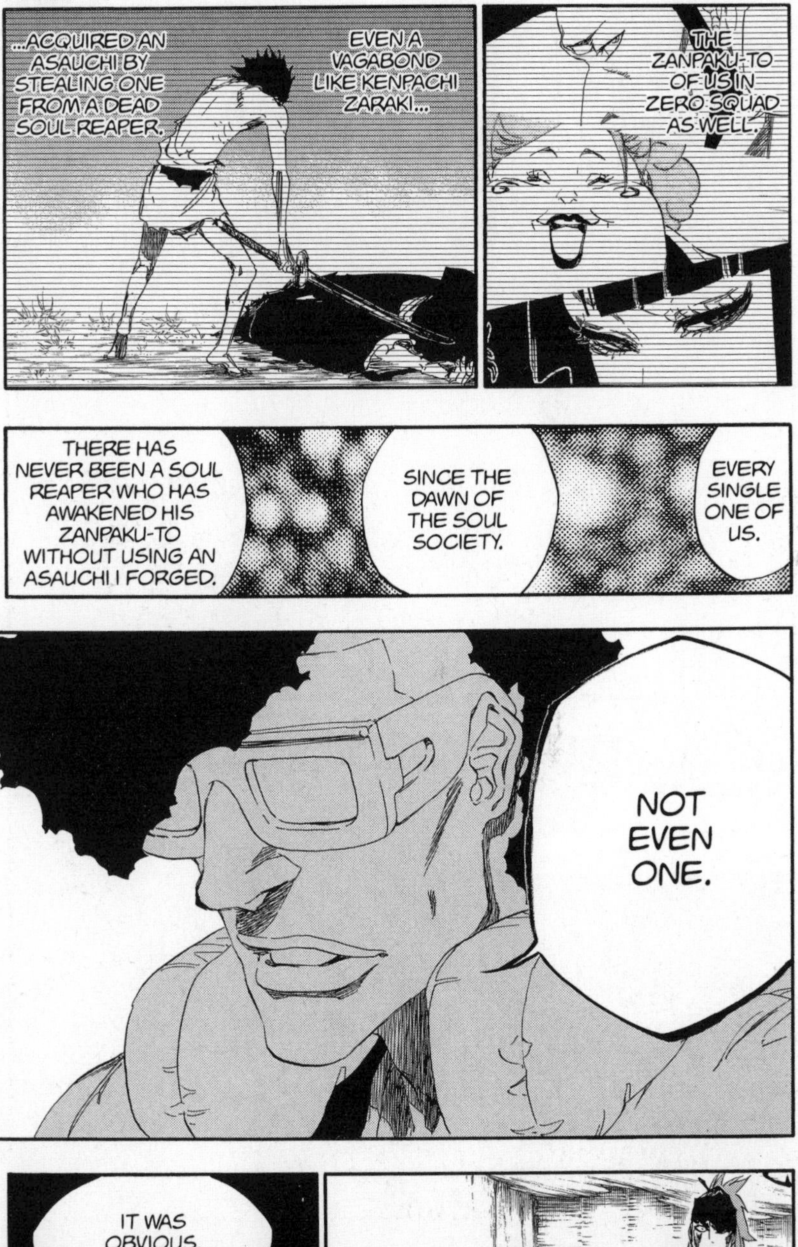
THE ZANPAKU-TO OF US IN ZERO SQUAD AS WELL.
EVEN A VAGABOND LIKE KENPACHI ZARAKI...
...ACQUIRED AN ASAUCHI BY STEALING ONE FROM A DEAD SOUL REAPER.
EVERY SINGLE ONE OF US.
SINCE THE DAWN OF THE SOUL SOCIETY.
THERE HAS NEVER BEEN A SOUL REAPER WHO HAS AWAKENED HIS ZANPAKU-TO WITHOUT USING AN ASAUCHI I FORGED.
NOT EVEN ONE.
IT WAS OBVIOUS.

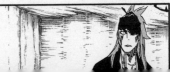

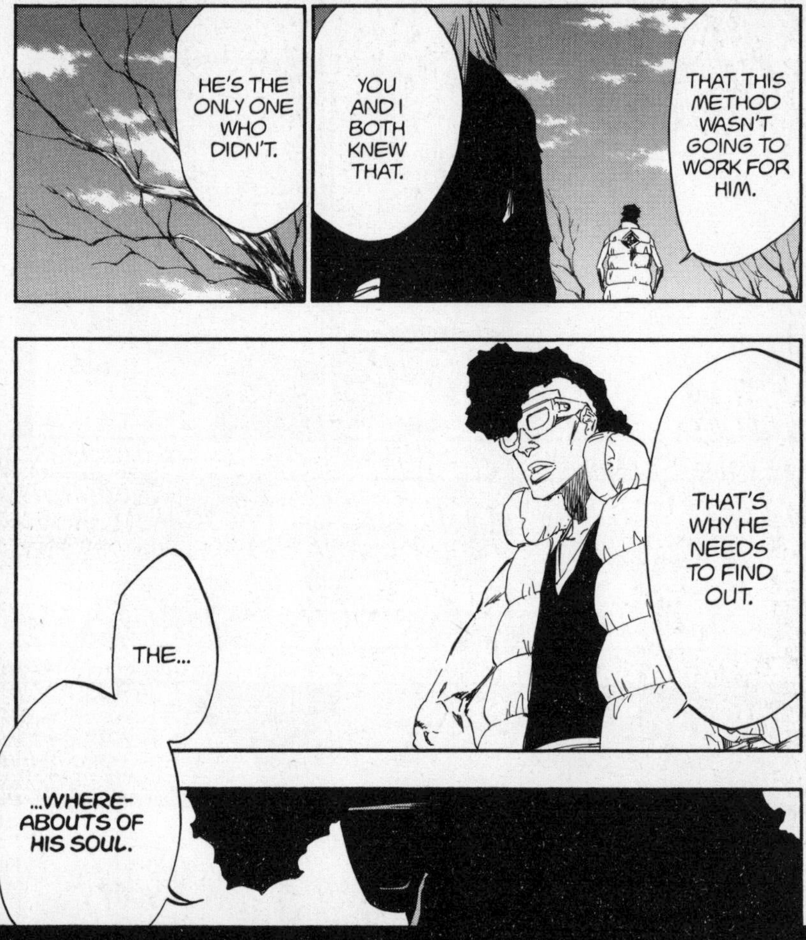
THAT THIS METHOD WASN'T GOING TO WORK FOR HIM.
YOU AND I BOTH KNEW THAT.
HE'S THE ONLY ONE WHO DIDN'T.
THAT'S WHY HE NEEDS TO FIND OUT.
THE...
...WHERE-ABOUTS OF HIS SOUL.

BLEACH 529.

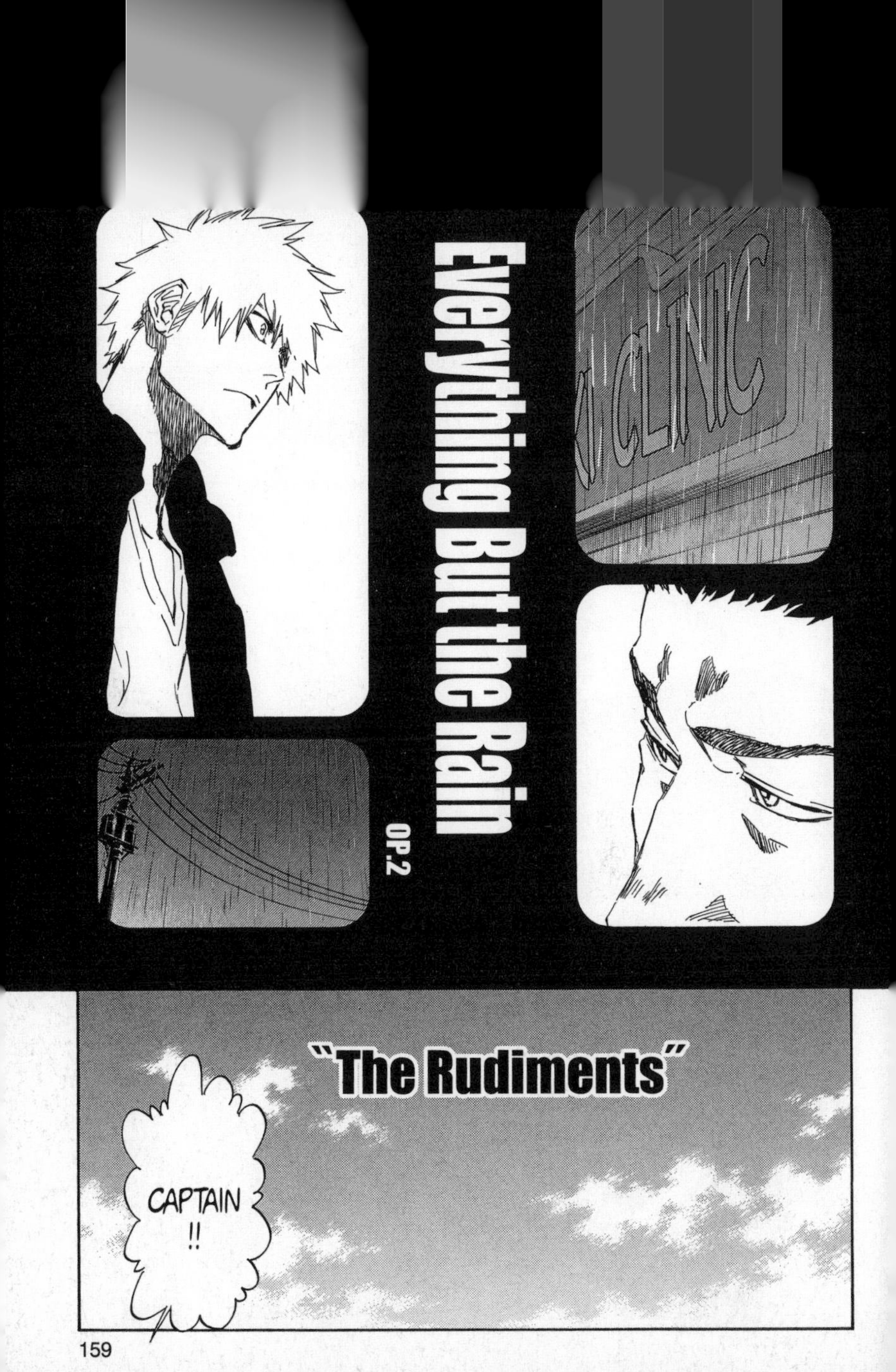

CLINIC
Everything But the Rain
OP.2
"The Rudiments"
CAPTAIN !!

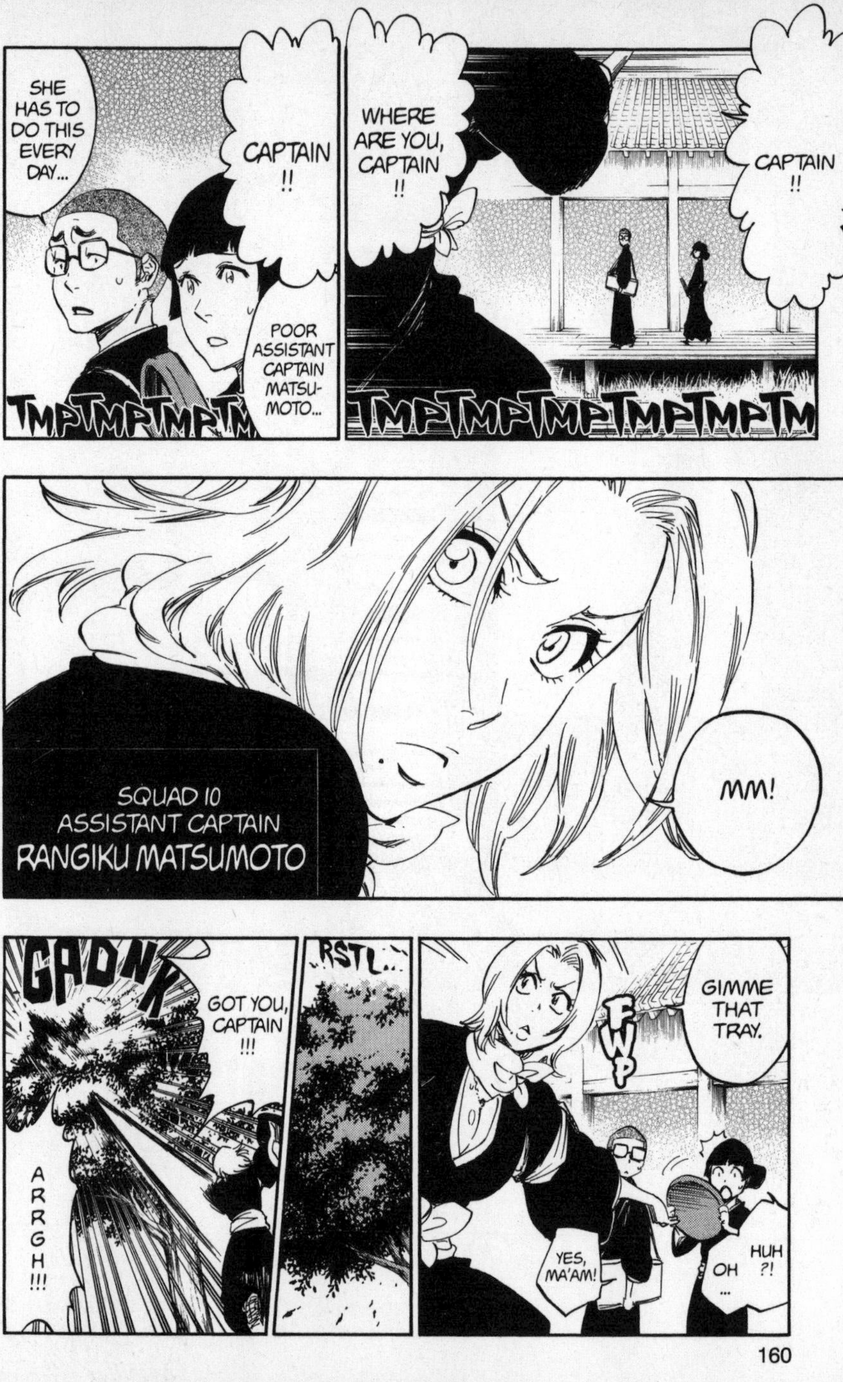
CAPTAIN !!
WHERE ARE YOU, CAPTAIN !!
TMPTMPTMPTMPTMPTM
CAPTAIN !!
SHE HAS TO DO THIS EVERY DAY...
POOR ASSISTANT CAPTAIN MATSU-MOTO...
TMPTMPTMPTM
MM!
SQUAD 10 ASSISTANT CAPTAIN RANGIKU MATSUMOTO
GIMME THAT TRAY.
FWP
HUH ?!
OH ...
YES, MA'AM!
RSTL...
GOT YOU, CAPTAIN !!!
GADONK
ARRGH!!!

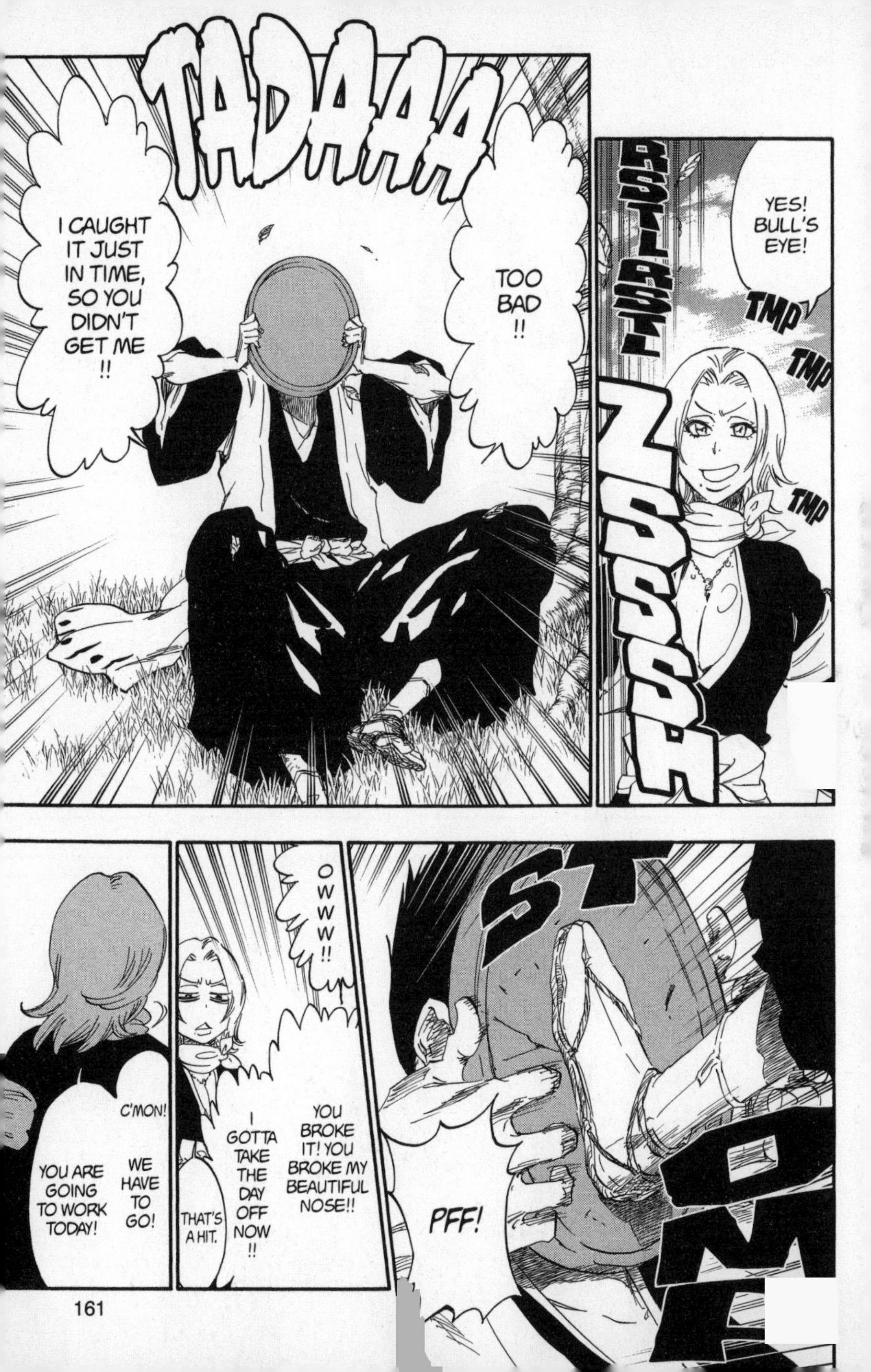
YES! BULL'S EYE!
RSTL RSTL
TMP
TMP
TMP
ZSSSH
TADAAA
TOO BAD!!
I CAUGHT IT JUST IN TIME, SO YOU DIDN'T GET ME!!
PFF!
OWWW!!
YOU BROKE IT! YOU BROKE MY BEAUTIFUL NOSE!!
I GOTTA TAKE THE DAY OFF NOW!!
THAT'S A HIT.
C'MON!
WE HAVE TO GO!
YOU ARE GOING TO WORK TODAY!

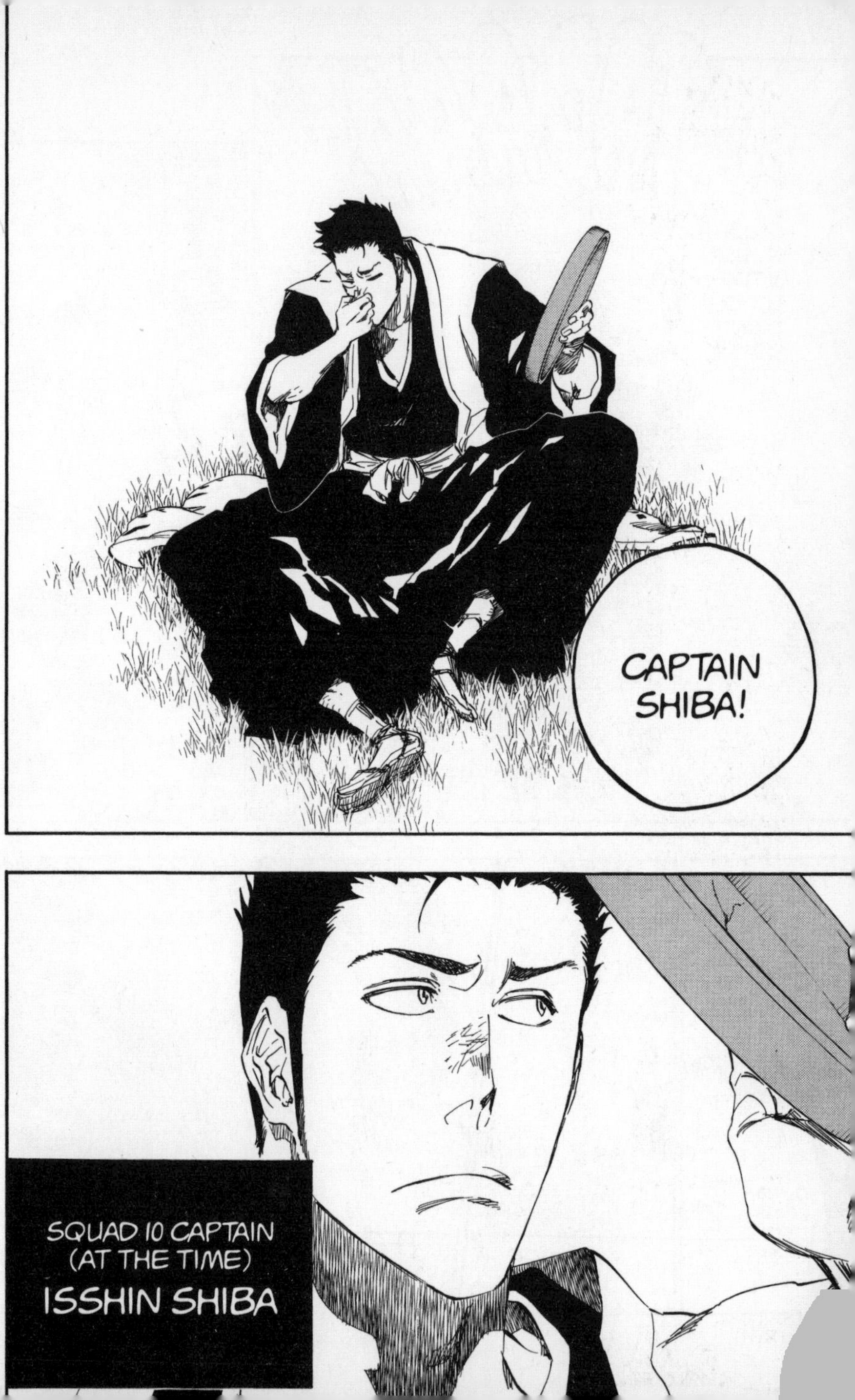
CAPTAIN SHIBA!
SQUAD 10 CAPTAIN (AT THE TIME)
ISSHIN SHIBA

READ THIS WAY

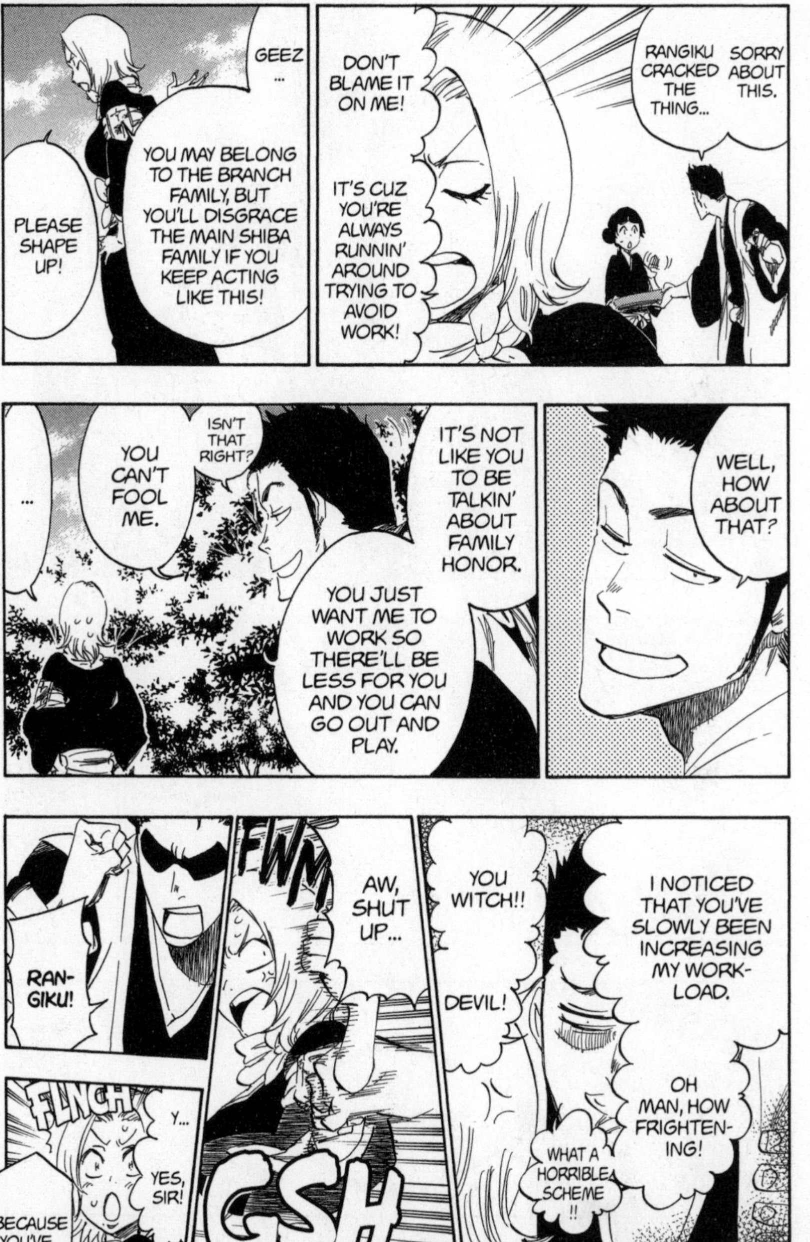
SORRY ABOUT THIS.
RANGIKU CRACKED THE THING...
DON'T BLAME IT ON ME!
IT'S CUZ YOU'RE ALWAYS RUNNIN' AROUND TRYING TO AVOID WORK!
GEEZ...
YOU MAY BELONG TO THE BRANCH FAMILY, BUT YOU'LL DISGRACE THE MAIN SHIBA FAMILY IF YOU KEEP ACTING LIKE THIS!
PLEASE SHAPE UP!
WELL, HOW ABOUT THAT?
IT'S NOT LIKE YOU TO BE TALKIN' ABOUT FAMILY HONOR.
YOU JUST WANT ME TO WORK SO THERE'LL BE LESS FOR YOU AND YOU CAN GO OUT AND PLAY.
ISN'T THAT RIGHT?
YOU CAN'T FOOL ME.
...
I NOTICED THAT YOU'VE SLOWLY BEEN INCREASING MY WORK-LOAD.
OH MAN, HOW FRIGHTEN-ING!
WHAT A HORRIBLE SCHEME!!
YOU WITCH!!
DEVIL!
FWM
AW, SHUT UP...
GSH
RAN-GIKU!
FLNCH
Y...
YES, SIR!
BECAUSE YOU'VE...

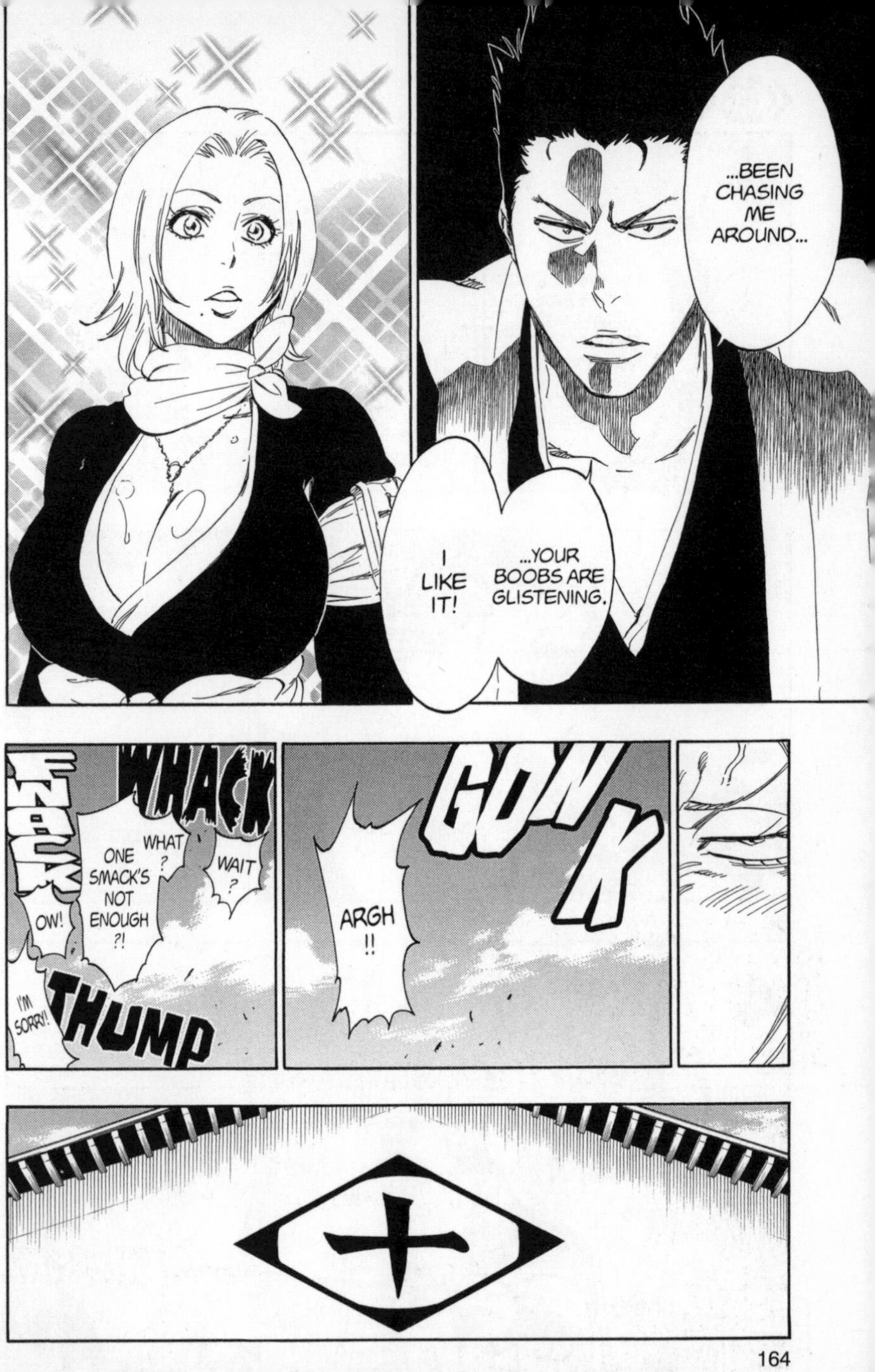
...BEEN CHASING ME AROUND...
...YOUR BOOBS ARE GLISTENING.
I LIKE IT!
GONK
ARGH!!
WHACK
WAIT?
WHAT?
ONE SMACK'S NOT ENOUGH?!
OW!
I'M SORRY!
THUMP
十

READ THIS WAY

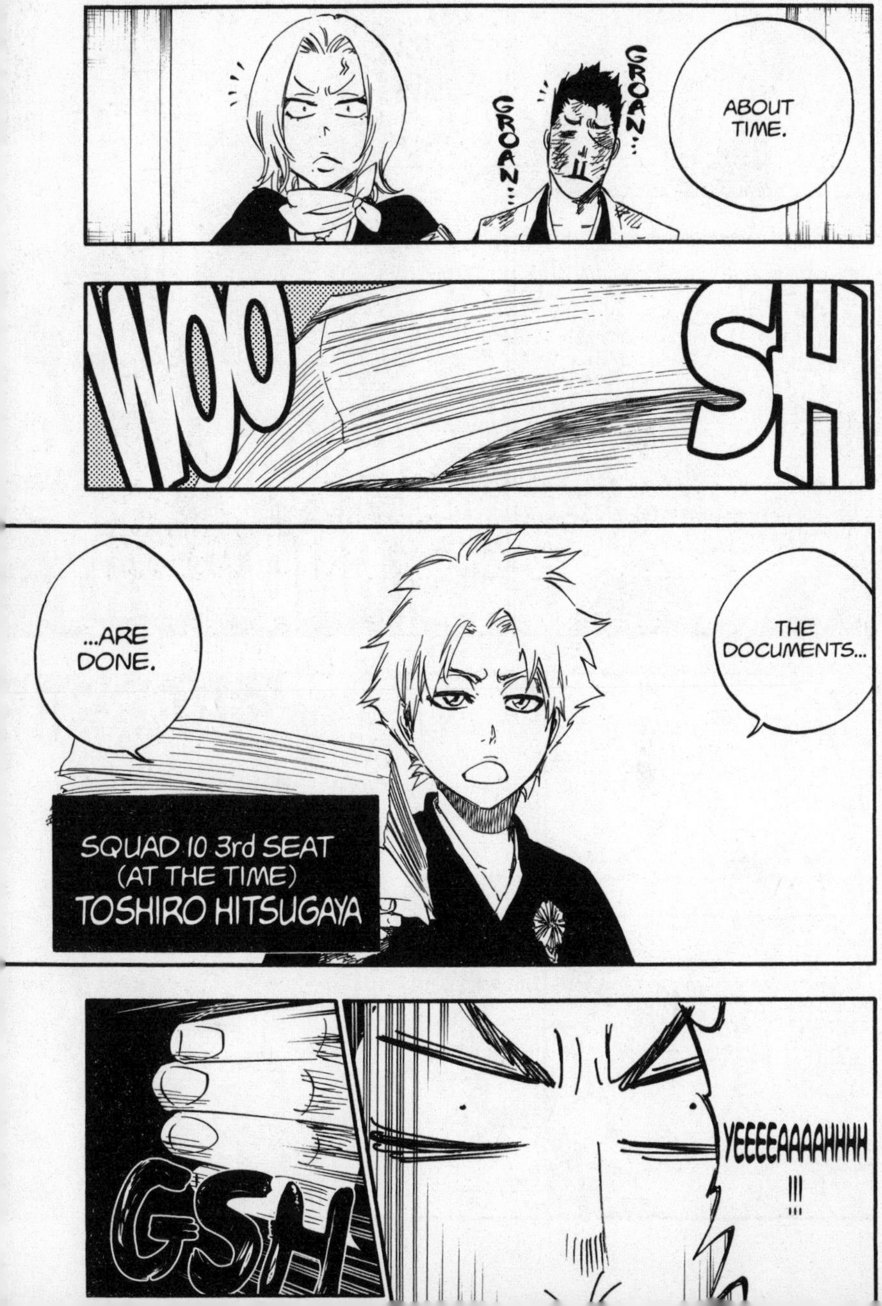
ABOUT TIME.
GROAN...
GROAN...
WOOSH
THE DOCUMENTS...
...ARE DONE.
SQUAD 10 3rd SEAT (AT THE TIME) TOSHIRO HITSUGAYA
YEEEEAAAAHHHH!!!
GSH

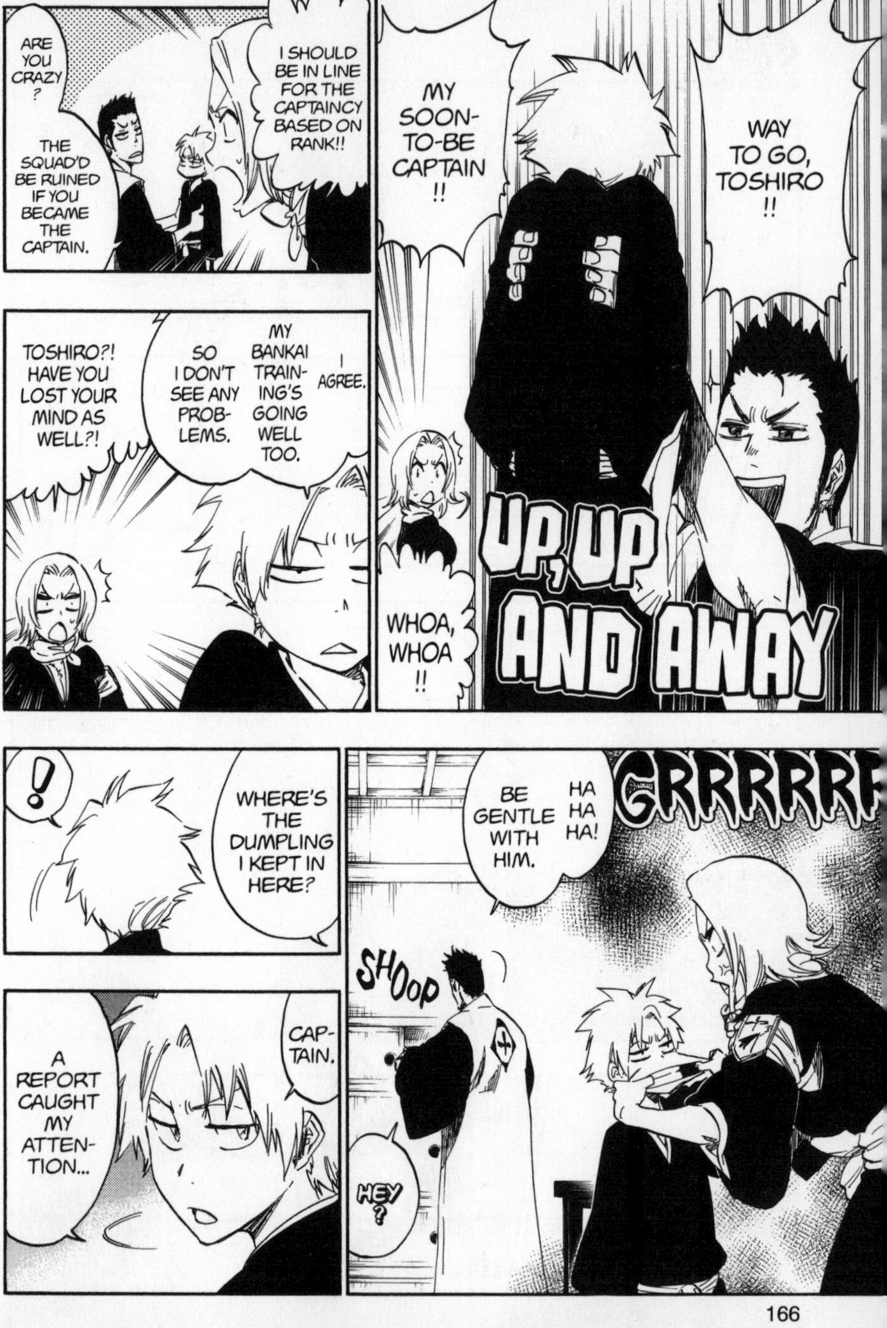
WAY TO GO, TOSHIRO!!
MY SOON-TO-BE CAPTAIN!!
UP, UP, AND AWAY
WHOA, WHOA!!
I SHOULD BE IN LINE FOR THE CAPTAINCY BASED ON RANK!!
ARE YOU CRAZY?
THE SQUAD'D BE RUINED IF YOU BECAME THE CAPTAIN.
I AGREE.
MY BANKAI TRAINING'S GOING WELL TOO.
SO I DON'T SEE ANY PROBLEMS.
TOSHIRO?! HAVE YOU LOST YOUR MIND AS WELL?!
GRRRRRR
HA HA HA!
BE GENTLE WITH HIM.
SHOOP
HEY?
WHERE'S THE DUMPLING I KEPT IN HERE?
!
CAPTAIN.
A REPORT CAUGHT MY ATTENTION...

READ THIS WAY

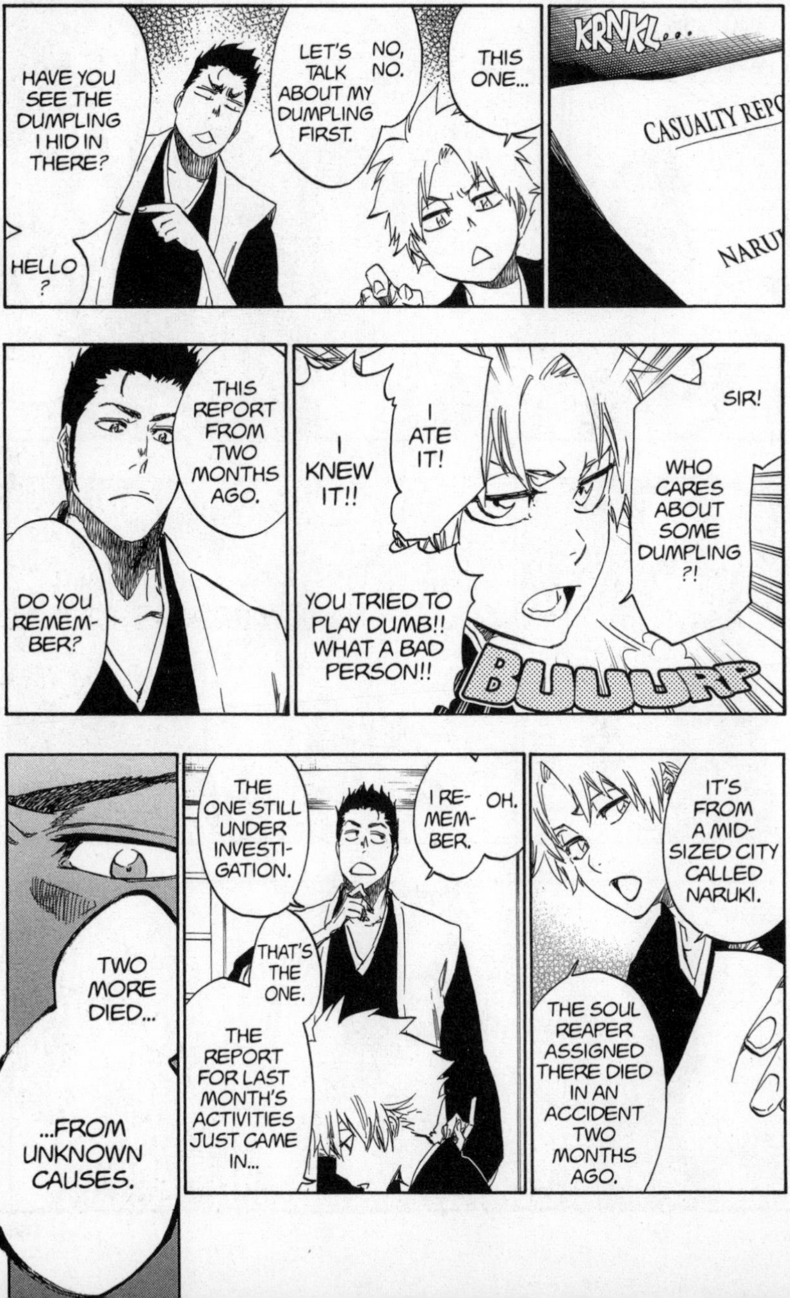
KRNKL...
CASUALTY REPO
NARU
THIS ONE...
NO, NO.
LET'S TALK ABOUT MY DUMPLING FIRST.
HAVE YOU SEE THE DUMPLING I HID IN THERE?
HELLO ?
SIR!
WHO CARES ABOUT SOME DUMPLING ?!
BUUURP
I ATE IT!
I KNEW IT!!
YOU TRIED TO PLAY DUMB!! WHAT A BAD PERSON!!
THIS REPORT FROM TWO MONTHS AGO.
DO YOU REMEMBER?
IT'S FROM A MID-SIZED CITY CALLED NARUKI.
THE SOUL REAPER ASSIGNED THERE DIED IN AN ACCIDENT TWO MONTHS AGO.
OH.
I REMEMBER.
THE ONE STILL UNDER INVESTIGATION.
THAT'S THE ONE.
THE REPORT FOR LAST MONTH'S ACTIVITIES JUST CAME IN...
TWO MORE DIED...
...FROM UNKNOWN CAUSES.

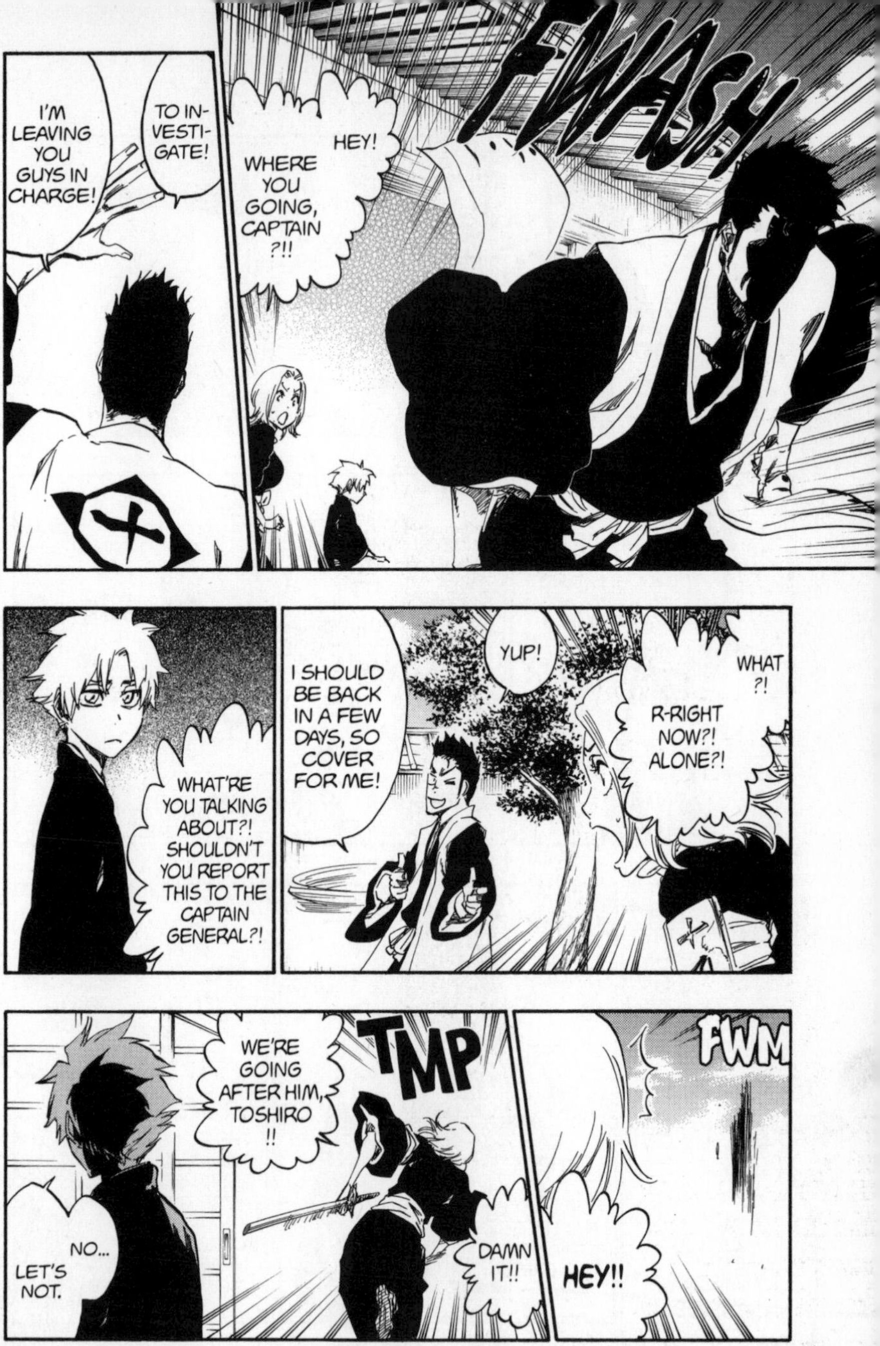
FWASH
HEY!
WHERE YOU GOING, CAPTAIN?!!
TO IN-VESTI-GATE!
I'M LEAVING YOU GUYS IN CHARGE!
WHAT?!
R-RIGHT NOW?! ALONE?!
YUP!
I SHOULD BE BACK IN A FEW DAYS, SO COVER FOR ME!
WHAT'RE YOU TALKING ABOUT?! SHOULDN'T YOU REPORT THIS TO THE CAPTAIN GENERAL?!
FWM
HEY!!
TMP
WE'RE GOING AFTER HIM, TOSHIRO!!
DAMN IT!!
NO... LET'S NOT.

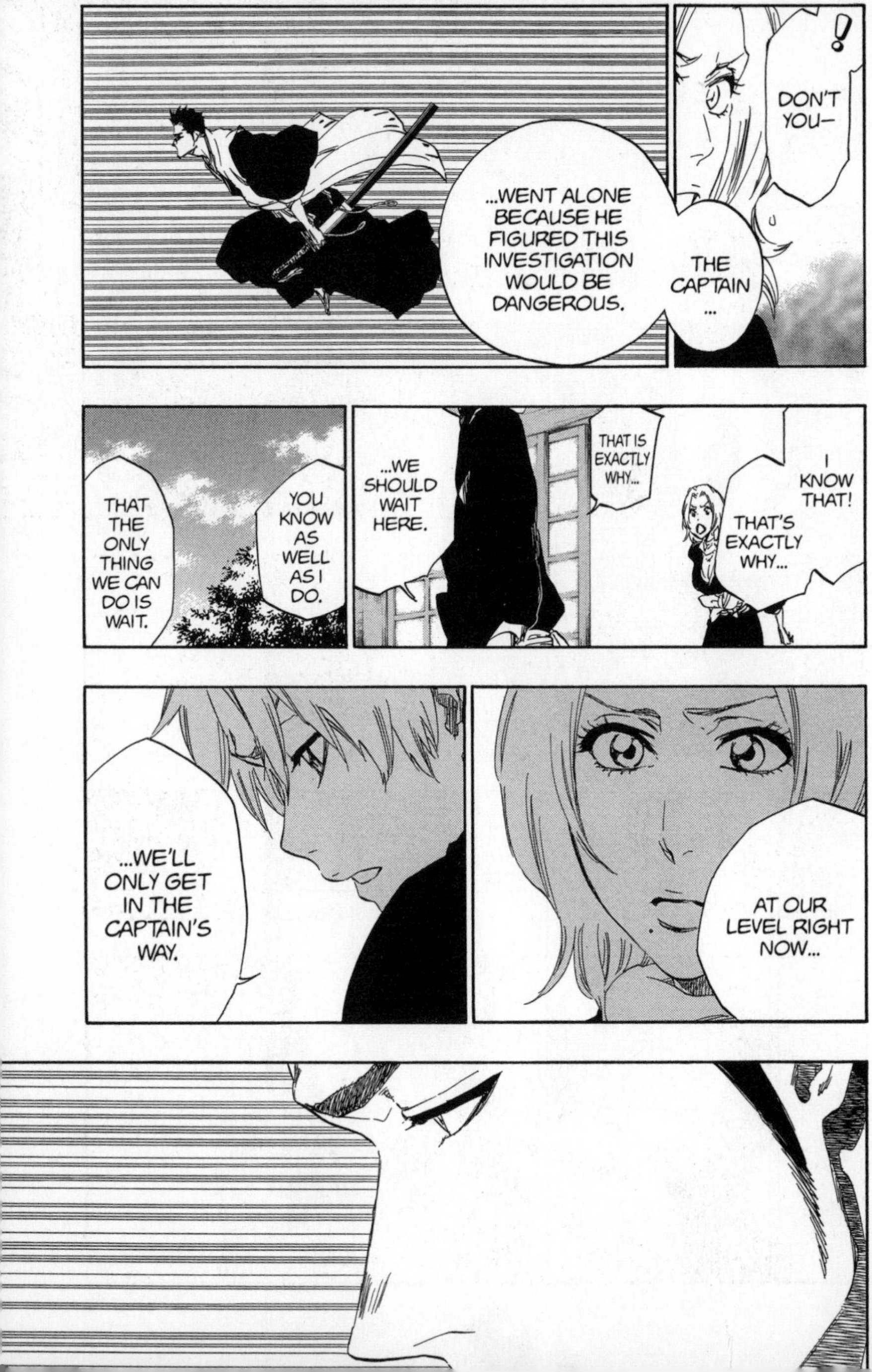
!
DON'T YOU—
THE CAPTAIN ...
...WENT ALONE BECAUSE HE FIGURED THIS INVESTIGATION WOULD BE DANGEROUS.
I KNOW THAT!
THAT'S EXACTLY WHY...
THAT IS EXACTLY WHY...
...WE SHOULD WAIT HERE.
YOU KNOW AS WELL AS I DO.
THAT THE ONLY THING WE CAN DO IS WAIT.
AT OUR LEVEL RIGHT NOW...
...WE'LL ONLY GET IN THE CAPTAIN'S WAY.

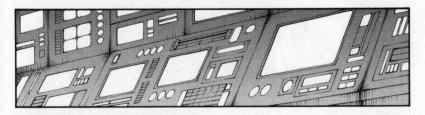

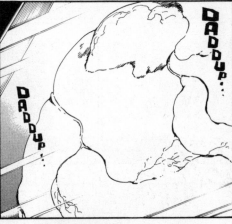

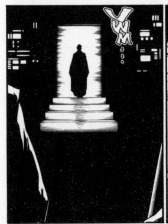

DADDUP...
DADDUP...
VWM
ANY PROGRESS?
NO.
NOT A LICK.
UNFORTUNATELY, NO...
WE'VE BEEN SUCCESSFUL EQUIPPING HOLLOWS WITH THE ABILITY TO HOLLOWFY TARGETS, BUT...
...THE TOXICITY IS TOO HIGH. COMMON KONPAKU, LET ALONE THE KONPAKU OF COURT GUARD OFFICERS, CAN'T HANDLE IT.
I SEE ...

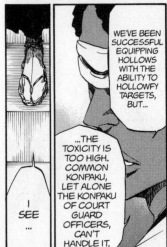

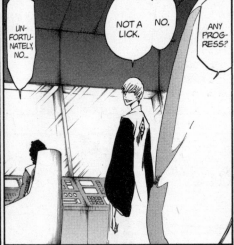

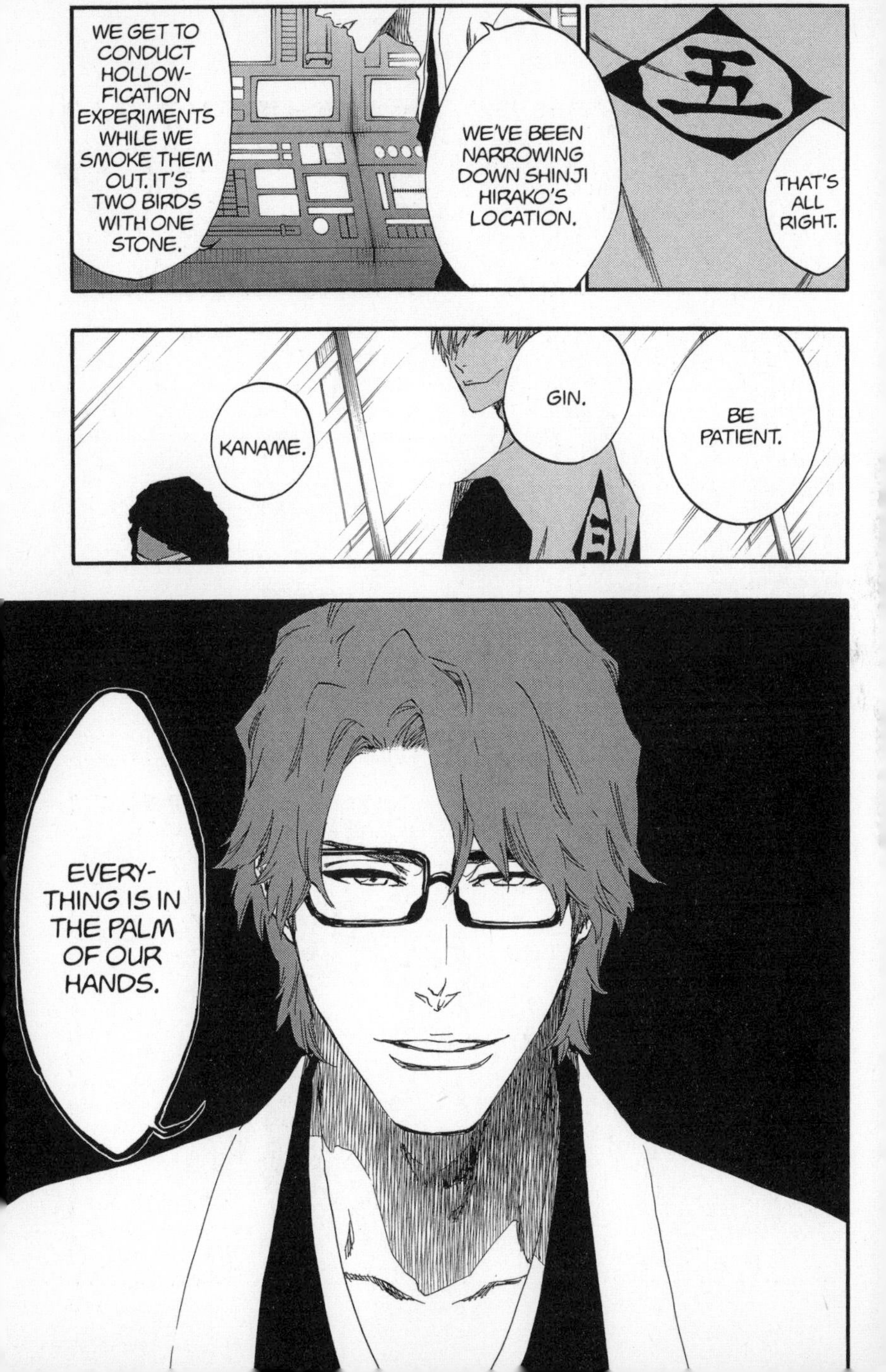
THAT'S ALL RIGHT.
WE'VE BEEN NARROWING DOWN SHINJI HIRAKO'S LOCATION.
WE GET TO CONDUCT HOLLOW-FICATION EXPERIMENTS WHILE WE SMOKE THEM OUT. IT'S TWO BIRDS WITH ONE STONE.
BE PATIENT.
GIN.
KANAME.
EVERY-THING IS IN THE PALM OF OUR HANDS.

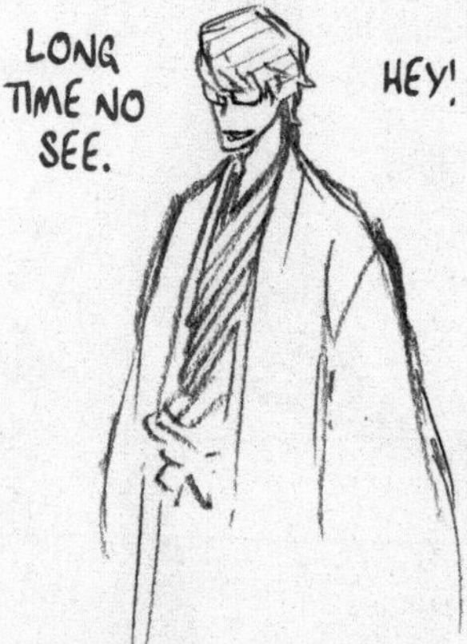
HEY!
LONG TIME NO SEE.

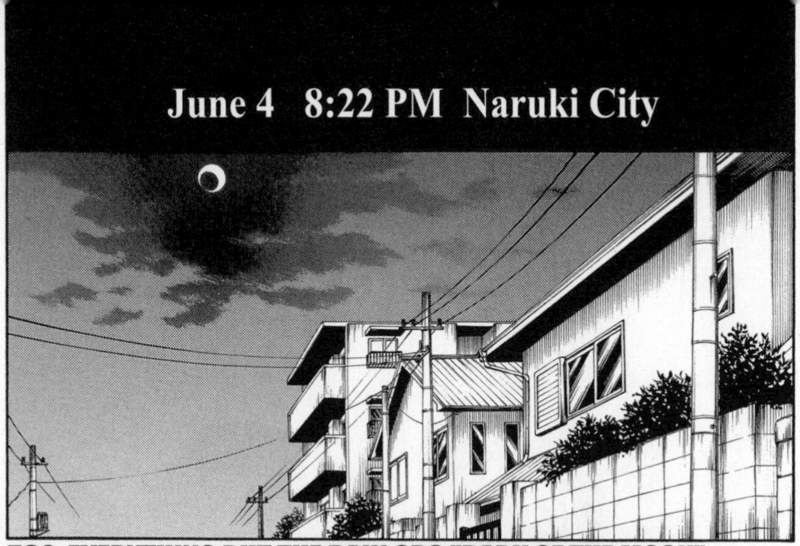
June 4 8:22 PM Naruki City

530. EVERYTHING BUT THE RAIN OP.3 "DARK OF THE MOON"

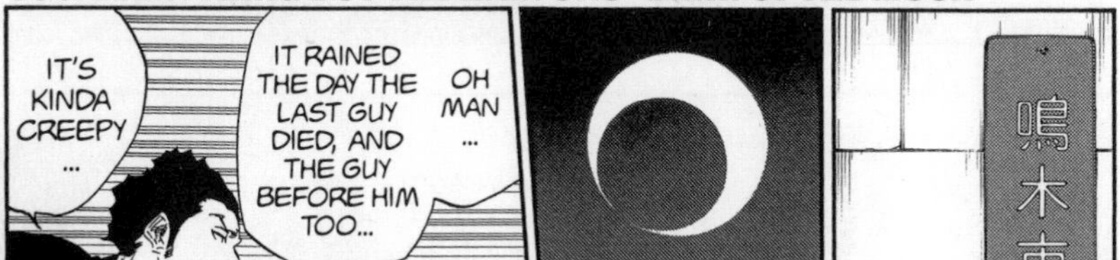
鳴木市 蝶原二丁目
鳴木市
IT'S GETTING CLOUDY...
OH MAN ...
IT RAINED THE DAY THE LAST GUY DIED, AND THE GUY BEFORE HIM TOO...
IT'S KINDA CREEPY ...
LET'S NOT TALK ABOUT IT...

*SIGN: NARUKI CITY CHOHARA 2-CHOME

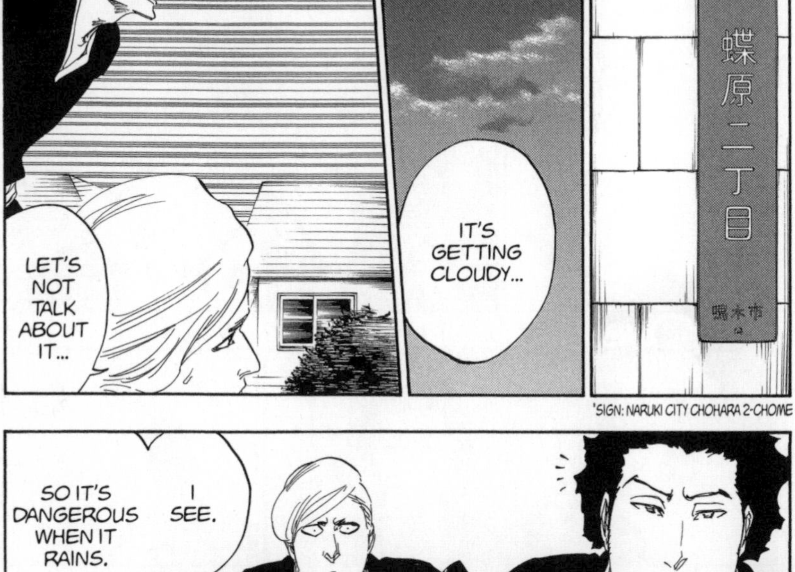
I SEE.
SO IT'S DANGEROUS WHEN IT RAINS.

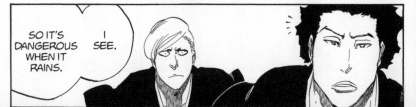

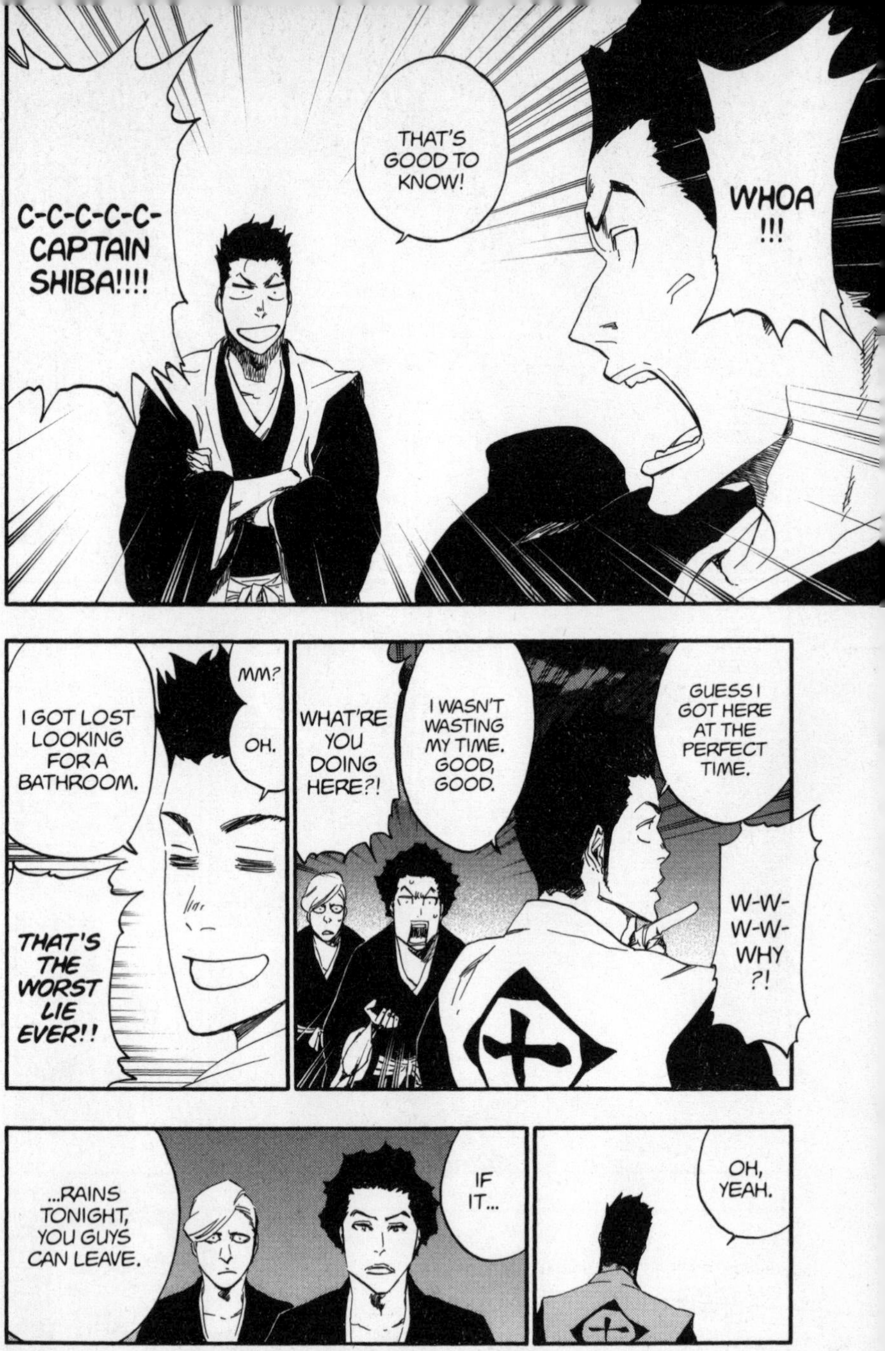
WHOA !!!
THAT'S GOOD TO KNOW!
C-C-C-C-C-CAPTAIN SHIBA!!!!!
GUESS I GOT HERE AT THE PERFECT TIME.
I WASN'T WASTING MY TIME. GOOD, GOOD.
W-W-W-W-WHY ?!
WHAT'RE YOU DOING HERE?!
MM?
OH.
I GOT LOST LOOKING FOR A BATHROOM.
THAT'S THE WORST LIE EVER!!
OH, YEAH.
IF IT...
...RAINS TONIGHT, YOU GUYS CAN LEAVE.

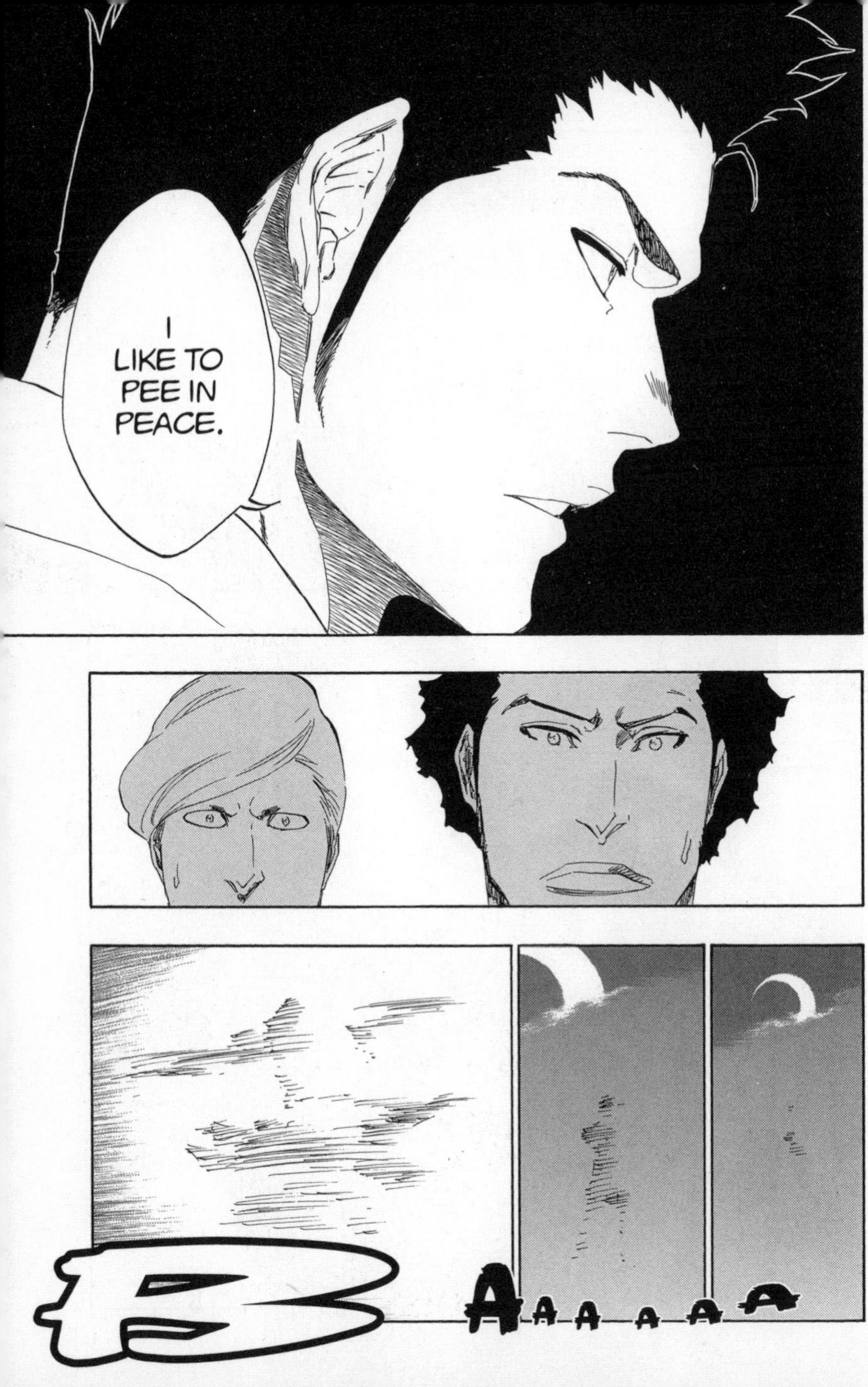
I LIKE TO PEE IN PEACE.
BAAAAAA

BLEACH 530.

Everything But the Rain op.3

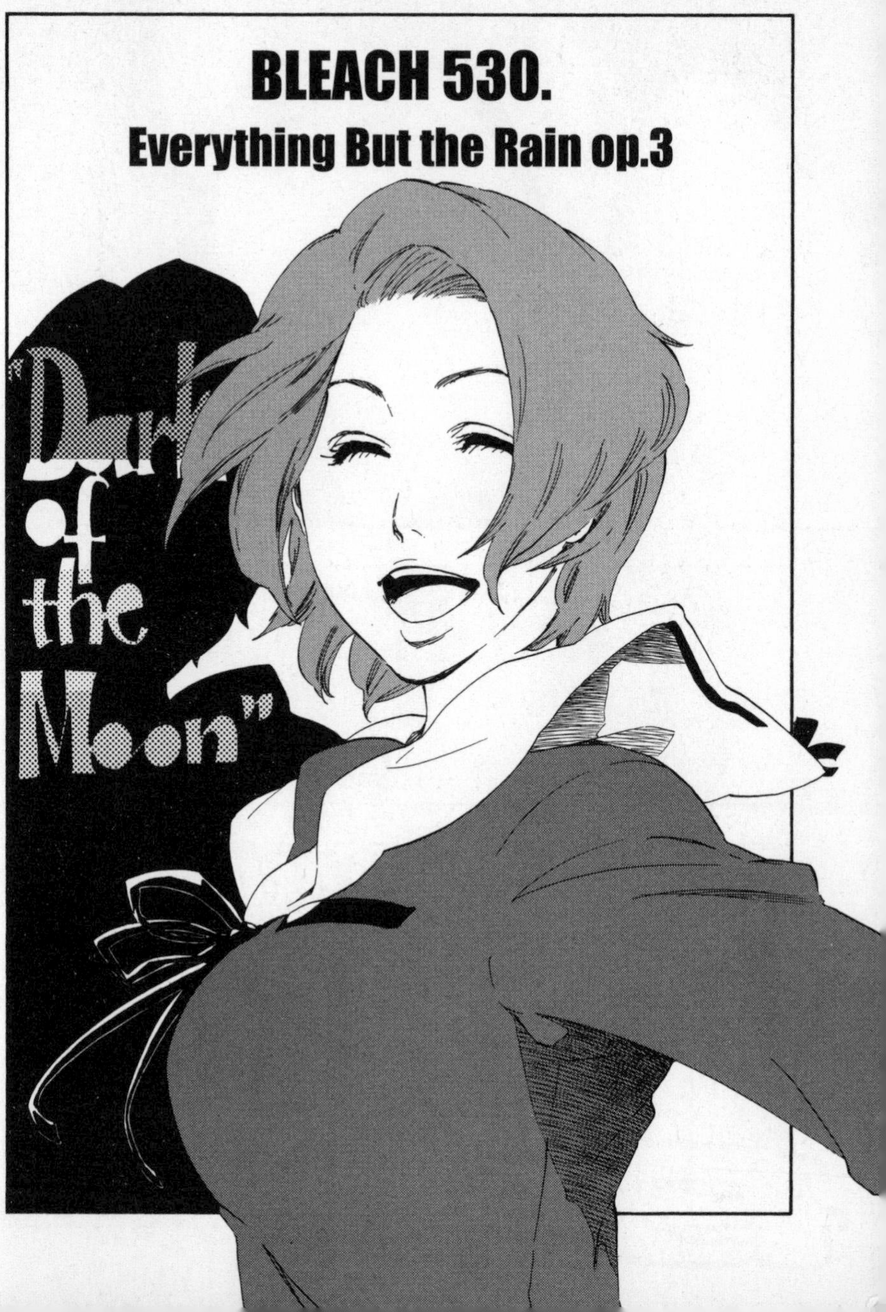
of the Moon"

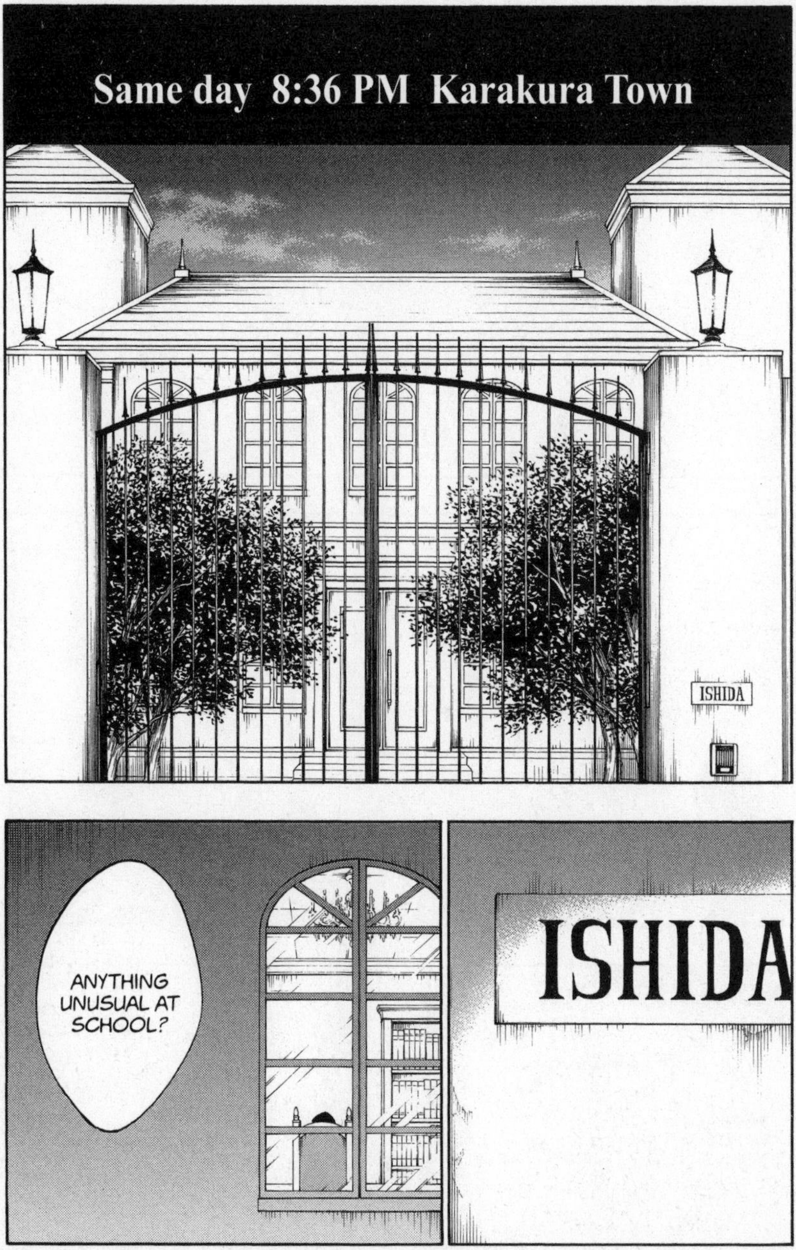
Same day 8:36 PM Karakura Town
ISHIDA
ISHIDA
ANYTHING UNUSUAL AT SCHOOL?

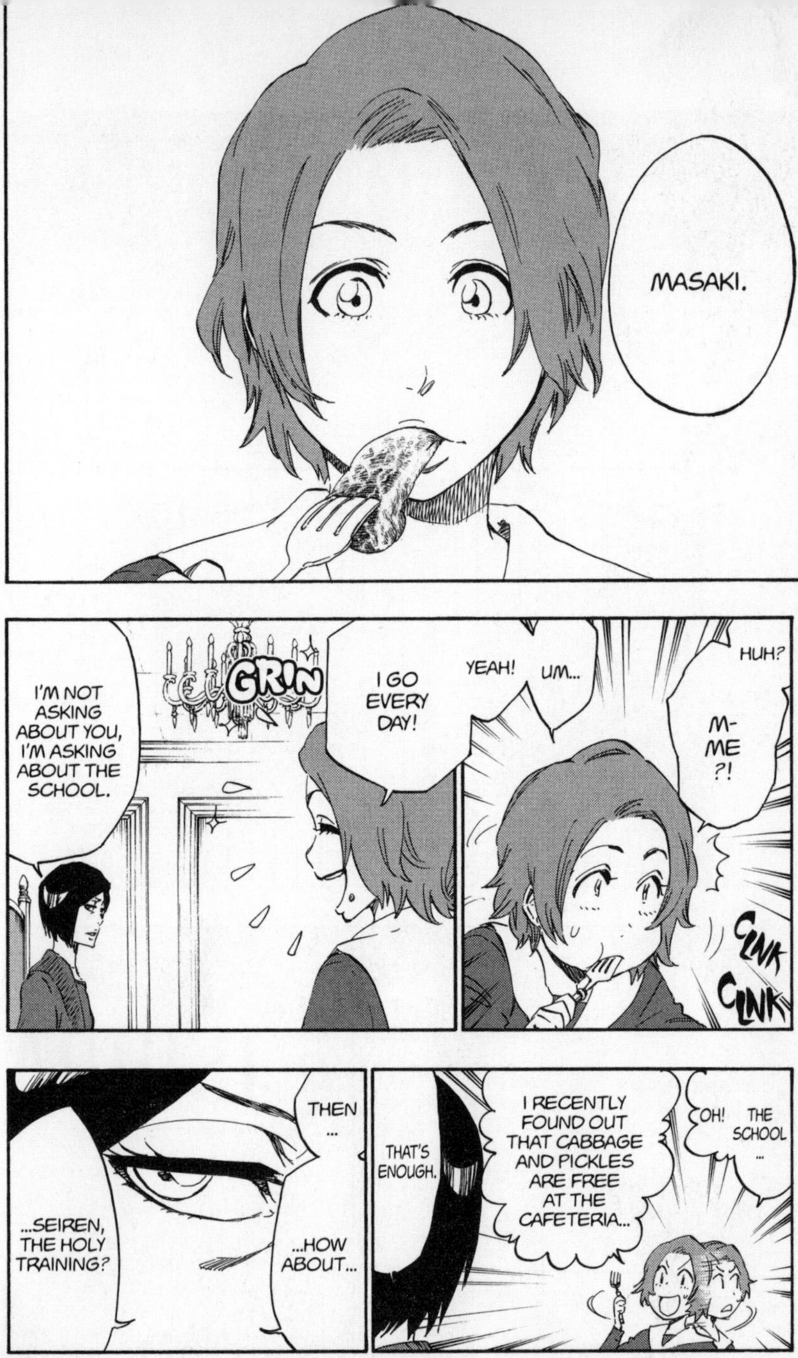

MASAKI.
HUH?
M-ME?!
CLINK
CLINK
UM...
YEAH!
I GO EVERY DAY!
GRIN
I'M NOT ASKING ABOUT YOU, I'M ASKING ABOUT THE SCHOOL.
OH! THE SCHOOL...
I RECENTLY FOUND OUT THAT CABBAGE AND PICKLES ARE FREE AT THE CAFETERIA...
THAT'S ENOUGH.
THEN...
...HOW ABOUT...
...SEIREN, THE HOLY TRAINING?

READ THIS WAY

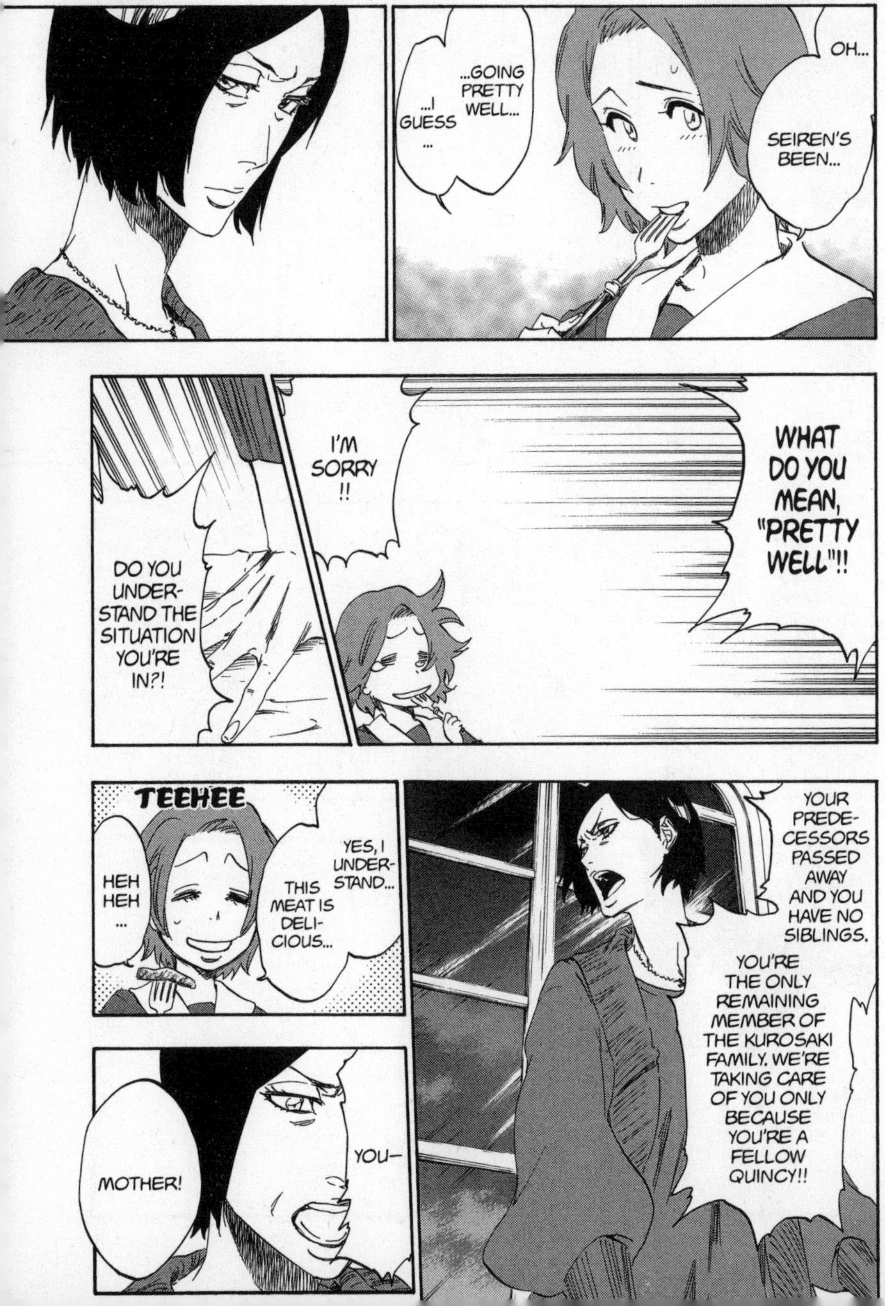
OH...
SEIREN'S BEEN...
...GOING PRETTY WELL...
...I GUESS ...
WHAT DO YOU MEAN, "PRETTY WELL"!!
I'M SORRY !!
DO YOU UNDER-STAND THE SITUATION YOU'RE IN?!
YOUR PREDE-CESSORS PASSED AWAY AND YOU HAVE NO SIBLINGS.
YOU'RE THE ONLY REMAINING MEMBER OF THE KUROSAKI FAMILY. WE'RE TAKING CARE OF YOU ONLY BECAUSE YOU'RE A FELLOW QUINCY!!
TEEHEE
YES, I UNDER-STAND...
THIS MEAT IS DELI-CIOUS...
HEH HEH ...
YOU—
MOTHER!

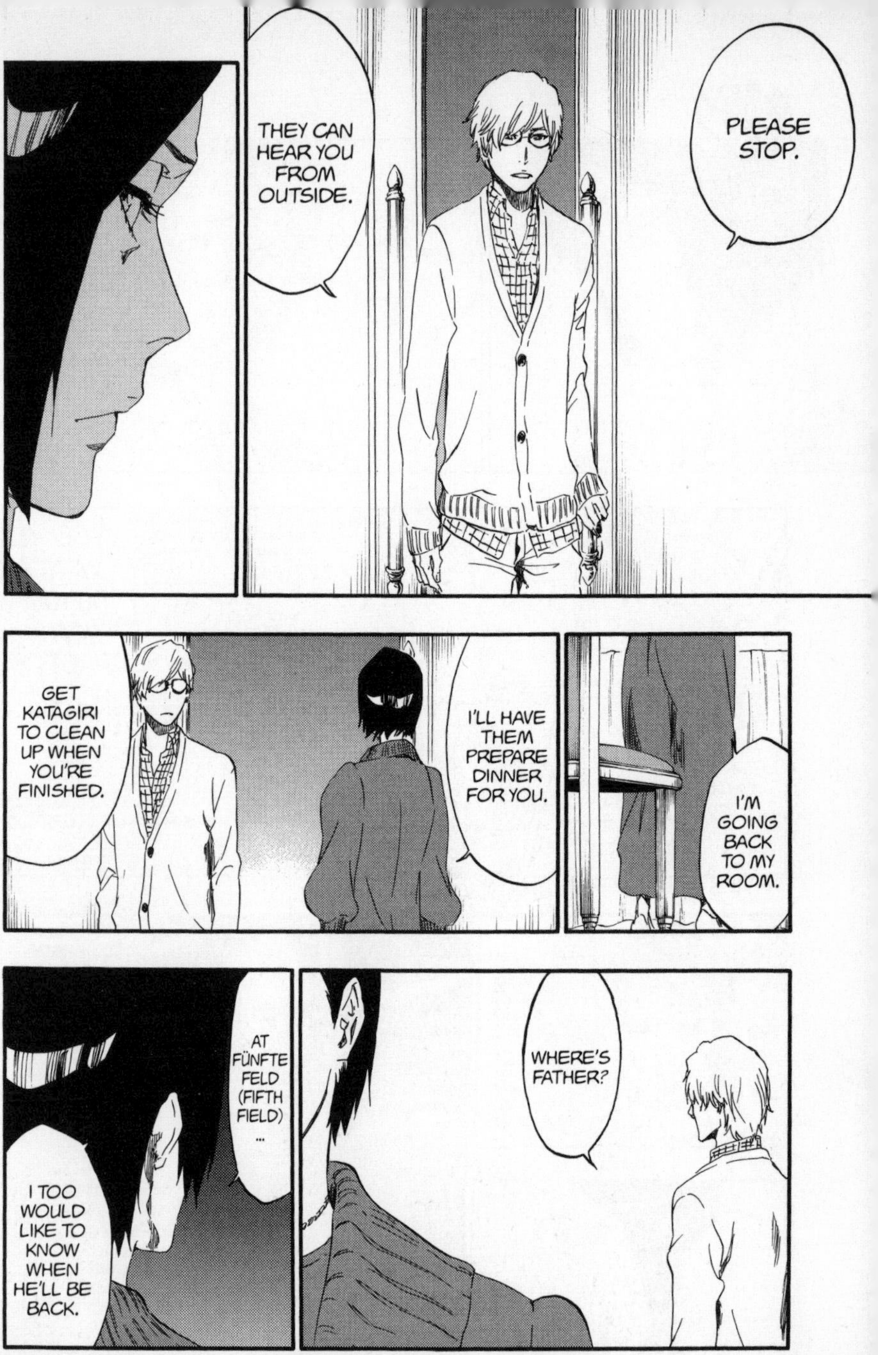
PLEASE STOP.
THEY CAN HEAR YOU FROM OUTSIDE.
I'M GOING BACK TO MY ROOM.
I'LL HAVE THEM PREPARE DINNER FOR YOU.
GET KATAGIRI TO CLEAN UP WHEN YOU'RE FINISHED.
WHERE'S FATHER?
AT FÜNFTE FELD (FIFTH FIELD) ...
I TOO WOULD LIKE TO KNOW WHEN HE'LL BE BACK.

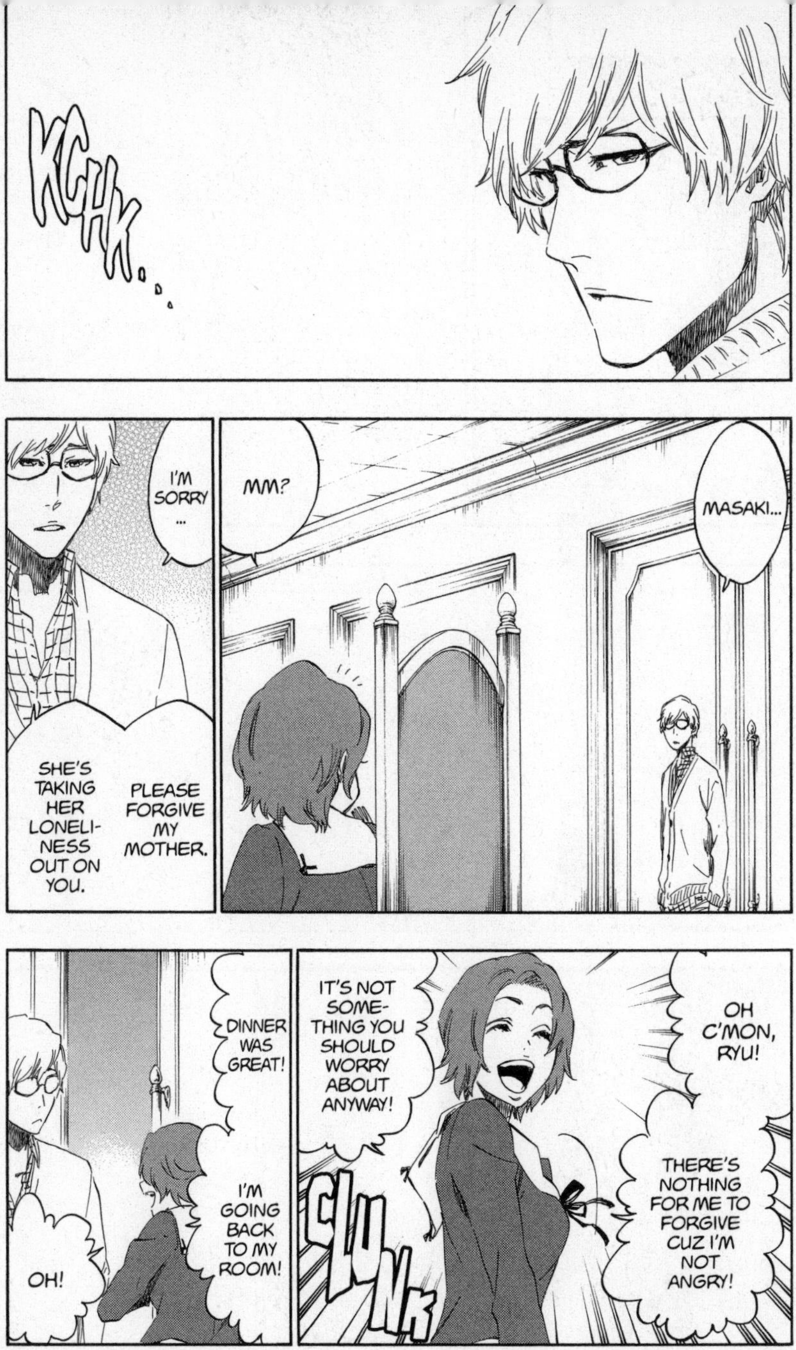
KCHK...
MASAKI...
MM?
I'M SORRY...
PLEASE FORGIVE MY MOTHER.
SHE'S TAKING HER LONELI-NESS OUT ON YOU.
OH C'MON, RYU!
THERE'S NOTHING FOR ME TO FORGIVE CUZ I'M NOT ANGRY!
IT'S NOT SOME-THING YOU SHOULD WORRY ABOUT ANYWAY!
CLUNK
DINNER WAS GREAT!
I'M GOING BACK TO MY ROOM!
OH!

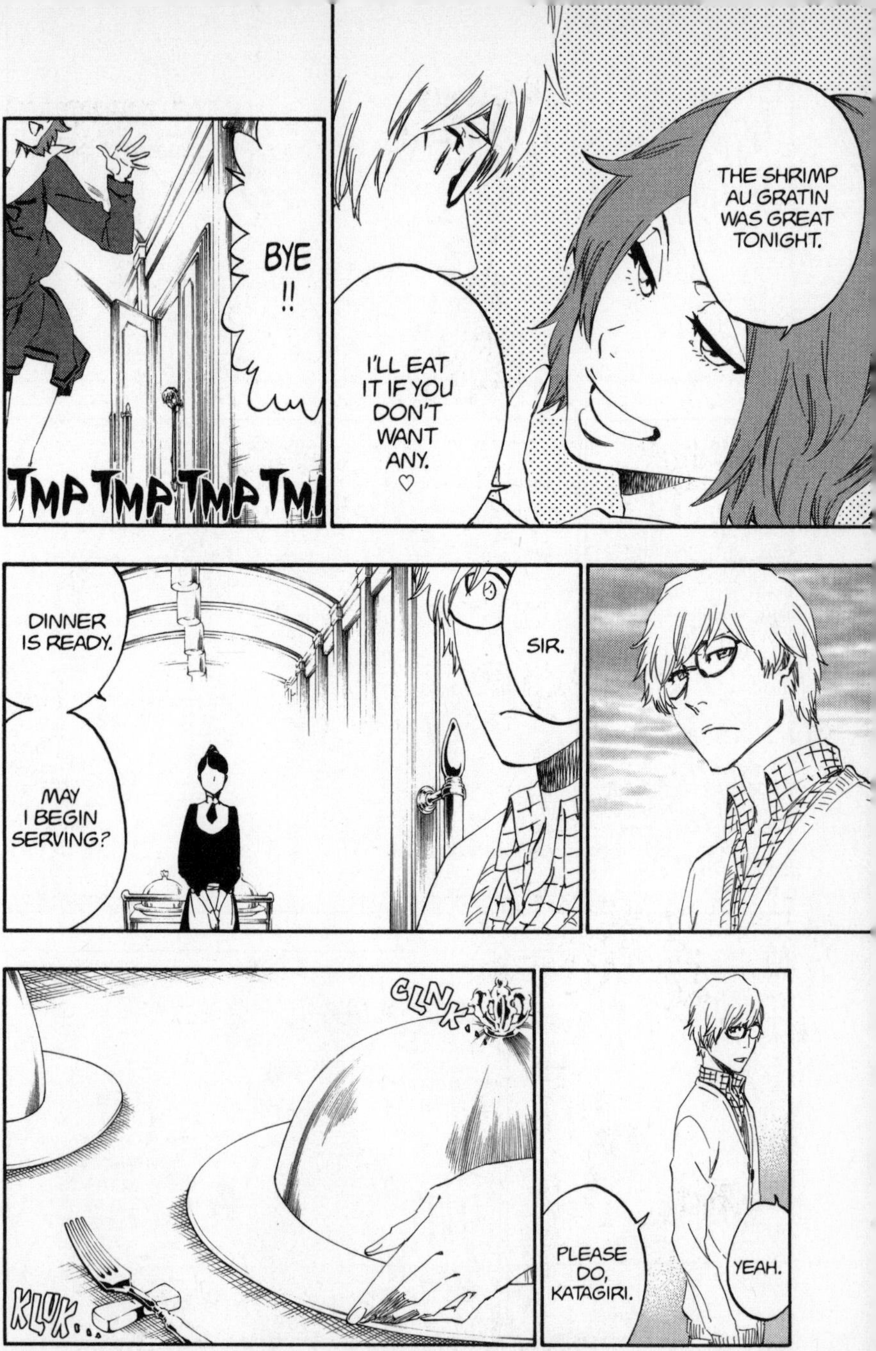
THE SHRIMP AU GRATIN WAS GREAT TONIGHT.
I'LL EAT IT IF YOU DON'T WANT ANY. ♡
BYE !!
TMP TMP TMP TM
SIR.
DINNER IS READY.
MAY I BEGIN SERVING?
YEAH.
PLEASE DO, KATAGIRI.
CLNK.
KLUK...

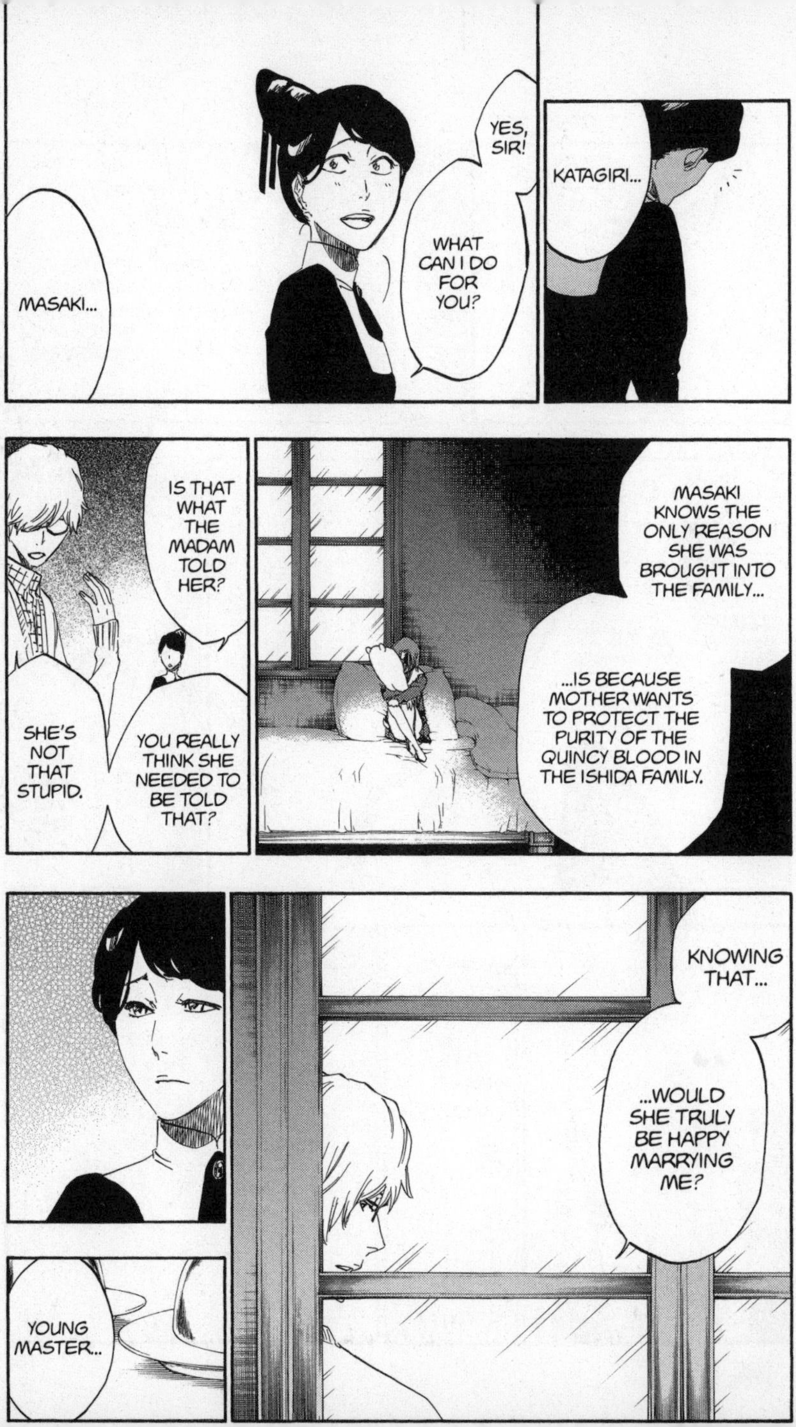
KATAGIRI...
YES, SIR!
WHAT CAN I DO FOR YOU?
MASAKI...
MASAKI KNOWS THE ONLY REASON SHE WAS BROUGHT INTO THE FAMILY...
...IS BECAUSE MOTHER WANTS TO PROTECT THE PURITY OF THE QUINCY BLOOD IN THE ISHIDA FAMILY.
IS THAT WHAT THE MADAM TOLD HER?
YOU REALLY THINK SHE NEEDED TO BE TOLD THAT?
SHE'S NOT THAT STUPID.
KNOWING THAT...
...WOULD SHE TRULY BE HAPPY MARRYING ME?
YOUNG MASTER...

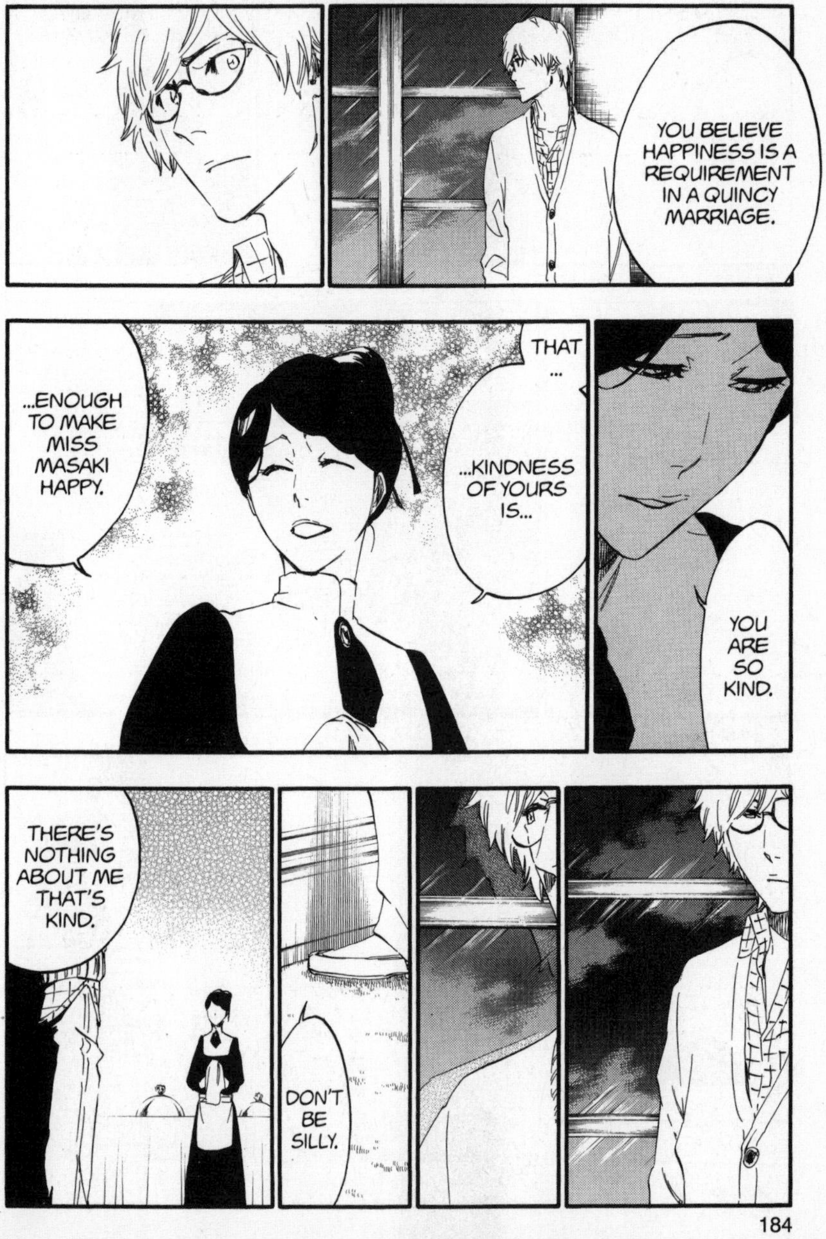
YOU BELIEVE HAPPINESS IS A REQUIREMENT IN A QUINCY MARRIAGE.
YOU ARE SO KIND.
THAT ... ...KINDNESS OF YOURS IS...
...ENOUGH TO MAKE MISS MASAKI HAPPY.
DON'T BE SILLY.
THERE'S NOTHING ABOUT ME THAT'S KIND.

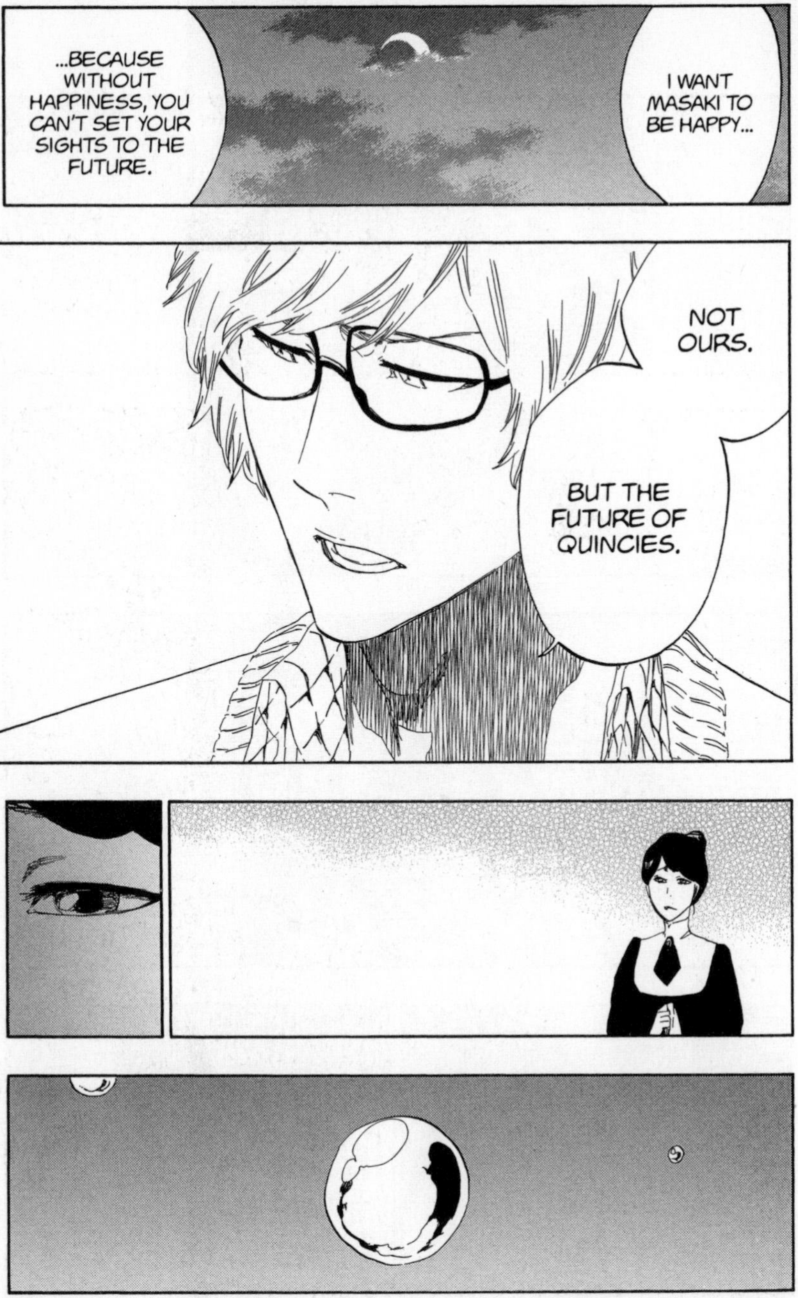
I WANT MASAKI TO BE HAPPY...
...BECAUSE WITHOUT HAPPINESS, YOU CAN'T SET YOUR SIGHTS TO THE FUTURE.
NOT OURS.
BUT THE FUTURE OF QUINCIES.

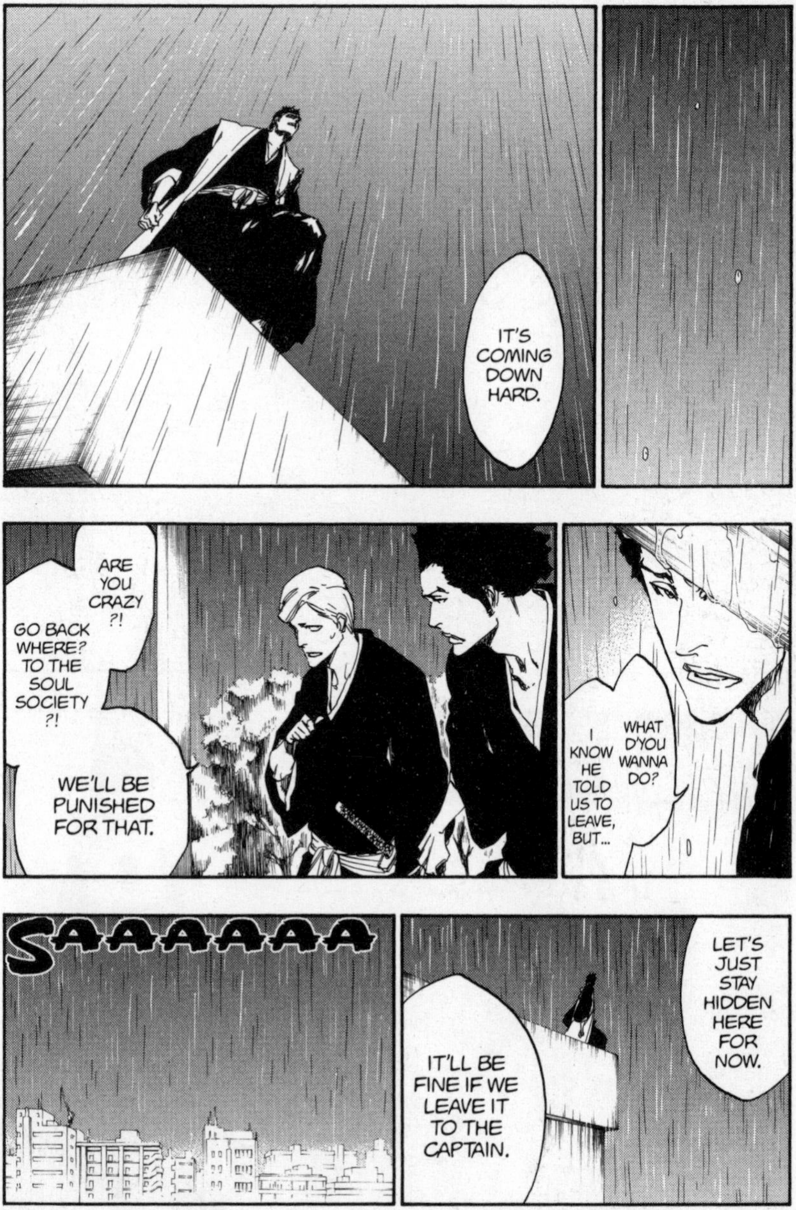
IT'S COMING DOWN HARD.
WHAT D'YOU WANNA DO?
I KNOW HE TOLD US TO LEAVE, BUT...
ARE YOU CRAZY?!
GO BACK WHERE? TO THE SOUL SOCIETY?!
WE'LL BE PUNISHED FOR THAT.
LET'S JUST STAY HIDDEN HERE FOR NOW.
IT'LL BE FINE IF WE LEAVE IT TO THE CAPTAIN.
SAAAAAA

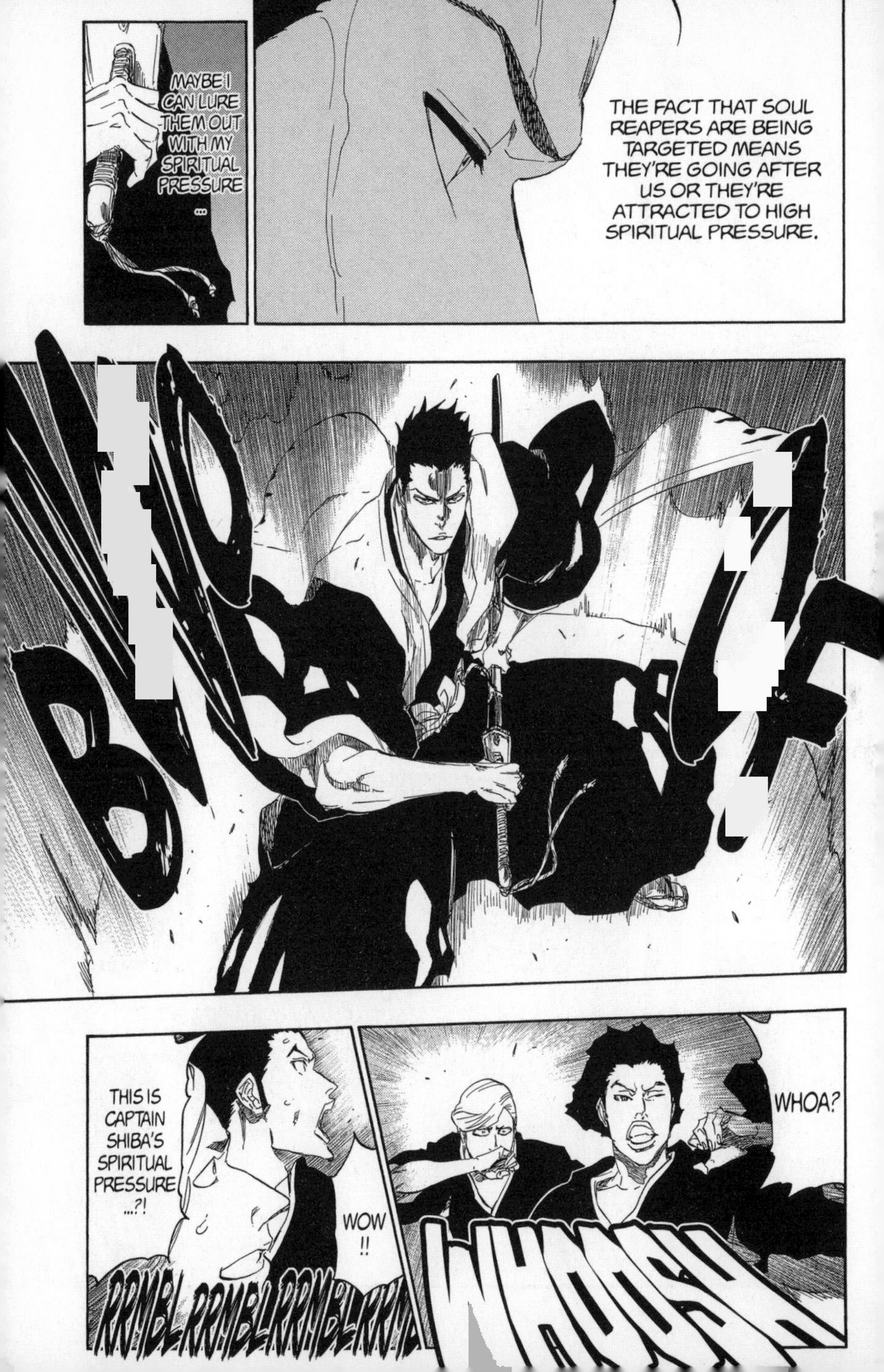
THE FACT THAT SOUL REAPERS ARE BEING TARGETED MEANS THEY'RE GOING AFTER US OR THEY'RE ATTRACTED TO HIGH SPIRITUAL PRESSURE.
MAYBE I CAN LURE THEM OUT WITH MY SPIRITUAL PRESSURE
...
WHOA?
WHOOSH
THIS IS CAPTAIN SHIBA'S SPIRITUAL PRESSURE ...?!
WOW !!
RRMBL RRMBL RRMBL RRMBL

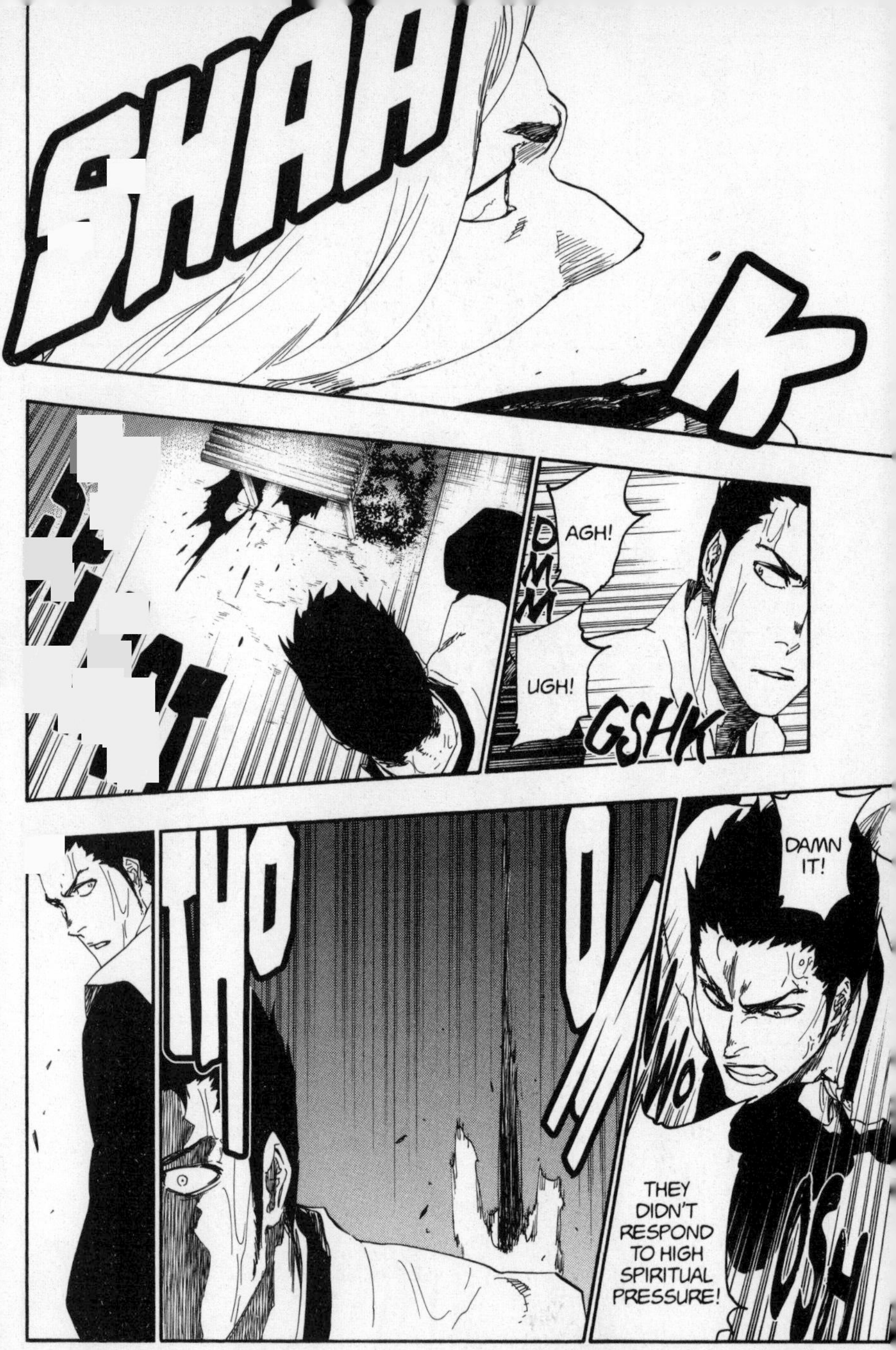
SHAA
K
AGH!
DMM
UGH!
GSHK
DAMN IT!
THEY DIDN'T RESPOND TO HIGH SPIRITUAL PRESSURE!
THO

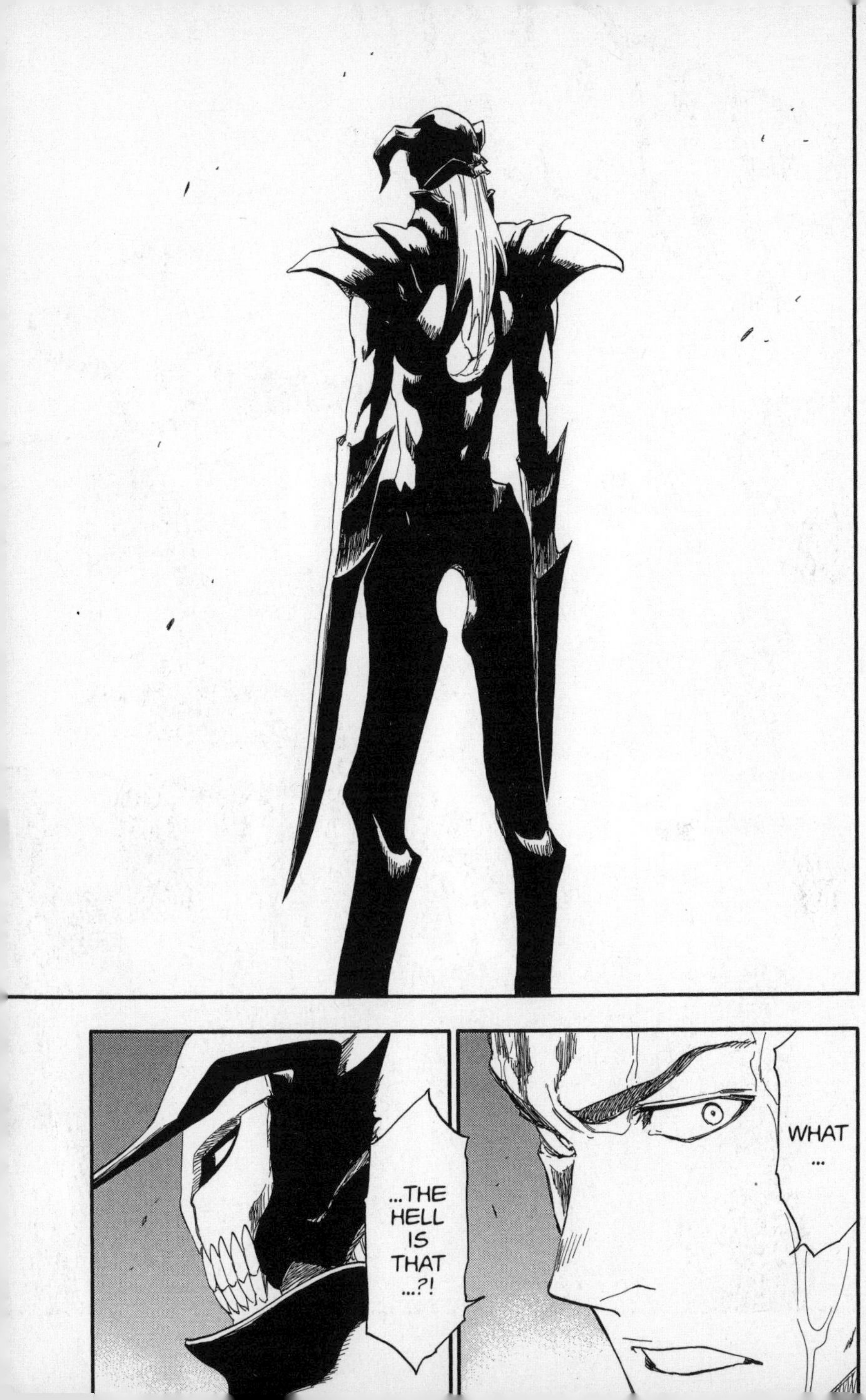
WHAT ...
...THE HELL IS THAT ...?!

CONTINUED IN BLEACH 60

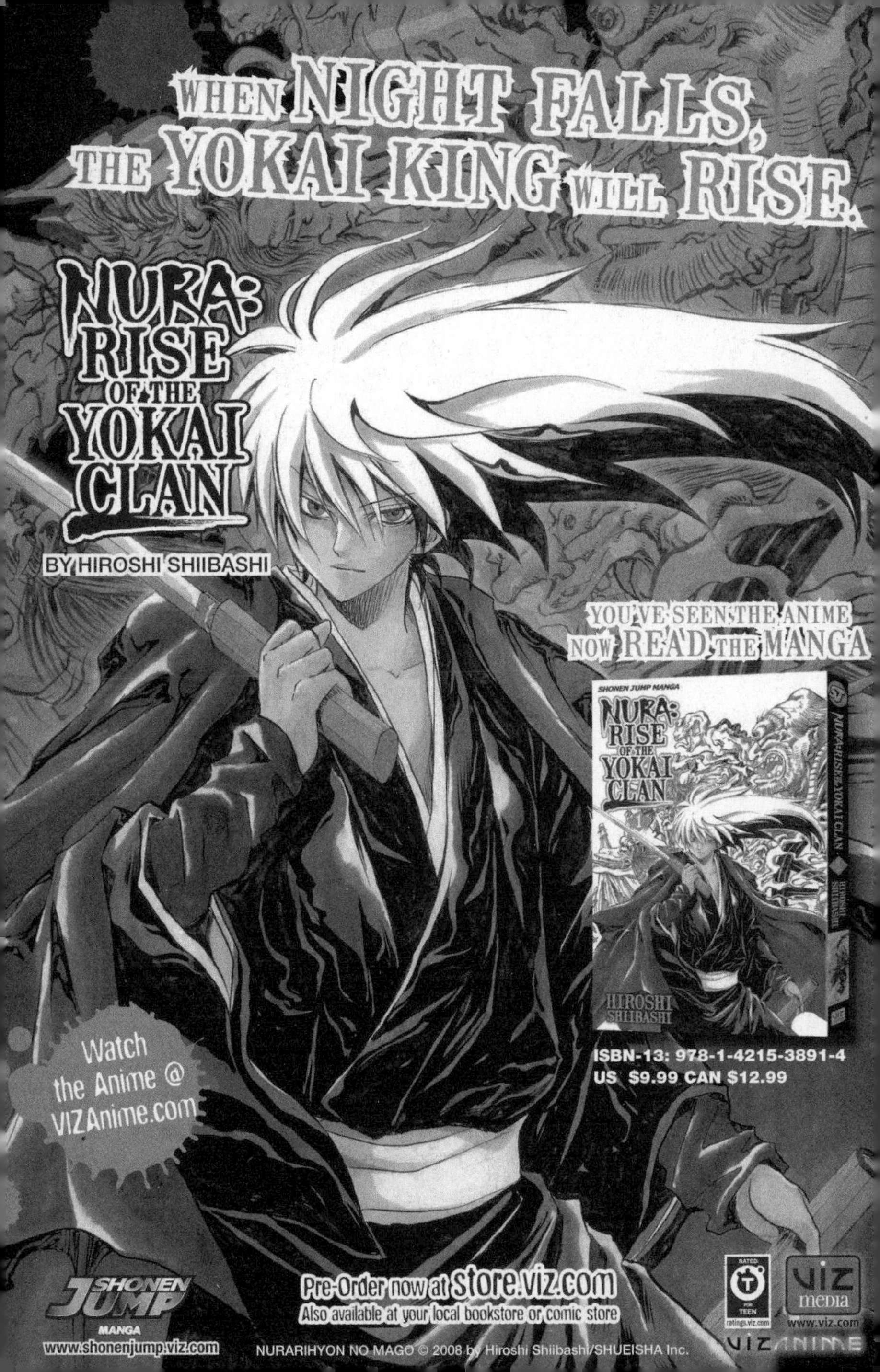
WHEN NIGHT FALLS, THE YOKAI KING WILL RISE.
NURA: RISE OF THE YOKAI CLAN
BY HIROSHI SHIIBASHI
YOU'VE SEEN THE ANIME NOW READ THE MANGA
SHONEN JUMP MANGA
NURA: RISE OF THE YOKAI CLAN
HIROSHI SHIIBASHI
ISBN-13: 978-1-4215-3891-4
US $9.99 CAN $12.99
Watch the Anime @ VIZAnime.com
SHONEN JUMP MANGA
www.shonenjump.viz.com
Pre-Order now at store.viz.com
Also available at your local bookstore or comic store
RATED T FOR TEEN
ratings.viz.com
VIZ media
www.viz.com
VIZ ANIME
NURARIHYON NO MAGO © 2008 by Hiroshi Shiibashi/SHUEISHA Inc.

You're Reading in the Wrong Direction!!

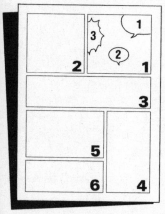

Whoops! Guess what? You're starting at the wrong end of the comic!

…It's true! In keeping with the original Japanese format, **Bleach** is meant to be read from right to left, starting in the upper-right corner.

Unlike English, which is read from left to right, Japanese is read from right to left, meaning that action, sound effects and word-balloon order are completely reversed… something which can make readers unfamiliar with Japanese feel pretty backwards themselves. For this reason, manga or Japanese comics published in the U.S. in English have sometimes been published "flopped"—that is, printed in exact reverse order, as though seen from the other side of a mirror.

By flopping pages, U.S. publishers can avoid confusing readers, but the compromise is not without its downside. For one thing, a character in a flopped manga series who once wore in the original Japanese version a T-shirt emblazoned with "M A Y" (as in "the merry month of") now wears one which reads "Y A M"! Additionally, many manga creators in Japan are themselves unhappy with the process, as some feel the mirror-imaging of their art skews their original intentions.

We are proud to bring you Tite Kubo's **Bleach** in the original unflopped format. For now, though, turn to the other side of the book and let the adventure begin…!

—Editor